W9-AZZ-587

workbook
FOR LECTORS AND GOSPEL READERS

Susan E. Myers

LTP

LITURGY
TRAINING
PUBLICATIONS

Liturgy Training Publications
1800 North Hermitage Avenue
Chicago, IL 60622-1101
1-800-933-1800
fax 1-800-933-7094
orders@ltp.org
www.ltp.org

Editor: David A. Lysik
Production editor: Bryan M. Cones
Cover art: Barbara Simcoe
Interior art: Steve Erspamer, SM
Original book design: Jill Smith
Revised design: Anna Manhart and Jim Mellody-Pizzato
Typesetting: Jim Mellody-Pizzato

Printed in the United States of America by Von Hoffmann Graphics, Inc.

ISBN 1-56854-329-8
WL01

CONTENTS

The Author

Susan E. Myers is a doctoral candidate in New Testament and early Christianity at the University of Notre Dame. She has degrees in theology and biblical studies, as well as experience in parish ministry and teaching. Susan's academic interests lie in all aspects of the beliefs, practices and prayer life of early Christians; her current research in early Christianity is concentrated in the region of eastern Syria. Her previous work with Liturgy Training Publications includes *At Home with the Word* (1997, 1998) and *Pronunciation Guide for the Sunday Lectionary* (1998). Susan brings to *Workbook for Lectors and Gospel Readers* a knowledge of biblical languages and exegesis, as well as knowledge of and participation in the pastoral and liturgical life of the Christian church.

INTRODUCTION

The Ministry of Proclaiming the Word of God

You were probably encouraged to become a lector in your parish or community by someone who knows you well and appreciates your love of God, or by someone who has witnessed your skills at public speaking. Or perhaps you volunteered for this ministry, moved by God's Spirit to share your gifts with others. Whatever brought you here, you are now part of the team of those who minister at liturgy. Some ministers have visible positions, such as the music director, the presider or the choir members, while others labor quietly behind the scenes: the members of the liturgy committee and its director, those responsible for the decor and presentation of the worship space, bread bakers, ushers and church maintenance crew members. Even the work of the pastoral ministers—RCIA catechists, religious education instructors, counselors, youth ministers, those involved in sacramental preparation—all comes together in the liturgy, the central event of our life as a church. It is through our gathering for prayer and praise that we celebrate who we are as God's people. When we come together for liturgy, we encounter God—in one another, in the sacramental actions (such as baptism or eucharist), and in the proclamation of the word of God.

You have the task of making God present in the liturgy of the word for your community. God has been among us in the past, especially in the person of Jesus. The prologue to the gospel of John says it best: "In the beginning was the Word, and the Word was with God, and the Word was God. . . . And the Word became flesh and lived among us." The Greek for "word" in this passage is *logos,* which can mean "reason"; it is what goes on in God's "head" and "heart." *Logos* can also mean "word," and that is how it is usually translated in this passage. It is the communication of the thoughts of God.

Jesus is God's word incarnate, but God's word is also spoken through others. God has spoken in the past through leaders and prophets, evangelists, apostles and many others. Today God speaks also through you as you proclaim in the assembly God's word as communicated through the individuals who composed the scriptures.

When the word of God is proclaimed in the assembly, it challenges and comforts, encourages and admonishes. Your task is to proclaim a living Word, not simply words on a page. When we read or hear the scriptures, we become part of the story they tell. We are part of the chosen people of God, struggling to understand God and ourselves, striving to be faithful, repenting when we fail. We are disciples of Jesus, following him and learning from his teachings. We are members of the Christian communities served by the evangelists and letter-writers of the New Testament. The word of God shapes our lives, teaching us, changing us, bringing us into an encounter with God.

In the liturgy, the Christian community depends on you, the lector or gospel reader, to mediate an encounter with God. In order to do this effectively, you must make the text come alive for your listeners. The job of making God present is an awesome responsibility, one that requires commitment and time. But do not worry. The Spirit of God will guide you in your ministry. You have been chosen.

Preparing to Proclaim

You can begin to bring God into your assembly by experiencing God's presence yourself, communicated through the words you are asked to read. Spend time with the selection you will proclaim. Read it several times. Pray about it. Allow God to speak to you through it.

Learn about the reading. The commentaries in this *Workbook* are intended to help you understand something about the purpose of the author who wrote the passage, as well as the historical setting out of which the passage arises. You might wish also to turn to your Bible and read the verses that precede and follow your selection, so that you can better understand its context. It might be helpful as well to read any introductory material in your Bible about the book from which the selection is taken, or consult a Bible commentary. The more you know about the reading, the more effectively you can share it with others.

Do not worry if the text does not completely make sense to you. Biblical scholars have long argued about the precise meanings of some passages and continue to find new information that adds to our understanding of the text. In addition, do not be alarmed if you find the reading confusing or bothersome. "There is nothing comfortable about the Bible" if we are truly engaged with it, as Thomas Merton has said. Remember that God has communicated this word to fallible human beings who sometimes inserted some of their own interests and biases into the text. Trust that God is bigger than any uncertainty or difficulty you have with the reading. If you are open to the movement of the Spirit of God in your life, you will enable the Spirit to move in your listeners in ways beyond your imaginings.

Preparation to proclaim the word of God ideally takes place in a group setting. Participants, usually other lectors and gospel readers, gather to discuss and summarize the readings, to practice together and to provide practical tips for one another. The sessions are most effective if a skilled leader directs them. If group meetings of lectors are not the norm in your parish, you might want to suggest that a group be formed or offer to organize one yourself. If you are unable to prepare with others, practice individually, but always try to have another person listen to you and offer suggestions at least once.

When you practice, it can be especially enlightening to have yourself videotaped or, if that is not possible, to create an audio tape of the reading. You will learn a great deal about your posture and vocal inflection, your phrasing and your pace by hearing and seeing yourself on tape. Always prepare with the microphone in the church and, if possible, with the same lectionary from which you will be reading. This *Workbook* is not suitable for use in the assembly; an elegantly bound lectionary, carried in procession, is the appropriate choice. Check also with your liturgy director or the presider for any special instructions, such as a choral refrain or other interlude, especially if you are preparing to read on a special feast day.

A microphone amplifies your every sound. It must clearly project your whispers, but not be too loud for forceful proclamation. Know how to adjust the microphone, how far away to stand from it and when to lean forward slightly or back away. Some microphones are very sensitive and should not be approached too closely. Especially avoid the popping of "p" and "b" sounds or the hissing of "s" and "z" that microphones tend to produce. Practice making these sounds subtly but clearly, so that your congregation will understand you but not be distracted by unwelcome noises. It is important that someone else listen to you and give you feedback when you are practicing with the microphone.

The Proclamation of God's Word

It is natural to approach the task of reading before an assembly with a bit of trepidation. Such nervousness, if controlled, can be to your advantage. God's word is powerful and active, and your energy can be channeled into a more effective proclamation. You are not giving a history lesson or telling a story but proclaiming the movement of God throughout history for the benefit of your listeners. The process of reading the scriptures does include some teaching, but you stand in the dual role of teacher and disciple. Most of all, you stand before your community as a believer. Proclaiming the word involves an active sharing of faith between the reader and the assembly; your community will sense your energy and will communicate back to you its trust in God's fidelity and love.

Despite the power of God's word, many of us adopt a monotone whenever we read before an assembly. Reading the word of God is unlike any other public proclamation, but it requires some of the same skills that are necessary for effective speeches, oral interpretation or debate. For many of us, the time we are most likely to put great expression into our oral reading is when reading children's books to a captive audience. Try adopting some (but not too much) of the inflection and exaggeration of reading to a child in your public proclamation. Although you may feel you are adding too much emphasis and inflection, it probably sounds quite differently to your listeners.

A small minority of people tend to exaggerate when reading in public. Although most of us need to "ham it up" more than might make us comfortable at first, we all need to remember that we are not entertaining. Proclaiming the word of God is a formal task, one requiring dignity and restraint. Avoid anything that might draw attention to you and away from the word you proclaim. This is not a performance but a noble ministry, entrusted to you by God and by your community.

Be careful, then, how you communicate through your body language. Stand erect and hold your head high. Move slowly and deliberately.

Plan your phrasing and know when you will pause. Be certain that you can pronounce all of the words you will read. Enunciate clearly; this is especially important in a church with a great deal of reverberation. If you do stumble while reading, correct yourself and then continue without drawing undue attention to your error. Your composure will allow the dignity of God's word to be retained.

When you approach the microphone, pause and wait for any activity in the assembly to die down. Take a moment to compose yourself. Be sure that you have the attention of your entire assembly before you begin. Proclaim in a strong voice, "A reading from . . ." and then pause. At the end of the reading, be sure you do not swallow "The word [or gospel] of the Lord." Instead, pause before the phrase and then proclaim it as something in which you take great pride. Your community will remind you through their response that they are as involved in this proclamation as you. If returning to your seat, move slowly and with dignity.

Eye contact is essential in a reading before an assembly. If you have practiced the reading well, you will be able to address your listeners directly during important phrases, and glance back at your text during pauses. You might want to keep your finger at the spot from which you are reading so that you do not lose your place, if you can do this without drawing attention to your movements. But remember that this is a reading of God's word, not a speech; there is no need for constant eye contact.

Trying to establish some eye contact can aid in achieving another objective of most readers: slowing down. In order for the members of your community to reflect on what you are proclaiming, they need time to digest the message. Many of us, in our nervousness, rush through a reading and return to our seats hurriedly. In everything you do, act slowly and deliberately, as is fitting for a proclamation of the majestic word of God. Your goal is to capture your assembly's attention so completely that its members will be transfixed by your words, experiencing God in their midst. Those who have the habit of reading along in a missalette or worship aid will leave the printed word behind and truly listen, with ears attentive to God's voice speaking through yours.

Your physical appearance should convey your respect for your ministry. Dress comfortably but nicely. Remember that you are not trying to draw attention to yourself, either by dressing shabbily or by trying to turn the liturgy into a fashion show. Before the liturgy begins, check your appearance in a mirror one last time so that you do not have to worry about how you look prior to or during the reading. And know that it is very difficult for your community to concentrate on your words if you have a tuft of hair sticking straight up during your proclamation.

Throughout everything, be confident. Know that you are not only capable of the task before you but have the guidance of the Spirit of God to assist you. If you are focused on God's word and have prepared well, you will be the vehicle through whom God speaks to your community.

Workbook for Lectors and Gospel Readers

Workbook includes the scripture readings for Masses on Sundays and feast days. It does not include the psalm selection, since that is properly sung, not proclaimed in the same manner as the readings.

Be sure that you know if you are to read a shorter version of the passage than that provided here. Shorter options are available for especially long readings, but this *Workbook* always gives the longer form.

The commentaries provided for each reading are intended to provide background information for the minister of the word. Historical and literary information is stressed, as well as suggestions for making your proclamation of the reading most effective. Understanding the reading is a first step toward proclaiming it.

Included to the left of the readings are margin notes with specific suggestions for your proclamation, as well as occasional information that will explain certain words and phrases or ancient practices. Pronunciations of difficult words are provided as well; refer to the pronunciation key that follows this section. Consult the *Pronunciation Guide for the Sunday Lectionary*, available from Liturgy Training Publications, for additional terms that are unfamiliar to you.

The italics evident in the text are intended to indicate an appropriate emphasis on certain words. Not all of the italicized words are to be stressed to the same degree. Instead, the italics provide a guide to the rhythm of the passage; truly significant words will need to be given added emphasis. The italics are provided as a service to readers, but there are other legitimate ways to convey the meaning of the text. If after careful preparation you find that another pattern of stress seems to communicate more effectively God's word as you understand it, feel free to adopt that pattern.

Since you will be reading from a lectionary and not from this *Workbook*, lectionary numbers are provided for each Sunday or other day in order to facilitate the location of the readings in the lectionary. You may wish to practice with the lectionary from which you will read as well as from this *Workbook*, since the layout of the reading might differ from that printed here. Anything you can do in order to be more confident in proclaiming the word will allow you to communicate God's presence more effectively.

Pronunciation Key

Most consonants in the pronunciation key are straightforward: The letter B always represents the sound B and D is always D, and so on. Vowels are more complicated. Note that the long I sound (as in kite or ice) is represented by *ī*, while long A (skate, pray) is represented by *ay*. Long E (beam, marine) is represented by *ee*; long O (boat, coat) is represented by *oh*; long U (sure, secure) is represented by *oo* or *yoo*. Short A (cat), E (bed), I (slim) and O (dot) are represented by *a, e, i* and *o* except in an unstressed syllable, when E and I are signified by *eh* and *ih*. Short U (cup) is represented by *uh*. An asterisk (*) indicates the schwa sound, as in the last syllable of the word "stable." The letters OO and TH can each be pronounced in two ways (as in cool or book; thin or they); underlining differentiates between them. Stress is indicated by the capitalization of the stressed syllable in words of more than one syllable.

bait = bayt
cat = kat
sang = sang
father = FAH-<u>th</u>er
care = kayr
paw = paw
jar = jahr
easy = EE-zee
her = her
let = let
queen = kween
delude = deh-L<u>OO</u>D
when = hwen
ice = īs
if = if
finesse = fih-NES

thin = thin
vision = VIZH-*n
ship = ship
sir = ser
gloat = gloht
cot = kot
noise = noyz
poison = POY-z*n
plow = plow
although = awl-<u>TH</u>OH
church = church
fun = fuhn
fur = fer
flute = fl<u>oo</u>t
foot = foot

Bibliography of Recommended Works

Guides for Proclaiming God's Word

Connell, Martin. *Guide to the Revised Lectionary.* Chicago, Illinois: Liturgy Training Publications, 1998.

Lector Training Program: This Is the Word of the Lord. Audio tapes and booklet. Chicago, Illinois: Liturgy Training Publications, 1988.

The Lector's Ministry: Your Guide to Proclaiming the Word. Mineola, New York: Resurrection Press, 1990.

Lee, Charlotte I., and Galati, Frank. *Oral Interpretation,* 9th ed. Boston, Massachusetts: Houghton Mifflin, 1997.

Myers, Susan E. *Pronunciation Guide for the Sunday Lectionary.* Chicago, Illinois: Liturgy Training Publications, 1998.

Proclaiming the Word: Formation for Readers in the Liturgy. Video. Chicago, Illinois: Liturgy Training Publications, 1994.

Rosser, Aelred R. *A Well-Trained Tongue: Formation in the Ministry of Reader.* Chicago, Illinois: Liturgy Training Publications, 1996.

——. *A Word That Will Rouse Them: Reflections on the Ministry of Reader.* Chicago, Illinois: Liturgy Training Publications, 1995.

——. *Guide for Lectors.* Chicago, Illinois: Liturgy Training Publications, 1998.

General Reference Works on the Bible

Boadt, Lawrence. *Reading the Old Testament: An Introduction.* New York, New York/Mahwah, New Jersey: Paulist Press, 1984.

Brown, Raymond E. *An Introduction to the New Testament* (The Anchor Bible Reference Library). New York, New York: Doubleday, 1997.

Collegeville Bible Commentary, Old Testament Series. Diane Bergant, general editor. Collegeville, Minnesota: The Liturgical Press, 1985.

Collegeville Bible Commentary, New Testament Series. Robert J. Karris, general editor. Collegeville, Minnesota: The Liturgical Press, 1991.

The Collegeville Pastoral Dictionary of Biblical Theology. Carroll Stuhlmueller, general editor. Collegeville, Minnesota: The Liturgical Press, 1996.

The New Jerome Biblical Commentary. Raymond E. Brown, Joseph Fitzmyer and Roland E. Murphy, editors. Englewood Cliffs, New Jersey: Prentice Hall, 1990.

New Testament Message: A Biblical-Theological Commentary. Wilfrid Harrington and Donald Senior, editors. Collegeville, Minnesota: The Liturgical Press, 1980.

The Women's Bible Commentary, expanded edition. Carol A. Newsom and Sharon H. Ringe, editors. Louisville, Kentucky: Westminster/John Knox Press, 1998.

Commentaries on the Gospel of Luke

Fitzmyer, Joseph A. *The Gospel according to Luke.* Garden City, New Jersey: Doubleday, 1981.

Kodell, Jerome. *The Gospel according to Luke.* Collegeville, Minnesota: The Liturgical Press, 1985.

LaVerdiere, Eugene. *Dining in the Kingdom of God: The Origins of the Eucharist according to Luke.* Chicago, Illinois: Liturgy Training Publications, 1994.

LaVerdiere, Eugene. *Luke* (New Testament Message). Collegeville, Minnesota: The Liturgical Press, 1990.

1ST SUNDAY OF ADVENT

Lectionary #3

READING I   Jeremiah 33:14–16

A reading from the book of the prophet Jeremiah

The *days* are *coming*, says the LORD,
    when I will *fulfill* the *promise*
    I *made* to the house of *Israel* and *Judah.*

In *those* days, in *that* time,
    I will *raise up* for David a *just shoot;*
    he shall do what is *right* and *just* in the land.

In those days *Judah* shall be *safe*
    and *Jerusalem* shall dwell *secure;*
    this is what they shall *call* her:
    "The LORD our *justice."*

Raise your voice in hope and encouragement. This is a solemn promise made by God.

Stress words dealing with justice and righteousness. This is no ordinary ruler, but one who will make all things right.

Lower your voice a bit, and speak in a more relaxed, assured tone. "In those days" even the name of Jerusalem will be changed to reflect the justice of God. Pause before the final line, then read slowly and carefully.

READING I In the time of the prophet Jeremiah, Jerusalem was besieged and eventually conquered by the Babylonians. Many of the leading members of the community were sent into exile. Jeremiah is remembered as a prophet of doom, warning of the impending fall of the kingdom of Judah.

Despite Jeremiah's harsh words, the book of Jeremiah also offers messages of hope and comfort. In Jerusalem's darkest days, shortly before the Babylonians conquered it, Jeremiah defies the prevailing wisdom and offers hope. God will not forsake this people, he says. Instead, God's righteousness will prevail, put into action by a descendant of the royal house of David.

Christians believe that Jesus fulfills the hopes spoken by Jeremiah. Proclaim this brief passage with eagerness for justice, confident that it is available in Christ.

READING II One of the ways we prepare for Christ's coming during Advent is by personal spiritual discipline. When Christ lives in us and inspires our words and actions, we more truly become the people God calls us to be. This is precisely what Paul exhorts the Thessalonians to do as well.

Paul expects Christ to return soon in glory, and he wants the Christians in his communities to be ready for that day. He instructs them to live holy and pure lives so

READING II   1 Thessalonians 3:12—4:2

A reading from the first letter of Saint Paul to the Thessalonians

These are Paul's words of endearment to the Thessalonians. Speak lovingly.

Brothers and *sisters*:
May the Lord make you *increase* and *abound* in *love*
    for one *another* and for *all*,

Emphasize "we" in this line. If it helps, think of Paul using it.

    just as *we* have for *you*,
    so as to *strengthen* your *hearts*,

Give strong emphasis to such terms as "blameless" and "holiness."

    to be *blameless* in *holiness* before our *God* and *Father*
    at the *coming* of our Lord *Jesus* with all his *holy* ones. Amen.

Finally, brothers and sisters,
    we earnestly *ask* and *exhort* you in the Lord *Jesus* that,

Pause before and after "that." Then read the next two lines (up to and including "God") a little more quickly, as an aside.

    as you *received* from *us*
    how you should *conduct* yourselves to *please* God
    —and as you *are* conducting yourselves—
    you do so even *more*.

Finally you conclude the thought begun at the start of the paragraph. Raise your voice a bit and speak this line slowly and firmly. Close with a reminder that this is not a new teaching.

For you *know* what *instructions* we gave you
    through the Lord *Jesus*.

---

that God might be pleased with their conduct. When their hearts overflow with love, they will be blameless before God. Paul is not chastising the Thessalonians, who look to him for leadership and guidance, but he does remind them that they have more to learn about living upright lives. Paul offers himself and the others who have ministered to the Thessalonians as models of Christian living.

Reflect on someone who has inspired you to lead a better life. Resolve to offer that same service to the people around you. And as you read these words encouraging holiness to the members of your community, pray that eventually all hearts might abound in love for one another.

GOSPEL   One of the comings of Christ we pray for during Advent is Christ's return as judge of the world. For the early Christians, the hope that Christ would

soon return in glory was alive and active. Believing that he was truly the Messiah, the chosen one of God who sits at God's right hand, the earliest Christians believed that Christ would return to bring judgment.

Jesus' words in today's passage from the gospel of Luke suggest that the last days will be a time of terrible tribulation for most of the world. Jesus asserts that the entire cosmos will be changed, and a sense of impending doom will prevail. For Christians,

GOSPEL   Luke 21:25–28, 34–36

A reading from the holy gospel according to Luke

Jesus said to his *disciples*:
"There will be *signs* in the *sun*, the *moon* and the *stars*,
   and on *earth nations* will be in *dismay*,
   perplexed by the *roaring* of the *sea* and the *waves*.
People will *die* of *fright*
   in *anticipation* of what is *coming* upon the *world*,
   for the *powers* of the heavens will be *shaken*.
And *then* they will see the *Son* of *Man*
   coming in a *cloud* with *power* and *great glory*.
But when these signs begin to *happen*,
   stand *erect* and *raise* your *heads*
   because your *redemption* is at *hand*.

"*Beware* that your hearts do not become *drowsy*
   from *carousing* and *drunkenness*
   and the *anxieties* of daily *life*,
   and that *day* catch you by *surprise* like a *trap*.
For that *day* will assault *everyone*
   who lives on the *face* of the *earth*.
Be *vigilant* at all times
   and *pray* that you have the *strength*
   to *escape* the tribulations that are *imminent*
   and to *stand* before the *Son* of *Man*."

Begin slowly and emphasize the various locations of the "signs." Pause briefly after "earth" before continuing with greater urgency.

Let some anxiety enter your voice.

With this line your voice should change. Speak slowly and with awe.

Offer these words as encouragement to your listeners. Speak with confidence.

Pause before beginning this section, and earnestly urge your community to reflect on matters of great importance.

Read this line quickly, as if the day is sneaking up on those who hear your words.

These final lines are key to this reading. Slow down and speak with encouragement and hope.

however, the last days will be a fulfillment of their hopes, if they live faithfully the life to which they have been called.

Jesus describes the glorious vision of the righteous judge, using words from the prophet Daniel. The members of Luke's community are instructed to welcome the last days with outstretched hands rather than cower in fright, as do those without hope. For Jesus' followers, the day will bring ransom and redemption, not fear. But this will be so only if they follow the exhortations in the final paragraph, keeping themselves pure and eagerly awaiting Christ's return.

In Advent, we too recall that there is more to life than our daily concerns. As we prepare for the celebration of Christmas, we must also prepare our hearts for Jesus' presence in them, and our lives for our own final judgment. Proclaim this reading as encouragement to your community to look toward that day with eagerness rather than loathing, ready to stand before God in purity and hope.

IMMACULATE CONCEPTION

Lectionary #689

READING I   Genesis 3:9–15, 20

A reading from the book of Genesis

Begin slowly. Allow God's question to sound genuine. In this story, God shows human attributes, even ignorance about what has happened.

After the man, *Adam*, had *eaten* of the *tree*,
　　the LORD God *called* to the man and *asked* him,
　　　　"Where *are* you?"
He answered, "I *heard* you in the *garden*;
　　but I was *afraid*, because I was *naked*,
　　so I *hid* myself."

The man is embarrassed.

Then he asked, "Who *told* you that you were *naked*?
You have *eaten*, then,
　　from the *tree* of which I had *forbidden* you to eat!"
The man replied, "The *woman* whom you put here *with* me—
　　she gave me *fruit* from the tree, and so I *ate* it."
The LORD God then asked the *woman*,
　　"Why did you *do* such a thing?"
The woman answered, "The serpent *tricked* me into it,
　　　　so I *ate* it."

God understands the situation now; let your voice express some indignation.

Adam sounds like a child trying to pass blame.

The woman's words also try to avoid responsibility.

Then the LORD God said to the *serpent*:
　　"Because you have *done* this, you shall be *banned*
　　from all the *animals*
　　and from all the wild *creatures*;
　　on your *belly* shall you *crawl*,
　　and *dirt* shall you *eat*
　　all the *days* of your *life*.
　　I will put *enmity* between *you* and the *woman*,

Speak God's words firmly but without overemphasis.

enmity = EN-mih-tee

READING I │ The stories in the early part of Genesis tell great truths about life. Today's reading gives an account of how sin entered the world and explains why human life can be difficult. Although God creates humans to dwell in paradise, this story indicates that we often overstep the boundaries of what is good for us, with dire results.

　　The story opens with a discussion between God and the man. When confronted with the truth of what he has done, the man instantly tries to blame the woman; the woman, in turn, points to the serpent. The sin was a social action; it was something the pair chose to do together. But they are embarrassed when it becomes known and want to deny it.

　　God directs the punishment at the snake. The author attempts to explain the natural world: The reason that snakes crawl and that humans and snakes have a natural aversion to one another is the result of what happened in the garden. In fact, the whole story suggests that everything wrong in the world is the result of the choice of human beings to reach beyond themselves, to act in ways that are reserved for God.

　　The final verse of the reading accords the woman great honor and is the reason this passage is chosen for today's feast. In a play on words ("Eve" means "life"), the woman is said to be the mother of all the living. This is somewhat similar to the promise of descendants given to Abraham; having many children was considered a great blessing to the Hebrews.

　　Mary, the new Eve, chose right instead of wrong and restored life where there was

and between *your* offspring and *hers*;
  he will *strike* at your *head*,
  while *you* strike at his *heel.*"

The man called his wife *Eve*,
  because she became the *mother* of all the *living*.

The tone changes here; pause. Read this last verse with a bit more warmth and hope.

READING II   Ephesians 1:3–6, 11–12

A reading from the letter of Saint Paul to the Ephesians

Brothers and sisters:
Blessed be the *God* and *Father* of our *Lord* Jesus *Christ*,
  who has *blessed* us in Christ
  with *every spiritual blessing* in the *heavens*,
  as he *chose* us in him, before the *foundation* of the *world*,
  to be *holy* and without *blemish* before him.

In *love* he destined us for *adoption* to himself
    through Jesus *Christ*,
  in accord with the *favor* of his *will*,
  for the *praise* of the glory of his *grace*
  that he *granted* us in the *beloved*.

In *him* we were also *chosen*,
  destined in accord with the purpose of the *One*
  who accomplishes *all* things according to the *intention*
    of his *will*,
  so that we might exist for the *praise* of his *glory*,
  we who first *hoped* in Christ.

Open with a resounding word of praise. Read this as a joyous proclamation of honor to God.

The tone changes a bit with the second paragraph, becoming more explanatory.

Our response to God's goodness is to offer praise and thanksgiving.

---

death. She reversed the downward spiral begun in Genesis by bearing the one who offers life to all. Because of her willingness to trust even what she did not understand, God truly made her the "mother of all the living."

READING II In a tone of praise and thanksgiving, the author of the letter to the Ephesians reflects on the many blessings God bestows on humanity in Christ. These are not mere physical blessings but are of a heavenly cast, and they

have been intended from the beginning. Even before creation, God chose us to be adopted children. The human choice to thwart God's plan for us, recounted in the first reading, was undone even before it occurred. God chooses us to inherit all the blessings that rightfully belong to Christ.

The goal of all this—indeed the goal of all creation—is to offer praise to God, who makes it all possible. Because of God's tremendous love for us, God blesses us

with an abundance that we could never claim to deserve. The only response possible is praise and gratitude.

Speak these words with a tone of great sincerity. Emphasize terms such as "blessing" and "granted" to stress the lavish generosity of God. Then lift your voice in praise, and give glory to God!

GOSPEL Although today's feast celebrates the conception of Mary, the gospel reading is an account

GOSPEL Luke 1:26–38

A reading from the holy gospel according to Luke

The angel *Gabriel* was sent from *God*
    to a town of *Galilee* called *Nazareth*,
    to a *virgin* betrothed to a man named *Joseph*,
    of the house of *David*,
    and the virgin's *name* was *Mary*.
And *coming* to her, he said,
    "*Hail*, full of *grace!* The *Lord* is *with* you."

But she was greatly *troubled* at what was said
    and *pondered* what sort of *greeting* this might *be*.
Then the angel said to her,
    "Do not be *afraid*, Mary,
    for you have found *favor* with *God*.
Behold, you will *conceive* in your womb and bear a *son*,
    and you shall name him *Jesus*.
He will be *great* and will be called *Son* of the *Most High*,
    and the *Lord God* will give him the *throne* of *David* his *father*,
    and he will *rule* over the house of Jacob *forever*,
    and of his *kingdom* there will be no *end*."

But Mary said to the angel,
    "How can this *be*,
    since I have no *relations* with a *man*?"

And the angel said to her in reply,
    "The *Holy Spirit* will come *upon* you,
    and the *power* of the *Most High* will *overshadow* you.
Therefore the *child* to be born
    will be called *holy*, the *Son* of *God*.

Pause slightly after "name" to give emphasis to Mary's name.

Speak these words with joy, but also with a sense of their importance.

Jesus' name is significant. Emphasize it.

Mary is puzzled.

---

of the conception of Jesus. Stories about Mary's own origins are relatively late, but she is remembered for her important role in giving life to the true life-giver. As we prepare our hearts for receiving Christ this season, this reading is appropriate and honors Mary for her trusting "Yes!" to God.

The story is familiar but deserves all the attention, preparation and fresh presentation one might give to any text. It is the story of a young girl who experiences a most extraordinary event—the appearance of an angel—and is given an even more extraordinary promise.

The angel Gabriel begins by indicating the favor God has bestowed on Mary and explains what this means: Her child will be given both honor and a mission. The name of this child—Jesus—bears special import. In Hebrew, the name means "he will save." The angel does not tell Mary what Jesus' saving actions will involve, only the glory due him. The pain that Mary will come to know remains shrouded in the dark silence of her womb.

Mary's question ("How can this be?") brings us back to the situation at hand. The angel explains that this is no ordinary child but will be called holy. Indeed, he will be the ruler in the line of David for whom Israel has longed. Writing long after Jesus' humiliating death and triumphant resurrection, the author knows that the reign of this child will not be earthly, nor will he be enthroned in a palace. But in him the hopes of Israel find true and lasting fulfillment.

Mary is confused, perhaps frightened, but in the end her response is firm: Yes, Lord,

And behold, *Elizabeth*, your *relative*,
    has *also* conceived a *son* in her *old age*,
    and this is the *sixth* month for her who was called *barren;*
    for *nothing* will be impossible for *God."*

Mary said, *"Behold,* I am the *handmaid* of the *Lord.*
May it be *done* to me according to your *word."*
Then the angel *departed* from her.

Pause before concluding. Then read Mary's words with solemn conviction.

whatever you will. Her humble response to this awesome message is an inspiration for all times. She simply, quietly, opens her heart to God's word and accepts her role in birthing the savior. Her trust in God's goodness will lead her down paths she could never have imagined.

As we honor Mary today, it is appropriate to remember her for her strength and conviction, the characteristics attributed to her in the gospel of Luke, from which most of our knowledge of Mary comes. Only a few verses after the conclusion of this story is Mary's Magnificat, a song of praise to God for turning the world on its head. Not only has God chosen a young Jewish girl to bear the hope of the world, but God has brought down the wealthy and powerful, giving honor to the lowly and disenfranchised. God is to be found not in palaces but in the humble hearts of those who have nothing.

Read this story as though for the first time. Allow the characters to come to life for you and for your assembly. And honor Mary by presenting her as the quietly forceful woman of conviction she was.

2ND SUNDAY OF ADVENT

Lectionary #6

READING I Baruch 5:1–9

A reading from the book of the prophet Baruch

Jerusalem, take *off* your robe of *mourning* and *misery*;
  put on the *splendor* of *glory* from God *forever*:
Wrapped in the cloak of *justice* from *God*,
  bear on your head the *mitre*
  that displays the *glory* of the eternal *name*.
For *God* will show *all* the earth your *splendor*:
  you will be *named* by God *forever*
  the *peace* of *justice*, the *glory* of God's *worship*.

Up, Jerusalem! *stand* upon the *heights*;
  look to the *east* and see your *children*
gathered from the *east* and the *west*
  at the *word* of the *Holy* One,
  rejoicing that they are *remembered* by *God*.
Led away on *foot* by their *enemies* they *left* you:
  but *God* will bring them *back* to you
  borne *aloft* in *glory* as on royal *thrones*.

For *God* has *commanded*
  that every lofty *mountain* be made *low*,
and that the age-old *depths* and *gorges*
  be *filled* to level *ground*,
  that *Israel* may advance *secure* in the *glory* of *God*.

Speak joyfully and urgently. This is a time for rejoicing, not for sorrow.

Let your voice reflect wonder at the beauty of these garments. But also emphasize the theme of justice, from which the clothing is fashioned.

Raise your voice with excitement, as though you are encouraging someone with spectacular news.

The humiliation of defeat and exile is reversed.

The author recounts how God has changed the desert terrain to prepare the way for the exiles' return. Speak with wonder at God's care for the people.

READING I The book of Baruch reflects back on the experience of the Babylonian exile of the Hebrew people. The Babylonians were able to conquer Jerusalem and take its leaders into captivity because of the sinfulness of the chosen people. But the Israelites learned from their experience. Today's passage joyfully recounts how personified Jerusalem is decked out in glory and awaiting her children as they return from their exile.

While the people were held captive in Babylon, Jerusalem lay in ruins. The image here is of a woman in mourning, wearing sackcloth. But she is told to leave her garments of sorrow behind and dress in splendid royal robes and a crown. Her clothes are not merely rich and beautiful, though; they are the garments of righteousness and God's glory, and they will give Jerusalem her new name, a sign of her restored existence.

Today's reading pictures a woman, Jerusalem, looking out from the heights at her children, the exiles, returning to her. God brings them back in glory, making the traveling easy, an honor that would be accorded royalty. It is a day of great rejoicing, and God's righteousness is evident.

It can be difficult to imagine Israel's experience of exile. Perhaps it helps to think of refugees driven from their homeland and yearning to return. Here, God's people are coming home to their beloved Jerusalem. In Advent, we are coming home, too. We journey through this season of darkness, yearning for the light. But we have hope that we will be restored, for we know that God's promises are true. Read this selection in joyful expectation of that glorious day when God's reign will be universally recognized, and justice and righteousness will prevail.

The *forests* and every fragrant kind of *tree*
  have *overshadowed* Israel at God's *command*;
for *God* is leading Israel in *joy*
  by the *light* of his *glory*,
  with his *mercy* and *justice* for *company*.

Close with a confident proclamation of God's goodness and righteousness.

READING II Philippians 1:4–6, 8–11

A reading from the letter of Saint Paul to the Philippians

Brothers and *sisters*:
I pray always with *joy* in my every *prayer* for *all* of you,
  because of your *partnership* for the *gospel*
  from the *first* day until *now*.

I am *confident* of *this*,
  that the one who *began* a good work in you
  will continue to *complete* it
  until the *day* of Christ *Jesus*.

God is my *witness*,
  how I *long* for all of you with the *affection* of Christ *Jesus*.
And *this* is my *prayer*:
  that your *love* may *increase* ever more and more
  in *knowledge* and every kind of *perception*,
  to *discern* what is of *value*,
  so that you may be *pure* and *blameless* for the day of *Christ*,
  filled with the *fruit* of *righteousness*
  that comes through *Jesus Christ*
  for the *glory* and *praise* of *God*.

Offer this as a prayer for your own community. Speak earnestly and with joy.

Raise your voice a bit, and speak more boldly.

Stress "long." Pause before continuing.

Speak forcefully, slowly and confidently from here to the end.

READING II Paul was very fond of the community in Philippi, as this reading makes clear. Here he expresses in a range of emotions how he feels about this church that he nurtured and guided. He is thankful for its members, confident of their progress in the faith, and longs to see them grow more and more in love and understanding. In that way, they will produce the "harvest of justice" that gives glory to God.

During Advent we reflect on God's promises, which we believe are fulfilled in Jesus. At the same time, we recognize that God's promises in Christ have yet to be fully

realized, and we joyfully await and work toward the time when God's righteousness will be evident to all.

Paul speaks of the same reality in his words to the Philippians. Christ has begun the "good work" in them, but it must be brought to completion. They, as we, are an Advent people, on a journey to greater recognition of the love of God. Paul prays that their love may increase. It is a fitting prayer for any community.

Offer this message to your own listeners with all the hope, joy and confidence that Paul expresses. Reflect on the ways that

your community lives the gospel, and speak tenderly in gratitude for such action. Pray also that each member of your assembly will continue to grow in love and will contribute to an abundant harvest of righteousness.

GOSPEL The gospel of Luke places Jesus squarely in the center of world history. Jesus is not simply a fringe character but alters the world and history forever. At the same time, he is the answer to the hopes of Israel. For this reason the author also stresses Jewish history in this

GOSPEL   Luke 3:1–6

A reading from the holy gospel according to Luke

Tiberius Caesar = tī-BEER-ee-uhs SEE-zer
Pontius Pilate = PON-shuhs PĪ-luht
Judea = joo-DEE-uh
Herod = HAYR-uhd
tetrarch = TET-rahrk
Galilee = GAL-ih-lee
Ituraea = ih-too-REE-ah
Trachonitis = trak-uh-NĪ-tis
Lysanias = lī-SAY-nee-uhs
Abilene = ab-uh-LEE-nee
Pause after "Caiaphas," then proceed
slowly and forcefully. This is the turning
point of the passage.
Annas = AN-uhs
Caiaphas = KĪ-uh-fuhs
Zechariah = zek-uh-RĪ-uh

Brighten your tone with this line. Exhort
your community to "prepare."

In the *fifteenth* year of the reign of Tiberius *Caesar*,
    when *Pontius Pilate* was *governor* of *Judea*,
    and *Herod* was tetrarch of *Galilee*,
    and his brother *Philip* tetrarch of the region
        of *Ituraea* and *Trachonitis*,
    and *Lysanias* was tetrarch of *Abilene*,
    during the high *priesthood* of *Annas* and *Caiaphas*,
    the *word* of *God* came to *John* the son of *Zechariah*
        in the *desert*.

John went throughout the *whole* region of the *Jordan*,
    proclaiming a *baptism* of *repentance* for the *forgiveness*
        of *sins*,
    as it is *written* in the book of the *words* of the prophet *Isaiah*:
    "A *voice* of one *crying out* in the *desert*:
    '*Prepare* the way of the *Lord*,
    make *straight* his *paths*.
    Every *valley* shall be *filled*
    and every *mountain* and *hill* shall be made *low*.
    The *winding roads* shall be made *straight*,
    and the *rough* ways made *smooth*,
    and *all flesh* shall *see* the *salvation* of God.'"

Close with a sense of joy and fulfillment.
This is what we are hoping and waiting for!

section, detailing the rulers of the various regions and the high priests of the Jewish temple. Jesus fulfills the expectations of the Hebrew people and answers the unrecognized need of the entire world as well. He is indeed the savior of all the world.

After situating the story of Jesus within history, the narrative turns to the person of John the Baptist. He is neither ruler nor priest, but one who fulfills the words of the prophets. His role is to prepare for the coming of God. In a rough, mountainous region, the claim that all roads will be made level

testifies to the importance of the person who is expected. The Lord is to be treated like royalty.

What John proclaims, however, is a "baptism of repentance for the forgiveness of sins." The most effective way to prepare for the Messiah is to repent. The person who receives John's baptism expresses a sincere sorrow for sin and a resolution to change, to turn a stone heart into one of flesh.

We spend Advent waiting, preparing. We prepare in practical ways for the celebration of Christmas, with its feasting, exchanges of gifts, and time spent with

loved ones. But we also prepare our hearts, creating a place for Jesus to dwell and examining our lives to prepare for that final day when we will meet God face to face. How can we best straighten the roads and level the paths, so that God may more easily come to us? John suggests one way: turning away from sin and starting fresh.

3RD SUNDAY OF ADVENT

Lectionary #9

READING I   Zephaniah 3:14–18a

Zephaniah = zef-uh-NĪ-uh

Raise your voice and proclaim this with joy.

A reading from the book of the prophet Zephaniah

Shout for *joy*, O daughter *Zion!*
 Sing *joyfully*, O *Israel!*
Be *glad* and *exult* with *all* your *heart*,
 O daughter *Jerusalem!*

There is comfort in these words.

The LORD has *removed* the *judgment against* you,
 he has turned *away* your *enemies*;
the *King* of Israel, the LORD, is in your *midst*,
 you have no further *misfortune* to *fear*.

Speak this as a promise of God's goodness.

On that *day*, it shall be said to *Jerusalem*:
 Fear *not*, O *Zion*, be not *discouraged!*
The LORD, your *God*, is in your *midst*,
 a mighty *savior*;

Again, lift your voice and exult in God's love.

he will *rejoice* over you with *gladness*,
 and *renew* you in his *love*,
he will sing *joyfully* because of you,
 as one *sings* at *festivals*.

READING I — Today, Gaudete Sunday, we raise our voices in praise of our God, who promises to come to us soon! The exultant words of the prophet Zephaniah ring in our ears, and we believe that the promises proclaimed here are addressed to us as well.

Zephaniah lived in a time when the kingdom of Judah enjoyed political independence; it was not responsible to any superior foreign power. It was a time of religious renewal as well, and much of Zephaniah's prophecy was directed toward this need. Today's reading, however, celebrates the new people formed by God. On the day when all God's people respond in faithfulness, God will cease to judge them and will proclaim them victorious.

As we approach the shortest days and darkest time of the year, when we are busy with the many demands of this season, it is good to be reminded that God is on our side. Proclaim this passage with enthusiasm and a tone of comfort, so that your community can be reminded of God's tremendous love for them. And rejoice! God is in our midst.

READING II — Paul reveals his fondness for the Philippian community in the words that begin our passage, words that fairly sing out, "Rejoice!" This proclamation reflects this Sunday's name, "Gaudete" Sunday (*gaudete* means "rejoice" in Latin). Paul is proud of the Philippian

The passage begins on a strong note. Be sure that you have the attention of your listeners before beginning. Then proclaim these words with all your energy.

Read this line slowly and with promise.

These words are meant to strengthen your community. Read them with sincerity and encouragement.

Pause, then continue with assurance of the peace available in God.

READING II   Philippians 4:4–7

A reading from the letter of Saint Paul to the Philippians

Brothers and sisters:
Rejoice in the Lord *always.*
I shall say it *again: rejoice!*

Your *kindness* should be known to *all.*
The *Lord* is *near.*
Have no *anxiety* at all, but in *everything,*
   by *prayer* and *petition,* with *thanksgiving,*
   make your requests *known* to *God.*

Then the *peace* of God that *surpasses* all *understanding*
   will *guard* your *hearts* and *minds* in Christ *Jesus.*

John's replies are solemn and demanding. Speak them slowly to allow their importance to sink in.

GOSPEL   Luke 3:10–18

A reading from the holy gospel according to Luke

The *crowds* asked John the *Baptist,*
   "What should we *do*?"
He said to them in *reply,*
   "Whoever has *two* cloaks
   should *share* with the person who has *none.*
And whoever has *food* should do *likewise.*"

Even *tax* collectors came to be *baptized* and they said to him,
   "Teacher, what should *we* do?"

church and commends the members of the community on their kindness. He further encourages them to offer their concerns to God in prayer and thanksgiving; in this way the community will come to know God's own peace. Paul expects the second coming of Christ to occur soon, and encourages his churches to be ready for it.

Reflect with fondness on your own community and the ways in which it makes God's presence known in the world. Then proclaim to your assembly the exultant message: Rejoice! Read the rest of the passage with gentle encouragement, so that your listeners will know that they can truly turn to God with every need.

At this hectic time of year, we need to hear the promise of peace for our hearts. Strive to do what Paul advocates—to let go

of anxieties and trust in God—so that you can communicate a sense of joyful peace to your assembly.

GOSPEL   John the Baptist was a popular preacher, a messenger of reform and renewed commitment to God. As today's gospel illustrates, he preached

He answered them,
　"*Stop* collecting *more* than what is *prescribed*."
Soldiers also asked him,
　"And what is it that *we* should do?"
He told them,
　"Do *not* practice *extortion*,
　do not falsely *accuse* anyone,
　and be *satisfied* with your *wages*."

Now the people were *filled* with *expectation*,
　and *all* were *asking* in their *hearts*
　whether *John* might be the *Christ*.
John answered them *all*, saying,
　"*I* am baptizing you with *water*,
　but one *mightier* than I is *coming*.
I am not *worthy* to *loosen* the *thongs* of his *sandals*.
He will baptize you with the *Holy Spirit* and *fire*.
His *winnowing* fan is in his *hand* to *clear* his *threshing* floor
　and to gather the *wheat* into his *barn*,
　but the *chaff* he will *burn* with unquenchable *fire*."
Exhorting them in many *other* ways,
　he preached *good news* to the *people*.

Stress the contrast between John and Jesus.

Let your voice grow in strength as John describes the one who is coming.

Pause after "fire," then conclude on a quieter note.

justice and proclaimed the dawn of a new age. To those who have plenty (two coats instead of one!), he notes the importance of sharing with those in need. People in positions of power—tax collectors, soldiers—are not to use their positions for their own advantage but are to accept only their due. The people hearing this are "filled with expectation." The vast majority of the people at the time were struggling to survive, burdened by extremely high taxes and living in uncertainty. John proclaims that things can change.

The followers of John and those of Jesus were apparently rivals for the attention of the masses. But in today's gospel, John makes it clear that he is not the one for whom the Hebrew people are waiting. One who is even greater than John is coming. John's baptism is with water only, but the Messiah will baptize with the Holy Spirit and fire. Finally, John speaks of a coming judge who will bring fire and burn what is not worthy or useful.

There is both comfort and challenge in this message. Offer this gospel to your assembly as a reminder to live justly, with concern for the powerless, in order to be counted among the righteous.

4TH SUNDAY OF ADVENT

Lectionary #12

READING I   Micah 5:1–4a

A reading from the book of the prophet Micah

Thus says the LORD:
You, Bethlehem-Ephrathah
    too *small* to be among the *clans* of *Judah*,
from *you* shall come *forth* for me
    one who is to be *ruler* in *Israel*;
whose *origin* is from of *old*,
    from ancient *times*.

Therefore the Lord will give them *up*, until the time
    when she who is to give *birth* has *borne*,
and the *rest* of his kindred shall *return*
    to the *children* of *Israel*.
He shall stand *firm* and *shepherd* his *flock*
    by the *strength* of the LORD,
    in the majestic *name* of the LORD, his *God*;
and they shall *remain*, for *now* his *greatness*
    shall reach to the *ends* of the *earth*;
    he shall *be peace*.

Bethlehem-Ephrathah = BETH-luh-hem–
EF-ruh-thuh
In the genealogical list of the descendants
of Judah, Ephrathah is given as the
wife of Caleb, mother of Hur. The family
lived in the area of Bethlehem, and
the entire region is known as Ephrathah.

Pause, then alter your voice slightly to
indicate that the quote has ended.

Speak warmly as you read this image of
a ruler who acts as a shepherd. This is
the legacy of David, the shepherd who
became the greatest ruler of Israel.
Read firmly and slowly, with a sense of
majesty.

Pause slightly before "shall be peace,"
and conclude with a strong voice to
emphasize the idea of peace.

READING I   The prophet Micah was
active during the time of
Assyrian threat against the kingdom of
Judah. Micah offers this prophecy of hope in
the Davidic line to a people fearing catastrophe. His advice is to trust that God will
work through the royal family, bringing a
ruler who will know how to care for the
people. In fact, Jerusalem did not fall to
the Assyrians.

This prophecy has special meaning for
Christians, who look to Jesus as its fulfillment. A descendant of David whose "origin
is from of old," he is the king Israel awaits,
and will rule as a shepherd, lovingly guiding
his flock. Jesus' reign is universal, and with
it comes profound peace.

As our Advent preparation draws to a
close, this passage offers hope and comfort
to an expectant people. Speak it with a sense
of gratitude and wonder. Tiny, insignificant
Bethlehem is the source of the greatest of
all gifts to the world! Finally, close with a

firm, confident proclamation that in Jesus is
true peace.

READING II   In a book that repeatedly
refers to the work of Christ
in terms reminiscent of the cult of Israel, this
passage from Hebrews claims that the offerings of the past are abolished. There is only
the pure offering of Christ, given "once for
all," unique and universal in its impact. The
author presents Christ speaking the words

READING II Hebrews 10:5–10

A reading from the letter to the Hebrews

Brothers and sisters:
When *Christ* came into the *world*, he said:
  "*Sacrifice* and *offering* you did not *desire*,
  but a *body* you *prepared* for me;
  in *holocausts* and *sin* offerings you took *no delight*.
  Then *I* said, 'As is *written* of me in the *scroll*,
  behold, I *come* to do your *will*, O God.'"

First he says, "*Sacrifices* and *offerings*,
  holocausts and *sin* offerings,
  you neither *desired* nor *delighted* in."
These are offered according to the *law*.
Then he says, "*Behold*, I *come* to do your *will*."
He takes *away* the first to *establish* the second.

By this "*will*," we have been *consecrated*
  through the *offering* of the *body* of Jesus *Christ* once for *all*.

Lift your voice as you begin the quotation. The author places the words of Psalm 40 in Jesus' mouth.

The passage is still quoting the psalmist. The "I" is now understood to be the statement of Jesus. Slow down for these lines, so that the significance of Jesus' claim to be doing God's will can be heard.

That is, the sacrifices of the Jewish law are no longer relevant, since Jesus has fulfilled the will of God.

---

of a psalm that rejects ritual sacrifice in favor of doing God's will.

This mention of God's will reminds us of Jesus' words in the Garden of Gethsemane just before his betrayal and arrest: "Not my will, but yours." In Christ is summed up the will of God; he was obedient even to the point of death. This reminder of Christ's obedience to death connects our celebration of Advent and Christmas to that of the Triduum. The

incarnation, the coming of God into the world in human form, is fulfilled in the triumph of the cross and the glory of the resurrection.

Keep in mind Jesus' sacrifice on the cross as you read this difficult passage. By doing so, you will remind your assembly that the central Christian feast is not Christmas but Easter. The purpose of Christ's coming into the world—which we celebrate on Christmas—was to die and, by his death and resurrection, to conquer death forever.

GOSPEL Last Sunday's gospel spoke of John's role as forerunner of the Messiah. Although John preached a message of radical newness and of righteous actions, he was pointing to the one who would be given dominion and power to judge the world. Today, in a passage from earlier in the same gospel, John has his first

GOSPEL Luke 1:39–45

A reading from the holy gospel according to Luke

Mary set *out*
> and traveled to the *hill* country in *haste*
> to a town of *Judah*,
>> where she entered the house of *Zechariah*
>> and greeted *Elizabeth*.

When *Elizabeth* heard Mary's *greeting*,
> the infant *leaped* in her *womb*,
> and Elizabeth, *filled* with the *Holy Spirit*,
> cried *out* in a loud *voice* and said,
> "*Blessed* are *you* among *women*,
> and *blessed* is the *fruit* of your *womb*.
And how does this happen to *me*,
> that the *mother* of my *Lord* should *come* to me?
For at the *moment* the sound of your *greeting* reached my *ears*,
> the *infant* in my *womb leaped* for *joy*.
Blessed are *you* who *believed*
> that what was *spoken* to you by the *Lord*
> would be *fulfilled*."

Convey Mary's haste by speaking somewhat quickly, but not at the expense of clarity. Continue at a normal, relaxed pace.
Zechariah = zek-uh-RĪ-uh

Give great emphasis to "leaped" and "filled." This is exciting news!
leaped = lept

Speak these familiar words slowly.

Elizabeth's question is humble and genuine. Raise your voice in question for the first "me," not the second.

Offer this as a real blessing from one joyful expectant mother to another who has trusted completely in God.

encounter with Jesus. Even in his mother's womb, John recognizes the superiority of Mary's child, and he is overjoyed at the coming of the Christ to the world.

This story's first encounter, however, occurs between the two pregnant women, filled with joy and hope. In her ecstatic blessing of Mary, Elizabeth speaks for all who await the coming of the Lord and expresses

her wonder at the presence of God on earth. It is this wonder that we experience as we come ever closer to the celebration of God's coming to earth as one of us.

Immediately following today's passage in the gospel of Luke is the Magnificat, Mary's beautiful song of praise. In it she envisions a world in which the wealthy and powerful are cast down, while the lowly are exalted. In this she anticipates the teaching

of John and of Jesus. Her child brings a righteousness that will transform the world.

Take care to proclaim this passage with the exuberance and awe that Elizabeth felt. It is worthy of special attention.

CHRISTMAS VIGIL

Lectionary #13

READING I Isaiah 62:1–5

A reading from the book of the prophet Isaiah

Let your voice be heard loud and clear; you are the prophet's mouthpiece.

For *Zion's* sake I will not be *silent*,
    for *Jerusalem's* sake I will not be *quiet*,
until her *vindication* shines *forth* like the *dawn*
    and her *victory* like a burning *torch*.

Jerusalem will shine forth in splendor for all to see. Proclaim these words with great joy.

Nations shall behold your *vindication*,
    and all the *kings* your *glory*;
you shall be *called* by a *new* name
    pronounced by the *mouth* of the LORD.
You shall be a glorious *crown* in the *hand* of the LORD,
    a royal *diadem* held by your *God*.

diadem = DĪ-uh-dem

Pause briefly before and after the words in quotation marks so that they can be heard as names.

No *more* shall people call you *"Forsaken,"*
    or your *land "Desolate,"*
but *you* shall be called *"My Delight,"*
    and your *land "Espoused."*
For the LORD *delights* in you
    and makes your *land* his *spouse*.

Let tenderness fill your voice.

As a young *man* marries a *virgin*,
    your *Builder* shall marry *you*;
and as a *bridegroom rejoices* in his *bride*
    so shall your *God* rejoice in *you*.

READING I Written at the end of the exile in Babylon, this passage declares the importance of the holy city Jerusalem for the Hebrew people and the renewed blessings God will bestow on it. The exile was understood as a punishment for wrongdoing; the destruction of Jerusalem and the temple gave witness to the barrenness of its former inhabitants. But all that is over; what matters now is that God has forgiven the sins of the people and Jerusalem is to be restored to glory. The

vindication of the city and its inhabitants is for all the world to know and see.

Jerusalem's "new name" is significant; the name of something indicates its very essence. Jacob's name was changed to Israel as a sign of the change in his life; Jerusalem's new titles indicate that the status of the city (and of the people who reside within it) has changed. Perhaps the most famous instance of assigning names of particular significance occurs in the story of the prophet Hosea, whose children bear names that reflect their mother's faithlessness (and by implication the faithlessness of

Israel). However, their names are altered in the end to represent the conversion of Israel after God woos the people into a new committed relationship of love.

The former names of Israel in today's passage are reflected also in an earlier passage of the book of Isaiah (54:1–8). There, exiled Judah is called barren and is compared with a desolate woman. Although the terms can also be applied to agricultural devastation, the introduction of a woman into

Antioch = AN-tee-ahk
Pisidia = pih-SID-ee-uh

Raise your voice over the crowd, just as Paul must have done.

Paul gives a brief history of Israel, concentrating especially on David and God's favor to him.

Although the Davidic dynasty no longer rules Israel, God's promises to David are realized in the person of Jesus.

Speak with humility and conviction.

READING II Acts 13:16–17, 22–25

A reading from the Acts of the Apostles

When *Paul* reached *Antioch* in *Pisidia* and entered
    the *synagogue,*
  he stood *up,* motioned with his *hand,* and *said,*

"Fellow *Israelites* and you *others* who are *God*-fearing, *listen.*
The *God* of this people *Israel* chose our *ancestors*
    and *exalted* the people during their *sojourn*
      in the land of *Egypt.*
With uplifted *arm* he led them *out* of it.

"Then he removed *Saul* and raised up *David* as *king;*
    of *him* he *testified,*
     'I have found *David,* son of *Jesse,* a man after my own *heart;*
    he will carry *out* my every *wish.'*

"From this man's *descendants God,* according to his *promise,*
    has brought to Israel a *savior, Jesus.*
John heralded his *coming* by proclaiming a *baptism* of *repentance*
    to *all* the people of *Israel;*
    and as John was *completing* his course, he would say,
    'What do you *suppose* that I *am*? I am *not* he.
Behold, one is coming *after* me;
    I am not *worthy* to unfasten the *sandals* of his *feet.'*"

the imagery and the play on the word for "married" reflect the status of women in Hebrew society. Marriage and children were seen as the greatest blessings a woman could receive, and the lack of them could be understood as punishment. But the use of terms related to commitment and the close bond of family ties is especially appropriate when applied to God's relationship of love and commitment with the chosen people.

Today's passage affirms the honor that will be given Jerusalem. It will be crowned and revered as royalty, espoused to God. The wedding of a monarch was always cause for great celebration in antiquity (as it often is today) and the passage reflects that joy. The desolation of old is left behind, and the bridegroom (God) professes delight with the bride. The restored Jerusalem will enter into a new and deeper relationship with God, a marriage marked by the passion of newlyweds.

Allow the joy of this passage to ring out in your words. Just as Christians joyfully celebrate the union of divine and human in the person of Jesus, so also the Hebrew people knew that they were to be intimately united with God. Let the newness of the marriage you announce remind your hearers of the renewed relationship possible with God, based as it is on the new covenant inaugurated by Jesus.

READING II The author of the Acts of the Apostles always depicts Paul proclaiming the gospel first in the Jewish synagogue, turning to the Gentiles only after being rejected there. Paul himself

GOSPEL   Matthew 1:1–25

A reading from the holy gospel according to Matthew

The *book* of the *genealogy* of Jesus *Christ*,
    the son of *David*, the son of *Abraham*.

Abraham became the *father* of *Isaac*,
    Isaac the father of *Jacob*,
    Jacob the father of *Judah* and his *brothers*.
Judah became the father of *Perez* and *Zerah*,
    whose *mother* was *Tamar*.
Perez became the father of *Hezron*,
    Hezron the father of *Ram*,
    Ram the father of *Amminadab*.
Amminadab became the father of *Nahshon*,
    Nahshon the father of *Salmon*,
    Salmon the father of *Boaz*,
    whose *mother* was *Rahab*.
Boaz became the father of *Obed*,
    whose *mother* was *Ruth*.
Obed became the father of *Jesse*,
    Jesse the father of *David* the *king*.

David became the father of *Solomon*,
    whose *mother* had been the *wife* of *Uriah*.
Solomon became the father of *Rehoboam*,
    Rehoboam the father of *Abijah*,
    Abijah the father of *Asaph*.
Asaph became the father of *Jehoshaphat*,
    Jehoshaphat the father of *Joram*,
    Joram the father of *Uzziah*.

Take a deep breath before beginning this long list of Jesus' ancestors. Take your time as you read, and convey the importance of family in what could otherwise be a wearying selection.

Perez = PAYR-ez

Zerah = ZEE-rah

Tamar = TAY-mahr

Hezron = HEZ-ruhn

Ram = ram

Amminadab = uh-MIN-uh-dab

Nahshon = NAH-shuhn

Salmon = SAL-muhn

Boaz = BOH-az

Rahab = RAY-hab

Obed = OH-bed

Pause briefly before beginning the next section.

Uriah = yoo-RI-uh

Rehoboam = ree-huh-BOH-uhm

Abijah = uh-BI-juh

Asaph = AY-saf

Jehoshaphat = jeh-HOH-shuh-fat

Joram = JOHR-uhm

Uzziah = uh-ZI-uh

---

gives us a quite different picture of his mission. Whatever the historical reality, the speech in today's reading provides Paul with the opportunity to indicate that the new revelation in Jesus is the fulfillment of God's promises to David. Jesus does not simply arrive in the world from nowhere, but was born into a people chosen by God and given protection and guidance through many travails. God promised eternal favor to the descendants of David.

Although the Davidic monarchy suffered through exile, foreign occupation and defeat, the Jews continued to hope that a descendant of David would arise and restore the people to right relationship with God. In today's speech, Paul indicates that Jesus is that descendant, the savior of Israel. And it was John, the revered preacher of repentance, who declared Jesus to be the one for whom Israel was waiting.

Read this passage as a claim that God's promises are always kept. Allow John's humble words to inspire you and your listeners,

so that you may celebrate the manifestation of God in the world in humility and joy.

| GOSPEL | The gospel writer today offers a message similar to that of |

Paul in Acts. Jesus came into the world as part of a particular people and a particular family. It is this particularity that is often baffling to non-Christians: How could God be present in such ordinariness? But that is what Christians claim, as we acknowledge

Jotham = JOH-thuhm

Ahaz = AY-haz

Hezekiah = hez-eh-KĪ-uh

Manasseh = muh-NAS-uh

Amos = AY-m*s

Josiah = joh-SĪ-uh

Jechoniah = jek-oh-NĪ-uh

Pause briefly before beginning the next section.

Shealtiel = shee-AL-tee-uhl

Zerubbabel = zuh-R<u>OO</u>B-uh-b*l

Abiud = uh-BĪ-uhd

Eliakim = ee-LĪ-uh-kim

Azor = AY-zohr

Zadok = ZAY-dok

Achim = AH-kim

Eliud = ee-LĪ-uhd

Eleazar = el-ee-AY-zer

Matthan = MATH-uhn

This is the announcement for which your assembly has been waiting. Slow down and proclaim it solemnly.

Uzziah became the father of *Jotham,*
  Jotham the father of *Ahaz,*
  Ahaz the father of *Hezekiah.*
Hezekiah became the father of *Manasseh,*
  Manasseh the father of *Amos,*
  Amos the father of *Josiah.*
Josiah became the father of *Jechoniah* and his *brothers*
  at the *time* of the Babylonian *exile.*

After the Babylonian *exile,*
  Jechoniah became the father of *Shealtiel,*
  Shealtiel the father of *Zerubbabel,*
  Zerubbabel the father of *Abiud.*
Abiud became the father of *Eliakim,*
  Eliakim the father of *Azor,*
  Azor the father of *Zadok.*
Zadok became the father of *Achim,*
  Achim the father of *Eliud,*
  Eliud the father of *Eleazar.*
Eleazar became the father of *Matthan,*
  Matthan the father of *Jacob,*
  Jacob the father of *Joseph,* the husband of *Mary.*
Of *her* was born *Jesus* who is called the *Christ.*

Thus the *total* number of generations
  from *Abraham* to *David*
  is *fourteen* generations;
  from *David* to the Babylonian *exile,*
  fourteen generations;
  from the Babylonian *exile* to the *Christ,*
  fourteen generations.

Jesus' human ancestry and proclaim that he truly is one of us.

The long genealogical list establishes Jesus as one who inherited both the blessings and the struggles of the Hebrew people. His lineage is traced back to Abraham, the original recipient of God's promises of favor and protection. He is the descendant of David as well, whose royal house was to endure forever. Jesus' ancestors survived the exile in Babylon, the humiliation of being deported to a foreign land, and the joy of returning home again. Jesus received all the hopes and dreams of his people at his birth:

the covenant established with Abraham; the Davidic dynasty; the struggles for independence from foreign powers. Jesus was fully human and profoundly Jewish.

While Luke emphasizes the role of Mary in the story of Jesus' conception and birth, the gospel of Matthew focuses on Joseph. Joseph is the noble one, unwilling to embarrass Mary, found pregnant before their marriage, and willing to accept God's will without fully understanding it. The divine messenger who appeared to Mary in

Luke appears instead to Joseph in Matthew with the astonishing news of an unusual conception. To Joseph is given the command to name the child Jesus, which means "he will save" in Hebrew.

Just as in the gospel of Luke, the purpose of the story of Jesus' conception and the angel's message is to assert Jesus' otherworldly origin. He is, as later Christians would articulate, fully human, descended from Abraham and David, and at the same time fully divine, conceived of the Holy Spirit. The author adds a final note, claiming that these events fulfill the scriptures, and quotes

Pause again before beginning the story about Joseph. Proceed with an animated voice.

Now *this* is how the birth of Jesus *Christ* came *about.*
When his mother *Mary* was betrothed to *Joseph,*
    but before they *lived* together,
    she was found with *child* through the Holy *Spirit.*

The Jewish law suggests that infidelity on the part of a betrothed woman is to be punished by stoning. Joseph, although he believes that Mary has been unfaithful, does not seek to disgrace her or hold her subject to such a penalty.

Joseph her *husband,* since he was a *righteous* man,
    yet *unwilling* to expose her to *shame,*
    decided to *divorce* her *quietly.*
Such was his *intention* when, *behold,*
    the *angel* of the *Lord appeared* to him in a *dream* and said,
    "*Joseph,* son of *David,*
    do *not* be *afraid* to take *Mary* your *wife* into your *home.*
For it is through the Holy *Spirit*
    that this child has been *conceived* in her.
She will bear a *son* and you are to name him *Jesus,*
    because he will *save* his *people* from their *sins.*"

All *this* took place to *fulfill*
    what the *Lord* had said through the *prophet:*
    "*Behold,* the *virgin* shall *conceive* and bear a *son,*
    and they shall *name* him *Emmanuel,*"
    which means "*God* is *with* us.*"*

When Joseph *awoke,*
    he *did* as the angel of the Lord had *commanded* him
    and took his *wife* into his *home.*
He had no *relations* with her until she bore a *son,*
    and he *named* him *Jesus.*

[Shorter: Matthew 1:18–25]

from the prophet Isaiah. This child is the manifestation of God on earth: Emmanuel.

Because of the long list of obscure names, this passage can be difficult to read. It is important to learn the pronunciations well and to practice them carefully. However, it is always more important to be confident in your proclamation than to do it without error. If you stumble or forget a pronunciation, try not to draw attention to your error, but continue as though nothing had happened. It is better to keep your listeners' attention

focused on the gospel than to distract them by your efforts to correct your mistakes.

The list of names is divided into three sets. Pause between the sets in order to provide a break for your listeners and to emphasize the structure of the passage. There is also a natural rhythm to the genealogical list; be sure that you do not allow your voice to become sing-song. This can happen when a reader becomes bored and does not focus on communicating the intent of the passage: to demonstrate Jesus' origins.

The account of Joseph can be told as a tender story of commitment and honor, as

well as an indication of the special character of this young child. As we celebrate this Christmas the incarnation of the divine Son of God, this story draws us into the events of 2,000 years ago. Offer it as a meditation on trust in God and a proclamation of the fact that, in Jesus, God is truly with us as never before.

CHRISTMAS MIDNIGHT

Lectionary #14

READING I   Isaiah 9:1–6

A reading from the book of the prophet Isaiah

Speak these words warmly and joyfully.

The *people* who walked in *darkness*
    have *seen* a great *light*;
upon those who *dwelt* in the land of *gloom*
    a *light* has *shone*.
You have brought them abundant *joy*
    and great *rejoicing*,
as they rejoice *before* you as at the *harvest*,
    as people make *merry* when dividing *spoils*.

For the *yoke* that *burdened* them,
    the *pole* on their *shoulder*,
and the *rod* of their *taskmaster*
    you have *smashed*, as on the day of *Midian*.

Midian = MID-ee-uhn

For every *boot* that tramped in *battle*,
    every *cloak* rolled in *blood*,
    will be *burned* as fuel for *flames*.

Begin anew, quietly but joyfully, then increase in volume and intensity until you fairly shout with joy the titles given to the ruler.

For a *child* is *born* to us, a *son* is *given* us;
    upon his *shoulder dominion* rests.
They name him *Wonder-Counselor*, *God-Hero*,
    Father-Forever, *Prince* of *Peace*.
His *dominion* is *vast*
    and *forever peaceful*,

Continue with confidence and conviction.

from David's *throne*, and over his *kingdom*,
    which he *confirms* and *sustains*

READING I Coming soon after Isaiah's promise that a child would be born who would be the answer to threats of doom, this passage seems to rejoice in the birth of that child. Isaiah was deeply committed to the promise made to David that his royal line would last forever. Despite adversity, he placed his hope in God's commitment to the Davidic monarch. He assured the king that God would never forsake Judah.

Today's passage came to represent the Jewish hope in a messianic savior. It

enlivened the thought of subsequent generations and provided fertile ground for the establishment of Christianity.

Christians have long held this passage as a favorite text, a hymn celebrating the qualities of Jesus the Christ. Indeed, as we gather during the darkest days of the year, we proclaim that it is precisely through the birth of a child that a piercing light, one that can never be extinguished, has shone through the darkness. The burdens placed on our shoulders are removed through the actions of this one sent by God. He fulfills all hopes for a royal Messiah. Even Solomon's

wisdom cannot compare with his; David's victories pale next to the heroic activity of God through him; he has inspired the patriarchs, the "fathers" of Israel, from the beginning; and his rule is marked by peace and justice. But his dominion is not that of any human king; he will rule forever in glory.

This familiar text is a joy to read in the assembly. Recall the exuberant majesty of Handel's *Messiah* as you share the source of Handel's inspiration. Let your words echo with joy and hope as you proclaim the fulfillment of God's promises in the God-child born in Bethlehem.

by *judgment* and *justice*,
    both *now* and *forever.*
The *zeal* of the L<small>ORD</small> of *hosts* will *do* this!

READING II   Titus 2:11–14

A reading from the letter of Saint Paul to Titus

Beloved:
The *grace* of *God* has *appeared*, saving *all*
    and training us to *reject* godless *ways* and worldly *desires*
    and to live *temperately, justly,* and *devoutly* in this age,
    as we *await* the blessed *hope,*
    the *appearance* of the *glory* of our great *God*
    and *savior* Jesus *Christ,*
    who *gave* himself for us to *deliver* us from all *lawlessness*
    and to *cleanse* for himself a people as his *own,*
    eager to do what is *good.*

GOSPEL   Luke 2:1–14

A reading from the holy gospel according to Luke

In those days a *decree* went out from Caesar *Augustus*
    that the whole *world* should be *enrolled.*
This was the *first* enrollment,
    when *Quirinius* was governor of *Syria.*

The meaning of Christmas is that God's graciousness is evident on earth.

That is, for Jesus to come again.

This is why he came to earth.

Caesar Augustus = SEE-zer aw-GUHS-tuhs

Quirinius = kwih-RIN-ee-uhs

READING II We celebrate today not simply the babe in the manger but the entry of God into human history in the person of Jesus. We know that Jesus' willingness to suffer and die, and his defeat of death, are the central salvific events in history. But today's passage suggests that salvation becomes a reality because of God's willingness to become human, to share in our struggles and our joys, our hopes and our dreams.

The gift God gives in being willing to become one of us also provides moral instruction. The passage suggests ways in which to live upright lives, adopting values that are instilled when we accept and give thanks for the gift of Jesus and look forward to his return. The gift of salvation comes first; righteous deeds follow.

This short passage can be difficult to read because of the long sentence in the opening section. There are three parts to the sentence: a statement about the "grace of God," an exhortation to holy living, and a closing declaration of praise (following the statement about waiting). Practice dividing the sentence according to parts, but do not rush the intervening material. Close with a sincere hope that your assembly will eagerly choose the good deeds desired by God.

GOSPEL As one of the best-loved passages in the New Testament, today's gospel has the ability to inspire children and adults alike. It is far more than a story about a cute baby, although the birth of this child is central to its proclamation. But the implications of the birth are far-reaching.

The text begins on a historical note, since the birth of this lowly child, wearing

Because Jesus was raised as Joseph's adopted child, he was considered of the same ancestral line as Joseph. Thus, he was of the royal line of David.

So *all* went to be *enrolled, each* to his own *town.*
And *Joseph* too went up from *Galilee* from the town of *Nazareth*
    to *Judea,* to the city of *David* that is called *Bethlehem,*
    because he was of the *house* and *family* of *David,*
    to be enrolled with *Mary,* his *betrothed,* who was with *child.*

While they were *there,*
    the time came for her to have her *child,*
    and she gave *birth* to her firstborn *son.*

Jesus was born in abject poverty.

She wrapped him in swaddling *clothes* and laid him in a *manger,*
    because there was no *room* for them in the *inn.*

Now there were *shepherds* in that region living in the *fields*
    and keeping the night *watch* over their *flock.*

The appearance of an angel and a bright light must have been terrifying. Try to convey some of that fear in your voice.

The *angel* of the *Lord appeared* to them
    and the *glory* of the Lord shone *around* them,
    and they were *struck* with great *fear.*
The angel said to them,

Speak reassuringly.

    "Do *not* be *afraid;*
    for *behold,* I proclaim to you *good news* of great *joy*
    that will be for *all* the people.

Slow down and proclaim this announcement with great solemnity.

For *today* in the city of *David*
    a *savior* has been born for you who is *Christ* and *Lord.*
And this will be a *sign* for you:
    you will find an *infant* wrapped in swaddling *clothes*
    and lying in a *manger.*"

And *suddenly* there was a *multitude* of the heavenly *host*
        with the angel,
    praising *God* and *saying:*
    "*Glory* to *God* in the *highest*

Raise your voice in joyful song.

    and on *earth peace* to those on whom his *favor* rests."

rags and sleeping in an animal's food trough, changes all of human history. The claims made about him are not about some fictitious figure, but about a real person, born at a particular time and place. The unattended birth of a baby in a stable inaugurates a new age in God's dealings with humanity and a new era of world history.

The journey of Joseph and Mary to Bethlehem, home of King David, is another way of claiming Jesus' royal ancestry and identifying him as the fulfillment of God's promises to David. This child will change human history, but he was sent precisely to answer the hopes of a particular people, the Jews.

A host of angels appears at Jesus' birth, offering praise to God for the wondrous event. But, as the rest of the gospel of Luke will make clear, the earth-shattering, life-changing, heart-warming event is one quite contrary to all expectations. The great Davidic ruler for whom Israel was waiting is born poor and unknown in a stable. No palace welcomes the Davidic ruler, no precious ointment caresses the skin of the anointed one of God. The announcement of his birth by a heavenly host, proclaimed as good news of joy for all people, is heard only by lowly, illiterate shepherds. The first visitors to the Messiah, the Savior and royal child, are not wealthy rulers or powerful elite, but unassuming guardians of sheep.

This is an exciting gospel to share with the members of your assembly. Try to read it as though for the first time. Share the quiet joy of the baby's birth, the exultation of the angels and the excitement of the shepherds. On this day is born a Savior, Christ the Lord.

CHRISTMAS DAWN

Lectionary #15

READING I   Isaiah 62:11–12

A reading from the book of the prophet Isaiah

The whole world will know the salvation given to Jerusalem. (Zion is another name for Jerusalem.)

See, the LORD *proclaims*
   to the *ends* of the *earth:*
say to daughter *Zion,*
   your *savior* comes!
Here is his *reward* with him,
   his *recompense before* him.

Your voice may become slightly quieter here, but still joyfully reassuring.

They shall be called the holy *people,*
   the *redeemed* of the LORD,
and *you* shall be called "*Frequented,*"
   a city *that* is *not forsaken.*

READING II   Titus 3:4–7

A reading from the letter of Saint Paul to Titus

Beloved:
When the *kindness* and generous *love*
   of God our *savior* appeared,
not because of any righteous *deeds we* had done
   but because of his *mercy,*

Pause briefly. The next line can be spoken a little faster; it is parenthetical.

READING I The end of the Babylonian exile brought about the joyous return of the Hebrew people to their beloved Jerusalem. The renewed city, rebuilt and restored, was the fulfillment of the people's hopes and the sign of God's favor. Although the exile was often understood as punishment for lack of faithfulness, the restoration of Jerusalem was proof of God's favor and Israel's vindication.

The song of joy in today's reading proclaims God's delight in the holy city, here called Zion, and in the people returning to dwell there. A name formerly appropriate for the city is changed: Zion is no longer "forsaken" but is now once again the dwelling place of many. These are the holy people, the redeemed of God. They have completed their time of exile and now can rejoice to return to their beautiful homeland.

Christians see the salvation of God offered most fully in the person of Jesus. It is he who makes us a holy people. Share this brief selection with your community as a song of praise and thanksgiving for what God has done for us in Jesus the Christ.

READING II This passage from the letter to Titus addresses the question of salvation in a uniquely Christian manner. It clarifies that salvation is a gift and does not result from any human actions. Instead, it is something God offers purely out of love for us, and it is effected through baptism. It is appropriate on this feast of the birth of the Savior that we reflect as well on our own rebirth in the waters of baptism.

Through baptism the Spirit of God is offered, a Spirit who gives us the strength to call out to God, not as a foreigner or a guest, but as a member of the household of God.

Slow down as you describe baptism, through which Christians receive the Spirit. Pause briefly after "Holy Spirit."

he *saved* us through the *bath* of *rebirth*
    and *renewal* by the Holy *Spirit*,
whom he richly poured *out* on us
    through Jesus *Christ* our *savior*,
so that we might be *justified* by his *grace*
    and become *heirs* in *hope* of eternal *life*.

GOSPEL   Luke 2:15–20

A reading from the holy gospel according to Luke

When the angels went *away* from them to *heaven*,
    the *shepherds* said to one *another*,
    "Let us *go*, then, to *Bethlehem*
    to *see* this thing that has taken place,
    which the *Lord* has made *known* to us."

The shepherds are eager and curious.

So they went in *haste* and found *Mary* and *Joseph*,
    and the *infant* lying in the *manger*.
When they *saw* this,
    they made known the *message*
    that had been *told* them about this *child*.
All who *heard* it were *amazed*
    by what had been told them by the *shepherds*.

Be careful of your phrasing here; pause after "Joseph" (so that Mary and Joseph do not seem to be lying in the manger!).

Speak with amazement in your voice.

And Mary *kept* all these things,
    reflecting on them in her *heart*.
Then the shepherds *returned*,
    glorifying and *praising God*
    for *all* they had heard and *seen*,
    just as it had been *told* to them.

Speak quietly and warmly about Mary, then enthusiastically as you describe the shepherds again.

We are heirs, recipients of the gift of life willed to us as children of God.

Offer this passage to your assembly as a confirmation that it is chosen by God. Read it with confidence and conviction. Because the passage is one long sentence, practice your phrasing so that you do not rush or run out of breath.

GOSPEL | This morning's gospel passage picks up and continues where the passage for the Mass at midnight left off. The shepherds have received from the angels the joyous announcement of

the birth of a child, a child who is proclaimed as the anointed one of God, Savior and Lord. In eagerness, they visit the child and share the angels' announcement with those they meet, including Mary and Joseph. The words of the angels are greeted with astonishment and awe. The earlier scene, with splendid light and a chorus of angels' voices, continues to inspire. For the gospel writer, everything about this event is amazing.

It is unlikely that Mary would find something new in the words of the shepherds; what is more interesting is what she does with the good news: She ponders it in

her heart. The shepherds, on the other hand, praise God and continue to proclaim the glad tidings.

Inspire the members of your assembly to join with the shepherds in going forth filled with wonder at the goodness of God, who did not deem it undignified to be born in a stable, to walk the earth as a human, to live among the poor and downtrodden. Convey as well the priceless treasure we celebrate today, so that the entire assembly might join with Mary as she ponders the good news in her heart.

CHRISTMAS DAY

Lectionary #16

READING I   Isaiah 52:7–10

A reading from the book of the prophet Isaiah

> **Speak in a gentle, peaceful tone, building as you approach the end of the sentence.**

How *beautiful* upon the *mountains*
   are the *feet* of him who brings glad *tidings*,
announcing *peace*, bearing good *news*,
   announcing *salvation*, and saying to *Zion*,
   "Your *God* is *King!*"

> **The guards on the towers are awaiting the coming of God to Jerusalem (here called Zion).**

Hark! Your *sentinels* raise a *cry*,
   together they *shout* for *joy*,
for they see *directly*, before their *eyes*,
   the LORD restoring *Zion*.

> **Speak with exuberance.**

Break out together in *song*,
   O *ruins* of *Jerusalem!*
For the LORD *comforts* his *people*,
   he *redeems* Jerusalem.
The LORD has *bared* his holy *arm*
   in the *sight* of all the *nations*;
all the *ends* of the *earth* will *behold*
   the *salvation* of our *God*.

> **Let your voice become quieter but still filled with conviction.**

READING I Announcing the end of the exile in Babylon and the restoration of Jerusalem, a messenger runs along the mountaintops, shouting out the good news that God rules over all the earth. During the Babylonian exile, it must sometimes have seemed that God was no longer in power and could not save the people of Judah, living in captivity. But the Persians under King Cyrus defeated the Babylonians, confirming the hopes of those who trusted in God.

The beautiful passage that forms today's reading also announces the end of the exile through the words of the guards in the towers above the city and even through the stones of the ruined city of Jerusalem. God was understood to be with the people as they returned to their beloved homeland. Throughout the exile, God remained with the people and now joins them in coming home, restored as well to the proper divine dwelling. It is time for rejoicing.

As Christians, we too rejoice that God is present in the birth of a child, which we celebrate today. We cry out in joy as we sing the good news that God reigns, confident that all the earth can come to know the salvation offered by our God.

Allow the joy of the speakers in the passage to fill your heart and your voice, so that the community may see and proclaim the wonders of God. Encourage the members of your assembly to see God's activity not only in Jesus but also in the story of the Hebrew people and in their lives today. God is active throughout all of human history.

A reading from the letter to the Hebrews

Brothers and sisters:
In times *past*, God *spoke* in partial and various *ways*
    to our *ancestors* through the *prophets*;
    in these *last* days, he has spoken to us through the *Son*,
    whom he made *heir* of all *things*
    and *through* whom he created the *universe*,
    who is the *refulgence* of his *glory*,
    the very *imprint* of his *being*,
    and who *sustains* all things by his mighty *word*.

When he had accomplished *purification* from *sins*,
    he took his *seat* at the right *hand* of the *Majesty* on *high*,
    as far *superior* to the *angels*
    as the *name* he has *inherited* is more *excellent* than *theirs*.

For to *which* of the angels did God ever say*:*
    "*You* are my *son*; this *day* I have *begotten* you"?
Or again:
    "I will be a *father* to him, and he shall be a *son* to me"?
And again, when he leads the *firstborn* into the *world*, he says:
    "Let *all* the angels of God *worship* him."

These terms and images were once applied to Lady Wisdom, and the preexistent Son is presented in much the same way that Wisdom is elsewhere.

The terminology recalls the actions of the Jewish high priests in the temple, offering expiation for the sins of the people.

Hebrews quotes several Old Testament passages; three are included here. The first (Psalm 2:7) was originally applied to a king, seen as God's son; the second (2 Samuel 7:14) designated the descendant of David; and the third (Deuteronomy 32:43 in the Greek version) comes from a song of Moses. Proclaim these words as statements of Christ's greatness.

READING II The opening verses of the letter to the Hebrews lay out the principal themes that will be addressed in the work. In terms similar to those in today's gospel, this passage declares that Christ the exalted Son reflects God's glory and was present at creation, referring to his salvific actions and his enthronement in heaven. This is one of the strongest statements in the entire New Testament regarding the preexistence of the Son, and it paves the way for development of the doctrine of the Trinity.

Initially, a contrast is made between the way in which God formerly communicated, through the prophets, and God's communication in the final age, through the Son. With amazing succinctness, the passage declares the special status of this Son, the one who is declared "heir of all things" and is above even the angels; he is, in fact, the imprint of the very essence of God.

The author goes on to discuss Christ's exaltation at the right hand of God. Here his superiority to the angels is revealed. He, unlike the angels, is called "Son."

The richness of this passage can make it difficult to proclaim. Be sure to read it slowly and deliberately, pausing briefly after each phrase so that the complexity of the passage will be clear to your listeners. Read the quotations as expressions of God's word and, as the author intends, proclamations of the greatness of Christ.

GOSPEL John 1:1–18

A reading from the holy gospel according to John

Speak very slowly, so that your listeners can follow the progression of thought.

In the *beginning* was the *Word,*
    and the Word was with *God,*
    and the Word *was* God.
He was in the *beginning* with *God.*
All things came to be *through* him,
    and *without* him *nothing* came to *be.*
What came to be through him was *life,*
    and this *life* was the *light* of the human *race;*
    the light *shines* in the *darkness,*
    and the *darkness* has not *overcome* it.

The image shifts here: The one through whom the world was created is also light for all people.

Change your tone and tempo to indicate the shift in subject. Make your voice lighter and less serious.

A man named *John* was sent from *God.*
He came for *testimony,* to *testify* to the *light,*
    so that *all* might *believe* through him.
He was *not* the *light,*
    but came to *testify* to the *light.*

The *true* light, which enlightens *everyone,*
    was coming into the *world.*
He was *in* the world,
    and the world came to be *through* him,
    but the world did not *know* him.

Slow down again, and speak with regret in your voice.

He *came* to what was his *own,*
    but his own *people* did not *accept* him.
But to those who *did* accept him
    he gave *power* to become *children* of *God,*
    to those who *believe* in his *name,*

Speak with hope and wonder.

GOSPEL The beautiful hymn that forms the prologue to John's gospel is a complex literary work. It is at once a hymn of creation, perhaps originally celebrating Wisdom as the cocreator of the world, and at the same time a proclamation of the incarnation. In its present state, it declares that the Word *(Logos)* presided at the creation of the world, bringing life and light to all people. The light is then personified and identified with Jesus, the Word made flesh, who is the only Son of God. Within this broad framework are inserted two digressive statements about John the Baptist, the one who gives witness to the coming of the light.

"In the beginning" recalls the creation story of Genesis, but the creation story is more complex than it appears at first, for with God at the beginning was the *Logos,* through whom God fashioned the world. The Greek term, usually translated "word," means a single word or story, or communication itself. It also signifies reason and intellectual capacity. To declare that the "Word was with God and the Word was God," then, is to speak of the communication of God's thought processes; the Word is divine, as intimately connected with God as a person's thought and speech are with that person.

After the digression concerning John the Baptist, the author resumes the discussion of the light. To explain to the original readers of the prologue (and to us today) why not everyone became a disciple of Jesus, the author claims that "his own" did not recognize or accept him. Surely this is

Communicate the awe of witnessing the glory of Christ.

Again there is a digression, as John is said to declare the superiority of the Word-made-flesh. When the hymn begins again, it continues with the same awe as before.

The passage closes with a statement of the closeness of the Son to God; the revealer knows intimately the one he reveals.

who were *born* not by natural *generation*
nor by human *choice* nor by a man's *decision*
but of *God.*

And the *Word* became *flesh*
and made his dwelling *among* us,
and we saw his *glory,*
the *glory* as of the Father's only *Son,*
full of *grace* and *truth.*

John *testified* to him and cried out, saying,
"This was *he* of whom I *said,*
'The one who is coming *after* me ranks *ahead* of me
because he existed *before* me.'"

From his *fullness* we have all *received,*
grace in place of *grace,*
because while the *law* was given through *Moses,*
grace and *truth* came through Jesus *Christ.*
No one has ever *seen* God.
The only *Son, God,* who is at the Father's *side,*
has *revealed him.*

[Shorter: John 1:1– 5, 9 –14]

an argument by the Jewish-Christian evangelist against the other Jews who did not follow Jesus. But, says the author, those who do follow Jesus become children of God, a relationship made possible because of the Word's special role as the very Son of God.

The claim that the divine could become flesh defies all human reason. The chasm between divine and human, especially evident to one unaccustomed to Christian claims, is great. But as Christians we believe that this *Logos* of God, active in creation and the bearer of life, was born as a human and lived on earth. A God who may at times appear remote has become one of us. The awesome wonder of the incarnation is ultimately beyond our understanding; we proclaim this with faith and gratitude, and with amazement at the tremendous love of a God who would share fully in our human life.

What a wonderful celebration of the incarnation you offer to your community as you read this awe-inspiring and poetic passage. Allow the sections about John to stand as the parenthetical statements they are; lower your voice a bit and increase your speed slightly in order to convey this. Meditate upon this gospel reading, so that the wonder it evokes in you can be heard as you proclaim it in the assembly.

HOLY FAMILY

Lectionary #17

READING I 1 Samuel 1:20–22, 24–28

A reading from the first book of Samuel

In *those* days Hannah *conceived*, and at the *end* of her term
 bore a *son*
 whom she called *Samuel*, since she had asked the LORD
 for him.
The next time her husband *Elkanah* was going up
 with the *rest* of his household
 to offer the customary *sacrifice* to the Lord and to fulfill
 his *vows*,
 Hannah did not go, explaining to her husband,
 "Once the child is *weaned*,
 I will *take* him to *appear* before the LORD
 and to *remain* there *forever*;
 I will offer him as a perpetual *nazirite*."

Once Samuel was *weaned*, Hannah brought him *up* with her,
 along with a *three*-year-old *bull*,
 an ephah of *flour*, and a skin of *wine*,
 and *presented* him at the temple of the LORD in *Shiloh*.
After the boy's *father* had sacrificed the young *bull*,
 Hannah, his *mother*, approached *Eli* and said:
 "*Pardon*, my lord!
As you *live*, my lord,
 I am the woman who stood *near* you here, praying to the LORD.

Pause before continuing with the story about Elkanah.
Elkanah = el-KAY-nah

Hannah speaks confidently, but pain must have filled her heart at the thought of separating from her son. Begin by speaking in a subdued voice, then grow in strength as you repeat Hannah's vow.
nazirite = NAZ-uh-rīt
A nazirite was one who was set apart, dedicated to the service of God.

ephah = EE-fah

Shiloh = SHĪ-loh

Eli = EE-lī
These words are addressed to Eli, the priest of the temple. Speak with confidence to communicate the strength and fortitude of this remarkable woman.

There are two choices for the first and second readings today. Speak with the liturgy coordinator or pastor to find out which readings will be used.

READING I **1 SAMUEL.** After the period when the judges governed the tribes of Israel, Samuel was recognized as the leader of the people. In fact, he anointed as monarch both the first king, Saul, and the successful and beloved King David. Today's story tells of the faithfulness and integrity of Samuel's mother, Hannah.

In verses just prior to the beginning of this reading, Hannah prays to God and asks for a son, promising to dedicate the child to God's service at the temple at Shiloh. True to her word, Hannah consecrates the child Samuel to God as soon as he is old enough to be separated from her. She turns Samuel over to the priest, so that he might serve in the temple and grow in wisdom. Hannah was later blessed with other children, but it was her first child who was destined for greatness in Israel.

The trust Hannah displays is inspiring. Although her heart longs for a child, she has confidence that she can plead her case before God. Earlier in the story, Hannah believes the word of Eli the priest and sets aside her sadness as soon as a child is promised to her. Finally, she allows Samuel to be raised by someone else, even though he is still young when she presents him in the temple. She is confident that God will provide for him.

Hannah keeps her word as well. No one but God had heard her vow. It would have been easy for her to forget it once she

"I prayed for this *child*, and the *Lord granted* my *request*.
Now *I*, in turn, *give* him to the LORD;
   as *long* as he *lives*, he shall be *dedicated* to the LORD."
Hannah *left* Samuel *there*.

Or:

READING I   Sirach 3:2–6, 12–14

A reading from the book of Sirach

God sets a *father* in *honor* over his *children*;
   a mother's *authority* he confirms over her *sons*.
Whoever *honors* his father atones for *sins*,
   and *preserves* himself from them.
When he *prays*, he is *heard*;
   he stores up *riches* who reveres his *mother*.
Whoever honors his *father* is gladdened by *children*,
   and, when he *prays*, is *heard*.
Whoever *reveres* his father will live a *long* life;
   he who *obeys* his father brings *comfort* to his *mother*.

My son, take *care* of your father when he is *old*;
   grieve him *not* as long as he *lives*.
Even if his mind *fail*, be *considerate* of him;
   revile him *not* all the *days* of his *life*;
kindness to a father will not be *forgotten*,
      firmly *planted* against the debt of your *sins*
      —a *house* raised in *justice* to you.

Sirach = SEER-ak

Both father and mother have authority and should be honored.

Respecting one's parents is not a burden but brings blessings.

The aged are to be given special consideration. Speak here in a gentle and encouraging tone.

bore her beloved son, but her integrity is too great to allow that. Still, it must have been heartbreaking for her to part with her young son. We can imagine her tender caresses and gentle words during the few years when Samuel remained in her care. Hannah's trust in God and her own dedication to the Lord give her the confidence to keep her vow.

Hannah's faithfulness and trust were matched only by those qualities in Mary, the mother of Jesus. Mary also trusted the promises made to her and taught her son to love and serve God. Hannah and Mary are examples of dedicated women who created families that were truly holy. As you proclaim this passage, keep in mind your own family's struggles to be holy, and let your voice reflect wonder and admiration at the deep devotion displayed by Hannah.

SIRACH. The book of Sirach is part of the wisdom tradition of Israel; it seeks to instruct people on how to live good and holy lives. Today's passage offers guidance for putting into practice the commandment to honor one's parents.

The authority of parents over their children is established by God. In keeping with a standard belief of Hebrew thought, good deeds are believed to result in blessings, including forgiveness of sins, riches, children and a long life. However, to honor one's father and mother is not only prudent behavior designed to ensure prosperity for oneself; it demonstrates recognition of a higher, divine authority.

It is important to note that the passage does not advocate blind acceptance of parental demands. Instead, it talks about

READING II   1 John 3:1–2, 21–24

A reading from the first letter of Saint John

Begin in a tone of amazement at the tremendous love of God.

Beloved:
See what *love* the Father has *bestowed* on us
    that we may be called the *children* of *God*.
And so we *are*.
The reason the *world* does not *know* us
    is that it did not know *him*.

Pause before and after "Beloved," and speak warmly. Continue in a warm tone, and add a bit of wonder to your voice as you contemplate what is yet to be.

Beloved, we are God's *children now*;
    what we *shall* be has not yet been *revealed*.
We *do* know that when it *is* revealed we shall be *like* him,
    for we shall *see* him as he *is*.

Speak more boldly.

Beloved, if our hearts do not *condemn* us,
    we have *confidence* in God and *receive* from him
        whatever we *ask*,
    because we *keep* his *commandments* and do what *pleases* him.
And his *commandment* is *this*:

Emphasize the commands of faith and love.

    we should *believe* in the *name* of his *Son*, Jesus *Christ*,
    and *love* one *another* just as he *commanded* us.
Those who *keep* his commandments *remain* in him, and *he*
    in *them*,

Slow down, concluding with peaceful confidence.

    and the way we *know* that he *remains* in us
    is from the *Spirit* he *gave* us.

Or:

---

giving honor and reverence to those who have given us life. For some, that may best be offered from afar. However, for most of us, honoring and revering our parents involves an active concern and willingness to provide for their needs, while continuing to respect their privacy and independence whenever possible.

The passage closes with reference to a parent who may be reaching old age and becoming increasingly vulnerable. This is an especially pertinent message in our day of longer life spans. Our age has also seen the public acknowledgment of the abuse of

the elderly, often by their own children.

Offer this passage both as a tribute to legitimate parental authority and as a challenge to the modern tendency to reject anything that is "old," including other human beings. Encourage all the members of your assembly to reflect on what they have learned from their parents and to resolve to give respect and honor in return.

READING II | **1 JOHN.** The Christian community is a "holy family," for we are all children of God. As if that is not

enough, the author of this reading goes on to say that there is even more that awaits us. When God is revealed, we will be not only children of God but truly like God!

In an intricate weaving of themes, the passage proceeds to an exhortation to right behavior. We can boldly ask God for what we need and be assured that God hears us precisely because we keep the commandments of God. Most important is the command to have faith, to believe in the revelation of God in the person of Jesus, and to love one another. And the result of believing in Jesus is the deep peace that comes

Speak warmly as you encourage your listeners to live virtuous lives.

Pause after each term, in order to let each one stand on its own.

Pause, then raise your voice a little as you reach the crowning virtue, love.

These lines require a delivery characterized by firm gentleness.

Reflect the richness of the message you proclaim. Speak with enthusiasm and conviction.

Once again, your voice can be warm and encouraging.

Try to emphasize the parallel structure of the passage, although the content is not parallel.

READING II   Colossians 3:12–21

A reading from the letter of Saint Paul to the Colossians

Brothers and sisters:
Put on, as God's *chosen* ones, holy and beloved,
  heartfelt *compassion*, *kindness*, *humility*, *gentleness*,
    and *patience*,
  bearing with one another and *forgiving* one another,
  if one has a *grievance* against another;
  as the *Lord* has forgiven *you*, so must you *also* do.
And over *all* these put on *love*,
  that is, the bond of *perfection*.
And let the *peace* of *Christ* control your *hearts*,
  the *peace* into which you were also *called* in one *body*.
And be *thankful*.

Let the *word* of Christ *dwell* in you *richly*,
  as in all *wisdom* you *teach* and *admonish* one another,
  singing *psalms*, *hymns*, and spiritual *songs*
  with *gratitude* in your hearts to *God*.
And *whatever* you do, in *word* or in *deed*,
  do *everything* in the name of the Lord *Jesus*,
  giving *thanks* to God the Father *through* him.

Wives, be subordinate to your *husbands*,
  as is *proper* in the *Lord*.
Husbands, love your *wives*,
  and avoid any *bitterness* toward them.
Children, obey your parents in *everything*,
  for this is *pleasing* to the *Lord*.

---

with resting or abiding in God. The Spirit, whose life in our hearts assures us that we are abiding in God, brings us that peace.

In proclaiming this passage, proceed slowly, so that your listeners can follow the progression of thought. Speak with warmth and confidence, in order to assure your community that it is indeed part of the family of God. And offer this message in an encouraging tone, so that God's peace might truly dwell in your assembly.

COLOSSIANS. In today's passage, after telling the Colossian community what not to

do in the previous verses, the author provides a list of virtues appropriate to the lives of Christians. The attributes are to be embraced not only because they are good advice, but because they are offered to people who are to respond as God's chosen ones. They are a holy people, beloved of God, and should live as such.

Stress each virtue in a way that will convey its importance, even when it is only one word. But give special attention to those that form the core of the passage: forgiveness and love. These are central to living as Christians, for they have been offered freely

to us by God. When these virtues are present and all are bound together by love, genuine peacefulness can be known.

The author goes on to encourage a life grounded in prayer. It is a natural outgrowth of allowing the word of Christ to take root in one's heart.

After offering poetic encouragement to holiness, the passage closes with a very specific admonition to members of a household: husbands and wives, children and parents, and (although not quoted here) slaves

Fathers, do not *provoke* your children,
    so they may not become *discouraged*.

[Shorter: Colossians 3:12–17]

GOSPEL   Luke 2:41–52

A reading from the holy gospel according to Luke

The story opens as a straightforward narrative.

Each *year* Jesus' *parents* went to *Jerusalem* for the feast
    of *Passover*,
  and when he was *twelve* years old,
  they went *up* according to festival *custom*.

After they had *completed* its days, as they were *returning*,
  the boy *Jesus* remained *behind* in *Jerusalem*,
  but his *parents* did not *know* it.
Thinking that he was in the *caravan*,
  they journeyed for a *day*
  and *looked* for him among their *relatives* and *acquaintances*,
  but not *finding* him,
  they *returned* to Jerusalem to *look* for him.

Let a bit of tension and anxiety be heard in your voice.

After *three days* they found him in the *temple*,
  sitting in the *midst* of the *teachers*,
  listening to them and asking them *questions*,
  and all who *heard* him were *astounded*
  at his *understanding* and his *answers*.

Speak with astonishment.

---

and masters. The importance of this section is to note the reciprocity involved in all these relationships. Although the specifics of what is required may seem foreign to us, there is always a balance between what each member of a family has to offer. At no time is it appropriate to read this to demonstrate the superiority of some people over others; the scriptures are never to be used to dominate other people.

Your task is to encourage your listeners to put into practice the admonition to live holy lives in love. Offer the reading as an example of one Christian's attempts to encourage others to live correctly. Do not shrink from the final section, but proclaim it simply as the author's example of how to put holy lives into practice.

| GOSPEL | The story of the boy Jesus in the temple is a story that |

brings understanding nods from almost any parent. A child who runs off without warning, whose precociousness amazes adults, and who simply cannot understand why anyone would be upset by an unexplained absence—there are many such children in the world! In some ways, the family of Jesus, Mary and Joseph is not so different from many "holy families" that argue and misunderstand, that struggle to live in harmony, and that love deeply and tenderly.

Of course, not all children are comfortable discussing divine law with religious leaders, as Jesus is. Placed between the story of his birth and the beginning of his ministry, this account provides a transition to the adult world in which Jesus will soon

Let Mary's reproach convey how upset she must have been.

Jesus responds with little concern for his parents' anxiety.

Read this with tenderness, and close the passage in a strong, confident tone.

When his parents *saw* him,
   they were *astonished*,
   and his *mother* said to him,
   "*Son*, why have you *done* this to us?
Your *father* and I have been *looking* for you with great *anxiety*."
And he said to them,
   "*Why* were you *looking* for me?
Did you not *know* that I must be in my Father's *house*?"
But they did not *understand* what he *said* to them.

He went *down* with them and came to *Nazareth*,
   and was *obedient* to them;
   and his *mother* kept all these things in her *heart*.
And Jesus *advanced* in *wisdom* and *age* and *favor*
   before *God* and *man*.

find himself. He is still a child, obedient to his parents, but his concerns are those of an adult with a message.

The portrait of Jesus' parents in this passage is fascinating. Although Joseph's name is not mentioned, both parents are portrayed as law-abiding, faithful Jews attending a feast in Jerusalem. The journey would have taken several days, but they made the trip annually, as the law commands. Since they are part of a large kinship group, they assume Jesus is safe with relatives or friends when they notice his absence. Then they search high and low, as any parents would, for their beloved child.

When they find him, it is Mary who speaks. She reproaches her son, as so many mothers do, for his thoughtlessness. Yet in the end, she holds the event and his response in her heart, pondering its meaning and wondering at the depth of devotion to God displayed by the child she bore. Her heart has yet to be pierced by the intense pain it will know when she witnesses the torture and death of her beloved son.

Offer this selection to your community as encouragement for each family's journey. Give as much life as possible to the speakers and to the contrast between Mary's concern and Jesus' lack thereof. Being a holy family is hard work, and it is comforting to know that Mary, Joseph and Jesus had to struggle with it just as we do.

MARY, MOTHER OF GOD

Lectionary #18

READING I   Numbers 6:22–27

A reading from the book of Numbers

The LORD said to *Moses:*
"Speak to *Aaron* and his *sons* and *tell* them:
    This is how you shall *bless* the Israelites.

"*Say* to them:
    The LORD *bless* you and *keep* you!
    The LORD let his *face shine* upon you,
        and be *gracious* to you!
    The LORD *look* upon you *kindly*
        and give you *peace!*

"So shall they *invoke* my *name* upon the *Israelites,*
    and I will *bless* them."

The family of Aaron had priestly responsibilities in ancient Israel.

Speak this blessing over your assembly with warmth and encouragement.

READING II   Galatians 4:4–7

A reading from the letter of Saint Paul to the Galatians

Brothers and sisters:
When the *fullness* of time had *come,* God sent his *Son,*
    born of a *woman, born* under the *law,*
    to *ransom* those under the law,
        so that we might receive *adoption* as *sons.*

God's Son was born of a woman, subject to the law of Moses.

READING I Today we celebrate Mary, the mother of Jesus, but we also gather as a people beginning a new calendar year. Offer the blessing in this reading over your community as it begins a new year in the hope that God will indeed look with kindness on this people.

This blessing is extremely ancient and is still being used today in many Jewish and Christian congregations. The blessing itself consists of three parts. The first asks God to provide for and protect the people. The second refers to God's "face" and asks that it be turned toward God's chosen ones, a way of asking for God's benevolence and graciousness. God's face shines like the sun, giving warmth and attention to the beloved of the Lord. The third part asks that God may bring peace to the people.

Speak the introductory words and conclusion with firmness; this is God's command. But look upon your assembly with gentle fondness as you warmly pray the words of the blessing.

READING II Paul wrote these words to remind the Galatians of their newfound status as Christians. He claims in an earlier passage that the Galatians were like slaves to sin prior to their reception of faith, lacking the freedom to act rightly. But when the Son came into the world, he freed us, allowing us to be called children of God.

For Paul, slavery was a fact of life. He freely refers to it to make his point. Because of the history of our nation, however, the mention of slavery brings to mind painful memories and unresolved tensions. Read this passage with sensitivity to the feelings of your listeners. At the same time, remind them of their status as Christians; they are

As *proof* that you are sons,
  God sent the *Spirit* of his Son into our *hearts*,
  crying out, *"Abba, Father!"*
So you are no *longer* a slave but a *son*,
  and if a *son* then also an *heir*, through *God*.

As proof of their new status, Paul appeals to the Galatians' own prayer: They call upon God as "Abba," the address of a child to its father.

GOSPEL Luke 2:16–21

A reading from the holy gospel according to Luke

The shepherds went in *haste* to *Bethlehem*
  and found *Mary* and *Joseph*,
  and the *infant* lying in the *manger*.
When they *saw* this,
  they made *known* the message
  that had been *told* them about this *child*.
All who *heard* it were *amazed*
  by what had been *told* them by the *shepherds*.

And Mary *kept* all these things,
  reflecting on them in her *heart*.
Then the shepherds *returned*,
  glorifying and *praising God*
  for *all* they had heard and *seen*,
  just as it had been *told* to them.

When eight *days* were completed for his *circumcision*,
  he was named *Jesus*, the *name* given him by the *angel*
  before he was *conceived* in the *womb*.

Pause after "Joseph," so that it does not seem that Mary and Joseph are lying with the baby in the manger!

Raise your voice to convey the excitement of all who heard the message.

Speak quietly and reflectively.

Again, raise your voice in joy and wonder.

---

truly God's children, free to approach God in intimacy and trust.

GOSPEL This selection was also used as the gospel reading for Christmas Mass at dawn. See that commentary for a fuller discussion.

Today's gospel reminds us of the wondrous event of the incarnation. It recalls the birth of a child who will inspire countless people to change their lives and acknowledge God's goodness. This child will grow to be a preacher and teacher, and will live his life in total obedience to God. This child will become a symbol of the overturning of the old order and a completely new offer of life from God. Finally, this child will one day be proclaimed as so intimately united with God that the child himself is divine.

The central mood of this passage is one of wonder. The shepherds are transformed, inspired to sing God's praises. More importantly, Mary quietly reflects on the events of the day and the words of the visitors.

The gospel closes with the account of Jesus' circumcision, a detail that reveals the importance of the Jewish law for his parents. The account of the circumcision also reminds us of the words of the angel to Mary at Jesus' conception. He is given the name that indicates what he will do: In Hebrew, the name Joshua (in Greek, Jesus) means "he will save."

Although this passage was used only a few days ago on Christmas, many in your assembly might not have heard it yet. Read it as though for the first time, emphasizing the awe of all involved, and especially concentrating on the tender trust of Mary as she ponders the significance of her son.

EPIPHANY OF THE LORD

Lectionary #20

READING I   Isaiah 60:1–6

A reading from the book of the prophet Isaiah

Rise up in *splendor*, Jerusalem! Your *light* has *come*,
the *glory* of the LORD shines *upon* you.
See, *darkness* covers the *earth*,
and thick *clouds* cover the *peoples*;
but upon *you* the LORD *shines*,
and *over* you appears his *glory*.

Nations shall walk by your *light*,
and *kings* by your shining *radiance*.
Raise your *eyes* and look *about*;
they all *gather* and *come* to you:
your *sons* come from *afar*,
and your *daughters* in the arms of their *nurses*.

Then you shall be *radiant* at what you *see*,
your *heart* shall *throb* and *overflow*,
for the *riches* of the sea shall be emptied out *before* you,
the *wealth* of *nations* shall be *brought* to you.
Caravans of *camels* shall *fill* you,
dromedaries from *Midian* and *Ephah*;
all from *Sheba* shall come
bearing *gold* and *frankincense*,
and proclaiming the *praises* of the LORD.

Sing out with joy and wonder at the splendors the author describes.

Lower your voice just a bit, then build to the end of the sentence.

Let your voice be filled with joy.

Midian = MID-ee-uhn
Ephah = EE-fah
Sheba = SHEE-buh

READING I The early Christians kept the feast of the Epiphany as the celebration of the incarnation and the manifestation of God to the world in the person of Jesus. The celebration of Christmas came later and is still secondary for many of the world's Christians. In today's feast we proclaim that God's glory is made known to all. This brings with it a responsibility to ensure that all peoples are welcome, that all needs are met.

The first reading is a joyous proclamation about the splendor of the holy city of Jerusalem. It is a beacon of light in a world of darkness, splendid and radiant as the sun. Its brightness guides not only its own sons and daughters (the people of Israel returning from exile) but even provides light for foreigners, who stream to the city, praising God and bearing riches from their own lands.

This selection also recognizes the responsibility Israel had to be a light to the nations, telling others of both the expectations and the blessings of God. Christians believe that the promises made to Israel are fulfilled in Jesus and that he is most fully the light for the nations. Jesus is like Jerusalem, radiant in glory, guiding all peoples and receiving gifts of wealth and honor.

Cry out with joy and excitement as you share this passage with your community. Let it inspire your listeners to rejoice in the splendors of God, now revealed in Jesus. Encourage them to be welcoming to all people, friend and foreigner, in order to become a new Jerusalem, shining for all to see.

READING II Paul's ministry was marked by controversy. Among the earliest followers of Jesus (all conscientious Jews, as was Jesus himself), there

The author claims that Paul's ministry to the Gentiles was undertaken in response to a revelation.

Close with strong emphasis on the equality of all in God.

There were people in the ancient Middle East who were known for their knowledge of the movement of stars. The gospel writer has them in mind here.

READING II   Ephesians 3:2–3a, 5–6

A reading from the letter of Saint Paul to the Ephesians

Brothers and sisters:
You have *heard* of the *stewardship* of God's *grace*
    that was *given* to me for your *benefit*,
    namely, that the *mystery* was made *known* to me
        by *revelation*.

It was *not* made known to people in *other* generations
    as it has *now* been *revealed*
    to his holy *apostles* and *prophets* by the *Spirit:*
    that the *Gentiles* are *coheirs*, members of the *same body*,
    and *copartners* in the promise in Christ *Jesus*
        through the *gospel.*

GOSPEL   Matthew 2:1–12

A reading from the holy gospel according to Matthew

When Jesus was born in *Bethlehem* of *Judea*,
    in the days of King *Herod*,
    behold, magi from the *east* arrived in Jerusalem, saying,
    "Where is the newborn *king* of the *Jews*?
We saw his *star* at its *rising*
    and have come to do him *homage.*"

---

arose a dispute about who could be saved. Paul and others argued that the salvation offered in Christ was available to all, regardless of race or religious heritage. The original view held that Jesus had come to his own people, the Jewish nation, and that it was necessary to be Jewish in order to be his follower. The letter to the Ephesians, written by an admirer of Paul, insists that God's blessings are for all; Gentiles together with Jews are recipients of the promises made to Israel and fulfilled in Jesus.

Today's passage recalls the ministry of Paul in establishing and serving churches composed primarily of non-Jews. The author uses the Pauline image of the body. Gentiles are pictured as a limb of the body of Israel. By being part of the same body, Gentiles are able to inherit all that belongs to the Israel, all that has been promised by God to the chosen people.

Since most of us are non-Jewish followers of Christ, we are the direct recipients of this Epiphany message. But just as the Jewish followers of Jesus were challenged to accept Gentiles, so also we cannot truly claim to follow Jesus unless we proclaim him to all the world without regard to race or class or appearance.

Your task is to present this challenge to your listeners by reading the concluding lines of the passage with special forcefulness. Encourage them to appreciate both the abiding nature of God's promises to the Jewish people and the inclusiveness that we must offer to others.

GOSPEL High drama now greets us as we turn from the adorable child in the manger and the choirs of angels celebrating his birth to the scheming of the

Herod the Great was a ruthless, greatly disliked puppet king. He jealously guarded his power and was afraid that he would be ousted from his throne.

When King Herod *heard* this,
    he was greatly *troubled*,
    and all Jerusalem *with* him.
Assembling all the chief *priests* and the *scribes* of the *people*,
    he *inquired* of them where the *Christ* was to be *born*.
They said to him, "In *Bethlehem* of *Judea*,
    for *thus* it has been written through the *prophet*:
    'And *you*, *Bethlehem*, land of *Judah*,
    are by *no* means *least* among the *rulers* of Judah;
    since from *you* shall come a *ruler*,
    who is to *shepherd* my people *Israel*.'"

Convey Herod's cunning.

Then Herod called the magi *secretly*
    and *ascertained* from them the time of the star's *appearance*.
He sent them to *Bethlehem* and said,
    "*Go* and search *diligently* for the child.
When you have *found* him, bring me *word*,
    that I *too* may go and do him *homage*."

They begin to "follow" the star at this point. Express the wonder and joy the wise men felt.

After their *audience* with the king they *set out*.
And *behold*, the *star* that they had seen at its rising
        preceded them,
    until it came and *stopped* over the place where the *child* was.
They were *overjoyed* at seeing the *star*,
    and on entering the *house*
    they saw the *child* with Mary his *mother*.

They *prostrated* themselves and did him *homage*.
Then they opened their *treasures*
    and offered him *gifts* of *gold*, *frankincense*, and *myrrh*.

And having been warned in a *dream* not to return to *Herod*,
    they *departed* for their country by another *way*.

king, who attempts to keep anyone from honoring this child. One of the reasons for the change in tone is the change in authors. Up to this point we have been reading the nativity story primarily from the gospel of Luke; we now turn to the gospel of Matthew. But it is also time to recognize the demands placed on us by that sweet babe, for Epiphany is a challenging feast. There is great joy in the proclamation that God is made known to the entire world in Christ Jesus, and great challenge to us to be as open and accepting of those who are different from us as the child Jesus was of his visitors.

The story is familiar, yet it has a timeless quality. People of great wealth and education, able to see the signs of the times concentrated in a single star, come to honor a poor, unknown baby born to parents far from home. Naturally they begin by seeking him in a palace, since they recognize that he is to be the king of the Jews. When King Herod attempts to trick them, they accomplish their mission and return home, thwarting his jealous plot.

On this feast of Epiphany, we celebrate the mission of these foreign people, who carried news of God's presence in Jesus back to their homelands. The significance of Jesus, unrecognized so often by his own people during his ministry, is clear to those who have never met him before.

Proclaim this gospel as the exciting story it is. Let the story challenge your listeners to be more accepting of those who are unfamiliar. We honor Jesus best today by resolving to do as the Magi did: bend our knees before the helpless; respect the young as well as the aged; offer our wealth to those with nothing.

Lectionary #66

READING I Isaiah 62:1–5

A reading from the book of the prophet Isaiah

Open with great enthusiasm.

For *Zion's* sake I will not be *silent*,
    for *Jerusalem's* sake I will not be *quiet*,
until her *vindication* shines *forth* like the *dawn*
    and her *victory* like a burning *torch*.

Nations shall behold your *vindication*,
    and all the *kings* your *glory*;
you shall be *called* by a *new* name
    pronounced by the *mouth* of the LORD.

Express with your voice the awe one feels when beholding something of great beauty. Pause at the end of the sentence. Speak earnestly and reassuringly.

You shall be a glorious *crown* in the *hand* of the LORD,
    a royal *diadem* held by your *God*.

No *more* shall people call you *"Forsaken,"*
    or your *land* *"Desolate,"*
but *you* shall be called *"My Delight,"*
    and your *land* *"Espoused."*
For the LORD *delights* in you
    and makes your *land* his *spouse*.

This closing section should be proclaimed with tenderness and deep joy.

As a young *man* marries a *virgin*,
    your *Builder* shall marry *you*;
and as a *bridegroom rejoices* in his *bride*
    so shall your *God* rejoice in *you*.

READING I Rejoicing in the shining glory of Jerusalem (also called Zion), this passage was written at the end of Israel's exile in Babylon. While the leading citizens of Jerusalem had been away, longing to return to their beloved city, the city itself had been lying in ruins. Now, however, God declares the importance of Jerusalem and the blessings that will be bestowed on it. Jerusalem will shine like the dawn; it will be as radiant as jewels. The splendor of God's chosen people, as depicted in the city itself, will be evident to all.

This passage was used also at the Christmas Vigil (see that commentary for further discussion). Its use today continues our celebration of Epiphany. On Epiphany, we proclaim that God's glory is manifest to all the world. This passage from Isaiah declares that the city of Jerusalem shines forth in splendor as a sign of God's greatness and love for the people of the city.

There are two aspects of this reading that require special emphasis today: Raise your voice joyfully as you proclaim the greatness of God, seen in the splendor of Jerusalem; and speak tenderly of the tremendous love and commitment of God toward this people, imaged in the love of newlyweds.

READING II This beautiful passage from Paul on the gifts of the Spirit is a celebration of what it means to live in a Christian community. Despite great diversity and different outlooks, there is one Spirit, who inspires all activity for the sake of the common good. Our challenge is to recognize both our own gifts and those of other members of our communities, in order to build up

A reading from the first letter of Saint Paul to the Corinthians

Brothers and sisters:
There are different kinds of spiritual *gifts* but the *same Spirit;*
    there are different forms of *service* but the *same Lord;*
    there are different *workings* but the *same God*
    who produces *all* of them in *everyone.*

To *each* individual the *manifestation* of the *Spirit*
    is given for some *benefit.*
To *one* is given through the Spirit the expression of *wisdom;*
    to *another,* the expression of *knowledge* according
        to the *same* Spirit;
    to *another, faith* by the same *Spirit;*
    to *another,* gifts of *healing* by the *one Spirit;*
    to *another,* mighty *deeds;*
    to *another, prophecy;*
    to *another,* discernment of *spirits;*
    to *another,* varieties of *tongues;*
    to *another, interpretation* of tongues.

But *one* and the same *Spirit* produces *all* of these,
    distributing them *individually* to *each* person as he *wishes.*

A reading from the holy gospel according to John

There was a *wedding* at Cana in *Galilee,*
    and the *mother* of Jesus was there.
Jesus and his *disciples* were *also* invited to the *wedding.*

Paul is trying to teach his community; speak accordingly. Proper stress is particularly important in this opening line. Give emphasis to "gifts," "service," and "workings," and especially to the word "same" throughout this section.

The Spirit is not given simply for personal use but for the entire community.

Although there is a similar presentation given to many of these gifts, each is unique. Try to provide some variety in your proclamation, so that each one stands out. Pause briefly after each gift.

Pause before proclaiming this line slowly and with a strong voice.

---

the entire community as lovingly and effectively as possible.

Paul continually needed to reprimand the members of the Corinthian community and guide them in their faith development. It was not that the Corinthians were faithless or wayward. Often the problem was precisely one of excessive enthusiasm. In worship, some were given spectacular signs of God's power in their lives, such as speaking in foreign tongues or prophesying God's messages. Paul must remind them that these are gifts from God and should not be sources of

personal pride. In addition, others also manifest God in their activities, even if their gifts are more subdued. Paul asserts that God, the source of all charisms, is one. There is one Spirit, one Lord (Jesus), one God. And the gifts given by the Spirit are given for the good of all.

Offer this message to your community as a reminder to appreciate the gifts of every member, young and old, male and female, whether rich or poor, educated or not. It is an assurance to those who do not see themselves as an integral part of the community

to know that their presence and their particular skills are essential for the church. And it is a reminder to those in leadership positions and those with more noticeable gifts that everything comes from God and that their gifts are no greater and no lesser than anyone else's.

GOSPEL   The gospel of John is filled with more symbolism and deeper meaning than first appears. In the story of the wedding at Cana, a simple account of an extraordinary event takes on

Jesus' mother is given few words here. How do you think she intends this? Is it simply an observation or is she concerned? Express it as you imagine her speaking.

Although Jesus' words are not meant to be harsh, he is asserting his authority over his mother's. Do not overemphasize "woman," but focus on the rest of the question.

Mary's words are confident and decisive.

Jesus is in charge. Although his words are few, they are spoken with authority.

This line is parenthetical. Speak it somewhat quickly.

There is amazement and perhaps a bit of reproach in his comment.

Speak with certitude.

When the *wine* ran short,
the mother of Jesus *said* to him,
"They have no *wine*."
And Jesus said to her,
"*Woman*, how does your concern affect *me*?
My *hour* has not yet *come*."
His mother said to the servers,
"Do *whatever* he *tells* you."

Now there were six stone *water* jars there for Jewish
ceremonial *washings*,
each holding twenty to thirty *gallons*.
Jesus told them,
"*Fill* the jars with *water*."
So they filled them to the *brim*.
Then he told them,
"*Draw* some *out* now and take it to the *headwaiter*."
So they *took* it.

And when the headwaiter *tasted* the *water* that had become *wine*,
without *knowing* where it *came* from
—although the servers who had *drawn* the water *knew*—
the headwaiter called the *bridegroom* and said to him,
"Everyone serves *good* wine *first*,
and then when people have drunk *freely*, an *inferior* one;
but *you* have kept the good wine until *now*."

Jesus did this as the *beginning* of his signs at *Cana* in *Galilee*
and so revealed his *glory*,
and his *disciples* began to *believe* in him.

---

even greater meaning when examined in light of the gospel as a whole. As the concluding lines claim, this first "sign" of Jesus is intended to display his glory. It is also an inspiration to faith.

Jesus responds to his mother's observation by asserting that his hour has not yet come. The "hour" in John's gospel is always that of Jesus' death on the cross, which manifests his glory. The story of Cana is thus linked with Jesus' sacrifice on the cross, suggesting that the water become wine should be interpreted in the same light. The "sign" that most fully reveals Jesus' glory is

the shedding of his blood on the cross. And the eucharistic wine is Jesus' blood, shed for all. For this reason, Christian art has long linked this story with the eucharist.

The jugs in which the water is poured are those used in Jewish ceremonial washings. Such purification rituals were—and are—very important for law-abiding Jews. Since Jesus himself is linked with the wine, the use of these jars for holding the wine suggests that salvation comes out of Judaism, with its extensive religious observances. At the same time, the new wine is better than the first, as the steward

observes. The new life brought by Jesus, himself fully Jewish, is superior to that available under the Jewish law.

Although this story is familiar, there is much here that is exciting to proclaim. Meditate on the passage's significance so that you will be able to proclaim it with a sincerity and exuberance.

3RD SUNDAY IN ORDINARY TIME

Lectionary #69

READING I   Nehemiah 8:2–4a, 5–6, 8–10

A reading from the book of Nehemiah

Ezra the *priest* brought the *law* before the *assembly*,
    which consisted of *men, women,*
    and those children *old* enough to *understand.*
Standing at one *end* of the *open* place that was before
        the *Water* Gate,
    he read out of the *book* from *daybreak* till *midday,*
    in the presence of the *men,* the *women,*
    and those children *old* enough to *understand;*
    and *all* the people listened *attentively* to the *book* of the *law.*
Ezra the *scribe* stood on a wooden *platform*
    that had been *made* for the *occasion.*

He *opened* the scroll
    so that *all* the people might *see* it
    —for he was standing higher *up* than any of the people—
    and, as he *opened* it, all the people *rose.*
Ezra *blessed* the LORD, the great *God,*
    and all the *people,* their hands raised *high,* answered,
    "Amen, amen!"
Then they bowed *down* and *prostrated* themselves
        before the LORD,
    their *faces* to the *ground.*

Ezra read *plainly* from the book of the *law* of *God,*
    interpreting it so that all could *understand* what was *read.*

Stress the length of this reading.

Lighten your voice and speak enthusiastically to stress the attentiveness of the people.

Let the enthusiasm of the people be heard.

READING I Ezra was a leading figure in the period following the rebuilding of the Jerusalem temple. The temple had been destroyed by the Babylonians and the leading members of Judean society taken into captivity in Babylon. When they returned, they set about building another temple and, as this passage attests, again devoted themselves to God. Ezra was instrumental in helping the people purify themselves, encouraging them to set aside any customs they had acquired from other peoples during the exile.

Ezra reads the law God gave to Moses to the gathered people. It is not entirely clear how much of the Pentateuch (the first five books of the Hebrew Bible) Ezra read, but it must have included some materials dictating proper conduct and ritual. It was certainly complex, since the Levites needed to interpret it so that the people could better understand it.

The response of the people is interesting. They stand transfixed, listening attentively to Ezra's words. When Ezra holds the sacred book for them to see, they bow down to worship God. But they also weep, whether in sorrow at their own failings or because they are touched by the words. Since Ezra tells them to act joyfully and to feast, it appears that they react in sorrow. At the same time it was the people who asked Ezra to read the law in the first place, and they listen for hours on end. They are eager to learn what they must do in order to serve God fully.

This attentiveness and love for the word of God is what we all wish for our own assemblies. Your task is to act as Ezra did,

Ezra read the law in Hebrew, and the Levites either offered instruction or translated Ezra's words into Aramaic, the language of the people.

Speak comfortingly.

Then *Nehemiah*, that is, His *Excellency*, and *Ezra*
the priest-*scribe*
and the *Levites* who were *instructing* the people
said to all the *people*:
"Today is *holy* to the LORD your *God*.
Do not be *sad*, and do not *weep*"—
for all the people were *weeping* as they heard the *words*
of the *law*.

He said further: "*Go*, eat rich *foods* and drink sweet *drinks*,
and allot *portions* to those who had nothing *prepared*;
for *today* is *holy* to our LORD.
Do not be *saddened* this day,
for *rejoicing* in the LORD must be your *strength!*"

READING II   1 Corinthians 12:12–30

A reading from the first letter of Saint Paul to the Corinthians

Brothers and sisters:
As a body is *one* though it has many *parts*,
and all the *parts* of the body, though *many*, are one *body*,
so also *Christ*.

For in *one Spirit* we were all *baptized* into one *body*,
whether *Jews* or *Greeks*, *slaves* or *free* persons,
and we were *all* given to drink of *one Spirit*.

Throughout this reading, give slight emphasis to the word "one" wherever it appears.

Speak firmly and decisively.

holding your listeners in rapt attention while you share God's word with them. You do this by the way you speak and move, and by the enthusiasm you bring to the reading. After all, hearing God's law is cause for rejoicing; it is not burdensome or tiring. Ezra declared that the day when Israel heard God's law was holy; it was a day for celebrating. Listening to God's word can be enlivening for us as well.

Today you are Ezra, sharing the word of God with the members of your assembly. Be sure you have their attention before you begin. Express with amazement the attentiveness of the crowd, and convey their sincerity as they hear the law. Proclaim with vigor the words of Ezra to go forth and celebrate. Let this instruction ring in the ears of your hearers today.

READING II Paul's beautiful metaphor of the church as a body whose parts must work in harmony picks up on last Sunday's reading. There Paul discussed the gifts of the Spirit, which God gives to each person in order to edify the entire community. It would be helpful to go back and read that passage first before continuing to prepare today's reading.

Just as the physical body has many parts, so also the community of Christians comprises many different people, each with different abilities and interests. But the one Spirit of God gives all of these various gifts. We become filled with this same Spirit in baptism. We must spend the rest of our lives

Imagine a foot or an ear actually talking, and read this section with that in mind. Then your voice will express the foolishness of claiming that some members are more important than others.

Now the body is not a *single* part, but *many*.
If a *foot* should say,
  "Because I am not a *hand* I do not *belong* to the body,"
  it does not for this reason belong any *less* to the body.
Or if an *ear* should say,
  "Because I am not an *eye* I do not *belong* to the body,"
  it does not for *this* reason belong any *less* to the body.
If the whole *body* were an *eye*, where would the *hearing* be?
If the whole *body* were *hearing*, where would the sense
    of *smell* be?

Now speak solemnly and slowly.

But as it *is*, God placed the *parts*,
  each *one* of them, in the body as he *intended*.
If they were all one *part*, where would the *body* be?
But as it *is*, there are *many* parts, yet *one body*.
The *eye* cannot say to the *hand*, "I do not *need* you,"
  nor again the *head* to the *feet*, "I do not need *you*."
Indeed, the *parts* of the body that *seem* to be *weaker*
    are all the more *necessary*,
    and *those* parts of the body that we consider less *honorable*
    we surround with *greater* honor,
    and our less *presentable* parts are treated with *greater* propriety,
    whereas our *more* presentable parts do not *need* this.

Offer these words with earnest compassion.

This is a key line. Give it great emphasis. It is only when all members of the community are truly appreciated that we can claim to be the body of Christ.

But *God* has so constructed the *body*
  as to give *greater* honor to a part that is *without* it,
  so that there may be no *division* in the *body*,
  but that the *parts* may have the same *concern* for one *another*.
If *one* part suffers, *all* the parts suffer *with* it;
  if one part is *honored*, all the parts share its *joy*.

appreciating our own gifts and the fact that the Spirit enlivens those around us, however different their skills and interests may be.

Paul provides a compelling argument for recognizing the various gifts each person has. There can be no question that the parts of the body must work in concert with one another in order for the entire body to function. No part is insignificant, and no part is so great that it can take the place of the others. As Paul says, if everything were an eye, how would we hear or smell? Even the parts of the body that embarrass us are

given honor, even honor greater than the other, less embarrassing parts.

Think of what this means when applied to the Christian community! Each task is necessary and noble, no one is insignificant, and no one can claim superiority over anyone else. And think of someone in your community who causes you embarrassment. Far from being shunned, that one is to be given greater honor! This message is both encouraging and challenging.

Paul was responding to a tendency in the Corinthian community to value some gifts, such as speaking in tongues, over

other, less spectacular ones. Paul's hierarchy reverses their expected order, placing the gift of speaking in tongues in the last position. How do you think Paul would respond to the hierarchies in our churches today? If he were to look at your community, would he be assured that all members were exercising their gifts? Would he need to correct some who consider themselves more important than others?

Proclaim this passage with sincerity and respect for each gift from God and for each member of your community. When Paul

Now *you* are Christ's *body*, and individually *parts* of it.
Some people God has *designated* in the church
  to be, first, *apostles*; second, *prophets*; third, *teachers*;
  then, mighty *deeds*;
  then gifts of *healing, assistance, administration,*
  and varieties of *tongues.*

Are *all* apostles? Are all *prophets*? Are all *teachers*?
Do *all* work mighty *deeds*? Do *all* have gifts of *healing*?
Do *all* speak in *tongues*? Do all *interpret*?

[Shorter: 1 Corinthians 12:12–14, 27]

Speak the questions slowly, although the negative answer to each is readily apparent. The passage ends rather abruptly. Read the final lines slowly, then provide a lengthy pause before returning to your seat.

GOSPEL   Luke 1:1–4; 4:14–21

A reading from the holy gospel according to Luke

Since *many* have undertaken to compile a *narrative* of the *events*
  that have been fulfilled *among* us,
  just as those who were *eyewitnesses* from the *beginning*
  and *ministers* of the *word* have handed them *down* to us,
  I *too* have decided,
  after investigating everything *accurately anew,*
  to write it down in an orderly *sequence* for you,
  most excellent *Theophilus,*
  so that you may realize the *certainty* of the *teachings*
  you have *received.*

Jesus returned to *Galilee* in the *power* of the *Spirit,*
  and *news* of him *spread* throughout the whole *region.*
He *taught* in their *synagogues* and was *praised* by *all.*

The author was clearly not an eyewitness to the events recorded in the gospel.

Theophilus = thee-OF-uh-luhs

Pause after "received" before beginning again on a strong note.

---

directly addresses the Corinthians ("you are the body of Christ"), offer these words to your own listeners. Finally, pray that you might touch their hearts so that the value of each member of the community might be known and the oneness envisioned by Paul created.

GOSPEL   Today we begin in earnest this liturgical year's journey through the gospel of Luke. We have heard from Luke before, during Advent and Christmas, and we shall occasionally read from other gospels in the months ahead, but it is the gospel of Luke that will predominate in our gospel readings during Ordinary Time.

The gospel of Luke opens, as does today's gospel reading, with an introduction that sets the stage for the rest of the two-volume work, the gospel of Luke and the Acts of the Apostles. The author writes in relatively polished Greek and uses many of the techniques employed in the Greek tradition of history writing. Although others have written similar accounts, our author claims to have researched the material and gained trustworthy witnesses before putting this information in writing. Indeed, all of the gospels are compositions written long after the events they record. Decades of oral tradition preceded the composition of even the earliest gospel. This two-volume work is dedicated to a certain Theophilus, whose name means "lover of God."

After the introductory paragraph, the lectionary skips to the beginning of Jesus' ministry. (The intervening material is the story of Jesus' birth and childhood.) The

Pause before and after "according to his custom."

Jesus seems to have chosen this passage. The entire gospel presents him as the fulfillment of it. Read the passage slowly and forcefully.

Speak this final line slowly and with great solemnity.

He came to *Nazareth*, where he had grown *up*,
    and *went* according to his custom
    into the *synagogue* on the *sabbath* day.

He stood up to *read* and was handed a *scroll* of the prophet *Isaiah*.
He *unrolled* the scroll and found the *passage* where it was *written*:
"The *Spirit* of the Lord is *upon* me,
    because he has *anointed* me
    to bring *glad tidings* to the *poor*.
He has *sent* me to proclaim *liberty* to *captives*
    and recovery of *sight* to the *blind*,
    to let the *oppressed* go *free*,
    and to *proclaim* a year *acceptable* to the *Lord*."

Rolling up the *scroll*, he handed it back to the *attendant* and
        sat *down*,
    and the eyes of *all* in the synagogue looked *intently* at him.

He *said* to them,
    "*Today* this *Scripture* passage is *fulfilled* in your *hearing*."

author paints a rosy picture of Jesus' popularity and influence. Ironically, today's passage ends immediately before the synagogue crowd in Nazareth turns against Jesus and tries to throw him off a cliff.

Jesus reads a passage from the prophet Isaiah in which the anointed of the Lord speaks, proclaiming good news to those who have been without favor. The poor, the captives, the blind, the prisoners—all those who are in pain, struggling and often rejected—will have their situations reversed. Indeed, the entire gospel of Luke is about change in the present reality, when what is expected is turned on its head. By reading this passage, Jesus not only offers himself as the anointed one of God, the fulfillment of God's promises, but also as a revolutionary. He is a preacher of a new world order in which the disenfranchised find favor and the despised are chosen.

Your proclamation of this passage sets the tone for much of the rest of this liturgical year. Let Jesus' words be forceful and prophetic, offering hope to those without hope. In this way, you may be able to offer the downtrodden in your own community the hope to carry on, knowing that Jesus came for their sake.

4TH SUNDAY IN ORDINARY TIME

Lectionary #72

READING I   Jeremiah 1:4–5, 17–19

A reading from the book of the prophet Jeremiah

The *word* of the LORD *came* to me, saying:
Before I *formed* you in the *womb* I *knew* you,
   before you were *born* I *dedicated* you,
   a *prophet* to the *nations* I *appointed* you.

But do you *gird* your *loins*;
   stand *up* and *tell* them
   all that I *command* you.
Be not *crushed* on their account,
   as though I would *leave* you *crushed* before them;
for it is *I* this day
   who have made you a fortified *city*,
a pillar of *iron*, a wall of *brass*,
   against the whole *land*:
against Judah's *kings* and *princes*,
   against its *priests* and *people*.
They will fight *against* you but not prevail *over* you,
   for *I* am *with* you to *deliver* you, says the LORD.

Speak tenderly.

Jeremiah is to be a prophet not only to the chosen people but to all nations.

The tone becomes more ominous here, as a battle ensues.

Lighten your voice a bit, and speak encouragingly.

End on a strong note.

READING I — The prophet Jeremiah's message often resonates with us because it flows from his own struggles with his ministry. He argues with God about his capabilities, but he also responds faithfully, even when threatened with death. Often remembered as a prophet of doom, he advised the king of Judah to accept foreign control in order for Judah to survive. Just as Jerusalem was about to fall to the Babylonians, Jeremiah offered encouraging words, stressing God's commitment to this people.

Today we read part of Jeremiah's call to ministry. Even before he was born, he was set aside for this task. God chose him not only to go to the people of Israel but to the Gentiles as well.

The task ahead of Jeremiah is daunting. There will be some who will oppose his message. But God will provide not only words but strength for the prophet. Even though he will challenge the most powerful people of the land, God assures Jeremiah that he will not be conquered.

The prophets of our own time know well what it is like to feel opposition, to take on the strong and powerful. But we can see in them (whether Martin Luther King Jr., Mother Teresa, Dorothy Day, or others) the iron will to resist and continue to proclaim God's love for all, even—and especially—the outcast.

The call of Jeremiah also has much in common with the beginning of Jesus' ministry. Jesus was chosen before he was born and sent to all the nations. He experienced conflict and resistance to his message. But we believe that God delivered him, that he

READING II   1 Corinthians 12:31—13:13

A reading from the first letter of Saint Paul to the Corinthians

Brothers and sisters:
Strive *eagerly* for the *greatest* spiritual gifts.
But I shall *show* you a still more *excellent* way.

If I *speak* in *human* and angelic *tongues*,
    but do not have *love*,
    I am a resounding *gong* or a clashing *cymbal*.
And if I have the gift of *prophecy*,
    and comprehend all *mysteries* and all *knowledge*;
    if I have all *faith* so as to move *mountains*,
    but do not have *love*, I am *nothing*.
If I give away *everything* I *own*,
    and if I hand my *body* over so that I may *boast*,
    but do not have *love*, I *gain* nothing.

Love is *patient*, love is *kind*.
It is not *jealous*, it is not *pompous*,
    it is not *inflated*, it is not *rude*,
    it does *not* seek its own *interests*,
    it is not quick-*tempered*, it does not *brood* over *injury*,
    it does not rejoice over *wrongdoing*
    but *rejoices* with the *truth*.
It *bears* all things, *believes* all things,
    hopes all things, *endures* all things.

Love never *fails*.
If there are *prophecies*, they will be brought to *nothing*;
    if *tongues*, they will *cease*;
    if *knowledge*, it will be brought to *nothing*.

Start each sentence on a hopeful note, then lower your voice with the words "but do not have love."

Pause, then begin again slowly, building in volume, speed and intensity as you proceed.

Pause. Stress the contrasts in the following lines.

---

has not been conquered despite all appearances to the contrary.

   As you proclaim today's reading, keep in mind the prophets in your own community or your own life. Speak tenderly to them, and offer them God's supportive words, so that this reading might be a source of strength for all who must challenge the powerful in order to work for justice.

READING II This intensely beautiful passage on the greatest gift, love, is an inspiration for all who read it.

Although it is often used at weddings, it is directed to all of us.

   There were several competing factions in the Corinthian community, and some members claimed to have greater gifts than others. These more spectacular charisms, such as speaking in tongues and prophesying God's messages, were the cause of much boasting. This teaching on love proclaims the goal of the Christian life and serves as a challenge to those who would claim superiority.

   Paul begins by declaring that spectacular spiritual gifts are useless unless they are grounded in love. Without love, everything else is lost. This is not a "warm and fuzzy" or romantic love, but a deep, abiding commitment to another. This love truly desires the best for the other and strives to make that a reality. The second section of the reading includes several statements about what love is (and is not). Proclaim this section even more slowly than usual, allowing each line to sink in. The conciseness of Paul's message reveals the depth of what he is expressing.

prophesy = PROF-uh-sī

For we *know partially* and we *prophesy partially*,
but when the *perfect* comes, the *partial* will pass *away*.
When I was a *child*, I used to *talk* as a child,
think as a child, *reason* as a child;
when I became a *man*, I put *aside* childish things.
At *present* we see *indistinctly*, as in a *mirror*,
but *then face* to *face*.
At *present* I know *partially*;
then I shall know *fully*, as I am fully *known*.

Close very slowly, stressing each of the three terms, and especially emphasizing the final word.

So *faith*, *hope*, *love* remain, these *three*;
but the *greatest* of these is *love*.

[Shorter: 1 Corinthians 13:4–13]

GOSPEL Luke 4:21–30

A reading from the holy gospel according to Luke

Jesus began speaking in the *synagogue*, saying:
"*Today* this *Scripture* passage is *fulfilled* in your *hearing*."
And all spoke *highly* of him
and were *amazed* at the gracious *words* that came
from his *mouth*.
They also asked, "Isn't this the son of *Joseph*?"

This is a solemn declaration. Speak slowly and forcefully.

He said to them, "Surely you will *quote* me this *proverb*,
'*Physician*, cure *yourself*,' and say,
'Do *here* in your *native* place
the things that we *heard* were done in *Capernaum*.'"

Try to convey the peoples' questioning of Jesus' teaching. How could the son of someone they knew have such authority?

Capernaum = kuh-PER-nee-*m

Paul goes on to speak of the lasting nature of love. Even if all else fails and passes away, love will remain. In the future, when all is brought to perfection in God, nothing of the things of this world will remain except love. All other gifts are imperfect, poor reflections of a greater reality. But love, together with faith and hope, will endure. And, as Paul says, the greatest of these is love.

Proclaiming this passage is both a joy and a challenge. Do not rush through it, but give each word due weight. Resist sentimentality, but read with seriousness and dignity. The passage has a natural rhythm to it, but be careful not to become sing-song. With plenty of practice and attentiveness to the message, you will be able to offer your listeners an eloquent lesson in love.

GOSPEL The gospel reading for today picks up and continues last Sunday's and repeats some of it. Jesus claims

that he fulfills the prophecy of Isaiah, in which the poor and disenfranchised receive blessings. This challenges Jesus' contemporary social reality, but the opposition he meets is directed primarily at his inclusion of non-Jews in his mission.

The Jewish people of Jesus' time based their self-understanding and social outlook on the knowledge that they were specially chosen by God. God established precepts, and Israel responded, sometimes faithfully, sometimes only with great struggle. But

This paragraph is a direct challenge to the divine favor that many claimed for Israel.

Elijah = ee-LĪ-juh

Zarephath = ZAYR-uh-fath
Sidon = SĪ-duhn

Elisha = ee-LĪ-shuh
Naaman = NAY-uh-muhn

Express clearly the anger of the crowd.

Jesus, blessed with divine protection, emerges unscathed. Speak with wonder, but also with certainty.

And he said, "*Amen*, I *say* to you,
  no prophet is *accepted* in his own native *place*.
Indeed, I tell you,
  there were many *widows* in Israel in the days of *Elijah*
  when the *sky* was closed for *three* and a half *years*
  and a severe *famine* spread over the entire *land*.
It was to *none* of these that Elijah was *sent*,
  but only to a widow in *Zarephath* in the land of *Sidon*.
Again, there were many *lepers* in Israel
  during the time of *Elisha* the *prophet*;
  yet not *one* of them was *cleansed*, but only *Naaman*
    the *Syrian*."

When the people in the synagogue *heard* this,
  they were all *filled* with *fury*.
They rose *up*, *drove* him out of the *town*,
  and led him to the *brow* of the *hill*
  on which their *town* had been *built*,
  to *hurl* him down *headlong*.
But Jesus *passed* through the *midst* of them and went *away*.

the very existence of this people was the result of God's initiative in establishing a covenant relationship with the Hebrew people. The Hebrew prophets likened the covenant between God and Israel to a marriage, which required total exclusion of all other parties. Israel was not to turn to other gods, and God was to remain always faithful to the chosen people.

Jesus' emphasis on the generosity of God to those outside the Jewish community,

then, comes as a shock to his hearers. He speaks of God turning aside from the needy within Israel and acting compassionately toward foreigners. On top of the outrageousness of the message, the one preaching it is a local boy, returning as an upstart after a little travel. Jesus' hearers find this unbearable, and they seize him by force and attempt to harm him. But his role as the anointed one of God extends beyond his preaching. God's power protects him, and he is given further opportunity to spread his revolutionary message.

There is drama in this passage, making it exciting to proclaim. In speaking Jesus' words, try to provide a sense of the opposition he faces. Read the closing paragraph with energy, expressing the anger of the people, before ending on a peaceful note.

5TH SUNDAY IN ORDINARY TIME

Lectionary #75

READING I   Isaiah 6:1–2a, 3–8

A reading from the book of the prophet Isaiah

Uzziah = uh-ZĪ-uh
Let your voice be filled with wonder as you describe the heavenly scene.

In the *year* King *Uzziah* died,
  I *saw* the LORD seated on a *high* and lofty *throne*,
  with the train of his *garment filling* the *temple*.
Seraphim were stationed *above*.

seraphim = SAYR-uh-fim

Cry out in praise of God.

They *cried* one to the *other*,
  "*Holy, holy, holy* is the LORD of *hosts!*
All the *earth* is *filled* with his *glory!*"
At the sound of that *cry*, the frame of the door *shook*
  and the house was *filled* with *smoke*.

Speak in despair and with humility.

Then I said, "*Woe* is *me*, I am *doomed!*
For I am a man of *unclean lips*,
  living among a *people* of unclean *lips*;
  yet my *eyes* have seen the *King*, the LORD of *hosts!*"
Then one of the seraphim *flew* to me,
  holding an *ember* that he had taken with *tongs* from the *altar*.

There is hope in the action and words of the seraph.

He touched my *mouth* with it, and said,
  "See, *now* that this has touched your *lips*,
  your *wickedness* is *removed*, your *sin purged*."

Then I heard the *voice* of the LORD saying,
  "*Whom* shall I *send*? *Who* will *go* for us?"
"Here I *am*," I said; "send *me!*"

Read these final words slowly and with eagerness.

READING I The call of Isaiah emphasizes the unworthiness of the human being in the presence of God. The setting is the heavenly court, where angels cry out in praise of God. There is majesty and an awesome power evident in this vision of God's abode.

Isaiah responds in fear-filled acknowledgement of his imperfections. No one is allowed to stand in the presence of God. The great law-giver Moses had spoken with God and was blessed with a partial view of God; he could hardly contain himself as a result. His face radiated the divine presence. No other ordinary human could ever survive such an experience. It would be overwhelming, burning in intensity.

But Isaiah is allowed to remain in God's presence. His lips are cleansed by a burning coal, and he is purified. The image recalls the purifying effects of fire, which burns away impurities from metal or clay. But let there be no mistake: Fire on human flesh is painful. Being made worthy to serve God is not an easy process.

When Isaiah's sins have been removed and he is cleansed, he is able to respond to the Lord's call. God requires a messenger; Isaiah volunteers eagerly. One senses that there was never any unwillingness on Isaiah's part, only a profound recognition of his own sinfulness. That is no longer an obstacle.

What a joyful, challenging and reassuring passage you share today! May we all join with Isaiah in humility before God and in eagerness to proclaim God's word. Describe with awe the heavenly scene, and let your voice be filled with remorse and anxiety

READING II   1 Corinthians 15:1–11

A reading from the first letter of Saint Paul to the Corinthians

Paul is reminding the Corinthians of things they already know.

I am *reminding* you, brothers and sisters,
   of the *gospel* I *preached* to you,
   which you indeed *received* and in which you also *stand.*
Through *it* you are also being *saved,*
   if you hold *fast* to the word I *preached* to you,
   unless you *believed* in *vain.*

Paul tries to encourage the community to remain faithful; speak supportively.

Lower your voice and proceed solemnly.

For I handed *on* to you as of first *importance* what I also *received*:
   that Christ *died* for our sins in *accordance* with the *Scriptures;*
   that he was *buried;*
   that he was *raised* on the third *day*
      in accordance with the *Scriptures;*
   that he appeared to *Cephas,* then to the *Twelve.*

Lift your voice a little as you speak of Christ's resurrection.

Cephas = SEE-fuhs
"Peter" means "rock" in Greek. *Cephas* is the Aramaic word for "rock."

After that, Christ appeared to more
      than five *hundred* brothers at *once,*
   most of whom are still *living,*
   though *some* have fallen *asleep.*
After that he appeared to *James,*
   then to *all* the apostles.

Pause before proclaiming humbly Paul's own experience.

Last of all, as to one born *abnormally,*
   he appeared to *me.*
For *I* am the *least* of the apostles,
   not *fit* to be *called* an apostle,
   because I *persecuted* the church of *God.*
But by the *grace* of God I *am* what I *am,*
   and his *grace* to me has not been *ineffective.*

Speak with fervent trust. Read "I am what I am" especially slowly so that it will not sound trite.

---

as you speak Isaiah's self-effacing words. But concentrate especially on the eagerness of his response to God's call, so that each member of your community might be inspired to respond similarly.

READING II   The passage you proclaim today provides a valuable insight into the earliest preaching of the Christian community. Paul's writings are the oldest Christian documents we have, and here he identifies traditions that were passed on to him, which he shares with the Corinthians. This passage contains the central teaching of Christianity: Jesus died for our sins, was buried, and rose again. This is the gospel in a nutshell, to which we assent every time we offer our "Amen" in the eucharistic assembly. Proclaim it solemnly and with certainty.

The details of Paul's account of Jesus' appearances are not the same as those recorded elsewhere. There are many stories of post-resurrection appearances, and various people are included among those present. The main point of the stories is that the early church experienced Jesus as having conquered death and that many witnessed his presence.

But Paul's theme is his own insignificance in comparison with the others. He, too, had an experience of the risen Lord, but he is the "least of the apostles." Like Isaiah in the first reading, he is aware of his own sinfulness and is especially sorrowful about

Indeed, I have toiled *harder* than *all* of them;
    not *I*, however, but the grace of *God* that is *with* me.

Therefore, whether it be *I* or *they*,
    so we *preach* and so you *believed*.

[Shorter: 1 Corinthians 15:3–8, 11]

GOSPEL   Luke 5:1–11

A reading from the holy gospel according to Luke

While the crowd was pressing *in* on Jesus and listening
    to the *word* of *God*,
  he was *standing* by the Lake of *Gennesaret*.
He saw two *boats* there alongside the *lake*;
  the *fishermen* had *disembarked* and were washing their *nets*.

Getting into *one* of the boats, the one belonging to *Simon*,
  he *asked* him to put out a short *distance* from the *shore*.
Then he sat *down* and taught the *crowds* from the *boat*.
After he had finished *speaking*, he said to *Simon*,
  "*Put* out into *deep* water and lower your *nets* for a *catch*."
Simon said in reply,
  "*Master*, we have worked hard all *night* and have
    caught *nothing*,
  but at your *command* I will lower the *nets*."
When they had *done* this, they caught a *great number* of fish
    and their *nets* were *tearing*.

Gennesaret = geh-NES-uh-ret

Pause briefly after these introductory verses.

Does Jesus speak as one with knowledge of what is to come? Or is his suggestion innocent? Phrase your proclamation according to your answer.

Peter is tired but trusting.

---

his role in persecuting Christians before his encounter with the risen Christ. But part of his humility is in being able to accept, as Isaiah did, the reality of being cleansed by God. He is not going to argue with God's choices. And in spite of his worthiness, he has worked harder than anyone to spread the gospel.

As proclaimer of God's word, you are in much the same position as Paul. You have received these traditions and are passing them on to your own community. It is an

awesome responsibility. Respond with Paul in humility and recognition of your own faults but also with certainty that God has chosen you. If you are truly able to make this message your own, you will effectively proclaim it to others. Speak with pride and confidence, but without boasting.

GOSPEL   Peter is one of the heroes of the gospel of Luke and the Acts of the Apostles, which together comprise a two-volume account of salvation history by the same author. Here the author of

the gospel presents Peter sympathetically, and Jesus' call of Peter is reminiscent of Isaiah's call in the first reading and Paul's in the second. The key theme is unworthiness in the face of the greatness of God. But Peter is called just as surely as the prophets and the other apostles.

The passage opens matter-of-factly, describing Jesus preaching from a boat. But the point of the story is not Jesus' preaching but the person of Simon (Peter). When Jesus tells Simon to put his fishing net into the water again, he is initially reluctant. He had

Present this account with excitement. Surely those fishing must have been overjoyed.

They signaled to their *partners* in the *other* boat
　　to come to *help* them.
They *came* and filled *both* boats
　　so that the boats were in danger of *sinking.*

When Simon Peter *saw* this, he fell at the *knees* of Jesus and said,

Speak Peter's words with humility and awe.

　　"*Depart* from me, Lord, for I am a *sinful man.*"

For *astonishment* at the catch of fish they had made *seized* him
　　and all those *with* him,
　　and likewise *James* and *John,* the sons of *Zebedee,*
　　who were *partners* of Simon.

Jesus speaks words of comfort.

Jesus said to Simon, "Do *not* be *afraid;*
　　from *now on* you will be catching *men.*"

When they brought their boats to the *shore,*

Pause briefly after "everything" in order to stress the magnitude of what they were leaving behind.

　　they left *everything* and *followed* him.

been fishing for hours without success, but he quickly agrees to try.

The success of Peter's fishing indicates several things. First, it points to Jesus' special relationship to God, revealed in his otherworldly knowledge or his miraculous abilities (the passage doesn't say which). The superior catch also provides Peter with the opportunity to express his awe in Jesus' presence and his knowledge of his own unworthiness. But Jesus assures him that he need not be afraid, and soon he and

his companions become disciples of Jesus. Finally, the record-breaking catch of fish indicates the success the gospel will enjoy when preached by Peter and the other apostles.

We are all called to lives of discipleship. Following Jesus requires recognizing our own sinfulness, but it also involves trusting in God's goodness and ability to use us as instruments of divine action. The gospel of Luke, read throughout Ordinary Time in this liturgical year, makes clear that discipleship is costly and difficult. But the knowledge of Jesus' magnificence makes it not only worthwhile but almost impossible to resist.

Proclaim this gospel with enthusiasm, and give plenty of expression to the words of Jesus and Peter. Offer it to your community as a commentary on what it means to know Jesus and to respond to God's call to proclaim the good news to all.

6TH SUNDAY IN ORDINARY TIME

Lectionary #78

READING I   Jeremiah 17:5–8

A reading from the book of the prophet Jeremiah

These are strong statements. Speak boldly, even with a hint of anger.

Thus says the LORD:
Cursed is the one who trusts in human *beings*,
    who seeks his *strength* in *flesh*,
    whose *heart* turns away from the LORD.
He is like a barren *bush* in the *desert*
    that enjoys no change of *season*,
but stands in a *lava* waste,
    a *salt* and empty *earth*.

Pause, then lighten your voice so that the contrast with what is above will be apparent.

Blessed is the one who *trusts* in the LORD,
    whose *hope* is the LORD.

Let your voice sound gentle and refreshing.

He is like a *tree* planted beside the *waters*
    that stretches out its *roots* to the *stream*:
It fears not the *heat* when it *comes*;
    its *leaves* stay *green*;
in the year of *drought* it shows no *distress*,
    but still bears *fruit*.

READING I   Jeremiah's strong words make clear the importance of trusting in God rather than human beings. Jeremiah spent his entire career making just that claim. Against those prophets who tried to assure the kings that they were always right and that Judah should assert itself with military power, Jeremiah preached the necessity of accepting limitations. Against those who saw only impending doom, Jeremiah preached hope. He did

so by practicing what he preaches here, by seeking God's favor rather than human favor.

The message is expressed in two sections, one chastising those who place human judgment above God's and one praising those who trust in God. The outcome of the former is devastation, but the one who turns to God in faith will prosper.

Stress the contrasts between the two figures you describe. Without overemphasizing, speak darkly of the fate of the former figure. Then raise your voice in hope as you reflect on the life-giving qualities available to those who hope in God.

READING II   As is so often true in Paul's correspondence with the Corinthian community, Paul here responds to an apparent misunderstanding on the part of some members of the community. Some people were denying the resurrection of the dead, perhaps reflecting on the fate of members of the community who had died before Christ's return. Since they expected Christ to reveal himself in glory during their own lifetimes, many thought that any Christian who had died would not be able to enjoy the splendor of that day.

READING II   1 Corinthians 15:12, 16–20

A reading from the first letter of Saint Paul to the Corinthians

Brothers and sisters:
If *Christ* is preached as *raised* from the *dead*,
    how can *some* among you say there is no *resurrection*
        of the *dead*?

If the *dead* are not *raised*, neither has *Christ* been *raised*,
    and if *Christ* has not been *raised*, your faith is *vain*;
    you are still in your *sins*.
Then those who have fallen *asleep* in Christ have *perished*.

If for *this* life *only* we have *hoped* in Christ,
    we are the most *pitiable* people of *all*.
But now Christ *has* been *raised* from the *dead*,
    the *firstfruits* of those who have fallen *asleep*.

Paul can hardly believe that anyone would say this. Speak with astonishment.

Read slowly and clearly, so that Paul's argument will be apparent.

Lift your voice in hope and confidence.

GOSPEL   Luke 6:17, 20–26

A reading from the holy gospel according to Luke

Jesus came down with the *twelve*
    and stood on a stretch of level *ground*
    with a great *crowd* of his *disciples*
    and a large *number* of the *people*
    from all *Judea* and *Jerusalem*
    and the coastal region of *Tyre* and *Sidon*.

Tyre = tīr
Sidon = SĪ-duhn

The idea of the resurrection of the dead was a point of contention for Jews of the time, and perhaps this discussion affected the Gentile Corinthian community. Whatever the source of the conflict, Paul cuts to the heart of the debate. To deny the resurrection of the dead is to deny the resurrection of Christ; the entire faith of Christians rests on belief in Christ's resurrection. Just as Christ has been raised, so also will those Christians who have died before his return rise again.

Christ is the "first fruits," the first offering to God of those who have died.

Although the immediate issue of this passage might not affect your community directly, Paul presents a wonderful opportunity to proclaim with certitude our belief that Christ has conquered death. Speak slowly so that the argument can be followed. But proclaim with vigor the final line, asserting its truth with confident faith.

GOSPEL   The "sermon on the plain" in the gospel of Luke is similar in many ways to the "sermon on the mount" in the gospel of Matthew. But it is also significantly different. While the Matthean account spiritualizes the sufferings of the blessed ("Blessed are those who hunger and thirst *for righteousness*"), the author of this passage speaks of the truly destitute. There is no reflection on spiritual longing, but a reference to the need for physical sustenance. In keeping with a theme

Read each beatitude slowly and brightly. Begin by proclaiming the unexpected recipient of the blessing with assurance, then lower your voice a bit as you conclude each line.

These are amazing words. Sound reassuring in the face of all this opposition.

Speak with sincere joy, then proceed calmly.

Let an ominous tone fill your voice. Grow slightly more forceful as you proceed through the woes.

Emphasize this final line, especially the term "false."

And raising his eyes toward his *disciples* he said:
"*Blessed* are you who are *poor*,
    for the kingdom of *God* is *yours*.
Blessed are you who are now *hungry*,
    for you will be *satisfied*.
Blessed are you who are now *weeping*,
    for you will *laugh*.
Blessed are you when people *hate* you,
    and when they *exclude* and *insult* you,
    and denounce your name as *evil*
    on account of the Son of *Man*.

"*Rejoice* and *leap* for *joy* on that day!
Behold, your *reward* will be great in *heaven*.
For their *ancestors* treated the *prophets* in the *same* way.

"But *woe* to you who are *rich*,
    for you have *received* your *consolation*.
Woe to you who are *filled* now,
    for you will be *hungry*.
Woe to you who *laugh* now,
    for you will *grieve* and *weep*.
Woe to you when all speak *well* of you,
    for their *ancestors* treated the *false* prophets in this *way*."

we shall see repeated throughout the gospel of Luke, the emphasis is on the downtrodden, the outcasts, those who struggle just to survive. Justice will be theirs.

Accepting Jesus' words is dangerous business. Those who do will be ostracized, hated and persecuted. But this should be cause for great rejoicing. Reflect on a time when you have stuck to your position even when all others disagreed. Does this description fit your experience? It is never easy to take an unpopular stand, but the author seems to say that true discipleship will not be popular.

Only in Luke's gospel are the beatitudes balanced by corresponding woes. Those who have everything that the others lack will lose it, while the poor, hungry and mourning will gain. Everything is turned upside down.

Stress the contrasts, speaking with encouragement at the beginning and challenging your listeners with the woes. And speak assuredly that those who are challenged for their faith are in good company.

7TH SUNDAY IN ORDINARY TIME

Lectionary #81

READING I   1 Samuel 26:2, 7–9, 12–13, 22–23

A reading from the first book of Samuel

In *those* days, Saul went down to the *desert* of *Ziph*
    with three thousand *picked* men of *Israel*,
    to search for *David* in the desert of *Ziph*.

So *David* and *Abishai* went among Saul's *soldiers* by *night*
    and found Saul lying *asleep* within the *barricade*,
    with his *spear* thrust into the ground at his *head*
    and *Abner* and his *men* sleeping *around* him.
Abishai whispered to *David*:
    "*God* has delivered your enemy into your *grasp* this day.
Let me *nail* him to the ground with *one* thrust of the *spear*;
    I will not *need* a *second* thrust!"
But David said to *Abishai*, "Do *not* harm him,
    for who can lay *hands* on the LORD'S *anointed*
        and remain *unpunished*?"

So David took the *spear* and the *water* jug from their place
        at Saul's *head*,
    and they got *away* without anyone's *seeing* or *knowing*
        or *awakening*.
All remained *asleep*,
    because the LORD had put them into a deep *slumber*.

Going across to an opposite *slope*,
    David stood on a remote *hilltop*
    at a great *distance* from *Abner*, son of *Ner*, and the *troops*.

Ziph = zif

Abishai = uh-BĪ-shī

Speak softly (but not so softly that you cannot be heard), as in a conspiratorial tone.

Speak David's words more forcefully.

Pause before proceeding.

READING I The relationship between Saul, the first king of Israel, and David, the second and greatest of all the kings of Israel, was marked by tension caused by Saul's mistrust of David. David distinguished himself as a youth and became close to the royal family. He was deeply devoted to Saul's son and even married Saul's daughter. But Saul saw him as a threat. David was well-liked and talented, and handpicked by God. Saul, by contrast, disobeyed God and increasingly fell into disfavor. Out of spite, he pursued David relentlessly and unjustly.

Today's reading is a story of one of the encounters between the two men. Saul is pursuing David, intent on destroying him, but David gains the upper hand by entering the king's camp at night. Yet David resists the temptation to kill his enemy. Instead, he chooses to prove his loyalty to the king God had anointed. Despite Saul's hatred for him and attempts to kill him, David still respects the divinely appointed ruler. He proves that Saul has nothing to fear from him.

David had already been anointed as the future ruler of Israel when this event occurred. Saul's death would not have left the people without a king. Surely he could have claimed that he was acting in self-defense or was following the rules of war in doing away with his pursuer. Yet more than once David rejected the opportunity to harm Saul, guided by a force greater than the human desire for retribution or safety. Here he acts with great magnanimity. Because David was not consumed with the desire for revenge, he was able to become a great and beloved ruler.

This is spoken over a great distance. Without shouting, raise your voice to convey this.

This line is delivered solemnly and with conviction.

Speak slowly in order to make Paul's argument clear. Stress "spiritual."

This is a key line. Read clearly and slowly.

Speak solemnly and with assurance of what awaits us.

He said: "*Here* is the king's *spear*.
Let an *attendant* come over to *get* it.
The LORD will *reward* each man for his *justice* and *faithfulness*.
Today, though the LORD *delivered* you into my *grasp*,
　I would not *harm* the LORD'S *anointed*."

READING II　1 Corinthians 15:45–49

A reading from the first letter of Saint Paul to the Corinthians

Brothers and sisters:
It is *written*, The *first* man, *Adam*, became a living *being*,
　the *last* Adam a life-giving *spirit*.
But the *spiritual* was not first;
　rather the *natural* and *then* the spiritual.

The *first* man was from the *earth*, *earthly*;
　the *second* man, from *heaven*.
As was the *earthly* one, so also are the *earthly*,
　and as is the *heavenly* one, so also are the *heavenly*.

Just as we have borne the *image* of the *earthly* one,
　we shall also bear the *image* of the *heavenly* one.

This story of compassion and forgiveness by one who has been wronged is inspiring even today. Read with intensity in order to convey the suspense of the story. Stress David's words of respect for Saul. Most of all, proclaim this remarkable story in such a way that your listeners will know that forgiveness is possible, no matter how serious the wrong.

READING II In today's second reading Paul continues his discussion of the issue of death and resurrection.

Some of the Corinthians had denied the resurrection of those in their community who had died. They expected Jesus to return soon and thought only those Christians living when he came would be able to share in the life he promised.

Paul had earlier argued that the resurrection of Jesus confirms the resurrection of the dead; denying the resurrection of those already dead means denying that Jesus has

truly conquered death. The discussion then turns to the nature of the resurrected body. It is not simply a physical body, with all the imperfections that bodies on earth have; it is a powerful spiritual vessel.

The two creation stories from Genesis provide a means for understanding this contrast. In the Jewish philosophical speculation of the time, the "first Adam" (Genesis 1) was a spiritual being, made in God's image, while the "second Adam" (Genesis 2) was an earthly creation, a "living soul." In today's reading, Paul corrects the order and insists

GOSPEL Luke 6:27–38

A reading from the holy gospel according to Luke

Jesus said to his disciples:
"To you who *hear* I say,
 love your *enemies*, do *good* to those who *hate* you,
 bless those who *curse* you, *pray* for those who *mistreat* you.
To the person who *strikes* you on *one* cheek,
 offer the *other* one as well,
 and from the person who takes your *cloak*,
 do not *withhold* even your *tunic*.
Give to everyone who *asks* of you,
 and from the one who *takes* what is *yours* do not demand
  it *back*.
Do to *others* as you would have *them* do to *you*.

"For if you *love* those who love *you*,
 what *credit* is that to you?
Even *sinners* love those who love *them*.
And if you do *good* to those who do good to *you*,
 what credit is *that* to you?
Even *sinners* do the *same*.
If you lend *money* to those from whom you expect *repayment*,
 what *credit* is that to you?
Even *sinners* lend to *sinners*,
 and get back the same *amount*.

Pause before "love," then let the full force of this surprising statement come through strongly. Perhaps a bit of astonishment in your voice can convey your own reaction to Jesus' words.

Do not rush through these instructions, but give each its due emphasis.

The "golden rule" is a traditional teaching found in many cultures. Pause before changing to a questioning tone.

This line is intentionally insulting.

---

that it is Jesus who is the second, heavenly Adam. He is the spiritual one.

The end of this short section draws us back to the issue of resurrection. Although we share the perishable body of the earthly Adam, we hope that we will someday bear the image of Christ, the heavenly one. In the final resurrection, our bodies will rise, as did Jesus' body, but they will not be the same. Just as Jesus walked and talked and shared meals, so also we will have real bodies. But Jesus also entered locked rooms and was not always recognizable to his friends. Our

frail bodies, too, will be transformed into glorious risen ones.

Proclaim this difficult passage slowly in order to allow your listeners to follow the argument as closely as possible. They will not have the same background you now have, so your task is to clarify the reading through your proclamation as much as possible. Stress the distinction between the first and the second Adams. Close with conviction; the final verses make Paul's point.

GOSPEL Continuing the Lukan theme of reversal (see the commentary on last week's gospel passage), today's gospel challenges us to do precisely the opposite of what comes naturally. The first words of Jesus cut to the heart of the matter: Love your enemies; bless those who curse you. This is not easy! But it is what discipleship requires.

The exhortations that open the passage become clearer as Jesus continues. Almost everyone responds favorably when loved; real merit lies in going beyond reciprocal goodness. If it is too easy, it is not enough.

Again, speak with solemnity, urging your listeners to respond by doing more than what seems reasonable.

This is an important line. Pause before and after it, and proclaim it with both compassion and urging in your voice.

Express your astonishment at the greatness of God's love.

But rather, *love* your *enemies* and do *good* to them,
　　and *lend* expecting nothing *back*;
　　then your *reward* will be *great*
　　and you will be *children* of the Most *High*,
　　for he himself is *kind* to the *ungrateful* and the *wicked*.
Be *merciful*, just as your *Father* is *merciful*.

"Stop *judging* and you will not be *judged*.
Stop *condemning* and you will not be *condemned*.
Forgive and you will be *forgiven*.
Give and gifts will be *given* to you;
　　a good *measure*, packed *together*, shaken *down*,
　　　and *overflowing*,
　　will be *poured* into your *lap*.
For the *measure* with which you *measure*
　　will in *return* be measured *out* to you."

But Jesus' words do not make good sense! What business could run without expecting payment? Who could survive in a world in which thieves not only escape punishment but are given more goods? Jesus does not explain; he simply instructs.

Even as we want to argue, something deep inside recognizes that those who generously provide for others will not go for long in need. And the thief who is treated kindly just might decide to act kindly toward others. But it is frightening; the risk is almost more than we can bear.

The closing paragraph illustrates the results of following the illogical instructions of the passage. We shall receive what we have given others. When we act with mercy and compassion, God will act similarly toward us. Going beyond what is required will inspire God to be equally generous. It is almost as though human actions determine those of God. Perhaps the point is that humans are simply unable to comprehend the lavish generosity of God. But when we learn to offer compassion and forgiveness to others, we will learn to trust what God is offering to us.

This passage offers an immense challenge to all who hear it. Proclaim it boldly, without softening its message. Close with a passionate rendering of the generous measure of love and forgiveness God bestows on all.

8TH SUNDAY IN ORDINARY TIME

Lectionary #84

READING I   Sirach 27:4–7

A reading from the book of Sirach

When a sieve is *shaken*, the *husks* appear;
    so do one's *faults* when one *speaks*.
As the test of what the potter *molds* is in the *furnace*,
    so in *tribulation* is the test of the *just*.

The *fruit* of a tree shows the *care* it has had;
    so too does one's *speech* disclose the bent of one's *mind*.
Praise *no* one before he *speaks*,
    for it is *then* that people are *tested*.

sieve = siv
Pause after the first line of each sentence, then lower your voice solemnly as you continue.

Slow down a bit for the last line.

READING II   1 Corinthians 15:54–58

A reading from the first letter of Saint Paul to the Corinthians

Brothers and sisters:
When this which is *corruptible* clothes itself
    with *incorruptibility*
  and this which is *mortal* clothes itself with *immortality*,
  then the word that is *written* shall come *about*:
  "*Death* is swallowed up in *victory*.
  Where, O *death*, is your *victory*?
  Where, O *death*, is your *sting*?"

Read slowly in order to make the point clear. Pause after each line.

Allow your voice to ring out as you proclaim Christ's victory over death.

READING I The book of Sirach provides some reflections on how to act wisely. Today's passage offers a brief collection of maxims, all pointing to the importance of testing someone in order to learn that person's true character. Its message is similar to "you can't judge a book by its cover." Here, a person's speech reveals his or her true character.

To illustrate, the author draws examples from everyday life. The first two images point out how stress can often bring out someone's true nature. It is easy to speak kindly and act rightly when things are going well; the real test is when things go wrong. When a sieve is shaken, all the good grain falls through; what is left are useless husks. The fire of the kiln reveals all imperfections. Stress and difficulty do the same to people, revealing their hidden faults.

Proclaim the wisdom of this short passage simply but sincerely.

READING II Paul's discussion here continues a line of argument that has been part of the second readings for the past two Sundays (see those commentaries). It might be helpful to look back at those earlier readings in order to understand this one better.

Paul responds to a discussion among the Corinthian Christians regarding the resurrection of the dead by asserting that indeed the dead will rise, just as Christ has. Here he closes the argument with a beautiful meditation on incorruptibility, ending with an exhortation to engage in the work of the Lord.

Speak solemnly but briefly.

Again, raise your voice, this time with gratitude.

End on a quiet, encouraging note.

The *sting* of death is *sin*,
　　and the *power* of sin is the *law*.
But *thanks* be to God who gives us the *victory*
　　through our *Lord* Jesus *Christ*.

Therefore, my beloved brothers and sisters,
　　be *firm*, *steadfast*, always fully *devoted* to the *work*
　　　of the *Lord*,
　　knowing that in the *Lord* your labor is not in *vain*.

GOSPEL　Luke 6:39–45

A reading from the holy gospel according to Luke

Jesus told his disciples a *parable*,
"Can a *blind* person guide a *blind* person?
Will not *both* fall into a *pit*?
No *disciple* is superior to the *teacher*;
　　but when fully *trained*,
　　　every disciple will be *like* his *teacher*.

"Why do you notice the *splinter* in your *brother's* eye,
　　but do not perceive the wooden *beam* in your *own*?
How can you *say* to your *brother*,
　　'Brother, let me remove that *splinter* in your *eye*,'
　　　when you do not even *notice* the wooden *beam* in your
　　　　own eye?
You *hypocrite! Remove* the wooden beam from *your* eye *first*;
　　then you will see *clearly*
　　　to remove the *splinter* in your *brother's* eye.

Pause before moving on to the next example. Although the guide and the teacher clearly refer to the same type of person, the images are distinct.

Pause again before continuing, then speak with incredulity and perhaps some indignation.

This is a strong condemnation. Do not try to soften it.

Just as Jesus conquered death by rising from the dead, so also each person will share in what Jesus has achieved. Resurrection means "incorruptibility" and "immortality." In other words, the human body will no longer decay, nor will death ever threaten us again. The words of the prophets are fulfilled in Jesus. Death has been vanquished, its power overcome by a far greater one.

Paul then briefly alludes to a teaching he makes elsewhere, linking sin and death. For Paul, faith in Jesus is the only thing that can lead to righteousness and life.

Proclaim Paul's message boldly. Speak comfortingly the prophetic words, and conclude with a call to action. Carefully proclaim Paul's various statements, offering assurance, comfort and challenge by your tone of voice.

GOSPEL　Jesus' teaching picks up on that found in the first reading. What is in one's heart reveals itself in one's actions, just as a tree shows its nature by its fruit. The earlier part of the reading provides lessons on discipleship and making judgments.

In a parable concerning the relationship between teachers and students, Jesus declares that the blind cannot lead the blind. Neither will reach the destination but will

Observe a lengthy pause before continuing in a bit softer tone.

"A *good* tree does not bear *rotten* fruit,
    nor does a *rotten* tree bear *good* fruit.
For *every* tree is known by its *own* fruit.
For people do not pick *figs* from *thornbushes*,
    nor do they gather *grapes* from *brambles*.

Speak encouragingly the words about the good person.

"A *good* person out of the store of *goodness* in his *heart*
       produces *good*,
    but an *evil* person out of a store of *evil* produces *evil*;
    for from the fullness of the *heart* the *mouth* speaks."

stumble on the way. Jesus highlights the importance of having clear vision and knowing the path to follow, especially for the leaders of a community. Leaders do not need to have all the answers, but they must know the basic direction to follow. Otherwise they are simply blind guides.

The same is true of leaders today. Are the people we admire visionaries? Or do they go through life with blinders on? It is important to choose our mentors wisely, for their example influences how we live and the choices we make.

Jesus' harsh words about the hypocrisy of attempting to remove the splinter in another's eye despite the log in one's own can really hit home. Although the image is humorous, the message is not. It is often much easier to recognize what changes someone else needs to make than to address our own faults and failings. Today's gospel provides a needed reminder that reform begins at home.

Proclaim this teaching of Jesus with vigor. Offer it as a challenge to yourself and to your community to concentrate on personal reform in order to produce good fruit.

ASH WEDNESDAY

Lectionary #219

READING I Joel 2:12–18

A reading from the book of the prophet Joel

Draw attention to the present need for repentance; stress "now." Then speak slowly and sincerely.

Even *now*, says the Lord,
    return to me with your *whole heart*,
        with *fasting*, and *weeping*, and *mourning*;
Rend your *hearts*, not your *garments*,
    and *return* to the Lord, your *God*.

Let the majestic nature of God's love shine through these words.

For *gracious* and *merciful* is he,
    slow to anger, *rich* in kindness,
        and *relenting* in punishment.

Speak with hope and awe.

Perhaps he will *again* relent
    and leave behind him a *blessing*,
Offerings and *libations*
    for the *Lord*, your *God*.

Read these short phrases forcefully. Be careful not to sacrifice clarity or to become sing-song.

Blow the *trumpet* in *Zion!*
    proclaim a *fast*,
        call an *assembly*;
Gather the *people*,
    notify the *congregation*;
Assemble the *elders*,
    gather the *children*
        and the *infants* at the breast;
Let the *bridegroom* quit his room,
    and the *bride* her *chamber*.

READING I We begin our annual season of repentance, prayer and renewal with a stark reminder of our need to turn our hearts and minds to God. The first reading, from the prophet Joel, calls us to a heartfelt conversion, a return to the presence of a God who is compassionate and loving. But this God is also powerful, able to bring judgment to an erring people, using any means available to draw them back into a loving embrace.

Joel wrote during a time of crisis in Israel. The political situation was peaceful, but Israel faced a severe locust plague and drought. Joel understands these conditions to be indicative of the Day of the Lord, the judgment of God. He believes that the people of Israel and the cultic leaders have become complacent, relying too much on rituals without the accompanying sincerity of heart that God desires. As a result, the locusts were sent as a sign of God's judgment.

But just when utter destruction seems inevitable and the end appears to be imminent, God extends the invitation that we read today. It is still possible to return to God, to weep before the Lord, to fast and pray. Joel offers the hope that the Day of the Lord will not only be a day of judgment but one of promise and vindication as well.

We gather today to acknowledge our own complacency before God, our own tendency to wander away from our home in the bosom of God, our own need to return to God with all our hearts. We too adopt the practices that Joel recommends: We fast and weep and repent, standing before God mindful of our sinfulness and trusting in God's mercy and love.

Between the porch and the altar
let the *priests*, the *ministers* of the Lord, *weep*,
And say, "*Spare*, O Lord, your *people*,
and make not your *heritage* a *reproach*,
with the nations *ruling over* them!
Why should they say among the peoples,
'*Where* is their *God*?'"

Then the Lord was *stirred* to *concern* for his land
and took *pity* on his people.

Proclaim this with sadness but also with dignity.

Pause, then let your voice ring with conviction as you proclaim God's compassionate response.

READING II   2 Corinthians 5:20—6:2

A reading from the second letter of Paul to the Corinthians

We are *ambassadors* for *Christ*,
God as it were appealing *through* us.
We *implore* you, in Christ's name:
be *reconciled* to God!
For *our* sakes God made him who did *not* know sin to *be sin*,
so that in *him* we might become the very *holiness* of God.

As your fellow *workers*
we *beg* you not to receive the grace of God in *vain*.
For he says,
"In an *acceptable time* I have *heard* you;
on a *day* of *salvation* I have *helped* you."
Now is the *acceptable time!*
Now is the *day* of *salvation!*

Plead for reconciliation.

Proclaim with wonder this willingness of Christ to take on responsibility for human sin.

You proclaim hope in God's promises, as well as the demand to put into practice the appeal for reconciliation. Speak with force and urgency.

Your task today is to proclaim, clearly and decisively, God's call to personal and communal conversion, and the urgency of leaving all else behind in order to respond. You have an awesome responsibility today. Let the solemnity of the occasion resonate in your words.

READING II The apostle Paul implores the Corinthians to turn to God and to recognize that salvation has been won in Christ. It is a fitting address to us as well, alerting us to our urgent need for reconciliation with God as we begin our journey through Lent.

Paul's relationship with the Corinthian church was a stormy one. The community was prone to factionalism. Sometimes Paul needed to be severe in his rebukes, resulting in strained relations with the Corinthians. Paul writes this letter after sending a delegate to the community to convey his message. He expresses in this letter his gratitude for their positive response.

Paul's appeal in this passage is urgent. Yet he does not clarify here what precipitates his message. This makes it especially available to us, living in a different time and place. The thrust of the appeal—"Be reconciled to God!"—applies to us just as to the Corinthians. But Paul also asserts that we are not engaged in this process on our own. In fact, the opportunity for holiness, for being united with God, is offered because of the salvific action of Christ. He has taken on our sinfulness, that tendency to stray from God,

GOSPEL   Matthew 6:1–6, 16–18

A reading from the holy gospel according to Matthew

Jesus said to his disciples:
"Be on *guard* against performing religious *acts*
        for people to *see.*
Otherwise expect *no recompense* from your heavenly Father.

When you give *alms,* for example,
do *not* blow a *horn* before you in *synagogues* and *streets*
        like *hypocrites* looking for *applause.*
You can be sure of *this* much, they are *already* repaid.
In giving *alms*
you are not to let your *left* hand
        know what your *right* hand is doing.
Keep your deeds of mercy *secret,*
and your *Father* who *sees* in secret will *repay* you.

"When you are *praying,*
do *not* behave like the *hypocrites*
who love to *stand* and pray in *synagogues*
or on *street corners* in order to be *noticed.*
I give you my *word,* they are *already* repaid.
Whenever *you* pray, go to your *room,*
close your *door,* and pray to your Father in *private.*
Then your *Father,*
who sees what *no* man *sees,* will *repay* you.

"When you *fast,*
you are not to look *glum* as the *hypocrites* do.
They *change* the appearance of their faces
so that others may *see* they are fasting.
I *assure* you, they are *already* repaid.

Introduce the gospel by reading these lines with solemn sincerity.

synagogues = SIN-uh-gogz
hypocrites = HIP-uh-krits

Emphasize the contrast between what the hypocrites do and what is admonished here. Raise your voice at the beginning of each practice—almsgiving, praying, fasting—and stress "You can be sure," and so forth.

so that we might be brought back into an intimate relationship with God. Quoting from the book of Isaiah regarding the servant of God, Paul indicates that divine aid is available to all those who serve God.

Paul says that he and his companions in ministry are ambassadors for Christ, as well as "fellow workers" with the members of the community. This is also an apt description of the role of the minister of the word, one who is part of the community but also entrusted with a noble task. You share

with Paul the responsibility and the dignity inherent in proclaiming God's message. You too announce that the time for reconciliation, for acceptance of the salvation offered in Christ, for turning to God, is now.

GOSPEL The gospel of Matthew was written for a community of Jews who believed in the saving action accomplished in Jesus' death and resurrection. This community of Jewish Christians found itself at odds with the larger Jewish

community. The entire gospel reflects a tension with the synagogue and its leaders, while preserving traditional Jewish practices and beliefs. Today's gospel passage adopts the hyperbole found in much of the gospel regarding the proper ways to act, in contrast to the deeds of the "hypocrites."

Prayer, fasting and almsgiving—the pillars of Lenten observance—were time-honored practices of the Jewish people. The author upholds them, suggesting that they are central to the Christian life as well. But

In reading this reversal of ordinary behavior, allow some amazement to enter your voice.

Slowly and warmly proclaim this promise.

When *you* fast,
see to it that you *groom* your hair and *wash* your face.
In *that* way no one can *see* you are fasting
but your *Father* who is *hidden;*
and your *Father* who *sees* what is hidden will *repay* you."

what is most striking is the author's insistence that all is to be done in secret.

These words challenge us as we solemnly begin a season in which we adopt practices of austerity and denial by marking our foreheads with ashes. We are called today to reflect on why we engage in these customs. Are we truly repenting, turning ourselves back to God with sincerity of heart? Or do we take pride in proclaiming to others what we are doing? Today's gospel insists that our duty is not so much to be examples for others, but rather to repent without drawing attention to ourselves: to care for the needs of others without recompense, to pray without being noticed, to fast and yet keep up our spirits.

The emphasis on private acts of piety comes at a time when we gather as community to begin our journey of 40 days. We know that we need one another. We come together to acknowledge our failings; we resolve, in the presence of others, to turn back to the path of righteousness. We also go forth from today's gathering to put into practice the exhortations of this gospel. Your task in proclaiming the gospel is to place God's invitation and demands before the community. Then step back and allow God to work in people's lives.

1ST SUNDAY OF LENT

Lectionary #24

READING I Deuteronomy 26:4–10

A reading from the book of Deuteronomy

Moses spoke to the *people*, saying:
   "The *priest* shall receive the *basket* from you
   and shall set it in *front* of the *altar* of the LORD, your *God*.

"Then you shall declare before the LORD, your *God*,
   'My *father* was a wandering *Aramean*
   who went down to *Egypt* with a small *household*
   and lived there as an *alien*.
But *there* he became a *nation*
   great, *strong* and *numerous*.
When the Egyptians *maltreated* and *oppressed* us,
   imposing hard *labor* upon us,
   we *cried* to the LORD, the God of our *fathers*,
   and he *heard* our cry
   and saw our *affliction*, our *toil* and our *oppression*.

"'He brought us *out* of *Egypt*
   with his strong *hand* and outstretched *arm*,
   with terrifying *power*, with *signs* and *wonders*;
   and bringing us into *this* country,
   he gave us this land *flowing* with *milk* and *honey*.

Aramean = ayr-uh-MEE-uhn

Speak forcefully as you recount God's wondrous deeds.

READING I The book of Deuteronomy (or "second law") purports to be the teachings of Moses given during Israel's wandering in the desert between the exodus from Egypt and the entrance into the Promised Land. In it, the entire law given at Sinai is repeated and reinterpreted. Today's instructions regard how the people are to conduct themselves after they enter the land of Canaan. Moses instructs the Israelites to offer the first fruits of the land as a thanksgiving to God. The offering of first fruits, long a part of ancient Hebrew tradition, is to continue every spring as a ritual for remembering God as the source of all blessings.

The agricultural festival of first fruits eventually became connected with the celebration of God's deliverance of Israel from the oppression of the Egyptians. This festival of Passover recalls God's liberation of the chosen people. Today's reading establishes the liturgical requirements of the feast and has been used in Passover celebrations for thousands of years. Jews continue to recount the exodus from Egypt as a sign of God's saving actions in their lives.

The "wandering Aramean" is Jacob, also called Israel, whose name was adopted to identify the entire people. Jacob and his family went to Egypt during a famine in the land of Canaan. The Israelites were enslaved there, but God delivered them and brought them home once again.

Notice that the passage does not recount only what God has done for Israel's distant ancestors. On the feast of Passover, each Jewish household recalls how God

Therefore, I have now brought you the *firstfruits*
of the products of the *soil*
which *you*, O LORD, have *given* me.'

"And having *set* them before the LORD, your *God*,
you shall bow *down* in his *presence*."

**Pause before concluding Moses'
instructions regarding the offering.**

READING II   Romans 10:8–13

A reading from the letter of Saint Paul to the Romans

Brothers and sisters:
What does *Scripture* say?

"The *word* is *near* you,
in your *mouth* and in your *heart*"
—that is, the word of *faith* that we *preach*—
for, if you *confess* with your mouth that *Jesus* is *Lord*
and *believe* in your *heart* that God *raised* him from the dead,
you will be *saved*.
For one *believes* with the *heart* and so is *justified*,
and one *confesses* with the *mouth* and so is *saved*.

For the Scripture says,
"No one who *believes* in him will be put to *shame*."
For there is no *distinction* between *Jew* and *Greek*;
the same *Lord* is Lord of *all*,
enriching all who *call* upon him.
For "everyone who calls on the *name* of the *Lord* will be *saved*."

**Emphasize these two aspects of faith,
explained more fully below.**

**Speak slowly and assuredly this central
claim.**

**The Christian faith is inclusive. It does not
judge some to be less worthy than others.**

"has brought *us* out of Egypt." The entire Jewish people identifies with both the plight of their ancestors in Egypt and the experience of the loving kindness of God, who delivers "with signs and wonders."

Christians also proclaim that God's saving deeds are not over but continue to touch our lives. Every time we celebrate the eucharist, we enter into the events of the past and make them present in our lives. Today we also identify with the Hebrew people of long ago and acknowledge God's saving deeds on their behalf and ours.

Proclaim this passage with great solemnity, especially as you recount the words that form the core of the Passover celebration. Change your voice appropriately as you recount the abuses of the Egyptians, the cry of Israel and God's gracious response, and, finally, the wondrous deeds of God.

READING II Paul wrote the letter to the Romans in large part to address the question of the relationship between the new faith in Jesus and its religious ancestor, Judaism. In today's passage,

he discusses the relationship between inner faith and its outward expression.

Lest anyone emphasize one aspect of the faith over another, Paul makes clear that both inner belief and a confession of faith are required. Outward expression alone is not enough; there must be a genuine inner trust that God has conquered death in Jesus. But the belief must also be verbalized. An unwillingness to voice one's faith that Jesus is Lord belies a weak faith indeed.

Emphasize the role of the Spirit, who guides Jesus.

GOSPEL Luke 4:1–13

A reading from the holy gospel according to Luke

Filled with the Holy *Spirit*, Jesus *returned* from the *Jordan*
   and was *led* by the Spirit into the *desert* for forty *days*,
   to be *tempted* by the *devil*.
He ate *nothing* during those days,
   and when they were *over* he was *hungry*.

The devil said to him,
"If you are the *Son* of *God*,
   command this *stone* to become *bread*."
Jesus answered him,
"It is *written*, 'One does not *live* on bread *alone*.' "

Then he took him up and *showed* him
   all the *kingdoms* of the world in a single *instant*.
The devil said to him,
"I shall *give* to you all this *power* and *glory*;
   for it has been handed over to *me*,
   and I may *give* it to whomever I *wish*.
All this will be *yours*, if you *worship* me."
Jesus said to him in reply,
"It is *written*:
   'You shall *worship* the LORD, your *God*,
   and him *alone* shall you *serve*.' "

Jesus responds to the devil with strength and conviction. Offer his words accordingly.

Again, speak Jesus' words firmly. He recognizes that only God deserves homage.

The confession "Jesus is Lord" was an early Christian liturgical proclamation. The term "Lord" was used to translate the divine name in the Greek translation of the Hebrew scriptures. Applying it to Jesus, then, is a way of claiming divine status for him. This confession of Jesus' divinity set Christianity apart from other religions in antiquity, and later persecutors would use it against the Christians. During periods of persecution, anyone who assented to belief in Jesus' divinity risked being tortured or even killed.

Paul closes with a declaration that anyone—Jew or Gentile—can benefit from the saving actions of God in Jesus.

Proclaim this reading as a lenten challenge to your listeners. Stress the twofold aspect of our faith—inward belief and outward expression—as well as the universal opportunity for salvation.

GOSPEL The story of Jesus' temptation in the desert affirms his full humanity. After his baptism, but before

he began his ministry, he was tempted just as we are. But in the end, Jesus prevailed.

The setting of the temptation story recalls the experiences of the Israelites as they wandered in the desert. Like his Hebrew ancestors, Jesus went into the wilderness, and his 40-day period of fasting and temptation recalls Israel's 40 years of wandering after the escape from Egypt. All of Jesus' responses come from the book of Deuteronomy, which summarizes the law parapet = PAYR-uh-pet

Then he led him to *Jerusalem*,
    made him stand on the *parapet* of the *temple*, and said to him,
"If you are the *Son* of *God*,
    throw yourself *down* from here, for it is written:
    'He will command his *angels* concerning you, to *guard* you,'
    and:
    'With their *hands* they will *support* you,
    lest you dash your *foot* against a *stone.*' "
Jesus said to him in reply,
"It *also* says,
    'You shall *not* put the LORD, your *God*, to the *test.*' "

When the devil had *finished* every *temptation*,
    he *departed* from him for a *time.*

Is Jesus angry, impatient or weary? Do not be afraid to express forcefully the emotion that you think best expresses Jesus' feelings.

God gave to Moses during Israel's wandering in the desert. Unlike the Israelites, however, Jesus resisted the temptation to rebel or take the easy way out. He chose to struggle with evil rather than give in to it.

The three temptations Jesus faced are familiar to us as well. We often desire comfort for ourselves, and a life free of effort in meeting our basic human needs. We also are tempted by the promise of power and sometimes sacrifice our values (which could be compared to worshiping the devil) to pursue it. Finally, we sometimes desire to test

God, thinking we can determine how God should communicate with us.

Jesus rejected all of these temptations, whether personal, political or religious. Although he could have had whatever he wanted, he chose to identify with the poor by being hungry, with the oppressed by rejecting displays of power, and with the unpretentious by refusing to demand that God save him. In fact, Jesus' entire life and his death reflect these values.

The conflict in this passage makes it an especially exciting one to proclaim. Allow

your voice to be filled with suspense. Speak the words of the devil with cunning but those of Jesus with conviction and strength. The knowledge that Jesus experienced temptation can be encouraging for us, who struggle with similar challenges.

2ND SUNDAY OF LENT

Lectionary #27

READING I   Genesis 15:5–12, 17–18

A reading from the book of Genesis

Abram = AY-br*m

Proclaim this as a solemn promise.

The Lord GOD took Abram *outside* and said,
 "Look up at the *sky* and count the *stars*, if you *can.*
Just so," he added, "shall your *descendants* be."
Abram put his *faith* in the LORD,
 who credited it to him as an act of *righteousness.*

He then said to him,
 "I am the LORD who brought you from *Ur* of the *Chaldeans*
 to give you this *land* as a *possession.*"

"O Lord *GOD*," he asked,
 "how am I to *know* that I shall *possess* it?"

This section, the account of the sacrifice, can be read more quickly.

He answered him,
 "Bring me a three-year-old *heifer*, a three-year-old *she*-goat,
 a three-year-old *ram*, a *turtledove* and a young *pigeon.*"
Abram *brought* him all *these*, split them in *two*,
 and placed each half *opposite* the *other*;
 but the *birds* he did not cut *up.*
Birds of prey *swooped* down on the *carcasses*,
 but Abram stayed *with* them.
As the *sun* was about to set, a *trance* fell upon Abram,
 and a deep, terrifying *darkness enveloped* him.

READING I In the covenant between God and Abram, God promises descendants and land. Abram (later called Abraham) and his wife were old and childless, but God vows to provide offspring. We know the great significance of this promise, aware that the life of Isaac, Abraham's son, was almost extinguished. We also know that the land possessed by Abraham and passed on to the Hebrew people has been ruled by many different nations and continues to be a source of dispute. The sincerity of the promises and the depth of Abraham's faith are even more striking when we reflect on our knowledge of what comes later.

In a time when few believed in an afterlife, having descendants promised immortality. This is why children were of such great importance in ancient Hebrew thought. Children carried on the traditions and name of the family, and could inherit the land and possessions of their parents.

God's promise to Abram included both descendants and land. Ancient covenants often involved the bestowal of land. Dwelling in the land given by God became both a blessing and a divinely assured right. In today's passage, God also reminds Abraham how he was brought to a new region and blessed with the gift of the land. God's generosity is not isolated but constant throughout the life of Abraham.

The covenant between God and Abraham reflects an ancient treaty between a powerful figure and a servant. The parties make promises and ratify the covenant with a sacrifice. In this case, however, God does all the promising. Abraham's response is faith in God's goodness and reliability.

This signifies that God accepts the sacrifice. Allow some awe to enter your voice.

When the *sun* had set and it was *dark*,
    there appeared a smoking *fire* pot and a flaming *torch*,
    which passed *between* those pieces.

It was on that *occasion* that the LORD made a *covenant*
        with *Abram*,
    saying: "To your *descendants* I give this *land*,
    from the Wadi of *Egypt* to the *Great* River, the *Euphrates*."

This again is a solemn vow.
Wadi = WAH-dee
Euphrates = yoo-FRAY-teez

READING II   Philippians 3:17—4:1

A reading from the letter of Saint Paul to the Philippians

Join with others in being *imitators* of me, brothers and sisters,
    and *observe* those who thus *conduct* themselves
    according to the *model* you have in *us*.
For *many*, as I have often told you
    and *now* tell you even in *tears*,
    conduct themselves as *enemies* of the *cross* of *Christ*.
Their end is *destruction*.
Their God is their *stomach*;
    their *glory* is in their *"shame."*
Their minds are occupied with *earthly* things.

Lower your voice and speak with sorrow.

Let a bit of anger enter your voice here.

But *our* citizenship is in *heaven*,
    and from it we also await a *savior*, the *Lord* Jesus *Christ*.
He will change our *lowly body*
    to *conform* with his *glorified body*
    by the *power* that enables him also
    to bring *all* things into *subjection* to *himself*.

Our human bodies are holy, but they will be changed and glorified.

Throughout the ages, the promises God made to Abraham have given hope to the Hebrew people. God chose a man, who responded with trust and obedience. God then promised that Abraham's descendants would be as numerous as the stars. Jews, Christians and Muslims alike consider themselves children of Abraham, heirs to the favor given him by God.

Today's passage is both a joy and a challenge to read. Concentrate your efforts on the promises God makes to Abraham, in order to convey God's great love and graciousness toward Abraham and all his descendants.

Although the story of Abraham's sacrifice is less intriguing, read it as an account of the reciprocal nature of the covenant relationship. God acts independently and decisively, but the human response is important. In this regard, Abraham can serve as a model for us in his willingness to respond to God in trust and faith.

READING II Paul's missionary churches were dear to his heart, and the Philippian community was especially beloved. Paul writes to the Philippians with

joy and gratitude, but also out of concern because of the false teachings they were receiving from some independent missionaries and perhaps even from members of their own community. In today's passage, Paul contrasts his teachings and reputation with those of the "enemies of the cross of Christ."

Paul exhorts the Philippians to look to the example of one person they know they can trust: Paul himself. Paul offers his life as an example because he knows that the Philippians need a model for proper behavior. He and his companions in ministry can be contrasted with those who are currently

Speak with tenderness and joy.

Therefore, my brothers and sisters,
　　whom I *love* and *long* for, my *joy* and *crown*,
　　in *this* way stand *firm* in the *Lord*.

[Shorter: Philippians 3:20—4:1]

GOSPEL　Luke 9:28b–36

A reading from the holy gospel according to Luke

Jesus took *Peter*, *John* and *James*
　　and went up the *mountain* to *pray*.
While he was *praying*, his face *changed* in *appearance*
　　and his *clothing* became dazzling *white*.

Emphasize the wonder of this sight.

And *behold*, two men were *conversing* with him, *Moses*
　　and *Elijah*,
　　who appeared in *glory* and spoke of his *exodus*
　　that he was going to *accomplish* in *Jerusalem*.

Peter and his *companions* had been overcome by *sleep*,
　　but becoming fully *awake*,
　　they saw his *glory* and the two men standing *with* him.

Peter's comment is impulsive and illustrates that he does not entirely understand what Jesus has been telling him. Allow his words to sound eager and perhaps a bit confused. Pause after them before continuing.

As they were about to *part* from him, *Peter* said to Jesus,
　　"*Master*, it is *good* that we are *here*;
　　let us make three *tents*,
　　one for *you*, one for *Moses*, and one for *Elijah*."
But he did not *know* what he was saying.

---

trying to influence the community. These latter missionaries are concerned more with personal comfort than with the higher good.

Paul reminds his readers that their true home is in heaven and that this reality should be reflected in their conduct. From that heavenly abode will come Jesus, who will transform all people and bring everything under his authority. Originally, Paul expected the return of Christ to occur during his own lifetime, but this passage presents only the hope that Christ will reign decisively at some point in the future. Paul closes the

passage with his characteristic love and joy for the church in Philippi.

You may feel uncomfortable advising your listeners to imitate you, but know that it is not self-aggrandizement. Remember that you are speaking for Paul, or think of someone who serves as a model for you, so that you can offer the passage as encouragement to your listeners. Offer it also as a challenge to look toward our future hope rather than rely only on the satisfaction of present, "earthly things." Finally, as you read Paul's closing words, allow your voice to be filled with satisfaction and joy.

GOSPEL　The account of the transfiguration is an awe-inspiring indication of the resplendent glory that belongs to Jesus as God's unique Son. It also points forward to Jesus' role as coming judge of the living and the dead.

The two figures who appear with the transfigured Jesus, Moses and Elijah, represent the Jewish law and the prophets. There was hope that Elijah and, later, Moses as well, would return, and there may be reference to the expected return of Jesus. What

Clouds often signal encounters with God.

Speak God's words lovingly.

While he was still *speaking*,
  a *cloud* came and cast a *shadow* over them,
  and they became *frightened* when they entered the cloud.
Then from the *cloud* came a *voice* that said,
  "*This* is my chosen *Son; listen* to him."
After the voice had *spoken*, Jesus was found *alone*.

They fell *silent* and did not at *that* time
  tell *anyone* what they had *seen*.

is clear, however, is that Jesus shares equal status with these historic figures. In fact, his authority exceeds even theirs, as the voice from heaven makes clear: Jesus is the beloved Son of God, to whom all are to listen.

What Moses and Elijah discuss with Jesus is his death, an event that would take place in Jerusalem. Both Moses and Elijah received glory without having to suffer an ignominious death, although both experienced resistance, even rejection, during their lives. In contrast, Jesus received glory only through suffering and dying.

This story of the glorification of Jesus follows Peter's declaration of faith in Jesus as the Messiah and Jesus' first teaching about his suffering and death. Here, Peter anticipates only a glorious reign for Jesus, as his impetuous comment about erecting tents (places to commune with God) suggests. But the author does not allow the community to linger at the mountaintop. Instead, the disciples keep silent and Jesus' ministry continues. But now the tenor of Jesus' teaching has changed. Increasingly,

there is discussion about the suffering and death that awaits Jesus, which all who follow in his footsteps must be willing to undergo. From this point on in the gospel, Jesus moves steadily toward his death.

Your task today is to announce the splendor of the transfiguration to your community, to proclaim the uniqueness of the one we call "Lord." At the same time, do not lose sight of the broader message of the gospel: One who follows Jesus must be willing to do what he did, renouncing glory in exchange for suffering.

3RD SUNDAY OF LENT

Lectionary #30

READING I   Exodus 3:1–8a, 13–15

A reading from the book of Exodus

Midian = MID-ee-uhn
Horeb = HOHR-eb

Moses was tending the flock of his father-in-law *Jethro*,
    the priest of *Midian*.
Leading the *flock* across the *desert*, he came to *Horeb*,
    the mountain of *God*.
There an *angel* of the LORD *appeared* to Moses in *fire*
    flaming out of a *bush*.
As he looked *on*, he was *surprised* to see that the *bush*,
    though on *fire*, was not *consumed*.

So Moses decided,
    "I must go over to *look* at this remarkable *sight*,
    and see why the *bush* is not *burned*."

Speak God's words forcefully. Moses responds to God with sincerity.

When the LORD saw him coming *over* to look at it more *closely*,
    God called *out* to him from the *bush*, "*Moses! Moses!*"
He answered, "*Here* I am."
God said, "Come no *nearer!*
Remove the sandals from your *feet*,
    for the place where you *stand* is *holy* ground.

"I am the *God* of your *fathers*," he continued,
    "the God of *Abraham*, the God of *Isaac*, the God of *Jacob*."
Moses *hid* his *face*, for he was afraid to *look* at God.

No one was able to see God directly and live. Strive to convey the awe Moses must have felt.

But the LORD said,
    "I have *witnessed* the *affliction* of my people in *Egypt*

READING I   After he was accused of killing an Egyptian, Moses fled Egypt and lived in the wilderness of the Sinai peninsula. While living there, he encountered God, as today's passage recounts, who called on Moses to lead the people of Israel out of bondage in Egypt and into the land God promised Abraham and his descendents.

    Moses experiences the presence of God on a mountaintop. Mountains often serve as locations for encounters with the divine. This mountain, Horeb, is sometimes identified with Mount Sinai, the place where Moses will later receive the divine commandments while leading the Israelites through the wilderness of the desert.

    God's presence is made known in great spectacle. A bush is aflame but does not burn up, and from it comes a voice calling to Moses. God tells Moses to remove his sandals out of respect for the holiness of the place. Moses hides his face, a sign of the awesome nature of the encounter.

    The conversation between Moses and God is intriguing. Although God does most of the speaking, Moses is not afraid to question God and seek clarification. God is revealed first and foremost as a God of relationship, the one known in the past to the ancestors of Israel. God is not a distant concept or an otherworldly being but one who has spoken to and guided the patriarchs. Twice in this passage, God affirms that the covenant relationship with Israel's ancestors sums up the divine identity. God spoke to Abraham, promising descendants and giving him the land. God cared for Isaac, Jacob and their children. And God remains active in the life of Israel, promising to relieve the suffering of the people and once again bring them into the land designated for them.

God speaks compassionately of the plight of Israel and forcefully about the deliverance in store for the people.

and have *heard* their cry of *complaint* against their
 slave drivers,
so I know *well* what they are *suffering*.
Therefore I have come down to *rescue* them
 from the *hands* of the *Egyptians*
 and lead them *out* of that land into a *good* and *spacious* land,
 a land *flowing* with *milk* and *honey*."

Moses shows boldness in daring to speak and must have been troubled about how to help the people believe his words.

Slow down your delivery and speak God's name with dignity.

Moses said to God, "But when I *go* to the Israelites
 and *say* to them, 'The God of your *fathers* has *sent* me to you,'
 if they *ask* me, 'What is his *name*?' what am I to *tell* them?"

God replied, "*I am* who *am*."
Then he added, "*This* is what you shall tell the *Israelites*:
 I AM sent me to you."

This is not a new god but one known to have acted before.

God spoke *further* to Moses, "*Thus* shall you say
 to the *Israelites*:
The LORD, the God of your *fathers*,
 the God of *Abraham*, the God of *Isaac*, the God of *Jacob*,
 has *sent* me to you.

"*This* is my name *forever*;
 thus am I to be *remembered* through all *generations*."

READING II 1 Corinthians 10:1–6, 10–12

A reading from the first letter of Saint Paul to the Corinthians

I do not want you to be *unaware*, brothers and sisters,
 that our *ancestors* were all under the *cloud*
 and all passed through the *sea*,

Paul refers here to the experience of the exodus, when a pillar of fire and cloud accompanied the people on their journey.

Although the original meaning of the four Hebrew letters that make up the divine name has been debated, there is no question about what the author understands it to mean: "I am who am." No further explanation is necessary or even possible. The name, then, evokes awe; it stresses the majesty and mystery of the divine. It also emphasizes God's ability to act freely, to grant favor and compassion on those chosen.

The key to proclaiming this passage well is to read slowly and deliberately, always aware of the great mystery you are communicating. Emphasize the majesty of

God as well as Moses' awe as he realizes who is speaking to him. At the same time, speak with compassion as you relate God's promise to act on behalf of the persecuted Israelites, pledging to bring them out of misery and into peace and prosperity.

READING II Paul addresses the church at Corinth concerning the actions of some members of the community. The Corinthians, in their enthusiasm as new Christians, often needed reminders and further instruction from Paul. They had a tendency to take Paul's teachings to extremes,

and Paul needed to communicate continually his ethical concerns as a corrective to their emphasis on freedom. In this passage, Paul appeals to the exodus story to remind his readers not to make the same mistakes that the Israelites made on their desert journey.

Paul understands the Israelites' passage through the Red Sea at the beginning of the exodus as a type of baptism. Just as the Israelites passed through the water of the Red Sea and were baptized into Moses, so Christians are baptized into Christ. But, despite Israel's experience of deliverance and "initiation" into the divine mysteries,

and all of them were *baptized* into *Moses*
    in the *cloud* and in the *sea.*
All *ate* the same spiritual *food,*
    and all *drank* the same spiritual *drink,*
    for they *drank* from a spiritual *rock* that *followed* them,
    and the *rock* was the *Christ.*

Yet God was not *pleased* with most of them,
    for they were struck *down* in the *desert.*

These things happened as *examples* for us,
    so that we might not desire *evil* things, as *they* did.
Do not *grumble* as some of *them* did,
    and suffered *death* by the *destroyer.*

These things happened to them as an *example,*
    and they have been written *down* as a *warning* to *us,*
    upon whom the *end* of the *ages* has *come.*
Therefore, whoever thinks he is standing *secure*
    should take *care* not to *fall.*

Moses procured water for the Israelites by striking a rock at God's command. Later tradition had the rock following the people.

Change your tone to convey God's displeasure.

Stress how your listeners can learn from the example of others.

This is a solemn warning.

GOSPEL   Luke 13:1–9

A reading from the holy gospel according to Luke

Some *people* told Jesus about the *Galileans*
    whose *blood* Pilate had mingled with the blood
        of their *sacrifices.*

Jesus said to them in reply,
    "Do you *think* that because these Galileans *suffered*
        in this way
    they were greater *sinners* than all *other* Galileans?

Pilate had the Galileans killed when they came to Jerusalem to offer sacrifice.

Speak emphatically Jesus' disagreement with the idea that they were worse sinners, as well as his warning to repent.

---

the people grumbled and complained as they continued their journey.

This, Paul asserts, is not to be the way Christians act. Baptism is the first significant encounter between God and the new Christian, an experience of divine favor and human commitment, but it is simply the first step on a long journey. It is essential to reaffirm the commitment and to avoid the pitfalls into which the Israelites fell. Their experience can be an example to the Christian, a warning of what to avoid.

During Lent we concentrate intently on our Christian journey. We also struggle and sometimes grumble. But if we take Paul's words to heart, learning from the mistakes of others, we can look forward to our Easter celebration, when we will renew our baptismal promises and welcome new members into our community.

Paul's unusual style of interpretation makes this passage a bit difficult to read. Reflect on the exodus story, and offer this selection as a warning to your listeners. In the second paragraph, emphasize especially the example intended by referring to this story from long ago. It is not simply a rebuke but an attempt to turn people—whether the original readers of the letter or your assembly—back to the right path.

GOSPEL   A common belief in ancient Hebrew thought was that blessings or misfortunes were the result of one's actions. Jesus does not question such an attitude in today's gospel, although he qualifies it. The parable, however, attests to God's tremendous patience, even with those who fail to bear fruit.

The terrible tragedies alluded to in today's selection are not corroborated by other sources, but they are easy to imagine.

By *no means!*
But I *tell* you, if you do not *repent,*
    you will all *perish* as *they* did!
Or those eighteen *people* who were *killed*
    when the *tower* at Siloam *fell* on them—
    do you think they were more *guilty*
    than everyone *else* who lived in *Jerusalem?*
By *no means!*
But I *tell* you, if you do not *repent,*
    you will all *perish* as *they* did!"

And he told them this *parable:*
    "There *once* was a person who had a *fig* tree planted
        in his *orchard,*
    and when he came in search of *fruit* on it but found *none,*
    he said to the *gardener,*
    'For three *years* now I have come in search of *fruit*
        on this *fig* tree
    but have found *none.*
So cut it *down.*
Why should it exhaust the *soil?'*

"He said to him in reply,
    'Sir, leave it for *this* year *also,*
    and I shall *cultivate* the *ground* around it and *fertilize* it;
    it may bear *fruit* in the *future.*
If *not* you can cut it *down.'"*

Again, speak strongly. Then pause before beginning the parable.

Offer the gardener's words with sincerity and hope.

Pilate was known for his cruelty and often directed it at the Galileans. And it is certainly possible that a tower could fall, whether as the result of shoddy construction or during an earthquake.

What is noteworthy in Jesus' treatment of these subjects is his placement of all the participants in the story on the same level. Far from being greater sinners and thus worthy of their tragic fates, those who died in the two incidents were much the same as Jesus' listeners. They did not bear greater guilt than others but neither were they completely innocent, as Jesus' address to his

listeners implies. The same fate could befall any who fail to repent and conform their lives to God's commands.

The value of repentance and God's forgiveness are the themes of the parable. Although the fig tree failed to produce fruit for three full years, it is given another chance. In the same way, we too can turn away from our fruitless lives and resolve to lead productive, beneficial ones. Just as the tree's fruit reveals its value, so also the worthiness of our lives is known through our actions. But

God is patient, forgiving even years of inactivity, if only we repent and change our lives.

In the end, the entire gospel reading affirms that a judgment is coming. It is not enough simply to say that one is no more sinful than another, or to hope in God's loving forgiveness. Before another tragedy occurs, before the tree is chopped down, action must be taken. The time to repent is now.

Proclaim this passage as encouragement to your listeners but also with a sense of urgency, offering a lenten wake-up call for a people who are sometimes complacent.

3RD SUNDAY OF LENT, YEAR A

Lectionary #28

READING I   Exodus 17:3–7

A reading from the book of Exodus

In *those* days, in their *thirst* for *water*,
    the people *grumbled* against *Moses*,
    saying, "*Why* did you ever make us leave *Egypt*?
Was it just to have us *die* here of *thirst*
    with our *children* and our *livestock*?"
So Moses cried out to the LORD,
    "What shall I *do* with this people?
A little *more* and they will *stone* me!"

The LORD answered Moses,
    "Go over there in *front* of the *people*,
    along with some of the *elders* of Israel,
    holding in your *hand*, as you *go*,
    the *staff* with which you struck the *river*.
I will be *standing* there in *front* of you on the *rock* in *Horeb*.
Strike the rock, and the water will *flow* from it
    for the people to *drink*."
This Moses *did*, in the presence of the *elders* of *Israel*.

The place was called *Massah* and *Meribah*,
    because the Israelites *quarreled* there
    and *tested* the LORD, saying,
    "Is the LORD in our *midst* or *not*?"

The people are upset, almost ready to revolt. Let their exasperation be heard in your words.

Moses is desperate.

Speak God's words calmly and firmly.

Massah = MAS-ah
Meribah = MAYR-ih-bah
Massah means "testing" and Meribah means "quarreling."

READING I   Life-giving water figures prominently in today's readings, as we prepare to welcome new members into the community through the waters of baptism on Easter.

Despite God's continual intervention on behalf of the Israelites wandering in the desert, the Pentateuch records their constant grumbling against the Lord whenever they meet with adversity. At times they even plan to return to Egypt; freedom, with its attendant struggles, can be even more threatening than slavery. This might seem to be the case for us too as we journey through the lenten wilderness. We would prefer to turn back rather than continue wandering with parched lips, longing for home. So today we are given refreshment to strengthen us on the way.

Although they have just been fed with quail and manna, the Israelites find the absence of water in the desert too much to bear. Although Moses rightly fears that he, as God's mouthpiece, is in danger of losing his life to the mob, the Israelites' revolt is really against God. As so often before, God instructs Moses to take symbolic action, and the result is a physical benefit for the Israelites. Here their thirst is met with water in abundance, but their rebellious actions are recorded forever in the names given to the places where they questioned God.

There is plenty of drama in this passage to make for an interesting presentation. Let the people's words sound defiant, and express Moses' fear, but make God's control throughout the situation evident. Challenge your listeners also to reflect on their own times of rebellion. Do we really believe that God will provide everything that we need? Through the waters of baptism we have

READING II   Romans 5:1–2, 5–8

A reading from the letter of Saint Paul to the Romans

Brothers and sisters:
Since we have been *justified* by *faith*,
    we have *peace* with God through our *Lord* Jesus *Christ*,
    through whom we have gained *access* by faith
    to this *grace* in which we *stand*,
    and we *boast* in hope of the *glory* of *God.*

And *hope* does not *disappoint*,
    because the *love* of God has been poured out into our *hearts*
    through the Holy *Spirit* who has been *given* to us.
For *Christ*, while we were still *helpless*,
    died at the appointed *time* for the *ungodly.*
Indeed, only with *difficulty* does one die for a *just* person,
    though *perhaps* for a *good* person one might even
        find *courage* to die.
But *God* proves his *love* for us
    in that while we were still *sinners* Christ *died* for us.

Begin strongly, but with a genuine peacefulness in your voice.

The word translated "boast" here is related to words meaning "rejoice" or "exult." Paul has been contrasting the presumptuous boasting of one who is overconfident with the certainty of one who genuinely trusts in God.

Stress words such as "difficulty," "just" and "perhaps" in order to emphasize how unusual it would be for someone to die for another—even for one who is good.

Pause briefly after "that." This reality is truly amazing; let your voice be filled with joy and awe.

---

become part of a community that commits itself to God, even as we know that God is completely committed to our welfare. Offer this reading to your assembly as a challenge to trust that God is indeed on our side.

READING II — This passage from Paul's letter to the Romans is filled with assurances about the great love of God. It spells out Paul's belief in the initiative taken by God for our sake, seen in the actions of Christ.

Paul begins this section by affirming one of his most cherished principles: We are made right ("justified") before God, brought back into relationship with God, not through anything we ourselves have done but through God's own gracious love. Because of this we can be at peace. Even in times of trial ("stand" in Paul's writings always means firmness in the face of adversity), we can turn to God in faith, knowing that God's glory will be revealed.

Our hope is not a false one. We can be confident because we know that God's love for us has been demonstrated in Jesus'

death. And that love has been poured out in abundance, filling our hearts to overflowing. It is through the Holy Spirit, given in baptism, that the overwhelming love of God for us is confirmed.

Jesus' actions demonstrate God's overflowing grace as well. Paul points out how rare it is for one person to die for another. We can think of instances when this happens, but usually it is a brave soul who saves a loved one or friend. It is much harder to imagine someone dying for the sake of an enemy. Yet that is what Jesus has done,

GOSPEL John 4:5–42

A reading from the holy gospel according to John

Sychar = SĪK-ahr

Jesus came to a town of *Samaria* called *Sychar*,
   near the plot of *land* that *Jacob* had given to his son *Joseph*.
Jacob's *well* was there.
Jesus, tired from his *journey*, sat *down* there at the *well*.
It was about *noon*.

A *woman* of *Samaria* came to draw *water*.
Jesus said to her,
   "Give me a *drink*."
His *disciples* had gone into the town to buy *food*.

Jesus' statement sounds rude and demanding. The woman does not understand it to be so. Phrase it in such a way that it sounds like a request rather than a demand.

In the gospel of John, the term "Jew" is usually applied to the religious leaders of the Jews. It is used of Jesus only here in this gospel.

The Samaritan woman said to him,
   "How can *you*, a *Jew*, ask *me*, a *Samaritan woman*,
     for a *drink*?"
—For *Jews* use nothing in common with *Samaritans*.—
Jesus answered and said to her,
   "If you knew the *gift* of *God*
   and who is *saying* to you, 'Give me a *drink*,'
   you would have *asked* him
   and he would have given you *living* water."

The woman is being practical and reasonable. In Greek the terms seem to refer to actual water.

Speak here with a bit of indignation and surprise at the notion.

The woman said to him,
   "*Sir*, you do not even have a *bucket* and the cistern is *deep*;
   where then can you get this *living water*?
Are you *greater* than our father *Jacob*,
   who *gave* us this cistern and *drank* from it himself
   with his *children* and his *flocks*?"

---

dying for us while we were caught in sin, having made ourselves enemies of God.

This is a solemn proclamation, yet the message is cause for great joy. Though we have done nothing to deserve it, God has given us the greatest gift of love. Inspire the members of your assembly to reflect on God's deep commitment and the tremendous love God offers us through Jesus. Encourage your listeners to stand firm in their faith in this season of Lent and always, knowing that God is always with us. In this there is truly a message of peace.

GOSPEL The story of the encounter between Jesus and the Samaritan woman at the well centers on the question of living water and the related significance of Jesus' identity. As always in the gospel of John, Jesus has full knowledge of his mission and identity, but his companions (here, primarily the woman, but also the disciples) have ordinary human knowledge, inadequate for fully comprehending what Jesus is saying. Here also, ordinary water—so important for sustaining life and for refreshment—gives way to living water, the kind of water necessary for eternal life.

As we prepare to approach the waters of baptism on Easter, whether to renew our baptismal commitment or to receive the life-giving waters, we are reminded of the source of our sustenance. It is through Jesus that we receive the water of life, essential for our thirsty souls.

Although Jesus could have avoided traveling through Samaria on his way to Galilee from Jerusalem, he finds himself in the heart of Samaritan territory. Samaritans and Jews, despite common roots, had long felt great animosity toward one another. Jews were convinced that "salvation is from

Jesus' words are solemn and carry deep meaning. Let them build so that the words sound like the bubbling water they describe.

Jesus answered and said to her,
　"Everyone who drinks *this* water will be thirsty *again*;
　but whoever drinks the water *I* shall give will *never* thirst;
　the water *I* shall give will *become* in him
　a *spring* of water welling *up* to *eternal life.*"

The woman said to him,
　"Sir, *give* me this water, so that I may not be *thirsty*
　or have to keep *coming* here to *draw* water."

Convey the woman's eagerness, although she still does not understand.

Jesus said to her,
　"*Go* call your *husband* and come *back.*"
The woman answered and said to him,
　"I do not *have* a husband."
Jesus answered her,
　"You are *right* in saying, 'I do not have a *husband.*'
For you have had *five* husbands,
　and the one you have *now* is *not* your husband.
What you have said is *true.*"

The woman said to him,
　"Sir, I can *see* that you are a *prophet.*
Our *ancestors* worshiped on this *mountain*;
　but *you* people say that the place to worship is in *Jerusalem.*"
Jesus said to her,
　"*Believe* me, woman, the hour is *coming*
　when you will *worship* the *Father*
　neither on *this* mountain nor in *Jerusalem.*

"*You* people worship what you do not *understand*;
　we worship what we *understand,*
　because *salvation* is from the *Jews.*

the Jews," and Samaritans held fast to the Pentateuch and viewed later traditions—such as worship in Jerusalem—as accretions to the true faith. For a Jewish teacher to speak at length (or at all!) with a Samaritan was unheard of.

For a Jewish teacher to speak in public with a woman—even a Jewish woman—was also unknown. The disciples' surprise when they returned and saw Jesus conversing with the Samaritan woman is to be expected. Jesus was defying the tradition that kept strict social barriers in place

between those of different nationalities, religious traditions and sexes. Jesus reached out to the woman and offered her what she did not even realize she needed.

The story begins simply; in one of the few instances in John's gospel in which he displays human weakness, Jesus is tired and thirsty after a morning of travel. When he requests a drink of the woman, she immediately hides behind the barriers she has always known. Jesus' response does not

address her issues, but rather turns the conversation to the question of water.

The term for "living" water can also mean "flowing," referring to water that is not stagnant but fresh and pure. The woman misunderstands and is skeptical of Jesus' claims. Although she recognizes him as a teacher, she is convinced that he could not possibly be greater than Jacob, whose well they are using. The reader anticipates what is coming: Jesus is, of course, far greater. However, Jesus again does not reply directly but allows her to draw her own conclusions.

But the hour is *coming*, and is now *here*,
when *true* worshipers will worship the Father
in *Spirit* and *truth*;
and indeed the Father *seeks such* people to *worship* him.
God is *Spirit*, and those who *worship* him
must worship in *Spirit* and *truth*."

The woman said to him,
"I *know* that the Messiah is *coming*, the one called the *Christ*;
when he *comes*, he will tell us *everything*."
Jesus said to her,
"*I* am *he*, the one *speaking* with you."

At that moment his disciples *returned*,
and were *amazed* that he was talking with a *woman*,
but still no one said, "What are you *looking* for?"
or "*Why* are you *talking* with her?"
The woman left her *water* jar
and went into the *town* and said to the *people*,
"*Come* see a man who told me *everything* I have *done*.
Could he *possibly* be the *Christ*?"
They went *out* of the town and *came* to him.
Meanwhile, the disciples *urged* him, "*Rabbi, eat*."
But he said to them,
"I have *food* to eat of which *you* do not *know*."
So the disciples said to one another,
"Could someone have *brought* him something to *eat*?"

Jesus said to them,
"My *food* is to do the *will* of the one who *sent* me
and to *finish* his *work*.
Do you not say, 'In four *months* the harvest will be *here*'?
I *tell* you, look *up* and see the fields *ripe* for the harvest.

Express the woman's excitement.

The disciples, like the woman, do not initially understand. This provides Jesus with an opportunity to teach them.

Jesus reveals that he has water for eternal life; the woman is intrigued. But she becomes convinced that he is no ordinary person when he has insight into her life and her character. Jesus brings her to fuller understanding of his identity by establishing a relationship with her.

It is especially appropriate to contemplate the "living water" offered by Jesus on this day when catechumens undergo their first scrutiny in preparation for Easter baptism. Recall that, as with the Samaritan woman, the life-giving water is something that is offered only through personal contact; one comes to know Jesus by encountering those who trust in him.

Just when it seems that their religious differences are irrelevant, Jesus affirms that "salvation is from the Jews." Here the gospel of John reveals itself as a document from a Jewish-Christian community. But, Jesus claims, the time soon approaches when true worship of God will be "in spirit and truth," rather than the rituals familiar to the Samaritans or the Jews. The evangelist is clearly alluding to Christian worship of the God who is revealed in Jesus. Jesus is truth, as the Johannine prologue asserts, and baptizes with the Holy Spirit. Although the old ways may have been valid in the past, the author leaves no doubt that a new way of living and worshiping is available in Jesus.

The woman's belief in a Messiah seems odd coming from a Samaritan. In fact, it is probably the Jewish expectation for a Davidic Messiah that is expressed, allowing Jesus to reveal himself as the fulfillment of that expectation.

The conversation is interrupted by the return of the disciples. Jesus continues his

The *reaper* is already receiving *payment*
    and gathering *crops* for *eternal life,*
    so that the *sower* and *reaper* can rejoice *together.*
For *here* the saying is *verified* that '*One sows* and another *reaps.*'
I sent you to *reap* what you have not *worked* for;
    others have done the *work,*
    and *you* are sharing the *fruits* of their *work.*"

Many of the *Samaritans* of that town began to *believe* in him
    because of the *word* of the *woman* who *testified,*
    "He told me *everything* I have *done.*"
When the Samaritans *came* to him,
    they invited him to *stay* with them;
    and he stayed there two *days.*
Many *more* began to believe in him because of *his* word,
    and they said to the woman,
    "We no *longer* believe because of *your* word;
    for we have heard for *ourselves,*
    and we *know* that this is *truly* the *savior* of the *world.*"

[Shorter: John 4:5–15, 19b–26, 39a, 40–42]

Close with an emphasis on the personal nature of faith, and on the title given Jesus.

enigmatic claims by asserting that he has food of which his disciples are not aware. He then launches into a discussion of ministry under the metaphor of harvest. As is so often true in agriculture and in life, the minister knows that it takes time for a seed to take root. The one who begins the work of evangelizing and nurturing faith is not always the one who sees that work come to fruition. We must recognize that no one individual or group can claim credit for success, precisely because we claim to be a community. One may plant the seed of faith, another may water it, and still another enjoy the fragrant blossoms of mature belief.

The Samaritan woman is sometimes remembered as the first evangelist. She ran to the town to tell others of her encounter with Jesus. Her neighbors came to believe, however, based on their own experience. Although others can introduce one to faith, each person must have his or her own encounter with Jesus.

This is an interesting and exciting story of faith. Allow the woman's sincerity and eagerness to be heard. Although Jesus' responses can be exasperating and elusive, use them as the teaching tools they are, drawing your listeners to a deeper level of understanding. Challenge your community of faith to reflect on its ministry and the necessity of coordinating efforts in order to witness the greatest gains. Finally, remember that it is often in quiet darkness that the seeds of faith are first sown. Trust that God is working even when all evidence seems to indicate otherwise.

4TH SUNDAY OF LENT

Lectionary #33

READING I   Joshua 5:9a, 10–12

A reading from the book of Joshua

The LORD said to *Joshua*,
  "*Today* I have removed the reproach of *Egypt* from you."

While the *Israelites* were encamped at *Gilgal* on the plains
      of *Jericho*,
  they celebrated the *Passover*
  on the *evening* of the fourteenth of the *month*.

On the day *after* the Passover,
  they *ate* of the *produce* of the *land*
  in the form of unleavened *cakes* and parched *grain*.
On that *same* day after the *Passover*,
  on which they ate of the *produce* of the *land*, the manna *ceased*.
No *longer* was there *manna* for the *Israelites*,
  who that year ate of the *yield* of the land of *Canaan*.

Read this as the solemn vow that it is before continuing with the story.
Gilgal = GIL-gahl

Passover is always held on the fourteenth of the spring month of Nisan.

READING II   2 Corinthians 5:17–21

A reading from the second letter of Saint Paul to the Corinthians

Brothers and sisters:
Whoever is *in Christ* is a *new creation*:
  the *old* things have passed *away*;
  behold, *new* things have come.

Speak with excitement in your voice.

READING I   After God delivered Israel from slavery in Egypt, Moses led the Israelites through the desert, but he died before entering the land of Canaan. In today's reading, Joshua has taken on Moses' role as the leader of Israel.

On this day, God declares that the experience of slavery in Egypt is finally over. It has been years since the Israelites were under the rule of the Pharaoh, but only now do they finally return home. While in the desert, they had been a nomadic people, without land or organized government. They had been rebellious, proving themselves still enslaved to idol worship and unwilling to trust in God's supreme goodness and care for them. But all that ends on this day, when they enter into the land God has designated for them. God and Israel renew their commitment to one another.

The exodus had begun with a celebration of Passover, and it ends with the same feast. Immediately after celebrating this Passover, the manna that God had provided to feed the Israelites on their journey ceases. They now have a rich land, a land "flowing with milk and honey," to provide for them. God no longer needs to supply their daily sustenance, but gives them the resources to provide for themselves.

It is the beginning of a new period in Israel's history. In time, a king will be chosen and a monarchy established. The loose organization that had characterized the years in Egypt and the time spent wandering in the desert is past. Israel will truly become a nation.

We, too, are wandering through the desert experience of Lent. Today's passage reminds us of the graciousness of God, who provides for our every need. Offer it to your

Proceed slowly through this section, giving due emphasis to the repeated words referring to reconciliation.

And all *this* is from *God*,
who has *reconciled* us to himself through *Christ*
and given us the *ministry* of *reconciliation*,
namely, God was *reconciling* the world to himself in *Christ*,
not counting their trespasses *against* them
and entrusting to *us* the *message* of *reconciliation*.

Speak as though you are begging your own community to set themselves on the right course.

So we are *ambassadors* for *Christ*,
as if God were *appealing* through *us*.
We *implore* you on behalf of *Christ*,
be *reconciled* to *God*.
For *our* sake he made him to be *sin* who did *not* know sin,
so that *we* might become the *righteousness* of God in *him*.

GOSPEL Luke 15:1–3, 11–32

A reading from the holy gospel according to Luke

Tax collectors and *sinners* were all drawing near to *listen* to Jesus,
but the *Pharisees* and *scribes* began to *complain*, saying,
"This *man* welcomes *sinners* and *eats* with them."

Give plenty of emphasis to this central accusation: Jesus is keeping bad company and the religious leaders judge him negatively.

So to them Jesus addressed this *parable*:
"A man had two *sons*, and the *younger* son said to his father,
'*Father* give me the *share* of your estate that should *come* to me.'
So the father divided the property *between* them.

"After a few days, the *younger* son collected all his *belongings*
and set off to a distant *country*
where he *squandered* his inheritance on a life of *dissipation*.

assembly as a simple story of God's goodness and love.

READING II Paul is convinced of the radical newness of all of life because of Jesus Christ. Today's reading expresses beautifully the new life available to the Christian and the promise of a new relationship with God effected in Christ.

For the person who abides in Christ, who is in Christ, everything is new. A principal characteristic of this new life is a new relationship with God. Through Christ the world is reconciled to God.

The reconciliation of humankind and God is made possible not by anything we have done but by Christ. Indeed, Paul says that God chooses not to count our transgressions against us, as we deserve. Instead Jesus, who was sinless, takes on the responsibility for our sins. By placing our faith in him, we are made right with God.

Paul recognizes that the gift of reconciliation is freely given but also knows that his readers have the responsibility to accept that gift and make it real. He thus implores the Corinthians to be reconciled to God. Although new life is fully available through

Christ, Paul asserts that we must actively seek to be in right relationship with God.

Paul declares himself and his companions to be "ambassadors for Christ." He sees himself speaking for God, enticing the members of his communities into an intimate relationship with God. In much the same way, you are an ambassador for Christ. You are entrusted with conveying God's message to the members of your assembly. Speak Paul's words as if addressed directly to your listeners, so that they too may embrace the new life offered in Christ and strive to be reconciled completely with God.

Allow the young man's plight to color your reading. Let your voice be filled with sadness, frustration and longing.

"When he had freely spent *everything*,
　a severe *famine* struck that country,
　and he found himself in dire *need*.
So he *hired* himself *out* to one of the local *citizens*
　who sent him to his *farm* to tend the *swine*.
And he *longed* to eat his fill of the *pods* on which the *swine* fed,
　but nobody gave him *any*.

"Coming to his *senses* he thought,
　'How many of my father's hired *workers*
　have *more* than enough food to eat,
　but here am *I*, *dying* from *hunger*.
I shall get *up* and go to my *father* and I shall *say* to him,
　"*Father*, I have sinned against *heaven* and against *you*.
I no longer *deserve* to be called your *son*;
　treat *me* as you would treat one of your hired *workers*."'

"So he got *up* and went back to his *father*.
While he was still a long way *off*,
　his father caught *sight* of him, and was filled with *compassion*.
He ran to his son, *embraced* him and *kissed* him.

Express the joy of this encounter.

"His son said to him,
　'*Father*, I have sinned against *heaven* and against *you*;
　I no longer *deserve* to be called your *son*.'
But his father ordered his *servants*,
　'*Quickly* bring the finest *robe* and put it *on* him;
　put a *ring* on his finger and *sandals* on his feet.
Take the fattened *calf* and *slaughter* it.
Then let us *celebrate* with a *feast*,
　because this *son* of mine was *dead*, and has come to *life* again;
　he was *lost*, and has been *found*.'
Then the celebration *began*.

Speak humbly and sincerely. The younger son does not expect any favor from the father.

The father's exuberance continues. He has barely heard his son's apology.

| GOSPEL | The story of the prodigal son (or, rather, the parable of the loving father) is a familiar one and will require a skilled storyteller to convey it in a fresh manner. We know the main points of the story well: One of two brothers asks for his inheritance, wastes it, and then returns home to his father, who greets him with joy and forgiveness. Such outpouring of love offends the other son, who has remained with the father. The story is simultaneously one of penitence, of God's love and forgiveness, and of the dangers of a judgmental attitude.

When understood as a story of penitence, the focus is on the younger son. The son was arrogant in demanding his share of his father's wealth, foolish in squandering it away, and deserving of his fate. Every Jew listening to the tale would have known that the younger son had indeed hit bottom, reduced to feeding pigs, the most unclean of animals. Finally, he recognizes his folly and humbly returns to his father, asking only to be treated as a servant.

The father in today's story rejoices to find the son who was lost. Clearly a metaphor for divine forgiveness and acceptance, this aspect of the tale leaves no doubt that the son's errant ways have been dismissed if not forgotten. The reader is left with the confidence that we, too, are forgiven completely whenever we sincerely leave behind our past life and turn in trust and humility to a God who loves us completely.

But the opening verses of today's passage suggest that the question of judgment of others is the real point of the story. The Pharisees and the scribes question Jesus' friendship with known sinners. Accusingly, they point out that Jesus actually shares meals with such delinquents, a sure sign

"Now the *older* son had been out in the *field*
and, on his way *back*, as he neared the *house*,
he heard the sound of *music* and *dancing*.
He called one of the *servants* and asked what this might *mean*.
The servant said to him,
'Your *brother* has *returned*
and your *father* has slaughtered the fattened *calf*
because he has him back *safe* and *sound*.'

The mood darkens as the older son becomes resentful.

"He became *angry*,
and when he *refused* to enter the *house*,
his *father* came out and *pleaded* with him.
He said to his father in reply,
'*Look*, all these *years* I *served* you
and not *once* did I disobey your *orders*;
yet you never gave me even a young *goat*
to feast on with my *friends*.
But when your *son* returns
who *swallowed up* your property with *prostitutes*,
for *him* you slaughter the fattened *calf*.'

Speak with loving reassurance.

"He said to him,
'My *son*, you are *here* with me *always*;
everything I *have* is *yours*.
But now we must *celebrate* and *rejoice*,
because your brother was *dead* and has come to *life* again;
he was *lost* and has been *found*.'"

that he shares in their sinfulness. It's as if they say, "You're known by the company you keep." Jesus not only challenges the assumptions made about him but turns the tables and demonstrates the dangers of their attitude in his parable. The older son is unable to forgive and rejoice. Although he has always done what is right, his heart is in the wrong place. The same could be said about the religious leaders who reject not only the well-known sinners in their midst but anyone who reaches out to such people.

For many of us who sincerely strive to lead upright lives, the story of the older son hits home. It simply isn't fair that someone who has wronged another should be welcomed with such lavish generosity, something never offered the upright son in the story. We too are tempted to feel "holier than thou" when we encounter others who do not strive as hard as we do to live the moral life. But Jesus' message is clear: It is those who are tempted to look down on the sinners in their midst who have the most to learn. God accepts all people.

We are never told if the older son finally accepts his father's explanation and joins in the celebration. Each one of us is left to identify with him and decide for ourselves. The party is the heavenly banquet, and our attendance requires only that we accept all who seek forgiveness.

Read this exciting story with new eyes, and strive to convey that freshness to your community. Pretend that you are reading it for the first time, giving full expression to the different characters in the story, so that your listeners might hear it anew, taking its message to heart.

4TH SUNDAY OF LENT, YEAR A

Lectionary #31

READING I   1 Samuel 16:1b, 6–7, 10–13a

A reading from the first book of Samuel

The LORD said to *Samuel:*
  "*Fill* your horn with *oil*, and be on your *way.*
I am sending you to *Jesse* of *Bethlehem*,
  for I have chosen my *king* from among his *sons.*"

As Jesse and his sons came to the *sacrifice,*
  Samuel looked at *Eliab* and thought,
  "*Surely* the LORD's *anointed* is here *before* him."
But the LORD said to Samuel:
  "Do *not* judge from his *appearance* or from his lofty *stature,*
  because I have *rejected* him.
Not as *man* sees does *God* see,
  because *man* sees the *appearance*
  but the LORD looks into the *heart.*"

In the *same* way Jesse presented *seven* sons before Samuel,
  but Samuel said to Jesse,
  "The LORD has not chosen *any one* of these."
Then Samuel asked Jesse,
  "Are these *all* the sons you have?"
Jesse replied,
  "There is still the *youngest*, who is tending the *sheep.*"
Samuel said to Jesse,
  "*Send* for him;
  we will not *begin* the sacrificial *banquet* until he *arrives* here."

Speak with confidence; Samuel is sure that this is God's chosen one.

Express Samuel's disappointment and confusion, then the exasperation in his next question.

Speak Jesse's words with an uncertain tone; he too must not have expected his youngest to be chosen over the others.

Samuel is firm.

READING I Saul, the first king of Israel, was chosen by the people against the advice of the prophet Samuel. But Samuel agreed to anoint him and supported him during his tenure as king, even while reprimanding him when he disobeyed God. But it was Saul's unwillingness to obey God in everything, and his inability to provide true leadership for the people, that led to his eventual downfall. In today's story, Samuel is sent to choose a successor for Saul, although the choice is kept secret and Saul remains in office until his death.

God sent Samuel to the insignificant town of Bethlehem to anoint the future king of Israel. Told that one of the sons of Jesse would be chosen by God to govern Israel, Samuel assumes that he should anoint the first and tallest son. When God rejects that one, Samuel examines six others, but none is God's choice for king. Only when the youngest is brought in from the fields is Samuel convinced that he has found the one to anoint.

This reading introduces the reader to the greatest king of Israel, David. God promises everlasting favor to David and his

descendants, and under David the kingdom prospers. But the blessings that await David are only hinted at here. In this passage, it is the importance of sight that dominates the discussion.

Just as the gospel reading will contrast the physical ability to see with genuine insight, so also this reading contrasts outward appearance with the qualities desired by God, qualities only God is able to see. For God does not see as humans do, but is able to look into the very heart of a person. The

Speak with fondness; David was much loved.

Jesse sent and had the young man *brought* to them.
He was *ruddy*, a youth *handsome* to behold
  and making a *splendid* appearance.

Speak slowly and emphasize this line.

The LORD said,
  "There—anoint him, for *this* is the *one!"*

David was anointed with God's spirit as well as with oil. Speak with excitement in your voice and emphasize David's name.

Then *Samuel*, with the horn of *oil* in *hand*,
  anointed *David* in the presence of his *brothers*;
  and from that day *on*, the *spirit* of the LORD
    rushed upon *David*.

READING II   Ephesians 5:8–14

A reading from the letter of Saint Paul to the Ephesians

Brothers and sisters:
You were once *darkness*,
  but *now* you are *light* in the *Lord*.
Live as *children* of light,
  for light produces every kind of *goodness*
  and *righteousness* and *truth*.

Speak encouragingly.

Try to learn what is *pleasing* to the Lord.
Take *no part* in the *fruitless* works of *darkness*;
  rather *expose* them, for it is *shameful* even to *mention*
  the things done by them in *secret*;
  but everything *exposed* by the light becomes *visible*,
  for everything that becomes *visible* is *light*.
Therefore, it says:

Offer this quote as an exciting promise.

  "Awake, O *sleeper*,
  and *arise* from the *dead*,
  and *Christ* will give you *light."*

---

qualities within David's heart were those that made him a great leader.

Read this captivating story from the point of view of Samuel. Express Samuel's certainty when he sees Eliab, his confusion when none of the seven is chosen, and his conviction when he sees David. Stress also the words of God.

READING II | Having discussed the fate of those who are disobedient, the author of Ephesians turns to discuss a positive way of life. Adopting the contrast of

light and darkness found in Jewish writings and other Middle Eastern materials, the author encourages Christians to live in the light, to walk uprightly.

A contrast is made as well between the present life of the Christians at Ephesus and their former lives as pagans. In the past, the recipients of the letter did not see the proper way to behave. Now, living in the light of Christ, they can act rightly. Formerly, they had embraced the darkness of the world around them, so that they could be said to be darkness; as Christians, the author says, they are bearers of the light. Their former

deeds are to be exposed—perhaps there is a reference to some type of public or private confession of sinfulness—so that they might be made light.

The final quotation from an unknown source is a vigorous call to live in the light of Christ. Mixing metaphors (as is done elsewhere in this passage), the author combines the idea that the former life was death as well as darkness. The quotation may come from a hymn or Christian prayer, or some other unknown document; it would have

GOSPEL   John 9:1–41

A reading from the holy gospel according to John

As Jesus *passed by* he saw a man *blind* from *birth.*
His disciples asked him,
  "*Rabbi,* who *sinned, this* man or his *parents,*
  that he was born *blind?"*

Jesus answered,
  "Neither *he nor* his parents sinned;
  it is so that the *works* of *God* might be made visible
    through him.
We have to do the *works* of the one who *sent* me while it is *day.*
Night is coming when *no* one can *work.*
While I am in the *world,* I am the *light* of the *world."*
When he had said this, he *spat* on the *ground*
  and made *clay* with the *saliva,*
  and *smeared* the clay on his *eyes,* and said to him,
  "Go *wash* in the Pool of *Siloam"* —which means *Sent.*
So he went and *washed,* and came back able to *see.*

His *neighbors* and those who had seen him *earlier*
    as a *beggar* said,
  "Isn't this the *one* who used to *sit* and *beg?"*
Some said, "It *is,"*
  but others said, "*No,* he just *looks* like him."
He said, "I *am."*
So they said to him, "How were your eyes *opened?"*
He replied,
  "The man called *Jesus* made *clay* and *anointed* my eyes
  and told me, 'Go to *Siloam* and *wash.'*
So I *went* there and *washed* and was able to *see."*

This was not a typical healing but an actual giving of light to one who had never seen it. Express the amazement of the man's neighbors. Their question implies not only that the man now had sight, but also that his former behavior of begging had been changed as well.

been especially appropriate for use in the celebration of baptism.

This reading applies to all of us as we strive to live lives that are pleasing to God. When we allow the brightness of Christ's love to shine in our hearts, we are able to see more clearly how to act justly and properly. Challenge your listeners to be fully alert in their Christian vocation, hiding nothing in darkness, but walking boldly in the light of day for all to see.

Offer this reading also for those who are preparing for initiation at Easter. We

sometimes refer to initiation as "illumination," and we pray that those seeking baptism will always find a well-lit path on which to travel. Proclaim this message as an encouragement, in the hope that those preparing for initiation will receive enlightenment. Charge them also to meet the challenge to practice deeds that can be exposed to the light rather than hidden away in shame.

GOSPEL | The giving of sight to the man born blind affirms one of the favorite truths of this gospel: Jesus is

the light and brings the ability to see with the eyes of faith to all who trust in him. It is this gift of insight that we desire for those who approach initiation at Easter. We pray that their eyes, and the eyes of all the faithful, will be opened more fully to appreciate the brightness of God's love and the glory of God revealed in Jesus.

Although the healing itself is told only briefly, great interest is shown in the question of Jesus' disciples. Traditional belief

And they said to him, "Where *is* he?"
He said, "I don't *know.*"

They brought the one who was once *blind* to the *Pharisees.*
Now Jesus had made *clay* and opened his *eyes* on a *sabbath.*
So then the Pharisees *also* asked him *how* he was able to *see.*
He said to them,
    "He put *clay* on my *eyes,* and I *washed,* and now I can *see.*"
So some of the Pharisees said,
    "This man is *not* from *God,*
    because he does not keep the *sabbath.*"
But *others* said,
    "How can a *sinful* man do such *signs?*"
And there was a *division* among them.

So they said to the blind man *again,*
    "What do *you* have to say about him,
    since he opened *your* eyes?"
He said, "He is a *prophet.*"

Now the Jews did not *believe*
    that he had been *blind* and gained his *sight*
    until they summoned the *parents* of the one
        who had gained his sight.
They asked them,
    "Is *this* your *son,* who you say was born *blind?*
How does he now *see?*"
His parents answered and said,
    "We *know* that this is our *son* and that he was born *blind.*
We do *not* know how he *sees* now,
    nor do we know *who* opened his *eyes.*
Ask *him,* he is of *age;*
    he can speak for *himself.*"

The blind man has an insight that is lost on the others: Jesus is a prophet because he performs signs.

Suspecting a fabrication, they try to investigate all possibilities.

held that a person was punished in this life for sins and rewarded with blessings for right behavior. In the absence of belief in an afterlife, affirmation of a just God required such belief. But, even before the development of hope in an afterlife, Jewish thought had been questioning the accuracy of this simple system of reward and punishment.

Jesus does not question the justice of the assertion that the man was being punished, whether for his own sin or that of his parents, nor does he appeal to the idea of an

afterlife. Instead, the occasion provides an opportunity for Jesus to demonstrate God's power. The affliction of the man allows the familiar Johannine themes of light and darkness to be played out literally for the blind man. Surprisingly, those with both eyesight and knowledge, the Pharisees, are the ones who are "blind" to the light.

Not only is the man given sight for the first time, but his behavior is so changed that his neighbors do not even recognize him. He affirms that he is indeed the one who used to sit and beg, and recounts what has happened to him. He tells his story a second

time, this time to the Pharisees. Although the Pharisees had no legal authority to declare a person cured, they were apparently consulted because of their religious knowledge.

The fact that the miracle occurred on the Sabbath immediately arouses suspicion in some of the Pharisees. After ascertaining what has happened, they accuse the man of being Jesus' disciple. Although some are open to the possibility that Jesus performs

The second questioning of the man is in a quasi-judicial hearing. The man speaks only of his own experience.

His parents said this because they were afraid
    of the *Jews,* for the Jews had already *agreed*
    that if anyone *acknowledged* him as the *Christ,*
    he would be *expelled* from the *synagogue.*
For this reason his parents said,
    "He is of *age;* question *him.*"

So a *second* time they called the man who had been *blind*
    and said to him, "Give *God* the *praise!*
We *know* that this man is a *sinner.*"
He replied,
    "If he is a *sinner,* I do not *know.*
One thing I *do* know is that I was *blind* and now I *see.*"
So they said to him,
    "What did he *do* to you?
    How did he *open* your *eyes?*"

The man becomes sarcastic when they again ask questions he has already answered.

He answered them,
    "I told you *already* and you did not *listen.*
Why do you want to hear it *again?*
Do *you* want to become his disciples, *too?*"

This is an accurate depiction of the Pharisees and a reason for them to be proud.

They *ridiculed* him and said,
    "*You* are that man's *disciple;*
    we are disciples of *Moses!*
We *know* that God spoke to *Moses,*
    but we do *not* know where *this* one is from."

The man answered and said to them,
    "*This* is what is so *amazing,*
    that you do not *know* where he is *from,*
        yet he opened my *eyes.*

The man speaks with great strength and conviction here. Express his words forcefully.

We *know* that God does not listen to *sinners,*
    but if one is *devout* and does his *will,* he *listens* to him.

signs as one sent from God (perhaps reflecting an openness to Jesus on the part of some Jewish leaders in the author's own day), the majority turn against the man. He unwaveringly states his belief that Jesus is a prophet, one endowed with a divine ability to perform miraculous signs.

    During the second questioning of the man, the atmosphere turns hostile. The Jewish leaders are harsh in their accusations, and the man responds with sarcasm

and contempt. He can tell only what he knows—that he was blind but can now see—and the Pharisees cling to their belief that they alone are best able to interpret the law of Moses. Finally the man speaks a truth that they refuse to believe: God, who does not listen to sinners, has acted decisively through Jesus. Far from being a sinner, Jesus must be a man of God. The one who was blind has real insight into Jesus' heavenly origin, while those who supposedly have the light of God's favor are in fact blind to God's servant.

    Rather than assist those less fortunate, the religious leaders would prefer to follow blindly the dictates of the law. Experts in the law, they refuse to help others understand what God asks of them, choosing instead to leave others in the dark. Although they think of themselves as enlightened leaders, they are seen in the end to be stumbling in darkness, and those they accuse of being filled with sin hold the lantern to guide them, if they would only open their eyes.

The man's strength of character is threatening, and they rely on the old line that he must have been sinful to have been born blind.

The man is open to faith, although he does not yet understand the significance of what has happened to him.

Speak reverently and sincerely.

This summarizes the entire passage: Those who do not see can be healed, but those who insist that they have not only working eyes but insight into God's will are in the end proven to be blind.

It is *unheard of* that anyone ever *opened* the eyes
  of a person born *blind.*
If this man were *not* from *God,*
  he would not be *able* to do *anything."*
They answered and said to him,
  "You were born *totally* in *sin,*
  and are *you* trying to teach *us?"*
Then they threw him *out.*

When Jesus *heard* that they had thrown him *out,*
  he *found* him and said, "Do you *believe* in the Son of *Man?"*
He answered and said,
  "Who *is* he, sir, that I may *believe* in him?"
Jesus said to him,
  "You have *seen* him,
  the one *speaking* with you is *he."*
He said,
  "I *do* believe, Lord," and he worshiped him.

Then Jesus said,
  "I came into this *world* for *judgment,*
  so that those who do *not* see might *see,*
  and those who *do* see might become *blind."*
Some of the *Pharisees* who were with him *heard* this
  and said to him, "Surely *we* are not also blind, *are* we?"
Jesus said to them,
  "If you were *blind,* you would have no *sin;*
  but *now* you are saying, 'We *see,'* so your sin *remains."*

[Shorter: John 9:1, 6–9, 13–17, 34–38]

This is an especially appropriate reading for us as we struggle through the dark days of Lent. We know that the light is available for us, if we but acknowledge it. With the catechumens, who are gradually being illuminated through their prayer and study, we pray that we will all grow in our ability to see Christ. Read this passage as a challenge to your community to proclaim Christ as the source of light for the world. Offer it also as encouragement to trust in the one who offers insight and enlightenment, even if those in power refuse to accept it. Finally, read this as a preparation for the baptismal promises of Easter, whether spoken for the first time by the newly initiated or renewed by the assembly.

5TH SUNDAY OF LENT

Lectionary #36

READING I   Isaiah 43:16–21

A reading from the book of the prophet Isaiah

> *The first section recalls God's actions during the exodus from Egypt.*

Thus says the LORD,
    who *opens* a way in the *sea*
    and a *path* in the mighty *waters,*
who leads out *chariots* and *horsemen,*
    a powerful *army,*
till they lie *prostrate* together, never to *rise,*
    snuffed *out* and quenched like a *wick.*

> *These are the words of God, introduced by the earlier "Thus says the Lord."*

> *This is the central proclamation of the passage. Speak as though you are letting your listeners in on a wonderful surprise.*

Remember *not* the events of the *past,*
    the things of long *ago* consider *not;*
see, I am doing something *new!*

Now it springs *forth,* do you not *perceive* it?
In the *desert* I make a *way;*
    in the *wasteland, rivers.*

Wild *beasts* honor me,
    jackals and *ostriches,*
for I put *water* in the *desert*
    and *rivers* in the *wasteland*
    for my chosen *people* to *drink,*
the people whom I *formed* for *myself,*
    that they might *announce* my *praise.*

> *Close with a strong assent to the idea of giving praise to God.*

READING I The section of the book of Isaiah starting with chapter 40 and including the passage used today is called Second Isaiah. Written centuries after the historical prophet Isaiah was active, it celebrates the end of the Babylonian exile. In the early part of the sixth century BCE the leaders of the kingdom of Judah were deported to Babylon; the city of Jerusalem lay in ruins. But by the year 540 BCE, it was clear that the Babylonian empire would be defeated and the anonymous prophet of this section believed that the exile would come to an end. It is a time of hope and joy, and of renewed commitment to God.

The exile in Babylon was a painful experience for Israel. The people longed to return to their homeland. Both the period of slavery in Egypt and the exodus had long influenced Israel's self-identity, but it must have become especially meaningful during the period of exile. Israel knew that it had been enslaved before but that God had brought the people out of bondage and into the Promised Land. Longing to return to that land, the prophets of this time saw the period of exile as a punishment for unfaithfulness.

But today the prophet has a new message and recalls God's actions on behalf of Israel. God made a way for the Israelites to pass through the waters of the Red Sea but brought destruction upon the Egyptian army. Yet that is no longer to be seen as the defining moment in God's dealings with Israel. God is inaugurating a new day and once again providing for this beloved people. The desert through which the exiles will return will no longer be parched but will be filled

A reading from the letter of Saint Paul to the Philippians

Begin strongly, then pause briefly after "loss," lowering your voice a bit for the words that follow.

Brothers and sisters:
I consider everything as a *loss*
    because of the supreme *good* of knowing Christ *Jesus* my *Lord.*
For his sake I have accepted the *loss* of all *things*
    and I consider them so much *rubbish,*
    that I may gain *Christ* and be found in *him,*
    not having any righteousness of my *own* based on the *law*
    but that which comes through *faith* in *Christ,*
    the *righteousness* from *God,*
    depending on *faith* to *know* him and the *power*
        of his *resurrection*
    and the *sharing* of his *sufferings* by being conformed
        to his *death,*
    if somehow I may attain the *resurrection* from the *dead.*

Throughout, speak slowly and clearly. Emphasize the idea that all righteousness comes from faith in Christ.

Build to this line.

It is not that I have already taken *hold* of it
    or have already *attained* perfect *maturity,*
    but I continue my *pursuit* in hope that I may *possess* it,
    since I have *indeed* been taken *possession* of by Christ *Jesus.*

Paul clarifies that resurrection is not a present reality but an object of hope.

Brothers and sisters, *I* for *my* part
    do *not* consider myself to have taken *possession.*
Just one thing: *forgetting* what lies behind
    but straining *forward* to what lies *ahead,*
    I *continue* my pursuit toward the *goal,*
    the *prize* of God's upward *calling,* in Christ *Jesus.*

Lift your voice again, expressing eagerness and the effort required to reach the goal.

with rivers. Wild animals will see the might of God and bow down in homage. All creation will honor God.

Praise for God will be the result of Israel's deliverance; Israel itself will sing praise. No longer will the people cry and mourn; they will instead shout out the glory of God.

Proclaiming this passage well requires a sensitivity to the actions of God in the past and an exuberant recounting of God's new creation. Begin with conviction, building as you proceed, until you announce with joy

the closing lines. Speak lovingly of God's choice of this people, and close strongly in a tone of praise.

READING II The community of Christians in Philippi was one of Paul's favorite churches. He writes its members with love and longing, but he is not afraid to rebuke them when necessary. In today's passage, he stirringly sums up the depth of his commitment to Christ.

Nothing else means anything compared with the opportunity to know Jesus Christ. Paul goes so far as to call everything else "rubbish," not because of its inherent lack of value but because in comparison with the righteousness made possible in Christ all else is worthless. Emphasizing a characteristic theme in his writings, Paul contrasts the Jewish law with faith in Christ and concludes that justification comes only by faith. God freely chooses to make people righteous; we are not saved by our own actions. Such a gift can only be accepted in faith.

GOSPEL   John 8:1–11

A reading from the holy gospel according to John

Jesus went to the Mount of *Olives*.
But early in the *morning* he arrived again in the *temple* area,
   and all the people started *coming* to him,
   and he sat down and *taught* them.

Then the *scribes* and the *Pharisees* brought a *woman*
   who had been caught in *adultery*
   and made her *stand* in the *middle*.
They said to him,
   "*Teacher*, this woman was caught
   in the very *act* of committing *adultery*.
Now in the *law*, Moses commanded us to *stone* such women.
So what do *you* say?"
They said this to *test* him,
   so that they could have some charge to bring *against* him.

Jesus bent *down* and began to write on the *ground* with his *finger*.
But when they continued *asking* him,
   he straightened *up* and said to them,
   "Let the one *among* you who is without *sin*
   be the *first* to throw a *stone* at her."
Again he bent down and wrote on the *ground*.

And in *response*, they went away *one* by *one*,
   beginning with the *elders*.
So he was left *alone* with the woman *before* him.

Here the drama really begins. Think about how the woman must have felt.

These are strong words. Speak in an angry, perhaps mocking, tone.

Jesus' words are solemn and bear a gentle forcefulness.

But faith is not simply assent to a principle or set of beliefs. Through it the Christian not only comes to know the power of Jesus' resurrection but also participates in Jesus' suffering. Faith in Christ means being willing to travel the same path Christ did. Paul hopes that the end of this journey will be the same for the Christian as it was for Christ: resurrection.

Against those who must have claimed that they were already living a heavenly life in company with the angels, Paul asserts that resurrected life remains a future reality. Resurrected life is Paul's great hope, but one he still awaits. He sees himself as a runner striving to complete a race, pressing ever forward with his goal—the resurrected life—in mind.

Proclaim this powerful passage with full attention to Paul's strong language. Begin in a somewhat subdued voice, reaching a crescendo with the phrase "the power of his resurrection." Lower your voice again before building to the end, then stress the wondrous prize that awaits the Christian, who

with Paul holds nothing dearer than knowing Christ Jesus.

GOSPEL   Today's gospel story of the woman caught in adultery was not originally part of John's gospel (the earliest manuscripts do not contain it). It was probably added during a period of controversy about forgiveness of serious sins committed after baptism.

Proceed especially slowly now. Jesus speaks with compassion, the woman with trust. Close firmly.

Then Jesus straightened *up* and *said* to her,
  "*Woman*, where *are* they?
Has no one *condemned* you?"
She replied, "*No* one, sir."
Then Jesus said, "Neither do *I* condemn you.
Go, and from now *on* do not sin any *more*."

The dramatic story about the woman's fate is a challenging story for people of any era. Its message is stark: No one has the right to condemn another, for we are all guilty of sin. Yet Jesus does not condone what the woman does. In fact, he knows that her actions were wrong and encourages her to leave behind her sinful ways.

The religious leaders were trying to trap Jesus, apparently by bringing before him a situation that had no easy legal resolution. The passion scene in the gospel of John makes it clear that the Roman occupiers forbid the Jews to put anyone to death. Since the Mosaic law advised stoning an adulterous woman, posing the question to Jesus placed him in a difficult position. He could neither deny the authority of the Jewish law, nor could he blatantly defy the Roman government.

Jesus' response to this challenge is inspiring. Instead of taking a stand on either side of the question, he seeks a change of heart, telling the woman not to sin again. But even more profound is the change demanded of the lynch mob that had brought the woman to him. Jesus' challenge to them—"Let the one among you who is without sin be the first to throw a stone at her"—forces them to look deep inside their own hearts.

Proclaim this moving tale with compassion and conviction. Allow the drama of the story to be heard in your voice, and give special weight to the words of Jesus.

5TH SUNDAY OF LENT, YEAR A

Lectionary #34

READING I Ezekiel 37:12–14

A reading from the book of the prophet Ezekiel

Thus says the Lord GOD:
O my *people*, I will *open* your *graves*
 and have you *rise* from them,
 and bring you *back* to the land of *Israel.*
Then you shall *know* that *I* am the LORD,
 when I *open* your *graves* and have you *rise* from them,
 O my *people!*

I will put my spirit *in* you that you may *live,*
 and I will *settle* you upon your *land;*
 thus you shall *know* that I am the LORD.
I have *promised*, and I will *do* it, says the LORD.

This is a message of comfort and love; speak with encouragement in your voice.

The exiles longed for their homeland.

This promise is especially inspiring; lift your voice and speak slowly and with conviction from here until the end.

READING II Romans 8:8–11

A reading from the letter of Saint Paul to the Romans

Brothers and sisters:
Those who are in the *flesh* cannot *please* God.
But *you* are *not* in the flesh;
 on the contrary, *you* are in the *spirit,*
 if only the Spirit of *God dwells* in you.

Pause slightly after the first line in order to provide a contrast with those (believers) who are not in the flesh.

READING I The prophet Ezekiel writes during the bleak years of Judah's exile in Babylon. Ezekiel's message is largely one of hope: God is with this people, wherever they are, and will one day restore them to their own land.

 Coming right after Ezekiel's vision of dry bones, today's passage speaks of the new life that God will give to the people. Both the vision and this selection picture a people coming to life again after having been dead, a people filled with God's spirit.

The message is one of hope: God will restore the nation and symbolically bring it back to life. The sad period of exile will end.

 Although it was several hundred years before the belief in an actual resurrection of the dead developed, this passage certainly sounds as though it promises such. In fact, the graves are symbolic of the nation's current state, and the promise is that the people will once again live in their own land. But it has also inspired many who hope for an afterlife, and this is the reason it is used in our liturgy today. The picture of graves opening and living people emerging fittingly

introduces the gospel story of the raising of Lazarus from the tomb.

 Offer this reading to your listeners on several levels. For those who are struggling, it is a message of hope that God will take care of them. Read it compassionately as a firm promise. For many of us, the passage can affirm our belief that this life is not final; we have hope in something greater. Finally, encourage the catechumens to reflect on the new life they are receiving in their Easter profession of faith. Allow God's promise of

Whoever does *not* have the Spirit of *Christ*
    does not *belong* to him.

But if Christ is *in* you,
    although the body is *dead* because of *sin*,
    the *spirit* is *alive* because of *righteousness.*

If the *Spirit* of the one who *raised* Jesus from the *dead*
      dwells in you,
    the one who raised *Christ* from the *dead*
    will give *life* to your mortal bodies *also*,
    through his *Spirit* dwelling *in* you.

Pause briefly after "dead."

Proclaim this with hope and confidence.

GOSPEL   John 11:1–45

A reading from the holy gospel according to John

Now a man was *ill*, *Lazarus* from *Bethany*,
    the village of *Mary* and her sister *Martha.*
Mary was the one who had *anointed* the Lord with perfumed *oil*
    and dried his *feet* with her *hair*;
    it was *her* brother *Lazarus* who was *ill.*

So the sisters sent *word* to Jesus saying,
    "*Master*, the one you *love* is *ill.*"
When Jesus *heard* this he said,
    "This *illness* is not to end in *death*,
    but is for the *glory* of *God*,
    that the *Son* of God may be glorified *through* it."

Mary is said to have anointed Jesus with costly oil, although the event has not yet been told in this gospel.

Emphasize the love Jesus had for Lazarus here and wherever it occurs.

What Jesus says of Lazarus here is much the same as his attitude toward his own death as presented in this gospel.

---

life in the Spirit to be addressed especially to them.

READING II   **Paul writes to the Christian community in Rome, whose members he had never met, in a theoretical rather than a personal tone. Here he contrasts the new life available in Christ with life in the "flesh."**

    When Paul speaks here of living in the flesh, he is talking about a mindset and a lifestyle. He contrasts living according to the dictates of the world with living as one who belongs to God. His addressees, he knows, are those who are committed to God, who are in the Spirit. The presence of the Spirit confirms whether one is Christian.

    But Paul recognizes also that resurrected life remains in the future. We live in an age that is still under the rule of sin and death, but the Christian is also infused with the Spirit of life. We live in two worlds in a sense, the world of death and the world of life in Christ. Obviously Paul's audience is not actually dead, but was still dwelling in a world under the sway of death. Yet the Romans could have hope, not only while in this life, but also after death, when they would be raised as Christ was. The hope is for an actual afterlife, although the life of the Spirit begins before death for the Christian.

    This passage offers the same hope in the indwelling of God's Spirit as the first reading, together with the same genuine belief in life after death evidenced in the gospel. Offer it to your community as an encouragement to recognize the life of the

Now Jesus *loved* Martha and her sister and *Lazarus*.
So when he heard that he was *ill*,
   he remained for *two* days in the place where he *was*.
Then after this he said to his disciples,
   "Let us go back to *Judea*."
The disciples said to him,
   "*Rabbi*, the Jews were just trying to *stone* you,
   and you want to go *back* there?"
Jesus answered,
   "Are there not *twelve* hours in a *day*?
If one walks during the *day*, he does not *stumble*,
   because he sees the *light* of this *world*.
But if one walks at *night*, he *stumbles*,
   because the *light* is not *in* him."

He said this, and then told them,
   "Our friend *Lazarus* is *asleep*,
   but I am going to *awaken* him."
So the disciples said to him,
   "*Master*, if he is *asleep*, he will be *saved*."
But Jesus was talking about his *death*,
   while they thought that he meant *ordinary* sleep.
So then Jesus said to them clearly,
   "*Lazarus* has *died*.
And I am *glad* for you that I was not *there*,
   that you may *believe*.
Let us *go* to him."
So *Thomas*, called Didymus, said to his fellow *disciples*,
   "Let us *also* go to *die* with him."

When Jesus *arrived*, he found that Lazarus
   had already been in the *tomb* for *four* days.
Now Bethany was *near Jerusalem*, only about *two* miles *away*.

This disciples must have been afraid for themselves and for Jesus; express their dismay effectively.

This author often plays on the contrast between light and darkness. This obscure statement is apparently Jesus' claim that he will not be swayed by the powers of darkness.

Although the euphemism "to fall asleep" is a common one, the disciples, as usual, misunderstand.

Pause briefly after "tomb."

Spirit within. It is an especially poignant promise to those who will be initiated into the community on Easter. But the new life offered is not contrasted only with the life prior to conversion or initiation, although it begins at initiation. We can all be more fully open to the Spirit of God in our hearts. Encourage your listeners to live more completely in Christ, with lives determined not by the values of the world around them, but by the Holy Spirit.

| GOSPEL | The story of the raising of Lazarus is inspiring and touching, and, most of all, it reveals Jesus' power over death. It is a precursor to Jesus' own death and resurrection, and inspires the characters within the story, as well as the reader of it, to accept the message that the opportunity for life is offered in Jesus. We also use this passage as an indication of the life that will be available to the newly initiated this Easter, as well as a promise of life after death.

The story, which appears only in the gospel of John, begins with an introduction of the sick man, Lazarus, later identified as especially beloved of Jesus, and his two sisters, Martha and Mary. Throughout, the author repeatedly insists on Jesus' profound love for Lazarus, Martha and Mary.

When Jesus learns of the illness of Lazarus, he responds with an enigmatic statement about giving glory to God. Oddly, he takes his time responding to the urgent message. The protests of the disciples when Jesus announces his decision to return to Judea make the reader aware of the perils

And many of the *Jews* had come to Martha and Mary
   to *comfort* them about their *brother.*
When *Martha* heard that Jesus was *coming,*
   she went to *meet* him;
   but *Mary* sat at *home.*
Martha said to Jesus,
   "*Lord,* if you had *been* here,
   my brother would not have *died.*
But even *now* I know that *whatever* you ask of *God,*
   God will *give* you."
Jesus said to her,
   "Your *brother* will *rise.*"

Martha said to him,
   "I *know* he will rise,
   in the *resurrection* on the last *day.*"
Jesus told her,
   "*I* am the resurrection and the *life;*
   whoever believes in *me,* even if he *dies,* will *live,*
   and everyone who *lives* and believes in me will n*ever* die.
Do you *believe* this?"
She said to him, "*Yes,* Lord.
I have come to *believe* that *you* are the *Christ,* the Son of *God,*
   the one who is *coming* into the *world.*"

When she had *said* this,
   she went and called her sister *Mary secretly,* saying,
   "The *teacher* is here and is *asking* for you."
As soon as she *heard* this,
   she rose *quickly* and *went* to him.
For Jesus had not yet come into the *village,*
   but was still where Martha had *met* him.

This is the central teaching of today's gospel. Read slowly and forcefully in order to give it due emphasis.

Speak Martha's declaration of faith with quiet but firm assurance.

inherent in the decision. The danger is underscored by Thomas' blustery remark, which indicates his willingness to die with Jesus.

As always in this gospel, Jesus speaks on a level deeper than that of his companions, and even his closest disciples misunderstand what he is saying. Jesus must finally spell out the situation, claiming that the entire event will be for their sake. Throughout this story, Jesus acts in order to instruct others, to inspire faith in the characters of the story and in the reader.

Both Martha and Mary seem to reproach Jesus for his delay, saying that Lazarus would not have died had he been present. But the statements may in fact be claims of faith; Martha's encounter with Jesus is especially telling. She immediately affirms that God will grant whatever Jesus asks, and the two discuss the resurrection of the dead, which leads to Martha's confession of faith in Jesus.

Whenever Jesus speaks, he offers fuller insight into his identity. Here he declares that he is the resurrection and the life. This is not simply a promise of a future resurrection of the dead, which Martha already accepts, but is a declaration of a present reality for the believer. Resurrected life begins now in faith, says the evangelist. Martha's response indicates a partial understanding; she recognizes that, in Jesus, the future hope has become present. Jesus is the Messiah for whom Israel has been waiting.

In a rare instance of human emotion in this gospel, Jesus is moved to tears when he sees the profound sadness of Mary. The reader, just like the Jewish visitors who were mourning with the family, is struck by the depth of Jesus' love for the dead man.

So when the *Jews* who were *with* her in the house *comforting* her
   saw Mary get up *quickly* and go *out*,
   they *followed* her,
   presuming that she was going to the *tomb* to weep *there*.

When Mary came to where *Jesus* was and *saw* him,
   she *fell* at his feet and *said* to him,
   "*Lord*, if you had *been* here,
   my *brother* would not have *died*."
When Jesus saw her *weeping* and the Jews who had come
       with her *weeping*,
   he became *perturbed* and deeply *troubled*, and said,
   "*Where* have you *laid* him?"
They said to him, "*Sir*, come and *see*."
And Jesus *wept*.
So the Jews said, "*See* how he *loved* him."
But some of them said,
   "Could not the one who *opened* the eyes of the *blind* man
   have done *something* so that *this* man would *not* have *died*?"

So *Jesus*, perturbed *again*, came to the *tomb*.
It was a *cave*, and a stone lay *across* it.
Jesus said, "Take away the *stone*."
Martha, the dead man's *sister*, said to him,
   "Lord, by *now* there will be a *stench*;
   he has been dead for *four days*."
Jesus said to her,
   "Did I not *tell* you that if you *believe*
   you will see the glory of *God*?"

So they took away the *stone*.
And Jesus raised his eyes and said,
   "*Father*, I *thank* you for *hearing* me.

Be sure to convey the great sorrow Jesus felt.

Pause after "wept." Jesus' love for Lazarus, and for Martha and Mary, ran deep. Let it sink in here for your listeners.

This is probably a wistful expression rather than criticism.

The mourners are not hostile to Jesus, which is evident in their expression of belief in his healing of the blind man.

The reality of Lazarus' death is affirmed once again through the words of Martha as Jesus approaches the tomb. As is typical in this gospel, Jesus' prayer is not for himself but for his listeners. He thanks God in advance for hearing him and responding in the raising of Lazarus.

When the dead man emerges from the tomb against all human expectations, those present respond with faith. The giving of life, an activity reserved for God, leads directly to the plot against Jesus in the verses that follow today's reading. The revelation of Jesus' person and mission, indeed the affirmation of his declaration to Martha that he is the resurrection and the life, is too threatening to the religious leaders in this gospel. The raising of Lazarus was accomplished for the glory of God. Jesus' death will also serve as the supreme moment of his revelation, when he is raised up in glory for all to see.

The superhuman knowledge of Jesus in this story—indeed, throughout this gospel— often makes it difficult to employ the best storytelling techniques to Jesus' words and deeds. But in this passage you are offered the words of others as well, and an indication that Jesus was deeply moved after his friend's death. Capitalize on these comments and proclaim the story with all its drama and emotion. Read Jesus' declarations regarding his person as statements intended to elicit faith, as they are intended.

Speak this command firmly and with authority.

I know that you *always* hear me;
   but because of the *crowd* here I have *said* this,
   that they may *believe* that you *sent* me."

And when he had *said* this,
   he cried out in a loud voice,
   "*Lazarus*, come *out!*"
The dead man came *out*,
   tied *hand* and *foot* with burial *bands*,
   and his *face* was wrapped in a *cloth*.
So Jesus said to them,
   "*Untie* him and let him *go*."

The story is meant to inspire us with more profound faith.

Now *many* of the Jews who had come to *Mary*
   and *seen* what he had done began to *believe* in him.

[Shorter: John 11:3–7, 17, 20–27, 33b–45]

PALM SUNDAY OF THE LORD'S PASSION

Lectionary #37

GOSPEL AT THE PROCESSION   Luke 19:28–40

A reading from the holy gospel according to Luke

Jesus proceeded on his *journey* up to *Jerusalem*.
As he drew near to *Bethphage* and *Bethany*
    at the place called the Mount of *Olives*,
    he sent *two* of his *disciples*.
He said, "*Go* into the village *opposite* you,
    and as you *enter* it you will find a *colt* tethered
    on which no one has ever *sat*.
Untie it and bring it *here*.
And if anyone should *ask* you,
    'Why are you *untying* it?'
    you will answer,
    'The Master has *need* of it.'"

So those who had been sent went *off*
    and found *everything* just as he had *told* them.
And as they were *untying* the *colt*, its owners *said* to them,
    "*Why* are you untying this *colt*?"
They answered,
    "The Master has *need* of it."
So they brought it to *Jesus*,
    threw their *cloaks* over the colt,
    and helped Jesus to *mount*.

Bethphage = BETH-fayj
Bethany = BETH-uh-nee

Jesus knows what will happen; he is in control.

Everything occurs just as Jesus had said.

PROCESSION GOSPEL Jesus' entrance into Jerusalem honors him as the awaited Messiah and indicates the favor accorded him by the crowds. In language recalling the nativity story in the gospel of Luke, Jesus' arrival is greeted by multitudes singing praise to God. Indeed, the entire cosmos joins in the praise: If his followers did not rejoice, the stones themselves would cry out.

The Mount of Olives was traditionally associated with the Messiah, the foremost "Anointed One" of God; the oil pressed from olives grown there was used to anoint Israel's rulers. Jesus' arrival in Jerusalem from the Mount of Olives is accompanied by shouts of blessings for one who "comes in the name of the Lord" (Psalm 118:26). He is both Messiah and king, fulfilling the words of Zechariah 9:9 ("Behold, your king comes to you; triumphant and victorious is he, humble and riding on a donkey, on a colt, the foal of a donkey"). The image fits well with the Lukan theme of reversal. The holy one of God, the one most deserving of honor and glory, arrives on a humble colt.

The story of procuring the colt, which occupies so much of today's selection, demonstrates Jesus' foreknowledge and provides a prophetic link. But it is the procession that is most dramatic. Your assembly will also join in a joyous procession shortly after hearing this gospel. In our retelling, as in the gospel of Luke, this event almost immediately precedes the passion account. It is ironic that Jesus is greeted now—by the crowds and by us—with joy and song, only to be abandoned during his hour of need.

Read the story of the colt as a straight-forward narrative of events. Hold nothing back, however, when you recount the procession itself. Lift your voice as you tell of

Let your voice gradually build as you describe the processional scene.

As he rode *along*,
> the people were spreading their *cloaks* on the *road*;
> and now as he was approaching the *slope* of the Mount
> > of *Olives*,
> the whole *multitude* of his disciples
> began to *praise* God aloud with *joy*
> for all the mighty *deeds* they had *seen*.
They proclaimed:

Sing out in joy.

> "*Blessed* is the *king* who comes in the *name* of the *Lord*.
> *Peace* in *heaven* and *glory* in the *highest*."

Some of the *Pharisees* in the crowd said to him,
> "*Teacher*, *rebuke* your disciples."
He said in reply,
> "I *tell* you, if *they* keep silent,
> the *stones* will cry out!"

Lectionary #38

A reading from the book of the prophet Isaiah

The Lord GOD has given me
> a *well*-trained *tongue*,
that I might know how to *speak* to the *weary*
> a word that will *rouse* them.
Morning after *morning*
> he *opens* my *ear* that I may *hear*;
and I have *not rebelled*,
> have not turned *back*.

Practice "well-trained tongue" until you can say it without swallowing any letters.

Read this with certainty and an eagerness to speak God's word.

I gave my *back* to those who *beat* me,
> my *cheeks* to those who plucked my *beard*;

Pause, then proceed in a tone of drama, emphasizing the torments experienced by the servant.

the reaction of the crowds to Jesus, and close with a triumphant tone.

READING I │ The servant songs from the book of Isaiah have long been understood to refer to Jesus' humility and willingness to endure pain and humiliation. This passage is especially poignant, followed in our liturgy by the reading of the passion narrative.

The servant sees himself as one who learns and then shares his knowledge with others. His task is to teach despite opposition.

He knows that the people are exhausted, that they continue to be in pain, but his own pain cannot silence him. He listens attentively to God, then instructs those who fear God.

The gospel accounts of Jesus' passion echo the description of the servant's sufferings. Jesus, like the servant, is struck, abused and insulted. Yet he does not give up, but knows that he will ultimately be vindicated.

Your task is similar to that of the servant: You are entrusted with God's word and asked to present it to your assembly, teaching and encouraging, continuing at all costs. Offer this reading to the members of your

assembly with an eye to the sufferings of Jesus. Speak of the suffering in a dark tone of pain, and close with an air of conviction and courage.

READING II │ Paul offers encouragement to the Philippians to be humble and obedient, just as Christ was. As a demonstration of Christ's humility, Paul quotes this hymn, celebrating the willingness of Christ to give up his rightful exalted state and be humiliated.

The hymn in Philippians is one of the earliest Christian passages that refers to the

Pause, then continue with a peaceful, trusting tone.

my *face* I did not *shield*
   from *buffets* and *spitting*.

The Lord GOD is my *help*,
   therefore I am not *disgraced*;
I have set my *face* like *flint*,
   knowing that I shall *not* be put to *shame*.

READING II   Philippians 2:6–11

A reading from the letter of Saint Paul to the Philippians

Christ *Jesus*, though he was in the *form* of *God*,
   did not regard *equality* with God
   something to be *grasped*.

Stress the contrast of these lines with what has gone before.

Rather, he *emptied* himself,
   taking the form of a *slave*,
   coming in human *likeness*;
   and found *human* in *appearance*,
he *humbled* himself,
   becoming *obedient* to the point of *death*,

Pause after this line, then change your tone to a lighter one.

   even *death* on a *cross*.

Because of this, God greatly *exalted* him
   and *bestowed* on him the *name*
   which is above *every* name,

Slow down and emphasize every phrase, allowing your voice to grow in intensity and wonder until you practically shout "Jesus Christ is Lord!" The final line is a bit more subdued but still emphasized; be careful not to rush.

   that at the name of *Jesus*
   every *knee* should *bend*,
   of those in *heaven* and on *earth* and *under* the earth,
   and every tongue *confess* that
Jesus Christ is *Lord*,
   to the *glory* of God the *Father*.

---

preexistence of Christ. Rather than laying claim to the exaltation of heaven, he humbled himself by becoming human and by being willing to die on the cross, only then to be glorified with God.

What is most exciting in this hymn is the name accorded Jesus. At the mention of his name, all honor will be given him, and everyone will proclaim that "Jesus Christ is Lord." The Greek word for "Lord" is the word that is used to translate the divine name from the Hebrew scriptures. Jesus can be addressed with the same title given to the creator of the world, the God who saved the

Israelites from their oppressors in Egypt, who was revealed at Sinai, who spoke through the prophets and restored the people after the exile in Babylon. The same God who acted on behalf of the Jewish people has now acted decisively for all the world.

Begin your reading, as does Paul, with an exhortation to proper behavior. Then recount solemnly the "emptying" of Jesus, giving special weight to the reference to his death. Speak triumphantly of his exaltation, allowing your voice to reach a crescendo with the proclamation that Jesus is Lord.

PASSION The passion account in Luke displays some characteristic themes of the gospel. Prominent are the themes of reversal and of the exaltation of the lowly. All expectations are turned upside down. The wealthy and powerful of the world are brought low while the poor and disenfranchised are honored. The theme of discipleship is emphasized as well: The Last Supper becomes an occasion for Jesus to teach about what it means to be his follower. Finally, at the climax of his life, Jesus displays the compassion characteristic of him in this gospel right to the end, comforting

PASSION   Luke 22:14—23:56

The Passion of our Lord Jesus Christ according to Luke

The reading of the passion begins without the customary introduction and responses.

(1) When the *hour* came,
    Jesus took his place at *table* with the *apostles*.
He said to them,
    "I have eagerly *desired* to eat this *Passover* with you
        before I *suffer*,
    for, I *tell* you, I shall not eat it *again*
    until there is *fulfillment* in the kingdom of *God*."

Speak Jesus' words with solemnity.

Then he took a *cup*, gave *thanks*, and said,
    "*Take* this and *share* it among *yourselves*;
    for I tell you that from this time *on*
    I shall not *drink* of the fruit of the *vine*
    until the kingdom of God *comes*."

Then he took the *bread*, said the *blessing*,
    broke it, and *gave* it to them, saying,
    "*This* is my *body*, which will be given for *you*;
    do this in *memory* of me."
And likewise the *cup* after they had *eaten*, saying,
    "This *cup* is the new *covenant* in my *blood*,
    which will be *shed* for you.

There is an ominous tone to these words. Speak accordingly.

(2) "And yet *behold*, the *hand* of the one who is to *betray* me
        is *with* me on the *table*;
    for the Son of Man indeed *goes* as it has been *determined*;
    but *woe* to that man by whom he is *betrayed*."
And they began to *debate* among themselves
    who among them would *do* such a deed.

(3) Then an *argument* broke out among them
    about *which* of them should be regarded as the *greatest*.

the mourning women and even granting forgiveness from the cross.

We are so accustomed to seeing depictions of the passion and speaking of the cross of Christ that we sometimes forget how offensive to Judaism the idea of a suffering and dying Messiah was. The cross was an instrument of torture, a symbol of degradation and humiliation. Even more, however, it was a sign of being cursed by God. For the Jew awaiting a Messiah who would overthrow the occupying forces, or a Messiah who would demonstrate God's victory and righteousness, or a Messiah who

would bring about peace and justice, the cross represented failure. Rather than acting decisively, God seemed to be silent. Rather than celebrating victory, the Messiah suffered helplessly. For the people of Jesus' time, the idea of a suffering Messiah was a contradiction in terms.

Although today's selection ends without an account of the resurrection, the passion narrative still proclaims the victory of Jesus. During the meal, he declares that his followers will share in his heavenly dominion. At his trial before the religious leaders he anticipates being seated at the right hand

of God. After Jesus' death, the centurion proclaims his innocence. We know, as does the author, that the ugly events recounted here are not the last word. There is more yet to come.

The method of reading the passion varies from parish to parish. Your parish may choose to have one well-prepared reader proclaim the entire passion, or a group of readers may proclaim the reading in parts. A group may choose to divide the reading by sections, or each individual might take a role. Sometimes the congregation is involved, although this unfortunately requires the

He said to them,
  "The *kings* of the *Gentiles* lord it *over* them
  and those in *authority* over them are addressed as
    'Benefactors';
  but among *you* it shall not be *so*.
Rather, let the *greatest* among you be as the *youngest*,
  and the *leader* as the *servant*.
For *who* is *greater*:
  the one *seated* at table or the one who *serves*?
Is it not the one *seated* at table?
I am among you as the one who *serves*.
"It is *you* who have stood by me in my *trials*;
  and I confer a *kingdom* on you,
    just as my *Father* has conferred one on *me*,
  that you may *eat* and *drink* at my *table* in my *kingdom*;
  and you will sit on *thrones*
  judging the twelve *tribes* of *Israel*.

Pause slightly, then speak solemnly.

There is an abrupt change in subject after this verse. Pause, then speak in a tone of warning.

(4) "*Simon, Simon*, behold *Satan* has demanded
  to *sift* all of you like *wheat*,
  but I have *prayed* that your *own* faith may not *fail*;
  and once you have turned *back*,
  you must *strengthen* your *brothers*."
He said to him,
  "*Lord*, I am prepared to go to *prison* and to *die* with you."
But he replied,
  "I *tell* you, Peter, before the cock *crows* this *day*,
  you will *deny* three *times* that you *know* me."

The mood lightens a bit.

(5) He said to them,
  "When I sent you *forth* without a *money* bag or a *sack*
    or *sandals*,
  were you in *need* of anything?"

entire assembly to read along throughout the passage rather than listen attentively. Perhaps a congregational antiphon will follow each section, indicating shifts in the narrative. However your community proclaims the passion, proper preparation is essential.

If several participants share the responsibility of reading, they should be chosen for their ability to make the reading come alive for their listeners. This involves reading the entire passion alone or in a group, discussing it and praying about it, allowing the tension and drama to sink into your very bones. Remember that in sharing this important reading with the rest of the assembly, you are helping your entire community to participate in the events described, making them present today.

All of the readers should have strong voices and clear diction. Although Jesus' words are few and his tone sometimes subdued, his speech is central; whoever reads them should have an especially strong voice. Determine in advance who will read what sections and practice together. Make sure each reader is comfortable with the difficult words and understands the significance of the action. Finally, practice in the place of worship. Know when you will move and where you will stand; be comfortable with the text and with the microphone. If there is to be music, practice with the musicians, so that you will all be familiar with the flow of proclamation and song. At least one person who is not reading or involved with music should be present to listen from various parts of the church to offer feedback regarding clarity and volume. When the details are settled in advance, all involved will be able to concentrate on the important ministry of proclaiming these central events of our salvation history.

"No, nothing," they replied.
He said to them,
    "But *now* one who has a *money* bag should *take* it,
    and likewise a *sack*,
    and one who does not have a *sword*
    should sell his *cloak* and *buy* one.
For I *tell* you that this *Scripture* must be *fulfilled* in me,
    namely, 'He was *counted* among the *wicked*';
    and *indeed* what is *written* about me is coming to *fulfillment*."

Then they said,
    "Lord, *look*, there are two *swords* here."
But he replied, "It is *enough!*"

Jesus speaks with exasperation. Pause before beginning a new scene.

(6) Then going out, he *went*, as was his *custom*, to the Mount
        of *Olives*,
    and the disciples *followed* him.
When he *arrived* at the place he said to them,
    "Pray that you may not undergo the *test."*

Jesus prays sincerely but not in anguish.

After *withdrawing* about a stone's *throw* from them and *kneeling*,
    he *prayed*, saying, *"Father*, if you are *willing*,
    take this cup *away* from me;
    still, not *my* will but *yours* be done."

And to *strengthen* him an angel from *heaven* appeared to him.
He was in such *agony* and he prayed so *fervently*
    that his *sweat* became like drops of *blood*
    falling on the *ground*.
When he *rose* from prayer and *returned* to his disciples,
    he found them *sleeping* from *grief*.
He said to them, *"Why* are you *sleeping*?
Get up and *pray* that you may not undergo the *test."*

(1) Jesus' passion, death and resurrection occurred at the time of the Jewish celebration of Passover, the commemoration of the Israelites' flight from Egypt. Passover is a celebration of new life, a proclamation of hope. It recalls God's action in preserving the lives of the Israelite children on the night of the last plague against Egypt, the death of the firstborn, and of bringing the people out of slavery and leading them to the land of promise. We recall the events of Jesus' passion, death and resurrection as offering rebirth, liberating us from lives held captive by sin.

The "hour" refers to the time when the Passover meal was celebrated. But it also designates the time when decisive events take place in Jesus' life. By sharing this meal with his disciples, Jesus transforms it into a reflection on the significance of his impending death, and commands his followers to continue sharing the meal, remembering him as they do so. He establishes a new covenant, similar to the covenants between God and the Hebrew people, especially the covenant established in the first Passover, when God led the people out of Egypt.

During this "hour" and until his death, the forces of evil are active. Satan has already entered Judas Iscariot. Later, vicious hatred will be so strong that it will, paradoxically, unite former enemies and alienate Jesus' friends. But evil and hatred do not prevail. Jesus will be vindicated in the end. Even during his time of helplessness, he acts as one in control, offering love and forgiveness to those in need of it.

The Passover meal has a forward-looking meaning. Jesus will not again share it with his friends on earth. But his words over the bread look forward to his passion

Allow tension to enter your voice.

(7) While he was still *speaking*, a *crowd* approached
　　and in *front* was one of the *Twelve*, a man named *Judas*.
He went up to Jesus to *kiss* him.
Jesus said to him,
　　"*Judas*, are you betraying the Son of *Man* with a *kiss*?"

His disciples *realized* what was about to *happen*, and they asked,
　　"*Lord*, shall we strike with a *sword*?"
And *one* of them struck the high priest's *servant*
　　and cut off his right *ear*.
But Jesus said in reply,
　　"*Stop*, no *more* of this!"
Then he *touched* the servant's ear and *healed* him.

Jesus is frustrated and angry. Pause slightly and change your tone as you proceed.

And Jesus said to the chief *priests* and temple *guards*
　　and *elders* who had *come* for him,
　　"Have you come out as against a *robber*, with *swords*
　　　　and *clubs*?
Day after *day* I was *with* you in the *temple* area,
　　and you did not *seize* me;
　　but *this* is your *hour*, the time for the power of *darkness*."

(8) After *arresting* him they led him *away*
　　and took him into the house of the high *priest*;
　　Peter was following at a *distance*.

They lit a *fire* in the middle of the *courtyard* and sat *around* it,
　　and *Peter* sat down *with* them.
When a *maid* saw him seated in the *light*,
　　she looked *intently* at him and said,
　　"*This* man *too* was with him."

Speak the accusations with increasing force, and express Peter's denials with vigor.

But he denied it saying,
　　"Woman, I do not *know* him."

and death, equating the bread with his body on the cross. In verses that are perhaps from another ancient tradition but have been added here, Jesus takes up a second cup and establishes the new covenant, again looking forward to his passion with reference to his blood. Yet he asks his disciples to continue the celebration of this special meal, looking back and remembering him.

(2) In Luke's gospel (unlike those of Matthew and Mark), Judas partakes of the bread and wine with the other disciples before he is revealed as Jesus' betrayer. This emphasizes the blame that he must bear as

one who was not only a disciple of Jesus but one who has shared in the covenant meal. Even this gospel of forgiveness proclaims "woe to that man" who turns against the Lord.

(3) The other disciples begin to wonder who among them could perform such a horrendous deed. But even in their shock at the possibility of betrayal, they cannot refrain from competing for greatness. Jesus reverses the usual expectations regarding greatness. The greatest ones are not those who exercise authority or enjoy leisure but those who serve others. Jesus provides the supreme

example of one who serves, and those who stand by him will, in yet another reversal, be granted authority in heaven, even judging the twelve tribes of Israel.

(4) Peter does not draw special attention to himself in this gospel but is singled out by Jesus. Satan is back in force, having been temporarily restrained after Jesus' temptation in the desert. During the events of the passion, Satan seems to prevail but in the end is vanquished. Peter rashly proclaims his willingness to die with Jesus, but the reader knows that Jesus' prediction of denial will prove to be true.

A short while *later* someone *else* saw him and said,
   "You *too* are one of them";
   but Peter answered, "My *friend*, I am *not*."

About an hour *later*, still *another* insisted,
   "*Assuredly*, *this* man *too* was with him,
   for he also is a *Galilean*."
But Peter said,
   "My *friend*, I do not *know* what you are *talking* about."
Just as he was *saying* this, the *cock* crowed,
   and the Lord turned and *looked* at Peter;
   and Peter *remembered* the word of the *Lord*,
   how he had said to him,
   "*Before* the cock *crows* today, you will *deny* me three *times*."
He went *out* and began to weep *bitterly*.

(9) The men who held Jesus in *custody* were *ridiculing* and
      beating him.
They *blindfolded* him and *questioned* him, saying,
   "*Prophesy!* Who is it that *struck* you?"
And they *reviled* him in saying many *other* things against him.

(10) When *day* came the council of *elders* of the people *met*,
      both chief *priests* and *scribes*,
      and they *brought* him before their *Sanhedrin*.
They said, "If you are the *Christ*, *tell* us,"
   but he replied to them, "If I *tell* you, you will not *believe*,
   and if I *question*, you will not *respond*.
But from this time *on* the Son of Man will be *seated*
   at the right *hand* of the power of *God*."
They all asked, "Are *you* then the Son of *God*?"
He replied to them, "*You* say that I am."
Then they said, "What further *need* have we for *testimony*?
We have *heard* it from his own *mouth*."

Slow your reading and let your voice be filled with sadness.

Pause in sorrow.

prophesy = PROF-uh-sī

Sanhedrin = san-HEE-druhn

Jesus speaks with authority.

---

(5) In chapter 10 of Luke's gospel, Jesus sends his followers out on the road with no provisions. They return overjoyed, declaring that even the demons submitted to them in Jesus' name. In these verses in the passion narrative, found only in Luke, they acknowledge that they had lacked nothing on that journey. Now, in this dark hour, the opposition is fierce. Jesus says that his followers must equip themselves for battle, even with swords. They will need all the strength they can get.

Jesus is speaking metaphorically of bags and swords, as is evident in his decisive response to their procurement of weapons: "Enough!" Violence is not what Jesus advocates but preparedness. Jesus' disciples must be ready for the opposition they will face. But, as they so often do, Jesus' disciples misunderstand him, unable to comprehend the nature of the battle they will face.

(6) The scene shifts as Jesus, followed by his disciples, goes to the Mount of Olives. In this gospel, prayer has marked every step of Jesus' ministry, and now, at the decisive moment, Jesus again turns to God in prayer.

The reference to the angel strengthening Jesus and his sweat like drops of blood are not found in the earliest manuscripts of this gospel and were probably added later. As it is, they emphasize Jesus' anguish in the face of death. But when they are removed, Jesus does not appear to be in great distress. He turns to God in trust, praying only once, not multiple times as in other gospels. He does not throw himself on the ground but kneels. Prayer gives Jesus all the strength he needs.

The disciples are portrayed in a more positive light in this gospel than in the others. Jesus rebukes them only once for sleeping, and their slumber is caused not by fatigue

Pilate is curious. He appears as a somewhat sympathetic figure in this gospel.

Galilean = gal-ih-LEE-uhn
Jesus' ministry had been centered in Galilee, where Herod was in charge.

Allow your tone to darken.

Speak with wonder at such an ill-favored friendship.

(11) Then the whole assembly of them *arose* and brought him
    before *Pilate*.
They brought *charges* against him, saying,
    "We found this man *misleading* our *people*;
    he *opposes* the payment of *taxes* to *Caesar*
    and maintains that *he* is the *Christ*, a *king*."

Pilate asked him, "Are *you* the king of the *Jews*?"
He said to him in reply, "*You* say so."
Pilate then addressed the chief *priests* and the *crowds*,
    "I find this man *not guilty*."
But they were *adamant* and said,
    "He is *inciting* the people with his teaching
        throughout all *Judea*,
    from *Galilee* where he began even to *here*."
(12) On hearing *this* Pilate asked if the man was a *Galilean*;
    and upon learning that he was under *Herod's* jurisdiction,
    he sent him to *Herod*, who was in *Jerusalem* at that time.

Herod was very *glad* to see Jesus;
    he had been *wanting* to see him for a long *time*,
    for he had *heard* about him
    and had been hoping to see him perform some *sign*.
He questioned him at *length*,
    but he gave him no *answer*.

The chief *priests* and *scribes*, meanwhile,
    stood by accusing him *harshly*.
Herod and his *soldiers* treated him *contemptuously*
        and *mocked* him,
    and after *clothing* him in resplendent *garb*,
    he sent him back to *Pilate*.
Herod and *Pilate* became *friends* that very *day*,
    even though they had been *enemies* formerly.

but by grief. Peter, James and John are not separated out from the others, but all the disciples are told to pray. The author claims that all followers of Jesus need to gain strength, as he did, from prayer.

(7) Events move quickly now. The sleeping disciples awaken to see a crowd. Judas indicates who Jesus is with an embrace; his act of treason is made even more bitter by his audacious use of a gesture of friendship. But Jesus retains his dignity and challenges Judas' deceit. The violent confrontation turns bloody when someone cuts off the ear of the high priest's servant. Jesus harshly rejects his followers' violence and even sets matters right by healing the severed ear, a miracle recounted only in this gospel.

Jesus addresses with anger the religious leaders who pursue him. He was not an armed robber, and he had never hidden from the authorities, yet they treat him as a common criminal. They have aligned themselves with the powers of darkness. Now is Satan's hour of triumph.

(8) We are not told what happens to the other disciples when Jesus is taken to the high priest's house. Only Peter follows. As Jesus had foretold, Peter turns his back on his friend and three times denies him, lying to save his own hide. But Peter does not curse and swear, as in other gospels. Instead, the scene becomes painfully poignant when Jesus makes eye contact with him, thus reminding Peter of his prediction and filling Peter with remorse.

(9) Immediately after his prediction regarding Peter is fulfilled, Jesus' accusers revile him and call on him to prophesy. The guards mock him, but Jesus meets the abuse with silence. The one who had rejected the sword, who preached forgiveness and reconciliation, suffers abuses but returns no insult.

(13) Pilate then summoned the chief *priests*, the *rulers* and
  the *people*
  and said to them, "You *brought* this man to me
  and accused him of *inciting* the *people* to *revolt*.
I have conducted my *investigation* in your *presence*
  and have *not* found this man *guilty*
  of the charges you have brought *against* him,
  nor did *Herod*, for he sent him *back* to us.
So no capital *crime* has been *committed* by him.
Therefore I shall have him *flogged* and then *release* him."

The assembly becomes ugly.

But all together they shouted out,
  "*Away* with this man!
  Release *Barabbas* to us."
—Now *Barabbas* had been imprisoned for a *rebellion*
  that had taken place in the *city* and for *murder*.—
Again Pilate addressed them, still wishing to *release* Jesus,
  but they *continued* their shouting,
  "*Crucify* him! *Crucify* him!"
Pilate addressed them a *third* time,
  "What *evil* has this man done?
  I found him *guilty* of no capital *crime*.
Therefore I shall have him *flogged* and then *release* him."

Barabbas = buh-RAB-uhs
The name, ironically, means "son of the father."

The tension mounts. Raise your voice in bloodthirsty rage.

With loud *shouts*, however,
  they *persisted* in calling for his *crucifixion*,
  and their voices *prevailed*.
The *verdict* of Pilate was that their demand should be *granted*.
So he *released* the man who had been imprisoned
  for *rebellion* and *murder*, for whom they *asked*,
  and he handed *Jesus* over to them to deal with as they *wished*.

Speak with sad resignation, then pause as the scene shifts.

(10) The account of the trial of Jesus before the supreme Jewish council, the Sanhedrin, is brief. There are no witnesses and no question about destroying the temple. Instead, the focus is on Jesus' identity: Is he indeed the awaited Messiah? But Jesus' response to their question is not limited to whether he is the Messiah. Jesus seems to affirm his identity as the Messiah, but he raises the stakes by declaring his heavenly status. Jesus combines Psalm 110:2 ("Sit at my right hand") with the exalted figure in Daniel 7 to acknowledge that he will act as heavenly judge, receiving dominion and glory.

Jesus' response to the next question posed by the council solidifies the forces of opposition arrayed against him. Although Jesus does not affirm that he is the Son of God, the way the question is asked seems to presume a positive response. The Jewish leaders themselves become responsible for the claim and the resulting decision to condemn him. It is ironic that, while completely powerless, Jesus responds with claims of total power; clearly his authority is not the kind we are accustomed to. The author presents Jesus as one wrongly charged and convicted, maltreated and subsequently executed as a criminal by the Romans. He is alone, stripped of dignity, yet he claims ultimate power.

(11) When Jesus is brought before the local Roman authority, Pilate, he resumes his silence, responding only with an ambiguous answer to Pilate's query. The Jewish leaders have altered the charge from one regarding Jesus' identity to political subversion: He opposes the payment of taxes and has made himself king. Indeed, the manner of

Cyrenian = sī-REE-nee-uhn

Jesus addresses the women tenderly,
even as he warns of impending danger.

(14) As they led him *away*
    they took hold of a certain *Simon*, a *Cyrenian*,
    who was coming in from the *country*;
    and after laying the *cross* on him,
    they made him *carry* it behind *Jesus*.

A large crowd of *people followed* Jesus,
    including many *women* who *mourned* and *lamented* him.
Jesus *turned* to them and said,
    "Daughters of *Jerusalem*, do not *weep* for *me*;
    weep instead for *yourselves* and for your *children*
    for indeed, the days are *coming* when people will say,
    'Blessed are the *barren*,
    the *wombs* that never *bore*
    and the *breasts* that never *nursed*.'

"At that time people will say to the *mountains*,
    '*Fall* upon us!'
    and to the *hills*, '*Cover* us!'
    for if these things are done when the wood is *green*,
    what will happen when it is *dry*?"

Now two *others*, both *criminals*,
    were led away *with* him to be *executed*.
(15) When they came to the place called the *Skull*,
    they *crucified* him and the *criminals* there,
    one on his *right*, the other on his *left*.

Then Jesus said,
    "*Father, forgive* them, they know *not* what they *do*."
They divided his *garments* by casting *lots*.

Jesus' execution—by crucifixion, a Roman form of capital punishment—indicates that he was convicted of being an enemy of the state. The gospel portrays Pilate as reluctant to crucify Jesus, although his cruelty and hatred for the Jewish people are well documented. Jesus gives Pilate the same response he gave the Jewish assembly, but Pilate understands it to indicate his innocence while the Jewish leaders concluded from it that he was guilty.

(12) Jesus' appearance before Herod Antipas (not the Herod of the infancy narrative) is told only in this gospel. The story takes some of the responsibility for Jesus' conviction away from Pilate. Jesus refuses to answer Herod's questions, whereupon Herod mocks him, attempting to ridicule Jesus' claim of royalty and heavenly status. But this gospel turns upside down the usual claims to power and authority. The one who is abused is truly the king of Israel.

(13) The practice of releasing a prisoner during the feast is unknown outside the gospels, as is the insurrection, although the Jews were often rebellious under Roman rule. Perhaps the crowd was disappointed that Jesus did not take up arms against the Romans and preferred one whose defiance of Rome had been demonstrated. But it is hard to imagine why the Roman governor would agree with them and release a dangerous rebel.

(14) In this gospel, Jesus makes his way to the place of crucifixion alone. Although Simon of Cyrene is mentioned in other gospels, here he becomes a true disciple of Jesus, following behind him as he bears some of the burden of the cross. A large crowd of women also follows, grieving and lamenting. Women are often noticeable figures in this gospel and here courageously

The tone is one of mocking and derision.

The people stood *by* and *watched*;
  the *rulers*, meanwhile, *sneered* at him and said,
  "He saved *others*, let him save *himself*
  if he is the *chosen* one, the *Christ* of *God*."

Even the *soldiers* jeered at him.
As they approached to offer him *wine* they called out,
  "If you are King of the *Jews*, save *yourself*."
Above him there was an *inscription* that read,
  "*This* is the King of the *Jews*."

Contrast with your voice the jeering of the first criminal with the sincere contrition of the second.

(16) Now one of the criminals *hanging* there *reviled* Jesus, saying,
  "Are you *not* the *Christ*?
  Save yourself and *us*."
The *other*, however, *rebuking* him, said in reply,
  "Have you no fear of *God*,
  for you are *subject* to the same *condemnation*?
And indeed, *we* have been condemned *justly*,
  for the sentence we received *corresponds* to our *crimes*,
  but *this* man has done nothing *criminal*."
Then he said,
  "*Jesus*, *remember* me when you come into your *kingdom*."
He replied to him,
  "Amen, I *say* to you,
  today you will be with me in *Paradise*."

(17) It was now about *noon* and darkness came
    over the whole *land*
  until *three* in the *afternoon*
  because of an *eclipse* of the *sun*.
Then the *veil* of the *temple* was torn down the *middle*.
Jesus cried *out* in a loud *voice*,
  "*Father*, into *your* hands I commend my *spirit*";
  and when he had *said* this he breathed his *last*.

Proclaim Jesus' words with force, then quietly conclude the scene. Observe a lengthy pause for meditation.

accompany Jesus on his path to death, providing an opportunity for Jesus to extend his compassion to them despite his own burden. Jesus tells the women to mourn not for him but for Jerusalem and the suffering of its people. The gospel was written shortly after Jerusalem and the temple were indeed destroyed by the Romans.

(15) Although Jesus' forgiveness of his persecutors is missing from some authorities, it does fit well with the tenor of this gospel. Even on the cross, Jesus looks with compassion on those around him and extends forgiveness to the guilty.

Given the title "King of the Jews," Jesus receives abuse from the leaders. They attempt to undermine the claim of royalty accorded Jesus, insulting and taunting him. What they do not realize is that the gospel inverts all claims to power and authority. Ironically, Jesus' vindication by God will demonstrate that all of the titles accorded him as derision are true.

(16) Although the crucifixion of two others with Jesus is recorded in all four gospels, only Luke contains the story of the penitent criminal. One of the criminals joins with the executioners and others who are mocking Jesus, but the other recognizes Jesus' innocence and his own guilt. In addition, he acknowledges Jesus' ability to lay claim to otherworldly authority by appealing to be remembered in Jesus' "kingdom." Jesus replies with characteristic forgiveness and the promise that the criminal will join him in paradise.

(17) The momentous nature of Jesus' crucifixion is evident in the supernatural phenomena that accompany it: At the sun's highest point, the sky is darkened, and when Jesus dies, the temple curtain is torn. This event is not simply an execution; it is a

centurion = sen-TYOOR-ee-uhn
Speak with conviction.

[Here all kneel and pause for a short time.]

(18) The *centurion* who *witnessed* what had happened *glorified*
    God and said,
  "This man was *innocent* beyond *doubt.*"
When all the *people* who had gathered for this spectacle *saw*
    what had happened,
  they returned *home* beating their *breasts;*
  but all his *acquaintances* stood at a *distance,*
  including the *women* who had followed him from *Galilee*
  and *saw* these events.

(19) Now there was a *virtuous* and righteous *man*
    named *Joseph, who,*
  though he was a member of the *council,*
  had not *consented* to their plan of *action.*
He came from the Jewish town of *Arimathea*
  and was *awaiting* the kingdom of *God.*
He went to *Pilate* and asked for the *body* of Jesus.
After he had taken the body *down,*
  he *wrapped* it in a linen *cloth*
  and *laid* him in a rock-hewn *tomb*
  in which no one had yet been *buried.*

It was the day of *preparation,*
  and the *sabbath* was about to *begin.*
The *women* who had come from *Galilee* with him
    followed *behind,*
  and when they had *seen* the tomb
  and the way in which his body was *laid* in it,
  they *returned* and prepared *spices* and perfumed *oils.*
Then they *rested* on the *sabbath* according to the *commandment.*

[Shorter: Luke 23:1–49]

Arimathea = ayr-ih-muh-THEE-uh

fulfillment of divine intent, a sign of the presence of God. The darkness indicates that the final Day of the Lord has arrived.

The rending of the temple veil probably indicates an abrogation of Jewish cultic practice. The author knew of the destruction of the temple in 70 CE by the Romans and saw it foretold in the events surrounding Jesus' death. It is also connected with the story about the centurion.

Although Jesus has kept his dignity throughout the story of the passion in the gospel of Luke, the account of his death still drains us of all energy when we hear it.

Jesus' final words can be spoken with confidence, but lower your voice in respect as you read of his death. A period of silent meditation customarily follows the death.

(18) The centurion is the Roman military official overseeing the crucifixion and thus is emblematic of the Gentile occupiers of Judea. For both Jewish and Gentile worlds, the cosmic nature of Jesus' death becomes evident. The centurion glorifies God and confesses the innocence of Jesus, drawing the reader to confess it as well.

(19) The story of Joseph of Arimathea requesting the body of Jesus serves several

purposes. It provides for the burial of Jesus before sundown, in accord with Jewish tradition, although it was not uncommon for victims of crucifixion to rot on the cross, having forfeited not only their lives but even their right to burial. The story also indicates that there were religious leaders of the Jews who were receptive to Jesus' message, despite the actions of some to have him executed. Finally, the stage is set for the visit of the women to the empty tomb on Easter morning, to hear the news that Jesus had risen.

HOLY THURSDAY: EVENING MASS OF THE LORD'S SUPPER

Lectionary #39

READING I   Exodus 12:1–8, 11–14

A reading from the book of Exodus

The LORD said to *Moses* and *Aaron* in the land of *Egypt*,
"*This* month shall stand at the *head* of your *calendar*;
   you shall reckon it the *first* month of the *year*.
Tell the whole community of *Israel*:
   On the *tenth* of this *month* every *one* of your *families*
   must procure for itself a *lamb*, one *apiece* for each *household*.
If a family is too *small* for a *whole* lamb,
   it shall join the nearest *household* in *procuring* one
   and shall *share* in the lamb
   in proportion to the number of *persons* who *partake* of it.

"The lamb must be a year-old *male* and without *blemish*.
You may take it from either the *sheep* or the *goats*.
You shall keep it until the *fourteenth* day of this *month*,
   and *then*, with the *whole* assembly of Israel *present*,
   it shall be *slaughtered* during the evening *twilight*.
They shall take some of its *blood*
   and apply it to the two *doorposts* and the *lintel*
   of *every* house in which they *partake* of the lamb.
That same *night* they shall *eat* its roasted *flesh*
   with unleavened *bread* and bitter *herbs*.

Nisan, in the spring, is the first month of the Hebrew calendar.

Passover has long been celebrated as a feast of hospitality.

The prescriptions concerning the sacrifice ensure that the animal is healthy and is consumed immediately after slaughter.

The foods recall the Exodus from Egypt. Unleavened bread was used because the people did not have time to allow the dough to rise; bitter herbs recall the bitterness of slavery.

READING I | Because the synoptic gospels of Matthew, Mark and Luke recall Jesus' last meal with his friends as a Passover meal, we also remember the origins of Passover on this night before we commemorate Jesus' death.

The passage from the book of Exodus tells of the instructions God gave the Israelites in Egypt before visiting the final and most severe plague, the death of the firstborn child, on the Egyptians. Adopting ancient rituals and reinterpreting them in light of the Exodus, the account recalls the preparations for the Passover meal, as well as the fulfillment of God's promises in freeing the Israelites from their oppressors.

The blood of an animal on the door of a dwelling was long understood as a means of warding off evil and protecting a household. In this case, it serves to keep the Israelite houses safe from the devastating plague brought by God. Blood is a sign of life; here it becomes a symbol of death being thwarted and of the "new" life now available.

The Hebrew people were instructed to remember this event always and to celebrate it faithfully. Indeed, Jews today continue to tell this story of their deliverance from tyranny. The events of long ago become present in the retelling and ritual sharing of the Passover meal.

Christians too recall Jesus' words at his last meal and celebrate them in a similar fashion, participating again at every eucharist in the meal Jesus shared with his friends. And just as the blood of the Passover lamb promised life for those protected by it, so also we celebrate the life available to us who share in the eucharistic meal of the Lamb of God, who died for our sake.

"This is how you are to *eat* it:
> with your loins *girt, sandals* on your *feet* and your *staff*
>> in *hand,*
> you shall eat like those who are in *flight.*
It is the *Passover* of the LORD.

"For on this *same* night I will go *through* Egypt,
> striking *down* every *firstborn* of the land, both *man* and *beast,*
> and executing *judgment* on all the *gods* of *Egypt*—I, the LORD!

"But the *blood* will mark the houses where *you* are.
Seeing the *blood,* I will pass *over* you;
> *thus,* when I strike the land of *Egypt,*
> no destructive *blow* will come *upon* you.

"This *day* shall be a memorial *feast* for you,
> which *all* your generations shall *celebrate*
> with *pilgrimage* to the LORD, as a perpetual *institution.*"

READING II   1 Corinthians 11:23–26

A reading from the first letter of Saint Paul to the Corinthians

Brothers and sisters:
I *received* from the Lord what I also handed *on* to *you,*
> that the Lord *Jesus,* on the night he was handed *over,*
> took *bread,* and, after he had given *thanks,*
> *broke* it and said, "*This* is my *body* that is for *you.*
Do this in *remembrance* of me."

In the same way *also* the *cup,* after *supper,* saying,
> "This *cup* is the *new* covenant in *my* blood.

Take care to give this passage the attention it deserves. Make the urgency and significance of the Passover story apparent. Speak with forcefulness God's promise not to destroy the Israelites. Close with firmness and confidence in a God who keeps that promise.

READING II Paul, quoting here from traditional material, gives us the earliest account of the eucharistic words of Jesus. The passage looks back to the death of Jesus but also looks forward to his coming again. Just as the Hebrew people celebrating Passover make present events of long ago, so also we participate in the ancient ritual of eucharist that becomes new every time we celebrate it. We too tell a story of freedom, a story that recalls the shedding of the blood of the Lamb for the safety and well-being of others, a story of God's love for this people.

Central to Paul's proclamation, here and elsewhere, is the death of Christ. An embarrassment, a source of confusion and ridicule, it is Jesus' death that is paradoxically the source of life for the world. It cannot be ignored or glossed over; it is to be proclaimed at every eucharist. As the Passover lamb was slaughtered and the bread broken, so too was Jesus' body broken on the cross. As the covenants of old were ratified in the blood of animals, the new covenant in Christ was ratified in his blood.

This is an extremely important selection and should be read with all solemnity. The beginning and ending lines are less familiar than the rest and should be emphasized. Speak Jesus' words quietly and forcefully, but without exaggeration. To you is

Take a breath before continuing with the last line. Speak it as though it was written for your assembly.

Do this, as often as you *drink* it, in *remembrance* of me."
For as often as you *eat* this bread and *drink* the *cup*,
  you proclaim the *death* of the Lord until he *comes.*

GOSPEL   John 13:1–15

A reading from the holy gospel according to John

Before the feast of *Passover*, Jesus *knew* that his hour had *come*
  to *pass* from *this* world to the *Father.*
He loved his *own* in the world and he *loved* them to the *end.*

Iscariot = is-KAYR-ee-uht

The devil had already induced *Judas*, son of Simon the *Iscariot*,
  to hand him *over.*
So, during *supper*,
  fully *aware* that the Father had put *everything* into his *power*
  and that he had *come* from God and was *returning* to God,
  he *rose* from supper and took off his outer *garments.*
He took a *towel* and tied it around his *waist.*
Then he poured *water* into a *basin*
  and began to *wash* the disciples' *feet*
  and *dry* them with the *towel* around his *waist.*

For a Passover meal, the group would have been reclining on couches. Although the Passover comes later in the gospel of John, this also was no ordinary meal.

He came to Simon *Peter*, who said to him,
  "*Master*, are you going to *wash* my *feet*?"
Jesus answered and *said* to him,
  "What I am *doing*, you do not understand *now*,
  but you will understand *later.*"
Peter said to him, "You will *never* wash *my* feet."
Jesus answered him,
  "Unless I *wash* you, you will have no *inheritance* with me."

Read Peter's words with a sense of both surprise and objection to the proposed action.

Jesus explains the meaning later in the narrative.

given the task of reminding the members of your assembly of the importance of what we do in every eucharist, when we gather to remember Jesus' death.

GOSPEL Washing the feet clean of the dust of the road when entering a home was common in Jesus' day. Usually one washed one's own feet, although another might wash the feet of a revered teacher. Jesus, acknowledging his role as teacher, reverses the custom and thus honors his disciples.

The account of Jesus washing his disciples' feet is found only in the gospel of John. It is placed in a setting in which Jesus' death is imminent, a death that gives Jesus the opportunity to show his love for "his own."

There are two interpretations of the footwashing within the passage. One emphasizes the importance of sharing in Jesus' life and especially in his death. Peter goes from refusing to permit Jesus to wash his feet to enthusiastic and excessive acceptance. The second section of the story stresses Jesus' revered status and his humility in serving

the disciples in this manner. Jesus calls on the disciples to join in the action; he has set the example.

The footwashing then has two meanings: It is both a sign of sharing in Jesus' fate and one of humble service to another. The second is usually emphasized in modern celebrations of the rite, but the use of this selection on the day preceding our commemoration of Jesus' passion and death suggests that we are asked to share in Jesus' death as well. Just as Paul insists on proudly

Continue speaking Peter's words with enthusiasm.

The author here interprets Jesus' words about cleanliness in terms of the presence of his betrayer within the community of disciples.

Stress the parallel between what Jesus does and what those who follow him are expected to do. Close with solemnity.

Simon Peter said to him,
  "*Master*, then not only my *feet*, but my *hands*
    and *head* as *well*."
Jesus said to him,
  "Whoever has *bathed* has no *need*
    except to have his *feet* washed,
  for he is clean all *over*;
  so *you* are clean, but not *all*."
For he knew who would *betray* him;
  for *this* reason, he said, "Not *all* of you are *clean*."

So when he had *washed* their feet
  and put his garments back *on* and reclined at *table* again,
  he said to them, "Do you *realize* what I have *done* for you?
You call me '*teacher*' and '*master*,' and rightly *so*, for indeed I *am*.
If *I*, therefore, the *master* and *teacher*, have washed *your* feet,
  you ought to wash one *another's* feet.
I have given you a *model* to *follow*,
  so that as *I* have done for *you*, *you* should *also* do.

proclaiming Jesus' death, so also does participation in the footwashing rite lead us directly into the darkness of Good Friday.

There is an ominous tone throughout the first part of the selection, but the words of Peter provide comic relief. Stress Peter's enthusiastic embrace of anything that brings him close to Jesus. Close with an exhortation to your own community to be willing to stoop before even the most lowly in whatever act of humble service is required.

In many parishes, the impression is sometimes given that these words are directed only to the ordained or those in liturgical ministries. They are not; they are for all Christians.

GOOD FRIDAY: CELEBRATION OF THE LORD'S PASSION

Lectionary #40

READING I Isaiah 52:13—53:12

A reading from the book of the prophet Isaiah

God is speaking here.

See, my *servant* shall *prosper*,
   he shall be raised *high* and greatly *exalted*.
Even as *many* were *amazed* at him—
   so *marred* was his look beyond human *semblance*
   and his *appearance* beyond that of the sons of *man*—
so shall he *startle* many *nations*,
   because of *him kings* shall stand *speechless*;
for those who have not been *told* shall *see*,
   those who have not *heard* shall *ponder* it.

The people speak now.

Who would *believe* what we have *heard*?
   To *whom* has the *arm* of the LORD been *revealed*?
He grew *up* like a sapling *before* him,
   like a *shoot* from the parched *earth*;
there was in *him* no stately *bearing* to make us *look* at him,
   nor *appearance* that would *attract* us to him.

The tone becomes very serious. Because the servant was not attractive in appearance, people treated him poorly.

He was *spurned* and *avoided* by people,
   a man of *suffering*, accustomed to *infirmity*,
one of those from whom people *hide* their *faces*,
   spurned, and we held him in *no esteem*.

Speak now with some hope but also regret for how the servant was regarded. Emphasize the strong verbs in this section.

Yet it was our *infirmities* that he *bore*,
   our *sufferings* that he *endured*,
while we thought of him as *stricken*,
   as one *smitten* by God and *afflicted*.

READING I One of the suffering servant songs of Second Isaiah, this passage depicts first God and then the people of Israel discussing one who served God so faithfully, despite ridicule and punishment, that others were able to benefit from it. The death does not appear to have been a physical one, but represents the pain and anguish of the Babylonian exile, when the rulers and elite of the kingdom of Judah were deported to Babylon. The servant accepted the exile, obediently experiencing it as just punishment for Israel's former sins. Others tried to flee the exile or settled in Babylon, but the servant, representing all of Israel, knew that it was a punishment for wrongdoing. The servant's actions allow the nation to continue to exist and eventually to return to Palestine. In the end, the servant is vindicated.

This passage has long been understood to foreshadow the work of the servant of God *par excellence:* Jesus. It is especially appropriate to read today, when we also hear the account of Jesus' passion from the gospel of John. There Jesus suffers, but he is exalted through his suffering, just as God claims of the servant in this reading. The words of the people describing the servant can easily be applied to Jesus. He was lowly in appearance yet was esteemed by God. He was rejected; he wrongly suffered; he died. But he did so in order that others might benefit. He silently offered his life for the sin of others. His punishment brought healing; it fulfilled God's will. In the end, God rewarded him.

On this solemn occasion, offer this selection to your assembly as a meditation

But he was *pierced* for our *offenses*,
   crushed for our *sins*;
upon *him* was the chastisement that makes us *whole*,
   by his *stripes* we were *healed*.

We had all gone *astray* like *sheep*,
   each following his own *way*;
but the LORD laid upon *him*
   the guilt of us *all*.

One who accepts mistreatment without objecting can be inspiring; such a one certainly catches people's attention. Express these lines with wonder at what the servant willingly endured.

Though he was harshly *treated*, he *submitted*
   and opened *not* his *mouth*;
like a *lamb* led to the *slaughter*
   or a *sheep* before the *shearers*,
   he was *silent* and opened *not* his *mouth*.

Oppressed and *condemned*, he was taken *away*,
   and who would have *thought* any more of his *destiny*?
When he was cut *off* from the land of the *living*,
   and *smitten* for the sin of his *people*,
a *grave* was assigned him among the *wicked*
   and a *burial* place with *evildoers*,
though he had done no *wrong*
   nor spoken any *falsehood*.
But the LORD was *pleased*
   to *crush* him in *infirmity*.

This perhaps refers to the exile and the plight of the servant, and all of Israel, separated from their homeland.

If he gives his *life* as an offering for *sin*,
   he shall see his *descendants* in a long *life*,
   and the will of the LORD shall be accomplished *through* him.

Pause before beginning this line. It is God who is again speaking.

Because of his *affliction*
   he shall see the *light*
   in fullness of *days*;

on the consequences that await one who truly serves God. Speak clearly and forcefully, inspiring your listeners to think especially of Jesus, but also to reflect on their own roles as God's servants.

READING II Jesus, as the great high priest, did what every high priest of the temple did: He offered a sacrifice in expiation for the people's sin. Yet he is enthroned in heaven, not as one unable to

understand our human frailties but as one who knows our weaknesses, who himself suffered and turned to God in prayer. It was through his suffering that he was perfected and because of it that he can offer salvation to all.

It is appropriate to reflect on this passage today. Jesus' passion was not without purpose. Read this as a reminder to your assembly of the fact that Jesus understands pain and can identify with the struggles of your community.

PASSION The gospel of John presents a distinctive portrait of Jesus, a portrait that reaches a climax in the passion narrative. In this gospel, Jesus does not hesitate to reveal himself, to speak of his mission and his relationship with God.

This gospel diverges from the others in recounting Jesus' ministry, but is more in line with them regarding the details of his passion and death. The accounts of the passion in the gospels show greater agreement than accounts of other events in Jesus'

through his *suffering*, my servant shall justify *many*,
and their *guilt* he shall *bear*.

Therefore I will give him his *portion* among the *great*,
and he shall divide the *spoils* with the *mighty*,
because he *surrendered* himself to *death*
and was *counted* among the *wicked*;
and he shall take *away* the sins of *many*,
and win *pardon* for their *offenses*.

Speak triumphantly; the servant is vindicated, even honored.

READING II   Hebrews 4:14–16; 5:7–9

A reading from the letter to the Hebrews

Brothers and sisters:
Since we have a great *high priest* who has passed
through the *heavens*,
Jesus, the Son of *God*,
let us hold *fast* to our *confession*.
For we do not have a *high priest*
who is *unable* to sympathize with our *weaknesses*,
but one who has similarly been *tested* in every *way*,
yet without *sin*.
So let us *confidently* approach the throne of *grace*
to receive *mercy* and to find *grace* for timely *help*.

In the days when *Christ* was in the *flesh*,
he offered *prayers* and *supplications* with loud *cries* and *tears*
to the *one* who was able to *save* him from *death*,
and he was *heard* because of his *reverence*.

Though heavenly high priest, Jesus was fully human and underwent trials and temptations.

Speak confidently, with a sure voice.

Jesus prayed to God with trust and sincerity, just as we can.

life. Jesus' suffering, death and resurrection formed the earliest core of the Jesus story. But the meaning of the events is told here in the distinctive style and with the particular interpretation and theological outlook of the fourth evangelist.

Throughout the gospel, Jesus hints at his own passion. He will be "lifted up"—in glory, on the cross. He lays down his life freely; he is not an abused victim but in control of events, the ruler of all. The cross provides the opportunity for Jesus to be revealed as king; it is his exaltation, his throne.

The suffering of Jesus is not denied but is his to embrace. The silent, pained Jesus of the other gospels is gone. The Jesus of the gospel of John boldly approaches the soldiers, heals while being arrested, and discusses his fate and his person with the religious and civil authorities. He is sure of himself, advancing to the cross as a victorious king marches to the triumphant shouts of throngs of admiring subjects.

John's gospel is marked by artful composition; the scenes of the arrest and trial are intertwined, and the crucifixion and death follow quickly. Peter's denial does not appear as a discrete unit but is embedded in the trial. The trial itself presents Pilate moving back and forth between the unruly crowd outside and the peaceful, composed figure of Jesus within the praetorium. The contrast is further heightened by the ugly demands of the religious leaders and the controlled discussion of Pilate and Jesus regarding kingship and truth.

The idea of obedience is central to this passage; stress it here and in the last line.

Son though he *was*, he learned *obedience* from what he *suffered*;
and when he was made *perfect*,
he became the source of eternal *salvation* for all who
obey him.

PASSION   John 18:1—19:42

The Passion of our Lord Jesus Christ according to John

Kidron = KID-ruhn

(1) Jesus went out with his *disciples* across the Kidron *valley*
to where there was a *garden*,
into which he and his disciples *entered*.
Judas his *betrayer also* knew the place,
because Jesus had often *met* there with his *disciples*.
So Judas got a band of *soldiers* and *guards*
from the chief *priests* and the *Pharisees*
and went there with *lanterns*, *torches*, and *weapons*.

Jesus is calm and in control, as he is throughout the passion narrative.

Nazarene = naz-uh-REEN

Jesus, knowing everything that was going to *happen* to him,
went out and said to them, "*Whom* are you *looking* for?"
They answered him, "Jesus the *Nazarene*."
He said to them, "*I AM*."
Judas his *betrayer* was *also* with them.
When he said to them, "*I AM*,"
they turned *away* and *fell* to the *ground*.
So he *again* asked them,
"*Whom* are you *looking* for?"
They said, "Jesus the *Nazarene*."
Jesus answered,
"I *told* you that *I AM*.

From the outset of this story, Jesus' power is evident. Rather than being dragged off by these armed guards, he controls their behavior.

Jesus is identified early in the gospel of John as the Lamb of God, and the image is especially apparent in the passion account. Jesus does not celebrate Passover with his disciples as in the other three gospels, but dies on the day of preparation for the feast. As a result, Jesus is crucified at the same time as the Passover lambs are being sacrificed in the temple. He is presented as the true Lamb whose blood offers life for those who believe. The evangelist even quotes from the regulations regarding the paschal lamb, noting that Jesus' legs were not broken, as were those of the criminals crucified with him.

The assertion that Jesus is the Passover lamb is combined with the image of the scapegoat from Leviticus. On the Day of Atonement, the scapegoat bore the sins of the Jewish people, cleansing them. The high priest's suggestion that Jesus die for the people is significant. As the one who presided over the Day of Atonement rituals, Caiaphas symbolically sent Jesus into the wilderness, bearing the sins of the people, just as he sent the scapegoat on Yom Kippur.

Although all the gospels suggest complicity between the Jewish religious authorities and the Roman governor in Jesus' execution, this gospel insists that the Jewish leaders are actually responsible; Pilate is presented as a pawn in their hands. This can be misleading.

All four gospels attest to the conflict between Jesus and the Jewish religious leaders. Indeed, the party of the Sadducees, in power at the time, may have been frightened by Jesus' popularity. The Sadducees were surely offended by his preaching about the resurrection of the dead, which they did

So if you are looking for *me*, let *these* men *go*."
This was to *fulfill* what he had *said*,
  "I have not lost *any* of those you *gave* me."

Then Simon *Peter*, who had a sword, *drew* it,
  struck the high priest's *slave*, and cut off his right *ear*.
The slave's *name* was *Malchus*.
Jesus said to Peter,
  "Put your *sword* into its *scabbard*.
Shall I not *drink* the *cup* that the Father *gave* me?"

(2) So the band of *soldiers*, the *tribune*, and the Jewish *guards*
      seized Jesus,
  bound him, and brought him to *Annas* first.
He was the father-in-law of *Caiaphas*,
  who was *high priest* that year.
It was *Caiaphas* who had counseled the Jews
  that it was better that *one* man should die
    rather than the *people*.

(3) Simon *Peter* and *another* disciple *followed* Jesus.
Now the *other* disciple was *known* to the *high priest*,
  and he entered the *courtyard* of the high priest *with* Jesus.
But *Peter* stood at the gate *outside*.
So the *other* disciple, the *acquaintance* of the high priest,
  went *out* and spoke to the *gatekeeper* and brought Peter *in*.
Then the maid who was the gatekeeper said to Peter,
  "*You* are not one of this man's disciples, *are* you?"
He said, "I am *not*."
Now the *slaves* and the *guards* were standing
      around a charcoal *fire*
    that they had made, because it was *cold*,
    and were *warming* themselves.
Peter was *also* standing there keeping *warm*.

Malchus = MAL-kuhs

The tribune was the chief officer of the cohort.

Annas = AN-uhs
Caiaphas = KĪ-uh-fuhs

Caiaphas said this after the raising of Lazarus; see John 11:49–50.
Pause briefly.

not accept. But the fact remains that Jesus was crucified by the Romans for political reasons, as the placard on the cross indicates, rather than stoned as a blasphemer by the Jewish authorities. In addition, although Pilate is known from other sources as having been particularly cruel to and contemptuous of the Jews, each gospel portrays Pilate somewhat sympathetically. This is particularly true of John's gospel, although it is unlikely that Pilate acted solely at the request of the Jewish leaders. Jesus may indeed have been delivered to Pilate by the Jewish authorities, but all evidence points to a Roman execution of an insurgent.

The negative portrait of the Jews in the gospel of John must also be qualified by the situation in the community of the evangelist. The Johannine Christians were Jews who proclaimed their belief in Jesus. At some point, the Jewish religious leaders had expelled these Jewish Christians from the synagogue for their unorthodox beliefs. The polemic against "the Jews" in this gospel, and against the Jewish leaders in particular, must be read in light of this conflict.

Reading the passion effectively is a challenging task. Take your time in order to do justice to the message you present. Allow a bit of wonder to enter your voice at the power and authority demonstrated by Jesus. Remember that Jesus is always in control, and attempt to convey that in your manner of speaking. Even on this dark day, when the vicious cries of the crowd attempt to drown out any seeds of compassion, this reading is triumphant.

(1) The meal Jesus had shared with his disciples is not a Passover meal in the gospel of John. This allows the evangelist to

Pause before continuing, to indicate a change in scene.

The high priest does not bring charges to be refuted, illustrating once again the total ineffectiveness of the Jewish authorities in this passion account. Instead, Jesus challenges them as to why he is being questioned at all.

Jesus does not flinch but responds in a calm, composed manner.

Pause briefly.

A connection is drawn between the encounter in the garden and this incident.

Observe a lengthier pause here.

praetorium = prih-TOHR-ee-uhm

(4) The high priest *questioned* Jesus
  about his *disciples* and about his *doctrine*.
Jesus answered him,
  "I have spoken *publicly* to the *world*.
I have always taught in a *synagogue*
  or in the *temple* area where all the Jews *gather*,
  and in *secret* I have said *nothing*. Why ask *me*?
Ask those who *heard* me what I *said* to them.
They know what I said."

When he had *said* this,
  one of the temple guards standing there *struck* Jesus and said,
  "Is *this* the way you answer the *high priest*?"
Jesus answered him,
  "If I have spoken *wrongly*, *testify* to the wrong;
  but if I have spoken *rightly*, why do you *strike* me?"
Then *Annas* sent him bound to *Caiaphas* the *high priest*.

(5) Now Simon *Peter* was standing there keeping *warm*.
And they said to him,
  "*You* are not one of his disciples, *are* you?"
He *denied* it and said,
  "I am *not*."
One of the *slaves* of the high priest,
  a *relative* of the one whose *ear* Peter had cut *off*, said,
  "Didn't I see you in the *garden* with him?"
Again Peter denied it.
And *immediately* the cock *crowed*.

(6) Then they brought Jesus from *Caiaphas* to the *praetorium*.
It was *morning*.
And they *themselves* did not enter the praetorium,
  in order not to be *defiled* so that they could eat the *Passover*.

present Jesus as the paschal lamb *par excellence*. There is also no agony in Gethsemane. The garden is simply a familiar meeting place for Jesus and the disciples. Jesus is in command in this scene; his self-assurance and power are visible.

Judas brings Roman soldiers and temple police with him to arrest Jesus. Simply by speaking, Jesus causes them all to fall to the ground in awe or fear. His enemies are powerless in his presence. He does not avoid arrest, but neither does he resign himself to it. In this gospel, Jesus offers himself for arrest. His only concern is for his

companions; their safety is preserved, not because they flee but in order to fulfill Jesus' own words.

The violent encounter between one of Jesus' followers and the slave of the high priest is given more detail in this gospel than elsewhere. The combatants are identified: Peter strikes the slave, whose name is Malchus. But Jesus rejects any attempts to deny him his opportunity for glory.

(2) There is no trial of Jesus before the Sanhedrin in the gospel of John. Jesus is instead taken to the home of the former high

priest, Annas. In addition to being the father-in-law of the current high priest, Annas also had five sons who served in the high priestly office. Therefore, he was still an influential figure in the management of the temple.

Caiaphas' proposal that one person die on behalf of the people ironically makes him suggest that Jesus fulfill the role of the scapegoat on Yom Kippur, the Day of Atonement. On that feast, the high priest symbolically placed the sins of the people on the back of a goat that was sent into the wilderness to die. Caiaphas continues to

So Pilate came *out* to them and said,
  "What *charge* do you bring against this *man?"*
They answered and said to him,
  "If he were not a *criminal,*
  we would not have handed him *over* to you."
At *this,* Pilate said to them,
  "Take him *yourselves,* and judge him according to *your* law."
The Jews answered him,
  "We do not have the right to *execute* anyone, "
  in order that the *word* of *Jesus* might be *fulfilled*
  that he said indicating the kind of *death* he would *die.*

(7) So Pilate went *back* into the *praetorium*
  and *summoned* Jesus and said to him,
  "Are *you* the *King* of the *Jews?"*
Jesus answered,
  "Do you say this on your *own*
  or have *others* told you about me?"
Pilate answered,
  "*I* am not a *Jew, am* I?
Your own *nation* and the chief *priests* handed you *over* to me.
What have you *done?"*
Jesus answered,
  "My *kingdom* does not belong to this *world.*
If my kingdom *did* belong to this world,
  my *attendants* would be fighting
  to *keep* me from being handed *over* to the Jews.
But as it *is,* my kingdom is not *here."*
So Pilate said to him,
  "Then you *are* a king?"
Jesus answered,
  "*You* say I am a *king.*

In this gospel, Pilate is sincerely trying to get information. The title "king" has not been suggested yet in the narrative, but it is the charge for which Jesus is crucified.

It is not clear if Pilate is speaking contemptuously or simply indicating his distance from the accusation.

Pilate's question could be spoken either by raising the voice at the end (indicating a genuine query) or by lowering it at the end (suggesting that the questioner knows that the answer is affirmative).

perform his high priestly function, but does so not with a goat but with Jesus. Jesus dies bearing the sins of the people.

(3) Although Peter is unknown to the high priest, the fourth evangelist provides a means to get him into the high priest's courtyard. The unnamed disciple is probably the same as the "one whom Jesus loved," and apparently represents John, son of Zebedee, who was revered by the community that produced this gospel. The scene is set for the first of Peter's three denials of Jesus.

(4) In this gospel, no witnesses are brought against Jesus; there is no charge of blasphemy or questions regarding Jesus' messianic status. Annas asks about his disciples and his teaching. Jesus responds somewhat harshly but truthfully, suggesting that the high priest consult those who have heard him preach. Jesus does not challenge the secretive nature of the arrest, as in the other three gospel accounts, but challenges the questioning itself.

(5) Peter denies that he knows Jesus two more times. The cock then begins to crow, confirming Jesus' words. The denial is

not as forceful here as in the other gospels, but the threefold rejection is underscored after Jesus' resurrection, when Jesus asks Peter three times "Do you love me?" Thus Peter is given the opportunity to right his wrong.

(6) Pilate moves between the inner court and the public space during the trial, between dialogue with Jesus and discussion with the Jewish officials eager to see the captive die. There are no charges brought against Jesus (implying that none were valid), only the weak claim that he must be a criminal or they would not have brought him

For *this* I was born and for *this* I came into the *world*,
  to *testify* to the *truth*.
Everyone who *belongs* to the truth *listens* to my *voice*."
Pilate said to him, "What is *truth*?"

(8) When he had *said* this,
  he again went out to the *Jews* and *said* to them,
  "I find no *guilt* in him.
But you have a *custom* that I release one *prisoner*
    to you at *Passover*.
Do you want me to *release* to you the *King* of the *Jews*?"
They cried out again,
  "Not *this* one but *Barabbas*!"
Now *Barabbas* was a *revolutionary*.

(9) Then Pilate took *Jesus* and had him *scourged*.
And the soldiers wove a *crown* out of *thorns*
    and placed it on his *head*,
  and *clothed* him in a purple *cloak*,
  and they *came* to him and said,
  "*Hail, King* of the *Jews*!"
And they struck him *repeatedly*.

(10) Once *more* Pilate went out and said to them,
  "*Look*, I am bringing him *out* to you,
  so that you may *know* that I find no *guilt* in him."
So Jesus came out,
  wearing the crown of *thorns* and the purple *cloak*.
And he said to them, "*Behold*, the *man*!"

When the chief priests and the guards *saw* him they cried out,
  "*Crucify* him, *crucify* him!"
Pilate said to them,
  "Take him *yourselves* and *crucify* him.

Pilate demonstrates that he is not one of those who knows the truth or he would listen to Jesus. Pause briefly.

Pilate is probably mocking the crowd with this question.

Barabbas = buh-RAB-uhs

The abuse of the soldiers lacks the bite of what is recorded in the other gospels. Jesus' response to it is not detailed.

Again, Pilate is probably mocking. His statement seems to be, "Look at this guy! How could he be dangerous?"

---

to Pilate. The claim that they could not put anyone to death does not fit the evidence from other periods but might have been true during Roman occupation.

(7) Pilate asks Jesus if he is the king of the Jews. The evangelist understands the ministry of Jesus in entirely nonrevolutionary terms: He is king, but not of an earthly realm. Anyone who recognizes the truth will recognize that Jesus bears witness to the truth. Pilate refuses to acknowledge the truth.

(8) Pilate appears as one who wants to save Jesus' life, offering to release Jesus. He mentions a custom known only to the gospels of releasing a prisoner at Passover. But the crowd demands the release of Barabbas instead. They choose a fighter over one who has just rejected violence.

(9) The abuse received by Jesus is told with less detail here than in the other gospels. Never is Jesus a spectacle for pity or revulsion. The royal fixtures—crown, royal robe and homage—are given to one whose kingdom lies elsewhere.

(10) Pilate repeatedly tries to free Jesus, but becomes fearful at the crowd's vehemence and its claim that Jesus made himself God's Son. Responsibility for Jesus' death is placed squarely on the shoulders of his Jewish accusers. In the gospels Jesus is executed for religious reasons rather than political ones.

(11) Pilate questions Jesus once again in an attempt to ascertain his origin, perhaps afraid that Jesus was a divine figure appearing as a human. Trying to assert his

I find no *guilt* in him."
The Jews answered,
  "We have a *law*, and according to that *law* he ought to *die*,
  because he made *himself* the Son of *God*."

(11) Now when Pilate heard *this* statement,
  he became even *more* afraid,
  and went back into the *praetorium* and *said* to Jesus,
  "Where are you *from*?"
Jesus did not *answer* him.

So Pilate said to him,
  "Do you not *speak* to me?
Do you not *know* that I have power to *release* you
  and I have power to *crucify* you?"
Jesus answered him,
  "You would have *no* power *over* me
  if it had not been *given* to you from *above*.
For *this* reason the one who handed me *over* to you
  has the *greater* sin."
(12) *Consequently*, Pilate tried to *release* him; but the Jews
    cried out,
  "If you *release* him, you are not a *Friend* of *Caesar*.
Everyone who makes himself a *king opposes* Caesar."

When Pilate heard *these* words he brought Jesus *out*
  and seated him on the *judge's* bench
  in the place called Stone *Pavement*, in Hebrew, *Gabbatha*.
It was *preparation* day for *Passover*, and it was about *noon*.
And he said to the Jews,
  "*Behold*, your *king!*"
They cried out,
  "Take him *away*, take him *away! Crucify* him!"

Pilate's question was apparently suggested by the statement that Jesus claimed to be God's Son.

"Friend of Caesar" was a title held by Pilate; here the crowd suggests that it is in jeopardy. Pause slightly before reading it to clarify the formal nature of the title.

Gabbatha = GAB-uh-thuh

Now Pilate mocks the crowd.

authority, Pilate is met with Jesus' calm discussion of power; there is no real power on earth, but all comes from God. It is evident that Jesus is the one endowed with divine authority, and from his lips comes a statement placing blame for his fate not on Pilate but on the Jewish authorities.

(12) This makes Pilate even more eager to free Jesus, but he is compelled to give in to the crowd according to this author. They no longer bring religious charges against

Jesus but appeal to Pilate's political vulnerability; if he frees this "king" he is aligning himself with an opponent of Caesar. Although Pilate taunts the crowd, he eventually consents to their wishes. The Jewish authorities profess their allegiance to Caesar, the ruler of the forces occupying their land and the chief obstacle to Jewish political, social and religious freedom. Indeed, there were Jewish leaders who were friendly with Rome. The Romans had originally been welcomed into the region to settle disputes.

(13) Jesus remains in control even on his path to crucifixion. He carries his own

cross. Nothing is said about taunts directed at him or abuse from the other criminals. Only the chief priests raise their voices, but this is in opposition to the title "King of the Jews" placed above the cross. Once again, Pilate dismisses them.

The crucifixion is recounted without great detail. Far from being a pathetic figure, Jesus is accorded honor. The religious leaders and, to a lesser extent, Pilate, are the characters to be pitied in this gospel.

At the time of Jesus' death there was no local king. The statement attributed to the chief priest is theological (denying Jesus' kingship). Pause before continuing.

Pilate said to them,
  "Shall I *crucify* your *king*?"
The chief priests answered,
  "We have *no* king but *Caesar.*"

(13) Then he handed him *over* to them to be *crucified.*

So they took *Jesus,* and, carrying the cross *himself,*
  he went out to what is called the *Place* of the *Skull,*
  in Hebrew, *Golgotha.*

Golgotha = GOL-guh-thuh

There they *crucified* him, and with him two *others,*
  one on either *side,* with Jesus in the *middle.*

Pilate also had an *inscription* written and put on the *cross.*
It read,
  "*Jesus* the *Nazarene,* the *King* of the *Jews.*"
Now *many* of the Jews read this *inscription,*
  because the place where Jesus was *crucified* was near the *city;*
  and it was written in *Hebrew, Latin,* and *Greek.*

So the chief *priests* of the Jews said to *Pilate,*
  "Do *not* write 'The *King* of the *Jews,*'
  but that he *said,* 'I am the *King* of the *Jews*'."
Pilate answered,
  "What I have *written,* I have *written.*"

For once, Pilate refuses to give in to the demands of the Jewish leaders.

(14) When the soldiers had *crucified* Jesus,
  they took his *clothes* and divided them into four *shares,*
  a *share* for each *soldier.*
They also took his *tunic,* but the tunic was *seamless,*
  woven in one *piece* from the top *down.*
So they said to one another,
  "Let's not *tear* it, but cast *lots* for it to see whose it will *be,*"

(14) Only the gospel of John mentions a seamless garment in the story of the soldiers dividing Jesus' clothing. Roman soldiers were allowed to confiscate the possessions (including the clothes) of those they executed; here, the action is seen as a fulfillment of Psalm 22:18, alluded to in the other passion accounts.

(15) The words of Jesus to his mother and the unnamed disciple make a statement about the church. The Acts of the Apostles indicates that Mary was present with the disciples in the early days of the Christian community. Jesus' words can be understood literally—that the disciple is to take Jesus' place and care for Jesus' mother—and figuratively. The disciple thus becomes the individual believer, while Mary represents the Christian church as a whole. Both interpretations have been a part of Christian tradition.

Although the other disciples are absent, Jesus is not alone. The women do not watch from afar but are close enough to speak with Jesus. In this gospel the disciple whom Jesus loved does not abandon Jesus but faithfully stands with the women.

(16) Even to his death, Jesus is in command of events. He determines that his time to die has come; he ensures that scripture is fulfilled. There is no cry of abandonment or pain. The author does not deny the reality of Jesus' death, but it remains a glorification rather than an ignominious fate.

Traditionally, a moment of reverent silence accompanied by bowing or kneeling follows at this point.

in order that the passage of Scripture might be *fulfilled*
    that says:
"They *divided* my garments *among* them,
    and for my *vesture* they cast *lots*."
This is what the soldiers *did*.

(15) Standing by the cross of *Jesus* were his *mother*
    and his mother's *sister*, *Mary* the wife of *Clopas*,
    and *Mary* of *Magdala*.

When Jesus saw his *mother* and the *disciple* there whom he *loved*
    he said to his mother, "*Woman*, *behold*, your *son*."
Then he said to the disciple,
    "*Behold*, your *mother*."
And from that *hour* the disciple *took* her into his *home*.

(16) After *this*, aware that everything was now *finished*,
    in order that the *Scripture* might be *fulfilled*,
Jesus said, "I *thirst*."
There was a *vessel* filled with common *wine*.
So they put a *sponge* soaked in *wine* on a sprig of *hyssop*
    and put it up to his *mouth*.
When Jesus had *taken* the wine, he said,
    "It is *finished*."
And bowing his *head*, he handed over the *spirit*.

[Here all kneel and pause for a short time.]

(17) Now since it was *preparation* day,
    in order that the *bodies* might not remain
    on the *cross* on the *sabbath*,
    for the *sabbath* day of *that* week was a *solemn* one,
    the Jews asked *Pilate* that their legs be *broken*
    and that they be taken *down*.

Clopas = KLOH-puhs
Magdala = MAG-duh-luh
There are four women here. Adjust your phrasing so there is no mistake that Mary the wife of Clopas is not identified with the sister of Jesus' mother.

Pause again.

hyssop = HIS-uhp
The use of the small hyssop plant for this is odd but connects the events with Passover. Hyssop was used to apply the lamb's blood to the doorposts of the Hebrews' houses before the exodus from Egypt.

Jesus died on a Friday and the Sabbath began that evening. This Sabbath, according to the gospel of John, was also the feast of Passover.

(17) In Jewish practice, a dead body was buried before sunset. The Romans had no such sensibilities; crucified corpses could be left on crosses to rot. Breaking the legs of the crucified was a merciful act, designed to hasten death. Jesus' legs were not broken because he was already dead, and this fact allows the author to apply to him the words spoken of the Passover lamb. The lamb was to be unblemished, with no broken bones. Once again the Jewish authorities are responsible. Pilate acts at their request.

The blood and water that flowed from Jesus' side have long been understood to refer to Christian eucharist and baptism, rituals connected with the saving death of Jesus. The author insists that a reliable witness observed the occurrence so that the reader might recognize its truth. The witness is probably the beloved disciple.

(18) The other gospels also attest to Joseph of Arimathea's role in burying the body of Jesus. Here he becomes a full-fledged follower of Jesus. Joining him in honoring the body is Nicodemus, whose nocturnal visit to Jesus is told only in this gospel. He anoints the body here, an act of tribute the women in the other gospels intended to do on Sunday morning. The stage is set for Mary Magdalene to arrive and find the empty tomb.

Breaking the legs of the crucified hastened death; they could no longer support their bodies but hung in exhaustion.

So the *soldiers* came and broke the legs of the *first*
    and then of the *other* one who was *crucified* with *Jesus.*
But when they came to *Jesus* and saw that he was *already* dead,
    they did *not* break his legs,
    but one soldier thrust his *lance* into his *side,*
    and immediately *blood* and *water* flowed *out.*

An eyewitness has *testified,* and his testimony is *true;*
    he *knows* that he is speaking the *truth,*
    so that you *also* may come to *believe.*

For this *happened* so that the *Scripture* passage might be *fulfilled:*
    "Not a *bone* of it will be *broken.*"
And again *another* passage says:
    "They will *look* upon him whom they have *pierced.*"

Arimathea = ayr-ih-muh-THEE-uh

(18) After *this,* Joseph of *Arimathea,*
    secretly a disciple of Jesus for *fear* of the *Jews,*
    asked Pilate if he could *remove* the body of Jesus.
And Pilate *permitted* it.
So he *came* and took his *body.*

Nicodemus = nik-oh-DEE-muhs
aloes = AL-ohz

Nicodemus, the one who had *first* come to him at *night,*
    also came bringing a mixture of *myrrh* and *aloes*
    weighing about one hundred *pounds.*
They took the *body* of Jesus
    and *bound* it with *burial* cloths along with the *spices,*
    according to the Jewish *burial* custom.
Now in the *place* where he had been *crucified* there was a *garden,*
    and in the *garden* a new *tomb,* in which *no* one
        had yet been *buried.*
So they *laid* Jesus there because of the Jewish *preparation* day;
    for the *tomb* was close *by.*

Only this gospel indicates that the tomb was near the place of crucifixion.

EASTER VIGIL

Lectionary #41

READING I   Genesis 1:1—2:2

A reading from the book of Genesis

In the *beginning*, when God created the *heavens* and the *earth*,
  the *earth* was a formless *wasteland*, and *darkness*
    covered the *abyss*,
  while a mighty wind *swept* over the *waters*.

Then God said,
  "Let there be *light*," and there was *light*.
God saw how *good* the light was.
God then *separated* the *light* from the *darkness*.
God called the *light* "*day*" and the *darkness* he called "*night*."
Thus *evening* came, and *morning* followed—the *first* day.

Then God said,
  "Let there be a *dome* in the middle of the *waters*,
  to separate *one* body of water from the *other*."
And so it *happened:*
  God made the *dome*,
  and it separated the water *above* the dome
    from the water *below* it.
God called the *dome* "the *sky*."
Evening came, and *morning* followed—the *second* day.

Then God said,
  "Let the *water* under the sky be *gathered* into a single *basin*,
  so that the dry *land* may appear."

Make "swept" sound like what it means.

Speak God's words in a strong, commanding tone.
Stress the word "good."

Pause slightly between "light" and "day."
Lower your voice in a concluding, satisfied tone.

Declare the success of God's command slowly and decisively.

Pause slightly after "dome."
Practice this line with a microphone until you are able to speak the difficult "second day" clearly, without swallowing any letters or sounding stilted.

READING I When you proclaim the creation story to your community, you set the mood for the readings and prayers that follow. You tell the story of primeval beauty and the plan of God in forming the earth. Read it with wonder and awe, inspiring your listeners to accept their role in protecting the earth, preserving it unblemished, reflecting its original goodness. Convey God's power over everything in being able to bring about such a wondrous creation, a universe twirling in a cosmic dance, carefully balanced, reflecting the greatness and goodness of its maker.

The story of the creation is poetic. It is similar to creation myths from other traditions, but unique as well. It establishes a six-day "work week," with a day devoted to rest. For the human the day of rest is appropriately devoted to marveling at the beauties of creation and giving praise to God for them and for all God's deeds.

In the creation story recounted here, God reigns supreme from beginning to end. There is no cosmic struggle for control, as in other creation accounts. The world begins in chaos, but God's spoken word brings order and beauty. As Christians we proclaim that God most fully communicates through the Son, the incarnate Word, through whom the world was made.

This story of creation announces the origin of the world from a dark void. God

Pause slightly after "land."

And so it *happened:*
 the *water* under the sky was *gathered* into its *basin,*
 and the dry land *appeared.*
God called the *dry land* "the *earth,"*
 and the basin of the *water* he called "the *sea."*
God saw how *good* it was.
Then God said,
 "Let the earth bring forth *vegetation:*
 every kind of *plant* that bears *seed*
 and every kind of *fruit* tree on *earth*
 that bears *fruit* with its *seed* in it."
And so it *happened:*
 the *earth* brought forth every kind of *plant* that bears *seed*
 and every kind of *fruit* tree on *earth*
 that bears *fruit* with its *seed* in it.

Speak sincerely and with satisfaction.
Take care not to swallow the "d" in "third."

God saw how *good* it was.
Evening came, and *morning* followed—the *third* day.

Then God said:
 "Let there be *lights* in the dome of the *sky,*
 to separate *day* from *night.*
Let them mark the fixed *times*, the *days* and the *years,*
 and serve as *luminaries* in the dome of the *sky,*
 to shed *light* upon the *earth."*
And so it *happened:*
 God made the *two* great *lights,*
 the *greater* one to govern the *day,*
 and the *lesser* one to govern the *night;*
 and he made the *stars.*
God *set* them in the dome of the *sky,*
 to shed *light* upon the *earth,*
 to govern the *day* and the *night,*
 and to separate the *light* from the *darkness.*

forms the world, beginning in the broadest possible way, by making light and darkness. From here, God proceeds to refine the work, making it ever more specific and detailed until finally reaching the creation of humanity. Human beings are the crown of creation because God declares them made in the divine image. This is both a declaration and a promise. We must fulfill God's word and reflect the divine in our words and actions.

Begin your proclamation by imagining the sound of a rushing wind, and try to convey that image as you read the introductory verses of this selection. Throughout the description of creation, speak as slowly and clearly as you can, careful always not to swallow any words or phrases. Never rush the repetition in the passage but draw attention to it. Emphasize the words describing the elements of creation: light, waters, earth, plants, fruit, birds, animals, and so on. Give

special emphasis to the creation of humans. Close with a quiet, satisfied voice.

There is a natural rhythm to this passage. Allow it to guide your proclamation, but try not to sound sing-song or too formal. Speak in a strong voice, and lift it a bit as you speak the words of God. Declare with warmth in your voice how good each aspect of creation is. Each "and so it happened"

Once again, speak sincerely and with satisfaction.

God saw how *good* it was.
*Even*ing came, and *morning* followed—the *fourth* day.

Then God said,
  "Let the water *teem* with an *abundance* of living *creatures*,
  and on the *earth* let *birds* fly beneath the *dome* of the *sky*."

Draw out "teem" in order to convey how many there were, then lift your voice and sound a bit excited as you describe the birds.

And so it *happened*:
  God created the great *sea* monsters
  and *all* kinds of *swimming* creatures with which
    the water *teems*,
  and *all* kinds of winged *birds*.

Practice this sentence until the phrasing is clear.

God saw how *good* it was, and God *blessed* them, saying,
  "Be *fertile, multiply*, and *fill* the water of the *seas*;
  and let the birds *multiply* on the *earth*."
*Even*ing came, and *morning* followed—the *fifth* day.

Say "blessed" in a confident tone and with the same satisfaction that you display when declaring the goodness of God's creation.

Then God said,
  "Let the earth bring *forth* all *kinds* of living *creatures*:
  cattle, creeping things, and wild *animals* of all *kinds*."
And so it *happened*:
  God made all *kinds* of wild *animals*, all kinds of *cattle*,
  and all kinds of *creeping* things of the *earth*.
God saw how *good* it was.

All of creation is made by God and is good, even those creatures we consider less than noble.
Pause before beginning this important proclamation, then lift your voice anew as you describe the creation of humanity.

Then God said:
  "Let us make *man* in our *image*, after our *likeness*.
Let them have *dominion* over the *fish* of the sea,
  the *birds* of the air, and the *cattle*,
  and over all the wild *animals*
  and all the *creatures* that crawl on the *ground*."
God created *man* in his *image*;
  in the image of *God* he created him;
  male and *female* he *created* them.

Stress "God."
Men and women are both made in God's image.

should be spoken after a slight pause and in a voice that expresses confidence rather than surprise. Pause slightly before and after the announcement of the day of the week ("evening" and "morning," "the first day," and so on). Read slowly, but with a tone of finality and satisfaction. Be sure to enunciate each word. Then pause before beginning the account of the succeeding day.

Your community might have the practice of beginning this reading in partial darkness, or the reading may be accompanied by a choral refrain or visual presentation. Be sure you understand what your liturgy committee or director has planned, and practice until you are confident that you can proceed smoothly, giving your entire attention to proclaiming the word of God.

You are given the task of announcing that the light has dawned, a message that will also be imparted through song and ritual. Pray about the passage. After you have reflected on the beauty of God's creation, you will be better able to convey your wonder and awe to your listeners.

God *blessed* them, saying:
"Be *fertile* and *multiply*;
fill the earth and *subdue* it.
Have *dominion* over the *fish* of the *sea*, the *birds* of the *air*,
and all the living *things* that move on the *earth*."

God also said:
"*See*, I give you every *seed*-bearing *plant* all over the *earth*
and every *tree* that has seed-bearing *fruit* on it to be your *food*;
and to all the *animals* of the land, all the *birds* of the air,
and all the living *creatures* that crawl on the *ground*,
I give all the green *plants* for *food*."
And so it *happened*.

God looked at everything he had *made*, and he found it
very *good*.
Evening came, and *morning* followed—the *sixth* day.

Thus the *heavens* and the *earth* and all their *array*
were *completed*.
Since on the *seventh* day God was *finished*
with the work he had been *doing*,
he *rested* on the *seventh* day from all the *work*
he had *undertaken*.

[Shorter: Genesis 1:1, 26–31a]

There is a purpose for everything, and all creation is in harmony.

Slow down as you read this, and stress the great goodness of creation.

Conclude the passage by reading slowly and with finality.

READING II Genesis 22:1–18

A reading from the book of Genesis

God put *Abraham* to the *test*.
He called to him, "*Abraham!*"
"*Here* I am," he replied.

Speak Abraham's name as if someone is calling him, then pause before giving his response.

READING II During our celebration of the Triduum, we reflect on the new covenant established in Jesus. It is appropriate, then, to learn about the covenant God first established with the patriarch Abraham. Today's passage follows the fulfillment of God's promise to Abraham and Sarah that they would have a child even though they were beyond childbearing years. Abraham's part of the covenant was to institute circumcision, while God promised to bless Abraham and his descendants. In today's passage, the breadth of God's promise is evident: Abraham and Sarah will have descendants as numerous as the stars of the sky and the sands of the seashore.

Before that promise is reiterated, Abraham demonstrates his faith in God by being willing to follow God's commands, even when they seem to contradict God's promises. The chilling story of the binding of Isaac shows just how far Abraham is willing to go. There is no doubt that Abraham loves his son; God's words make that clear. Yet he responds in faith, and it is for that faith that he is rewarded with the promise of many descendants. Written before a belief in an afterlife developed, this is the closest the text can come to speaking of immortality.

Speak slowly, and stress "only" and "love" in order to emphasize what a great gift this child was to Abraham and Sarah. Moriah = moh-RĪ-uh

Then God said:
  "Take your son *Isaac*, your *only* one, whom you *love*,
    and go to the *land* of *Moriah*.
There you shall *offer* him up as a *holocaust*
  on a *height* that I will point *out* to you."

Early the next *morning* Abraham saddled his *donkey*,
    took *with* him his son *Isaac* and two of his *servants* as well,
    and with the *wood* that he had cut for the *holocaust*,
    set *out* for the *place* of which God had *told* him.

The tension begins to mount as Abraham and Isaac approach the mountain.

On the *third* day Abraham got *sight* of the place from *afar*.
Then he said to his servants:
  "Both of you stay *here* with the *donkey*,
    while the *boy* and I go on over *yonder*.
We will *worship* and then come *back* to you."
Thereupon Abraham took the *wood* for the *holocaust*
    and laid it on his son Isaac's *shoulders*,
    while he *himself* carried the *fire* and the *knife*.

Isaac carries the wood just as Jesus will carry his cross.

As the two walked on *together*, Isaac *spoke*
      to his father Abraham:
  "*Father!*" Isaac said.
"*Yes*, son," he replied.
Isaac continued, "Here are the *fire* and the *wood*,
    but where is the *sheep* for the *holocaust*?"
"*Son*," Abraham answered,
    "God *himself* will provide the *sheep* for the *holocaust*."
Then the *two* continued going *forward*.

Although Isaac's words can be spoken lightly, allow some sadness to fill Abraham's responses.

This is not to be spoken matter-of-factly. Let your voice display some tightness in order to indicate what is coming.

Read these four lines slowly and allow tension to fill your voice.

When they came to the place of which God had *told* him,
    Abraham built an *altar* there and arranged the *wood* on it.
Next he *tied up* his son *Isaac*,
    and put him on *top* of the wood on the *altar*.

Although the idea of a father sacrificing his son to God is horrifying, the purpose of the story is actually to assert that the God of Abraham does not require such an action. The gods of neighboring peoples accepted human sacrifice, but this God does not. God wants a demonstration of faith but rejects the violence practiced by the nations.

Read this dramatic account with a tone of tension and horror just below the surface. Although it begins matter-of-factly, the story quickly threatens our sensibilities and

causes us anxiety. Be aware of the discomfort that may be present in your assembly, but do not attempt to soften the message. When reading the dialogue, speak Isaac's words innocently, but allow some sorrow as well as nervousness to enter your voice as you read Abraham's words. Let the suspense build until the angel intervenes. Allow your voice to reflect relief when Abraham finds the ram, but continue to speak God's promise in a strong yet comforting tone.

READING III The book of Exodus is the story of the plight of the Israelites in Egypt and their escape from the army of Pharaoh as it chased them into the desert. Today's passage begins shortly after the journey has begun, just as Pharaoh's army is approaching the Israelite procession. As they would do so many times on this journey to their Promised Land, the Israelites turn against Moses and lose heart. They regret the decision to flee Egypt, preferring to live in slavery than to die in the wilderness.

Speak very slowly and deliberately, with a tone of subdued horror. Then pause at length. When you begin again, speak with urgency and pick up your pace.

Although these are solemn words, you may speak with relief.

The tension continues to subside.

Yahweh-yireh = YAH-way–YEER-ay

This is a solemn promise, spoken with great sincerity.

Speak the final line slowly and with emphasis.

Then he reached *out* and took the *knife* to *slaughter* his son.
But the LORD's *messenger* called to him from *heaven*,
 "*Abraham, Abraham!*"
"*Here* I am," he answered.
"Do *not* lay your hand on the *boy*," said the messenger.
"Do not do the *least thing* to him.
I know *now* how *devoted* you are to God,
 since you did not *withhold* from me your *own* beloved s*on*."
As Abraham looked *about*,
 he spied a *ram* caught by its *horns* in the *thicket*.
So he went and *took* the ram
 and offered it *up* as a *holocaust* in place of his *son*.
Abraham named the site *Yahweh-yireh*;
 hence people *now* say, "On the *mountain* the LORD will *see*."

Again the LORD's messenger called to Abraham from *heaven*
 and said:
 "I *swear* by *myself*, declares the LORD,
 that because you acted as you *did*
 in not *withholding* from me your beloved *son*,
 I will *bless* you *abundantly*
 and make your *descendants* as *countless*
 as the *stars* of the *sky* and the *sands* of the *seashore*;
 your *descendants* shall take possession
 of the *gates* of their *enemies*,
 and *in* your descendants *all* the *nations* of the *earth*
 shall find *blessing*—
 all *this* because you *obeyed* my *command*."

[*Shorter: Genesis 22:1–2, 9a, 10–13, 15–18*]

The current selection follows immediately after Moses tries to reassure the people.

The Israelites know that Pharaoh's army is near, but God seems far away. But the divine presence is manifested when the two camps approach the sea. The presence of God in the angel and in the pillar of cloud separates the Egyptians from the Israelites and protects them, then strikes the Egyptians and frightens them. When Moses follows God's instructions, the waters of the sea open for the Israelites but close again over the army of Pharaoh.

The spectacular account of God's intervention during the flight from Egypt ends with a song of praise to God. It is appropriate for us to join our voices with those of the Israelites today, for God's promise to care for the Israelites gives glory to God and brings favor to the Israelites. In addition to giving God glory, the exodus event provides salvation for the Hebrew people and convinces them of the great power of God.

This key reading is understood by Christians as being especially important on this holy night, when we proclaim that Jesus has passed through death to life. In

addition, the Israelites' crossing of the sea is understood as an image of baptism, when the Christian passes through the waters to new life. Paul's understanding of baptism in his letter to the Romans, which follows shortly, speaks of dying in baptism with the promise of new life. Paul uses the exodus event to explain Christian baptism. For the Israelites and for Christians, going through the waters and leaving the former life behind acknowledges the salvation offered by God.

READING III   Exodus 14:15—15:1

A reading from the book of Exodus

The LORD said to *Moses,* "Why are you crying *out* to me?
Tell the *Israelites* to go *forward.*
And *you,* lift up your *staff* and, with hand *outstretched*
over the *sea,*
split the sea in *two,*
that the Israelites may pass *through* it on dry *land.*
But I will make the *Egyptians* so *obstinate*
that they will go in *after* them.
Then I will receive *glory* through *Pharaoh* and all his *army,*
his *chariots* and *charioteers.*
The *Egyptians* shall know that *I* am the LORD,
when I receive *glory* through *Pharaoh*
and his *chariots* and *charioteers.*"

The angel of *God,* who had been *leading* Israel's *camp,*
now *moved* and went around *behind* them.
The column of *cloud also,* leaving the *front,*
took up its place *behind* them,
so that it came *between* the camp of the *Egyptians*
and that of *Israel.*
But the *cloud* now became *dark,* and thus the night *passed*
without the rival *camps* coming any closer *together*
all night *long.*

Then Moses *stretched* out his *hand* over the *sea,*
and the LORD *swept* the sea
with a strong east *wind* throughout the *night*
and so turned it into dry *land.*

It is for God's glory that these events have been recorded. That is also the reason we recall them today.

The angel and the pillar of cloud had signified God's presence, leading the Israelites on the journey. Now they separate the Israelites from the Egyptians, offering protection and assistance.

Raise your voice and speak majestically of God's intervention.

There is a great deal of excitement in the story about the Israelites' flight from Egypt. Begin by speaking God's words forcefully; emphasize the glory that rightfully belongs to God. Let your voice reflect some of the anxiety that must have accompanied the Israelites as they passed through the sea, and allow it to grow in intensity until the Egyptians are finally vanquished. Speak triumphantly of the safety of the Israelites, and proclaim joyfully the victory song of the people.

The key theme of this reading is God's constant presence and care for the people, despite their grumbling. Offer it to your assembly as a commentary on God's continual care and the necessity of passing through tribulations, even death, on the path to true life.

READING IV Chapters 40–55 of Isaiah are often called Second Isaiah because they were written centuries after the prophet Isaiah was active. The prophet Isaiah had counseled the king of Judah when Jerusalem was threatened by the Assyrians. Second Isaiah comes from a time near the end of the Babylonian exile, when the people were eagerly awaiting the chance to return to their homeland. Jerusalem had been destroyed and its inhabitants led away, but they kept alive the hope that they would one day return. As the political events of the day indicated that the time was drawing near, a prophet wrote these reassuring words. God speaks of the exile as a time of punishment that is drawing to a

When the *water* was thus *divided*,
    the Israelites *marched* into the *midst* of the sea on dry *land*,
      with the water like a *wall* to their *right* and to their *left*.

Pick up the pace a bit, as the Egyptians follow in hot pursuit.

The *Egyptians* followed in *pursuit*;
    all Pharaoh's *horses* and *chariots* and *charioteers*
      went *after* them
right into the *midst* of the *sea*.
In the night *watch* just before *dawn*

This line can be tricky; prepare your phrasing well.

    the LORD *cast* through the *column* of the fiery *cloud*
    upon the Egyptian *force* a *glance* that threw it into a *panic*;
    and he so *clogged* their chariot *wheels*
    that they could hardly *drive*.

Two explanations are given for Pharaoh's defeat. Here the wheels of the chariots became clogged, but in the next paragraph the Egyptians drown when the waters return.

With *that* the Egyptians sounded the *retreat* before *Israel*,
    because the LORD was *fighting* for them against the *Egyptians*.

Then the LORD told *Moses*, "*Stretch* out your *hand* over the *sea*,
    that the water may flow *back* upon the *Egyptians*,
    upon their *chariots* and their *charioteers*."
So Moses *stretched* out his hand over the *sea*,
    and at *dawn* the sea flowed *back* to its normal *depth*.

Increase your speed here.

The Egyptians were fleeing *head on* toward the *sea*,
    when the LORD *hurled* them into its *midst*.
As the water flowed *back*,
    it covered the *chariots* and the *charioteers*
      of Pharaoh's whole *army*
    which had *followed* the Israelites into the *sea*.
Not a single *one* of them *escaped*.

This is spoken with satisfaction. The danger has passed.

But the *Israelites* had marched on dry *land*
    through the *midst* of the *sea*,
      with the water like a *wall* to their *right* and to their *left*.
Thus the LORD *saved* Israel on that day
    from the *power* of the *Egyptians*.

close. God also eagerly awaits the return of the chosen people to Jerusalem, to the holy mountain of Zion.

God speaks throughout today's reading, first as a husband filled with love for a wife he had abandoned. Brimming with compassion, he calls her back. God was angry, but the moment of anger was brief and has passed. The image of Israel as a bride of God is expressed most poignantly in another prophet, Hosea; there God is faithful always, despite Israel's waywardness. Here God seems to regret the momentary anger,

although elsewhere the exile is seen as a necessary period of instruction and testing.

God's word is forceful in the next section of the passage, as the author recalls the story of the flood in the days of Noah. At that time God also spoke, declaring never again to destroy the earth. Now the prophet proclaims that nothing can interfere with God's tremendous love for this people. Even if the mountains move and the hills quake, God will remember the covenant with Israel.

Finally, God addresses the city of Jerusalem directly. The city is lying in waste after the defeat by the Babylonians, and God promises to renew its splendor, decorating it with precious stones. Israel thought of the city of Zion as the one place that could not be defeated by the enemies of God. Even with Jerusalem in ruins, that hope is renewed here, for God will care for the city.

The people will also be renewed, taught by God and established in righteousness. In everything, God will offer protection and love.

When Israel saw the Egyptians lying *dead* on the *seashore*
and beheld the great *power* that the LORD
had *shown* against the *Egyptians*,
they *feared* the LORD and *believed* in him
and in his servant *Moses*.

Then *Moses* and the *Israelites* sang this *song* to the LORD:
I will *sing* to the LORD, for he is *gloriously triumphant*;
horse and *chariot* he has cast into the *sea*.

As will so often happen on this journey, Israel is in awe of God's tremendous deeds.

Speak this with great joy, giving glory to God.

READING IV   Isaiah 54:5–14

A reading from the book of the prophet Isaiah

The One who has become your *husband* is your *Maker*;
his name is the LORD of *hosts*;
your *redeemer* is the Holy One of *Israel*,
called *God* of all the *earth*.
The LORD calls you *back*,
like a wife *forsaken* and grieved in *spirit*,
a wife married in *youth* and then cast *off*,
says your God.

For a brief *moment* I *abandoned* you,
but with great *tenderness* I will take you *back*.
In an outburst of *wrath*, for a *moment*
I hid my *face* from you;
but with enduring *love* I take *pity* on you,
says the LORD, your *redeemer*.

Convey the intimacy of the relationship between God and Israel.

There is hope here, but sadness in the following lines.

Speak with regret.

Convey the tender love of God in a warm but firm voice.

Speak quietly but joyfully as you read these reassuring promises. Address this beautiful statement of God's commitment directly to the members of your assembly. Offer it as an assurance that God always wants to live in intimacy and love with this people. Remind them that times when God may seem distant are temporary, but God's love is eternal.

READING V | This passage from Isaiah follows almost immediately after the verses of the fourth reading. It is an invitation to eat and drink and be satisfied. It is offered to all, even to those who cannot afford to purchase the food necessary to prepare the feast. This food is available to anyone because it is not food for physical sustenance but nourishment for the spirit. Just as we often gather together to celebrate momentous occasions by sharing in a banquet, so also the banquet is spread here in order to invite people to consume the food of wisdom.

In fact, the invitation to come and eat sounds very much like the invitation of Wisdom in the book of Proverbs. There, Lady Wisdom entices her listeners, inviting them to share a meal with her and drawing them especially to embrace her and act always in accordance with her instruction.

A new idea begins here. Lift your voice as though starting afresh.

This is for me like the days of *Noah,*
  when I *swore* that the *waters* of Noah
  should *never again* deluge the *earth;*
so I have *sworn* not to be *angry* with you,
  or to *rebuke* you.
Though the *mountains* leave their *place*
  and the *hills* be *shaken,*
my *love* shall never *leave* you
  nor my covenant of *peace* be *shaken,*
  says the LORD, who has *mercy* on you.

Speak this as a solemn oath.

God speaks tenderly to Jerusalem.

Let your voice grow in intensity as you describe the majesty of Jerusalem.

O *afflicted* one, *storm*-battered and *unconsoled,*
  I lay your *pavements* in *carnelians,*
  and your *foundations* in *sapphires;*
I will make your *battlements* of *rubies,*
  your *gates* of *carbuncles,*
  and all your *walls* of precious *stones.*

Speak these final lines in a sure, commanding voice. They are a promise of peace and justice.

All your *children* shall be taught by the LORD,
  and *great* shall be the *peace* of your *children.*
In *justice* shall you be *established,*
  far from the *fear* of *oppression,*
  where *destruction* cannot come *near* you.

READING V   Isaiah 55:1–11

A reading from the book of the prophet Isaiah

Thus says the LORD:
All you who are *thirsty,*
  come to the *water!*
You who have no *money,*

Speak this invitation quietly but clearly. Stress "come" throughout the reading in a way that sounds like you are eager for the guests to arrive.

In today's passage, God invites a people living in exile to feast. The author recognizes that the end of the exile is near and the people will soon be restored to their homeland. The covenant that God established with David is still valid despite the exile; it will be renewed as an everlasting covenant. Israel will once again be a light to all the nations of the world.

One of the lessons of the exile was the necessity to repent for wrongdoing. God again invites the wicked to forsake their deeds, to turn to God and learn. All of Israel needs to hear this (as do we), and to recognize that God's ways are fundamentally different from the ways of humans. But those who listen to God's word will recognize this, for like the rain and the snow that cause the earth to produce vegetation, God's word is effective and brings forth new life.

We accept God's call today to come to the waters. We come not for physical refreshment, but to reaffirm our commitment to the one who provides life-giving water. For those in your community who are approaching the waters of baptism, as well as for those renewing their baptismal commitment, offer this selection as an invitation to approach with confidence and trust, knowing that God

Sound eager and encouraging. It is free!

These are reassuring words. Continue to sound inviting but in a firmer tone.

Speak these words with great promise.

Pause before beginning this line, and lower your voice again, gently urging your listeners to seek God.

This is meant to be encouraging, not disdainful. Do not give undue emphasis to "scoundrel."

Pause before this line, then speak with majesty.

come, receive *grain* and *eat*;
come, without *paying* and without *cost*,
   drink *wine* and *milk!*
Why spend your *money* for what is not *bread*,
   your *wages* for what fails to *satisfy*?
Heed me, and you shall eat *well*,
   you shall *delight* in rich *fare*.
Come to me *heedfully*,
   listen, that you may have *life*.
I will *renew* with you the everlasting *covenant*,
   the *benefits* assured to *David*.

As I made him a *witness* to the *peoples*,
   a *leader* and commander of *nations*,
so shall *you* summon a *nation* you knew *not*,
   and *nations* that knew you *not* shall *run* to you,
because of the LORD, your *God*,
   the *Holy* One of *Israel*, who has *glorified* you.

Seek the LORD while he may be *found*,
   call him while he is *near*.
Let the scoundrel *forsake* his *way*,
   and the wicked man his *thoughts*;
let him *turn* to the LORD for *mercy*;
   to our *God*, who is generous in *forgiving*.

For *my* thoughts are not *your* thoughts,
   nor are *your* ways *my* ways, says the LORD.
As *high* as the heavens are *above* the earth,
   so *high* are *my* ways above *your* ways
   and my *thoughts* above *your* thoughts.

will teach them and work through them. God has also spread a feast in the eucharist that we will soon share. Invite your community to partake of the sustenance that satisfies more than physical hunger. Read with a welcoming tone and a reassuring voice as you become the vessel through whom God's word is sown.

| READING VI | The book of Baruch, like Second Isaiah, was written in connection with Israel's exile in Babylon

and expresses a hope for return to the Promised Land. The present section is a poem in honor of wisdom, a pastiche of quotes from the Hebrew scriptures designed to draw the reader to recognize that wisdom is found in living according to the commandments of God.

The author begins by declaring that Israel's exile is a punishment for forsaking God and disobeying God's commands. Exile is such a humiliation that it can be compared with dwelling among the dead. Such is the destiny of those who abandon wisdom.

Wherever there is wisdom, there is strength and understanding, but also a long and happy life. Wisdom is a grammatically feminine term and is elsewhere personified as a woman. Yet wisdom is not easy to find. Fortunately for Israel, God has found her and given her as a gift to this chosen people.

Hebrew wisdom literature speaks of Lady Wisdom as the joint creator of the universe with God. Although that specific teaching is not present in this passage, it

This final section is a promise. It is one long complex sentence and will have to be carefully prepared. Read it slowly, knowing when you will pause for breath.

With "so shall" you begin the fulfillment of the promise. Pause before this line and speak it and what follows slowly and forcefully.

For *just* as from the *heavens*
    the *rain* and *snow* come *down*
and do not *return* there
    till they have *watered* the *earth,*
    making it *fertile* and *fruitful,*
giving *seed* to the one who *sows*
    and *bread* to the one who *eats,*
so shall my *word* be
    that goes *forth* from my *mouth;*
my *word* shall not return to me *void,*
    but shall do my *will,*
    achieving the *end* for which I *sent* it.

READING VI   Baruch 3:9–15, 32—4:4

Baruch = buh-ROOK

Speak as though a herald, calling from the rooftops.

Do not end this long question by raising your voice at the end. It is rhetorical; God knows how and why the people went into exile.

Here is the answer to the question. Speak it forcefully.

A reading from the book of the prophet Baruch

Hear, O Israel, the commandments of *life:*
    listen, and know *prudence!*
How *is* it, Israel,
    that you are in the *land* of your *foes,*
    grown *old* in a foreign *land,*
defiled with the *dead,*
    accounted with those *destined* for the *netherworld?*
You have *forsaken* the fountain of *wisdom!*
Had you *walked* in the way of *God,*
    you would have *dwelt* in enduring *peace.*

does recall the creation account in Genesis. The one who created the universe knows Wisdom and bestowed her upon Israel. Through this people she has dwelt on earth.

In a move that is somewhat surprising (developed to an even greater extent in the book of Sirach), Lady Wisdom is now identified with the Torah, the law given to Moses. The gift of wisdom is the same as the gift of the law. To keep the commandments of the law is to hold on to wisdom and to have life. Israel can rejoice in having received the law. Through it Israel knows how to please God.

Christians have long understood the reference to Lady Wisdom living on earth among humans to refer to the incarnate Son of God, Jesus. He is truly Wisdom, from whom we learn about God and ourselves. We embrace the gift God has given us in Jesus and pledge our commitment to hold fast to him, so that we might live.

This is both an invitation and a bold challenge to the members of your community. Speak in encouraging tones as you coax them ever closer to the source of all life and knowledge.

Lower your voice a bit and speak encouragingly.

Learn where *prudence* is,
    where *strength*, where *understanding*;
that you may know *also*
    where are length of *days*, and *life*,
    where *light* of the *eyes*, and *peace*.

Wisdom is hard to find.

Who has *found* the place of *wisdom*,
    who has *entered* into her *treasuries*?

The One who knows *all* things knows *her*;
    he has *probed* her by his *knowledge*—
the One who established the *earth* for all *time*,
    and *filled* it with four-footed *beasts*;

What follows is a brief recapitulation of the Genesis creation account. As in Genesis, God is the one in control of everything.

    he who *dismisses* the light, and it *departs*,
    calls it, and it *obeys* him *trembling*;
before whom the *stars* at their *posts*
    shine and *rejoice*;

The stars speak eagerly and joyfully.

when he *calls* them, they answer, "*Here* we *are!*"
    shining with *joy* for their *Maker*.

Such is our *God*;
    no *other* is to be *compared* to him:
he has *traced* out the *whole* way of *understanding*,

Pause before beginning this section, then read with great conviction.

    and has *given* her to *Jacob*, his *servant*,
    to *Israel*, his beloved *son*.

Since *then* she has appeared on *earth*,
    and *moved* among *people*.
She is the *book* of the *precepts* of *God*,
    the *law* that endures *forever*;

Israel believes that wisdom resides in the law.

all who *cling* to her will *live*,
    but those will *die* who *forsake* her.

Turn, O Jacob, and *receive* her:
    walk by her *light* toward *splendor*.

Slow your pace and speak tenderly, joyfully and encouragingly from here to the end.

READING VII Ezekiel was a prophet during the Babylonian exile. He rebukes Israel for its unfaithfulness to God, which resulted in the destruction of Jerusalem and the deportation of its leaders to a foreign land. Yet his is also a strong voice of hope that the exile would soon end and Israel would be restored.

The present passage is written entirely in God's words. God details the sins for which the punishment of the exile occurred. A new claim is added: The people in exile have profaned God's name simply by the fact that they are living in exile. God gave them a land, but the exile made it appear that God was unable to care for the chosen people as promised. As a result, God pledges to return them to their homeland regardless of their worthiness. Israel's God acts to protect the divine name, to display holiness for all the nations to see.

The passage closes with a beautiful promise that God will not only restore the people to the land but will also make them worthy, cleansing them and removing idols from among them. God vows to place within the people a new heart, a heart of flesh to replace their stone-cold heart. God will also put God's own spirit in them, instructing them in the correct ways to live.

See this selection both as a historical lesson and as a challenge to your listeners to recognize God's greatness and to pledge to live as God's people. Raise your voice to read the final fifteen or so lines—the promise of God to reestablish the people. Inspire your community to open its heart to God, to rejoice in its homecoming, and to be willing to live according to the statutes of God.

Give not your *glory* to *another*,
 your *privileges* to an alien *race*.
Blessed are *we*, O Israel;
 for what *pleases* God is *known* to us!

READING VII   Ezekiel 36:16–17a, 18–28

A reading from the book of the prophet Ezekiel

The *word* of the LORD came to me, saying:
 Son of *man*, when the house of *Israel* lived in their *land*,
 they *defiled* it by their *conduct* and *deeds*.
Therefore I poured out my *fury* upon them
 because of the *blood* that they poured out on the *ground*,
 and because they *defiled* it with *idols*.
I *scattered* them among the *nations*,
 dispersing them over foreign *lands*;
 according to their *conduct* and *deeds* I *judged* them.

But when they came among the *nations* wherever they *came*,
 they served to *profane* my holy *name*,
 because it was said of them: "*These* are the people of the LORD,
 yet they had to *leave* their *land*."

So I have *relented* because of my holy *name*
 which the house of *Israel profaned*
 among the *nations* where they *came*.
Therefore *say* to the house of *Israel: Thus* says the Lord GOD:
 Not for *your* sakes do I act, house of Israel,
 but for the sake of my holy *name*,
 which you *profaned* among the *nations* to which you *came*.

"Son of man" simply refers to someone who is human. It is God's favorite form of address to Ezekiel.

Lower your voice and let anger enter into it as you express God's wrath.

Let "scattered" sound like what it means.

Give emphasis to the statement about profaning God's name. As if their lawless deeds were not enough, the exile itself sullied God's name.

Pause before this line and then speak calmly and reassuringly.

Speak forcefully, increasing your volume.

EPISTLE   In keeping with his emphasis on the cross of Christ, Paul's classic treatment of baptism also emphasizes the death of Christ and the believer's share in that death. In baptism, the old self is left behind, indeed crucified, in order to embrace the promise of a new life. And the resurrection is, for Paul, always a future hope, something to be sought.

On this night, we begin our celebration in the darkness of death. But we are expectant and hopeful, knowing that our Lord is risen. Tonight we welcome into our community new members who have long been preparing for this day. We recall as well our own baptism and renew our baptismal promises. It is fitting that we be reminded of Paul's understanding of baptism and reflect on its significance in our lives.

It is your task tonight to remind the members of your community of their baptismal pledge to leave sin behind. Urge them also to look forward, as does Paul, to the promise of being united with Christ in his resurrection. Proclaiming that Christ is risen allows us also to acknowledge that we shall rise with him.

This passage is not easy to proclaim and will require careful preparation. Stress the central concepts and terms: death, life, resurrection, freedom from sin. Close by offering Paul's exhortation to the Romans to be alive in Christ Jesus as a direct appeal to your own community.

This is a solemn promise.

I will prove the *holiness* of my great *name*,
    profaned among the *nations*,
in whose *midst* you have *profaned* it.
Thus the *nations* shall know that *I* am the LORD,
    says the Lord GOD,
when in their *sight* I prove my *holiness* through *you*.

The emphasis returns to what God will do for Israel. Speak with comfort.

For I will take you *away* from among the *nations*,
    gather you from all the foreign *lands*,
and bring you *back* to your own *land*.

The sprinkling of water symbolizes purity. It reminds Christians of baptism.

I will sprinkle clean *water upon* you
    to *cleanse* you from all your *impurities*,
and from all your *idols* I will *cleanse* you.

Speak tenderly and encouragingly.

I will give you a new *heart* and place a new *spirit within* you,
    taking from your bodies your *stony* hearts
and giving you *natural* hearts.
I will put my spirit *within* you and make you *live* by my *statutes*,
    careful to *observe* my *decrees*.

Close with a tone of solemn satisfaction.

You shall *live* in the land I gave your *fathers*;
    you shall be my *people*, and *I* will be your *God*.

EPISTLE   Romans 6:3–11

A reading from the letter of Saint Paul to the Romans

Brothers and sisters:
Are you *unaware* that we who were *baptized* into Christ *Jesus*
    were *baptized* into his *death*?

This is a rhetorical question and can be read either with or without raising your voice at the end.

GOSPEL The gospel of Luke (together with its sequel, the Acts of the Apostles) has a unique approach to the significance of Jesus and the events of his life. Instead of being understood simply as an itinerant Jewish preacher in Roman Palestine, the author of Luke sees Jesus as a person with a message of significance for the entire world. Although he was born and lived in a particular place and time, his life and death change all of history. Although sent to the Jewish people, the chosen race,

he offers life to members of every nation. At the same time, the author of the gospel proclaims the centrality of the promises of God to the Jews and the importance of the holy city of Jerusalem. From this people and this place comes the promise of salvation and life for all people.

The story of Christ's triumph over death—the defining moment in salvation history—is told also from this unique perspective in the gospel of Luke. All of the appearances of Jesus in the gospel of Luke occur in or near Jerusalem. Before his ascension (as described at the beginning of the

Acts of the Apostles), Jesus commissions the community of disciples to be his witnesses first in Jerusalem and then to the ends of the earth. Jerusalem is the center of the earth, the source of the message of everlasting significance. And Easter is the dawn of a new age.

The proclamation of Jesus' resurrection and the story of the empty tomb, told in today's gospel passage, together with the story of Jesus' ascension, are the chief

We were indeed *buried* with him through *baptism* into *death*,
    so that, just as Christ was *raised* from the *dead*
    by the *glory* of the *Father*,
    we *too* might live in *newness* of *life*.

This is the hope that Paul has; lighten your voice and read with an expectant expression.

For if we have grown into *union* with him
    through a *death* like his,
    we shall also be *united* with him in the *resurrection*.
We know that our *old* self was *crucified* with him,
    so that our sinful *body* might be done *away* with,
    that we might no *longer* be in *slavery* to *sin*.
For a *dead* person has been *absolved* from sin.
If, then, we have *died* with Christ,
    we believe that we shall also *live* with him.

Paul begins with what is past and moves on to the hope of sharing life with Christ. Stress the contrasts.

We know that *Christ*, *raised* from the dead, dies no *more*;
    death no longer has *power* over him.
As to his *death*, he died to sin *once* and for *all*;
    as to his *life*, he lives for *God*.
Consequently, you *too* must think of yourselves
    as being *dead* to *sin*
    and *living* for *God* in Christ *Jesus*.

Speak with firm conviction.

Make all of the contrasts clear.

GOSPEL   Luke 24:1–12

A reading from the holy gospel according to Luke

At *daybreak* on the *first* day of the *week*
    the *women* who had come from *Galilee* with Jesus
    took the *spices* they had *prepared*
    and went to the *tomb*.

---

means by which the author conveys the central Christian belief that Jesus has conquered death and is glorified with God. The humiliation and agony of the passion give way to the glory of the resurrection. An intense light dispels all darkness, and Jesus' followers are able to see once again.

This was not all immediately clear to Jesus' friends, however, as the confusion of the women and the disbelief of the male apostles makes clear. In the accounts of Jesus' appearances to his friends, he must explain to them the necessity for his death before they are able to acknowledge that he

is risen. He is changed beyond their ability to recognize him. But he is also the same person they once knew, and he reveals himself in the familiar ritual of sharing a meal.

Today's selection opens with the story of the female disciples from Galilee who had been with Jesus until the end and had seen where his body was laid. They arrive to perform a burial ritual in order to honor their friend. To their amazement, they are able to enter the tomb with ease, but do not see

Jesus' body. They apparently recognize the men in dazzling garments as angelic messengers because they bow in homage and understandable astonishment. The messengers offer the central proclamation that stirs our hearts on this day: The living one has no place among the dead. Death has been conquered, and its companion—sin—has been vanquished. Evil has been overcome by the powerful forces of good, embodied in the broken flesh of this man from Galilee. God is triumphant.

They found the *stone* rolled *away* from the tomb;
  but when they *entered*,
  they did not find the *body* of the Lord *Jesus*.

Let your voice express astonishment and awe.

While they were *puzzling* over this, *behold*,
  two *men* in dazzling *garments appeared* to them.
They were *terrified* and bowed their *faces* to the *ground*.
They said to them,
  "Why do you seek the *living* one among the *dead*?

Pause before this line. Then read slowly and forcefully.

He is not *here*, but he has been *raised*.
Remember what he *said* to you while he was still in *Galilee*,
  that the Son of *Man* must be handed over to *sinners*
  and be *crucified*, and *rise* on the third *day*."
And they *remembered* his *words*.

Then they *returned* from the tomb
  and announced *all* these things to the *eleven*
  and to all the *others*.
The women were Mary *Magdalene*, *Joanna*,
    and Mary the mother of *James*;
  the *others* who accompanied them *also* told this
    to the apostles,

The number of women present is unclear. There were several more than those named.

  but their *story* seemed like *nonsense*
  and they did not *believe* them.

But *Peter* got up and ran to the *tomb*,
  bent *down*, and saw the burial cloths *alone*;

Read this line with awe.

  then he went home *amazed* at what had *happened*.

The messengers remind the women that Jesus had spoken of the necessity of his suffering, but had foreseen that his humiliation would not be the final word. In their excitement, they run to tell the others, but the news is too much. The others must see for themselves. Peter sees the empty tomb himself; others will observe Jesus' wounds and talk with him. From this point forward, all is changed.

The task of proclaiming this gospel passage is both joyful and awesome. In this liturgy, we listen to the stories of God's action throughout history. We reflect on the significance of our own initiation into the mysteries and will soon welcome new members. And most of all we proclaim that God acts most fully in the person of Jesus, offering life and wholeness to a broken world. Today, after the deafening silence of recent weeks, the gospel proclamation is preceded by the return of the "Alleluia" in all its joy-filled splendor. In majestic procession, the gospel is brought before the assembly, which awaits the word with eager anticipation.

Approach this text with the recognition that it is the climactic proclamation of the liturgical year. Prepare carefully, so that you will be able to offer it with power and enthusiasm. God is speaking through you a message of victory. Proclaim it forcefully, so that you might be able to draw your entire assembly into praise for God's goodness and glory.

EASTER SUNDAY

Lectionary #42

READING I Acts 10:34a, 37–43

A reading from the Acts of the Apostles

Peter proceeded to *speak* and said:
"*You know* what has happened all over *Judea*,
    beginning in *Galilee* after the baptism
    that *John* preached,
    how God *anointed* Jesus of *Nazareth*
    with the *Holy Spirit* and *power.*
He went about doing *good*
    and *healing* all those oppressed by the *devil*,
    for God was *with* him.

"We are *witnesses* of all that he *did*
    both in the country of the *Jews* and in *Jerusalem.*
They put him to *death* by hanging him on a *tree.*
This man God *raised* on the third *day* and granted
        that he be *visible,*
    not to *all* the people, but to *us*,
    the *witnesses* chosen by God in *advance,*
    who *ate* and *drank* with him after he *rose* from the *dead.*

"He *commissioned* us to *preach* to the people
    and *testify* that he is the one appointed by *God*
    as *judge* of the *living* and the *dead.*
To *him* all the prophets bear *witness,*
    that everyone who *believes* in him
    will receive *forgiveness* of sins through his *name.*"

Peter's speech begins here. Lift your voice and speak slowly, especially at the beginning, in order to make this sound like a speech.

Pause.

Here is the core of the Christian faith. Emphasize it, especially stressing "raised."

Everyone who believes—both Jew and Gentile—will receive the salvation wrought by Jesus.

READING I The speech of Peter to the household of Cornelius, the first Gentiles to be included among the followers of Christ, contains in a nutshell the truths of the Christian faith. Peter speaks about the ministry of Jesus on earth, as well as the core of Christian faith—Jesus' death and resurrection and his appearances to the disciples—and closes with a statement of belief in Christ as the heavenly judge in whom sins are forgiven. It is appropriate to proclaim this message on this central feast of our liturgical year.

Peter's speech follows his realization that the salvation offered in Christ is available to all people, Jews and Gentiles alike. He also claims to be a witness to Jesus' ministry, as well as to Jesus' death, and claims to have experienced the risen Jesus. The author makes it clear that Peter's testimony is reliable.

The command to preach about Jesus paves the way for the readings at our liturgies during the Easter season. In the coming weeks, we will hear about the early growth of the new community of believers and will be challenged to share the message of the risen Christ with those we meet.

Read this speech as a direct proclamation to your assembly. It provides you with a chance to remind your listeners of the core of their faith, a faith based on the testimony of prophets, apostles and "everyone who believes in him."

READING II   Colossians 3:1–4

A reading from the letter of Saint Paul to the Colossians

Brothers and sisters:
If then you were *raised* with Christ, seek what is *above*,
    where Christ is *seated* at the *right hand* of *God*.
Think of what is *above*, *not* of what is on *earth*.
For you have *died*, and your life is *hidden* with Christ in *God*.
When *Christ* your life *appears*,
    then you *too* will appear with him in *glory*.

Or:

READING II   1 Corinthians 5:6b–8

A reading from the first letter of Saint Paul to the Corinthians

Brothers and sisters:
Do you not *know* that a *little* yeast leavens *all* the *dough*?
Clear *out* the *old* yeast,
    so that you may become a *fresh* batch of dough,
    inasmuch as you are *unleavened*.
For our paschal *lamb*, *Christ*, has been *sacrificed*.
Therefore, let us *celebrate* the feast,
    not with the *old* yeast, the yeast of *malice* and *wickedness*,
    but with the *unleavened* bread of *sincerity* and *truth*.

Challenge your listeners to set their sights on heavenly goals.

The ideas progress quickly here. Pause before continuing.

Pause again.

Speak with enthusiasm.

There is a choice of second readings today. Speak with the liturgy coordinator or pastor to find out which reading will be used.

READING II   **COLOSSIANS.** For Paul, resurrection is always in the future. But here, in an apparent reference to the experience of baptism, the author (an admirer of Paul who wrote in his name) claims that the Christian has already been raised with Christ. "You have died"— probably in the waters of baptism, but surely to a past sinful life—and must therefore live as one who is already sharing in the heavenly life of Christ enthroned with God. The splendor of resurrected life is not yet revealed to all but will be when Christ appears in glory.

Offer this exhortation to your community as it was first offered to the Colossians: Encourage your listeners to strive for high goals in their behavior, remembering always that they have a share in the life available in Christ.

1 CORINTHIANS. Paul exhorts the Corinthians to live new, pure lives by referring to the feast of Passover and using the metaphor of leavened and unleavened bread. Even Gentiles would understand the domestic metaphor, although they probably did not understand leaven to be impure as the Jews did.

Paul assumes that his readers understand the way yeast or leaven is used: A small amount of leavened dough is saved and used to start a new loaf, providing the agent that will make the new dough rise. If left too long, the dough will ferment too much and begin to smell. Unleavened bread,

GOSPEL   John 20:1–9

A reading from the holy gospel according to John

Magdala = MAG-duh-luh

The passage began quietly, but the pace picks up with this line. Increase your speed slightly and allow your voice to indicate amazement.

Mary is a bit distraught; reflect this in your voice.

On the *first* day of the week,
　　Mary of *Magdala* came to the *tomb early* in the morning,
　　while it was still *dark*,
　　and saw the *stone removed* from the tomb.
So she *ran* and went to Simon *Peter*
　　and to the *other* disciple whom Jesus *loved*, and *told* them,
　　"They have taken the *Lord* from the *tomb*,
　　and we don't know *where* they *put* him."

So *Peter* and the *other* disciple went out and came to the *tomb*.
They both *ran*, but the *other* disciple ran *faster* than Peter
　　and arrived at the tomb *first*;
　　he bent *down* and *saw* the burial cloths there, but did
　　　not go in.

When Simon *Peter* arrived *after* him,
　　he went *into* the tomb and saw the *burial* cloths there,
　　and the *cloth* that had covered his *head*,
　　not with the burial cloths but rolled up in a *separate* place.
Then the *other* disciple *also* went in,
　　the one who had arrived at the tomb *first*,
　　and he *saw* and *believed*.

Emphasize this line; read slowly and forcefully.

For they did not yet *understand* the Scripture
　　that he had to *rise* from the *dead*.

---

in contrast, is a flat bread whose dough does not rise. Every Passover, Jews discard all yeast products from their homes and prepare unleavened bread, just as the Israelites did before fleeing Egypt.

　　Paul suggests that the moral life of the Christian is like the dough used to make bread. Wicked thoughts and actions can mushroom, negatively affecting a person or an entire community. Paul encourages the Corinthians to be like unleavened bread,

free of any undesirable qualities. The mention of unleavened bread reminds him of the feast of Passover, when Jesus was crucified and became the "paschal lamb," the one who brought freedom through his death.

　　Encourage your community to purify itself this Easter season and to recognize the new life available to it. We too are celebrating the feast on which our paschal lamb gave us life; let us live in a manner worthy of our calling.

> The gospel from the Easter Vigil may be read at any Mass on Easter Sunday, at any time of the day. The gospel for the Third Sunday of Easter, Year A, may be used at an afternoon or evening Mass (see lectionary #46).

GOSPEL | The gospel of John recounts several appearances of the risen Jesus to his followers. They, together with the witness of the empty tomb, provide touching, powerful testimony to our Easter proclamation: Jesus is risen. Alleluia!

Lectionary #46

AFTERNOON GOSPEL   Luke 24:13–35

A reading from the holy gospel according to Luke

That *very* day, the *first* day of the *week*,
   two of Jesus' *disciples* were going
   to a *village* seven miles from *Jerusalem* called *Emmaus*,
   and they were *conversing* about *all* the things
     that had *occurred.*
And it happened that while they were *conversing* and *debating,*
   Jesus himself *drew near* and walked *with* them,
   but their eyes were *prevented* from *recognizing* him.

He asked them,
   "What are you *discussing* as you walk *along?"*
They *stopped,* looking *downcast.*
One of them, named *Cleopas,* said to him in reply,
   "Are you the *only* visitor to Jerusalem
   who does not *know* of the things
   that have taken *place* there in these *days?"*

And he replied to them, "What *sort* of things?"
They said to him,
   "The things that happened to *Jesus* the *Nazarene,*
   who was a *prophet* mighty in *deed* and *word*
   before *God* and all the *people,*
   how our *chief priests* and *rulers* both *handed* him *over*
   to a sentence of *death* and *crucified* him.
But *we* were *hoping* that he would be the one to redeem *Israel;*
   and besides all this,
   it is now the *third* day since this took *place.*

Emmaus = eh-MAY-uhs

All the resurrection appearances of Jesus indicate that he had been transformed; he was no longer easily recognizable.

Jesus' question seems innocent, but the response is one of frustration and sorrow.

Cleopas = KLEE-oh-puhs

They recognized him as a prophet and had hoped that he was the Messiah.

Mary Magdalene, remembered in many sources as an especially close friend of Jesus and the first to encounter the risen Christ in the gospel of John, approaches the tomb but runs away when she sees that the stone has been removed. Understandably, she believes that the body has been stolen. Peter and the beloved disciple (probably John), the most prominent of the Twelve in this gospel, follow. Although the author indicates that the beloved disciple "saw and believed," the statement that the disciples did not yet understand that Jesus was to rise from the dead, as well as the witness of the other gospels, suggests that the women—in this gospel, Mary Magdalene—were the first to encounter both the empty tomb and the risen Lord.

The story of Peter and the beloved disciple racing to the tomb is exciting. This gospel passage moves quickly, with much to catch the assembly's attention. Read it as though for the first time, and make the story come alive with your telling. This reading provides not only a testimony of faith to the resurrection of Jesus, but most of all shows the tender love shared by Jesus and his followers.

AFTERNOON GOSPEL The story of the encounter between Jesus and two of his disciples on the road to Emmaus is touching, inspiring and revealing. It recounts the disciples' sadness and confusion in the beginning, their joy at recognizing Jesus, and their need to

Women were clearly members of the group of Jesus' disciples and were the first to recognize that Jesus had risen.

Some *women* from our group, however, have *astounded* us:
    they were at the tomb *early* in the morning
    and did *not* find his *body*;
    they came *back* and *reported*
    that they had indeed seen a *vision* of *angels*
    who announced that he was *alive.*

"Then *some* of those with us *went* to the tomb
    and found things *just* as the women had *described,*
    but *him* they did not *see.*"

Speak Jesus' words with tired sadness and a bit of frustration.

Although we know the answer, speak this as a real question.

And he said to them, "Oh, how *foolish* you are!
How *slow* of heart to believe *all* that the prophets *spoke!*
Was it not necessary that the *Christ* should *suffer* these things
    and *enter* into his *glory*?"

Then beginning with *Moses* and all the *prophets,*
    he *interpreted* to them what *referred* to him
    in all the *Scriptures.*
As they *approached* the village to which they were *going,*
    he gave the impression that he was going on *farther.*
But they urged him, "*Stay* with us,
    for it is nearly *evening* and the day is almost *over.*"
So he went in to *stay* with them.

And it happened that, while he was *with* them at *table,*
    he took *bread,* said the *blessing,*
    broke it, and *gave* it to them.

Speak with amazement. It is through sharing food that the disciples come to know who their companion is.

With *that* their eyes were *opened* and they *recognized* him,
    but he *vanished* from their sight.

Then they said to each other,
    "Were not our hearts *burning within* us
    while he spoke to us on the *way* and opened the *Scriptures*
      to us?"

---

understand what the prophets had said about him, as well their recognition of his presence in their lives. It is written for Christians of any age or era, and provides inspiration for embracing an Easter faith.

On the first Easter, two disciples discuss all they have experienced. The gospel writer suggests that the events of the crucifixion and death of Jesus were known to the residents of Jerusalem and to the pilgrims who had traveled there for the Passover festival. The two proceed to tell Jesus about himself: his deeds in life, their belief in him as a prophet, and his death, which crushed their hopes that he was the Messiah. Even though they knew the story of the empty tomb and of angels saying that Jesus was alive, they did not understand its meaning. They were clearing pondering these matters as they walked along the road.

When Jesus appears to them as a stranger and explains the scriptures to them, they experience their hearts "burning within" them. The disciples' need to have Jesus' mission explained to them suggests how important it is to comprehend the faith in order to believe truly. Education is imperative in order to have informed believers who really understand what they claim. But knowing that the prophets had predicted all that had to happen to the Messiah is not enough for these disciples. It is only through a personal encounter with Jesus that their faith is able to come to life.

There is great excitement in this announcement. Apparently the male disciples, previously unwilling to believe the women, now accept what Peter says.

End on a quiet note.

So they set out at *once* and returned to *Jerusalem*
    where they found gathered *together*
    the *eleven* and those with them who were *saying,*
    "The *Lord* has truly been *raised* and has appeared to *Simon!*"

Then the *two* recounted
    what had taken *place* on the *way*
    and how he was made *known* to them in the *breaking* of *bread.*

Although Jesus appears to be continuing through the village, the disciples reach out to him in hospitality, inviting him to join them for a meal. It is this meal encounter that finally opens their eyes. Sharing in something as ordinary as a meal provides a powerful opportunity for enlightenment to occur. It is for this reason that we gather to share the eucharist: to read the scriptures, to teach and understand, and finally to recognize Jesus in the breaking of the bread.

Your task today is made particularly enjoyable by the interesting, exciting story you are privileged to share with your community. Read it with plenty of expression, conveying the diciples' surprise that the stranger did not know about the events that had recently occurred. Express the disciples' disappointment and Jesus' exasperation at their lack of understanding, and finally the joy of the encounter and of the other disciples. Offer the story to your community as a loving challenge to recognize Jesus in its midst, especially in the eucharist and the assembly gathered to share it.

2ND SUNDAY OF EASTER

Lectionary #45

READING I   Acts 5:12–16

A reading from the Acts of the Apostles

Speak with awe.

Many *signs* and *wonders* were done among the people
    at the *hands* of the *apostles*.
They were *all together* in Solomon's *portico*.
None of the others dared to *join* them, but the people
    esteemed them.

Emphasize the large numbers of new converts.

Yet more than *ever*, believers in the *Lord*,
    great *numbers* of men and women, were *added* to them.
Thus they even carried the *sick* out into the *streets*
    and laid them on *cots* and *mats*
    so that when *Peter* came by,
    at least his *shadow* might fall on *one* or *another* of them.

Close with a note of triumph.

A large number of *people* from the towns
    in the *vicinity* of Jerusalem *also* gathered,
    bringing the *sick* and those disturbed by unclean *spirits*,
    and they were all *cured*.

READING I   The author of the Acts of the Apostles characterizes the earliest days of the Christian community as a period of harmony and success in preaching the gospel. Continuing in the manner of Jesus, the believers are able to heal the sick and those possessed by demons. In addition, as faithful Jews, they continue to pray and gather in the area of the temple in Jerusalem, just as Jesus had.

Peter's prominence in the Acts of the Apostles is seen in this passage in his ability to heal without even touching the sick person. Peter becomes the mouthpiece for the author's message that Jesus is the fulfillment of God's promises to Israel and is the savior of the world.

Apparently because of their healing ministry, many people from Jerusalem and the surrounding area come to visit the followers of Jesus and become believers.

Although there are some tensions in this early community, the gospel is always triumphant and new believers in the risen Jesus abound. The Christian community is expanding, both in numbers and in space, extending into the towns around Jerusalem.

Speak triumphantly yet contentedly as you recount the success of the first followers of Jesus.

READING II   Revelation 1:9–11a, 12–13, 17–19

"Revelation," not "Revelations."

Patmos = PAT-muhs

Speak with wonder at this vision.

The risen Christ offers words of comfort but also speaks with authority.

A reading from the book of Revelation

I, *John*, your *brother*, who share with you
    the *distress*, the *kingdom*, and the *endurance* we have
        in *Jesus*,
    found myself on the island called *Patmos*
    because I proclaimed God's *word* and gave *testimony* to Jesus.
I was caught up in *spirit* on the *Lord's* day
    and heard behind me a *voice* as loud as a *trumpet*, which said,
    "Write on a *scroll* what you *see*."

Then I turned to see whose *voice* it was that *spoke* to me,
    and when I *turned*, I saw seven gold *lampstands*
    and in the *midst* of the lampstands one like a *son* of *man*,
    wearing an ankle-length *robe*, with a gold *sash*
        around his *chest*.

When I caught *sight* of him, I fell down at his *feet* as though *dead*.
He *touched* me with his right hand and said, "Do *not* be *afraid*.
I am the *first* and the *last*, the one who *lives*.
Once I was *dead*, but now I am *alive forever* and *ever*.
I hold the keys to *death* and the *netherworld*.
Write *down*, therefore, what you have *seen*,
    and what is *happening*, and what will happen *afterwards*."

READING II John, the author of the book of Revelation, here recounts his ecstatic experience of being commissioned by God to proclaim individual messages to seven churches. They are messages of correction and instruction, as well as encouragement.

John writes to others who share his belief in Christ but who also know the reality of persecution. He was presumably exiled to the island of Patmos because of his faith in the "word" of God and the "testimony" of Jesus.

On the "Lord's day," Sunday, John has a vision in which he receives the command to write what he sees. He also encounters a glorified human figure who inspires great awe. John's description of the glorified person is reminiscent of the human figure from the book of Daniel who is given dominion over all the earth. Although John falls to the ground in awe, the glorified person encourages him. This person then describes himself as the "first" and the "last," one who

was dead but now lives, and one who even controls the entrances to the regions of the dead. John depicts Christ as having all authority; he is judge of the world and even wears clothes that designate him priest and king.

This exalted one instructs John to proclaim the present situation of the church—the reality of persecution, the faithfulness or the errors of each community—as well as its future. For the seven churches, what is coming immediately is a period of greater testing that carries with it the opportunity to "conquer." In the end, the entire book of

GOSPEL   John 20:19–31

A reading from the holy gospel according to John

On the *evening* of that *first* day of the *week,*
  when the doors were *locked,* where the *disciples* were,
  for fear of the Jews,
  Jesus came and stood in their *midst*
  and said to them, "*Peace* be with *you.*"
When he had *said* this, he showed them his *hands* and his *side.*
The disciples *rejoiced* when they saw the *Lord.*
Jesus said to them again, "*Peace* be with *you.*
As the *Father* has sent *me,* so *I* send *you.*"

And when he had *said* this, he *breathed* on them and said
    to them,
  "*Receive* the Holy *Spirit.*
Whose *sins* you forgive are *forgiven* them,
  and whose sins you *retain* are *retained.*"

Thomas, called *Didymus,* one of the *Twelve,*
  was not *with* them when Jesus *came.*
So the *other* disciples said to him, "We have *seen* the *Lord.*"
But he said to them,
  "Unless I see the mark of the *nails* in his *hands*
  and put my *finger* into the *nailmarks*
  and put my *hand* into his *side,* I will not *believe.*"

Now a week *later* his disciples were *again* inside
  and Thomas was *with* them.
Jesus came, although the doors were *locked,*
  and stood in their midst and said, "*Peace* be with *you.*"

Speak Jesus' words with genuine peacefulness and tenderness in your voice.

Didymus = DID-ih-muhs

The other disciples are ecstatic.

Thomas is hesitant; he does not want to be misled by idle tales.

Again, offer Jesus' words with gentleness.

Revelation speaks of the triumph of Christ and those who remain faithful.

The book of Revelation, with its fantastic images and bizarre figures, inspires awe in its readers. Draw on that sense of wonder as you share this passage with your assembly. Read the words of the exalted figure with authority.

GOSPEL The stories of the appearances of the risen Jesus in the gospel of John differ somewhat from those found elsewhere. In all the resurrection accounts, Jesus is changed and must

make himself known, even to his intimate companions. In this scene, Jesus is able to walk through closed doors, a feature unknown to the other gospel writers, and he reveals himself not by sharing a meal with his followers but by showing the marks of his wounds and greeting his friends with a message of peace.

The hallmark of the presence of the risen Jesus is his gift of the Spirit to his disciples. After initially cowering in fear, the disciples are strengthened to preach the

good news through the power of the Spirit. Jesus commissions them to go forth, and they are given the authority to forgive or retain sins. This scene provides us with the Johannine vision of the origin of the Christian community, the body of believers in the risen Lord that is sent forth to preach and serve in the power of the Spirit.

The story of Thomas follows the initial account of Jesus' appearance to his followers. Thomas was absent when Jesus came to inspire (literally, "breathe into") his followers to belief in him. As a result, Thomas finds it hard to accept what the others tell

Thomas is awestruck.

This is offered to your community.

Then he said to *Thomas*, "Put your finger *here* and see my *hands*,
    and bring *your* hand and put it into my *side*,
    and do not be *unbelieving*, but *believe*."
Thomas answered and said to him, "My *Lord* and my *God*!"

Jesus said to him, "Have you come to *believe*
    because you have *seen* me?
Blessed are those who have *not* seen and have *believed*."

Now Jesus did many *other* signs in the presence of his disciples
    that are *not* written in this *book*.
But *these* are written that you may come to *believe*
    that *Jesus* is the *Christ*, the Son of *God*,
    and that through this *belief* you may have *life* in his *name*.

him. He does not stubbornly refuse to believe the obvious but, like so many of us, does not want to be misled by easy answers or mere gossip. He tries to assess the validity of the claims being made and, because the disciples' story seems so unlikely, he needs to see for himself. Just as Mary Magdalene was told by Jesus at the empty tomb not to touch him, so also Thomas does not actually touch Jesus, although Jesus invites him to do so. In the end, what opens Thomas' eyes is not the proof he had said he needed but rather the entire encounter with the risen Lord.

Thomas' experience is much like our own; we want to believe but have never actually heard the risen Jesus speak or seen him in the flesh. In the story about Thomas, however, the author proclaims that even those who are removed from the events he describes and who have not personally known Jesus can still believe in him. Thomas' statement of confession ("My Lord and my God") vindicates him and erases his doubt; it is one of the strongest statements of the divinity of Jesus in the New Testament.

Read this exciting story with plenty of expression. Give Thomas a strong voice as he first insists on empirical evidence and especially when he proclaims his faith. Allow Jesus to speak directly to your assembly the blessing on those who have not seen and yet believe.

3RD SUNDAY OF EASTER

Lectionary #48

READING I   Acts 5:27b–32, 40b–41

A reading from the Acts of the Apostles

When the *captain* and the court *officers* had brought
   the apostles *in*
and made them stand before the *Sanhedrin*,
the high priest *questioned* them,
"We gave you strict *orders*, did we *not*,
to stop *teaching* in that *name*?
Yet you have *filled* Jerusalem with your *teaching*
and want to bring this man's *blood* upon *us*."

But Peter and the apostles said in reply,
"We must obey *God* rather than *men*.
The God of our *ancestors* raised *Jesus*,
   though you had him *killed* by hanging him on a *tree*.
God *exalted* him at his *right hand* as *leader* and *savior*
   to grant Israel *repentance* and forgiveness of *sins*.
We are *witnesses* of these things,
   as is the Holy *Spirit* whom God has given to those who
     obey him."

The Sanhedrin *ordered* the apostles
   to stop speaking in the name of *Jesus*, and *dismissed* them.
So they *left* the presence of the Sanhedrin,
   rejoicing that they had been found *worthy*
   to suffer *dishonor* for the sake of the *name*.

Sanhedrin = san-HEE-druhn

Speak Peter's words with boldness and conviction.

Draw attention to Jesus' name, which carries power and inspires faithfulness.

READING I The rosy picture of the early church painted in the first part of the Acts of the Apostles begins to darken. Not all goes well for these first followers of Jesus, as they continue to teach and preach in the area of the temple in Jerusalem. They attract the ire of the temple leaders and are brought before the Sanhedrin, the Jewish legal council. The high priest understands their teaching to implicate the religious leaders in the death of Jesus.

Although several of the apostles are arrested, it is Peter, the hero of the first part of the Acts of the Apostles, who acts as their mouthpiece. Peter was also the one who spoke for the believers before the Sanhedrin when they were arrested the first time for preaching the resurrection of the dead. At that time, they were thrown into prison and ordered not to teach in the name of Jesus. They violated that order and so were arrested again.

In today's passage, Peter proclaims that Jesus was raised from the dead and exalted to the right hand of God. After a council member suggests adopting a wait-and-see attitude (in intervening verses not found in today's reading), the apostles are again released and rejoice to have suffered for the name of Jesus.

Jesus' name of has profound power; it is teaching in his name that gets the disciples into trouble in the first place. By speaking Jesus' name the apostles are able to heal the sick. Jesus' name has an authority and power that goes beyond simply a memory of him; it is active and forceful. The Sanhedrin recognizes the power of the name and orders that it not be spoken.

READING II   Revelation 5:11–14

A reading from the book of Revelation

I, *John*, *looked* and *heard* the voices of many *angels*
    who surrounded the *throne*
    and the living *creatures* and the *elders*.
They were *countless* in number, and they cried out
      in a loud *voice*:
    "*Worthy* is the *Lamb* that was *slain*
    to receive *power* and *riches, wisdom* and *strength,*
    honor and *glory* and *blessing*."

Then I heard every creature in *heaven* and on *earth*
    and *under* the earth and in the *sea,*
    everything in the *universe,* cry out:
    "To the one who sits on the *throne* and to the *Lamb*
    be *blessing* and *honor, glory* and *might,*
    forever and *ever*."
The four living creatures answered, "*Amen,*"
    and the *elders* fell down and *worshiped*.

GOSPEL   John 21:1–19

A reading from the holy gospel according to John

At *that* time, Jesus revealed himself *again* to his disciples
    at the Sea of *Tiberias*.
He revealed himself in *this* way.
Together were Simon *Peter, Thomas* called Didymus,
    Nathanael from Cana in Galilee,
    Zebedee's sons, and two *others* of his disciples.

As you read this selection, emphasize the importance of Jesus' name in the charges brought against the apostles and in their response. Proclaim Peter's speech boldly.

READING II   The seer John continues to describe his heavenly vision, a description that we will read throughout the season of Easter. Today's passage follows upon John's vision of the Lamb who has been slaughtered but found worthy to open the scroll of God. At first John had thought that no one could be worthy of such

an honor, but he is told that the descendant of Judah has already conquered and is worthy. Opening the scroll will inaugurate an era of tribulation, but in the end the righteous will triumph.

When the Lamb takes the scroll, all creation breaks out in song. The passage reflects an ancient understanding of the division of the cosmos into three sections, with the earth sandwiched between heaven and the netherworld. The angels in heaven

proclaim the Lamb's greatness, while all the creatures on the earth and under it sing the praises of the enthroned one and the Lamb.

The language in the book of Revelation is highly symbolic. Clearly, the enthroned figure is God, judge and ruler of all. The Lamb who was slain is Jesus the Christ in his role as paschal lamb, slaughtered in order to give life to all. The four living creatures are beings near the throne of God and resemble animals, although one has human features as well. Twenty-four elders also surround God's throne, sitting in thrones of their own and probably representing the

Simon Peter said to them, "I am going *fishing*."
They said to him, "We *also* will come *with* you."
So they went *out* and got into the *boat*,
    but that night they caught *nothing*.

When it was already *dawn*, Jesus was standing on the *shore*;
    but the disciples did not *realize* that it was Jesus.
Jesus said to them, "*Children*, have you caught anything to *eat*?"
They answered him, "*No*."
So he said to them, "Cast the net over the *right* side of the boat
    and you will *find* something."
So they *cast* it, and were not able to pull it *in*
    because of the number of *fish*.

So the disciple whom Jesus *loved* said to Peter, "It is the *Lord*."
When Simon Peter heard that it was the *Lord*,
    he tucked in his *garment*, for he was lightly *clad*,
    and *jumped* into the *sea*.
The *other* disciples came in the *boat*,
    for they were not *far* from *shore*, only about a hundred *yards*,
    dragging the net with the *fish*.

When they climbed out on *shore*,
    they saw a charcoal *fire* with *fish* on it and *bread*.
Jesus said to them, "Bring some of the *fish* you just *caught*."
So Simon Peter went *over* and *dragged* the net *ashore*
    full of one hundred fifty-*three* large *fish*.
Even though there were so *many*, the net was not *torn*.
Jesus said to them, "*Come*, have *breakfast*."
And *none* of the disciples dared to *ask* him, "Who *are* you?"
    because they *realized* it was the *Lord*.
Jesus came *over* and took the *bread* and *gave* it to them,
    and in *like* manner the *fish*.

Jesus' words are tender and kind.

Read this line with quiet excitement in your voice.

The image is humorous. Read the line as though you were telling a child. Speak in a low voice about Peter's clothing, then raise your voice and emphasize "jumped."

twelve tribes of Israel and the twelve apostles. Everyone who has breath proclaims the greatness of God and the righteousness of the Lamb, who was killed for the sake of the world.

Although the images in the book of Revelation are sometimes bizarre, the purpose of the work and especially of today's selection is to give glory and praise to God. Lift your voice with the angels and creatures as you too sing the praises recorded here. Speak with awe and reverence for the majesty of the Lamb.

GOSPEL
The appearances of the resurrected Jesus often have something to do with meals. In the ordinary but life-sustaining act of sharing food, Jesus' friends learn to recognize him. Today's story begins with the apostles going fishing. In fact, it is the miracle of the unexpected great catch of fish that leads Peter to recognize Jesus. As elsewhere, Jesus' appearance is changed; his friends do not immediately recognize him, yet they come to know that it is he.

The story itself is from a section of the gospel of John that might have been added later. It does not seem to recognize that Jesus had already revealed himself to his followers and breathed the Spirit into them. In addition, it takes place in Galilee rather than Jerusalem. Finally, it provides an opportunity to focus on a figure who was important among the early Christians, Peter.

The central story of the passage is the poignant conversation between Jesus and Peter. Just as Peter had three times denied Jesus before Jesus' death, so Peter is now asked to affirm his love for Jesus three

Read this touching story with sincerity and compassion.

This was now the *third* time Jesus was *revealed* to his disciples
  after being *raised* from the *dead*.

When they had finished *breakfast*, Jesus said to Simon Peter,
  "*Simon*, son of *John*, do you *love* me more than *these*?"
Simon Peter answered him, "*Yes*, Lord, you *know* that
    I love you."
Jesus said to him, "*Feed* my *lambs*."

He then said to Simon Peter a *second* time,
  "*Simon*, son of *John*, do you *love* me?"
Simon Peter answered him, "*Yes*, Lord, you *know* that
    I *love* you."
Jesus said to him, "*Tend* my *sheep*."

Jesus said to him the *third* time,
  "*Simon*, son of *John*, do you *love* me?"
Peter was *distressed* that Jesus had said to him a *third* time,
  "Do you *love* me?" and he said to him,
  "*Lord*, you know *everything*; you *know* that I *love* you."
Jesus said to him, "*Feed* my *sheep*.

"Amen, amen, I *say* to you, when you were *younger*,
    you used to dress *yourself* and go where you *wanted*;
  but when you grow *old*, you will stretch out your *hands*,
    and someone *else* will dress you
    and lead you where you do *not* want to *go*."
He said this signifying by what kind of *death* he would
    glorify *God*.
And when he had said this, he said to him, "Follow *me*."

[Shorter: John 21:1–14]

Peter is insistent, perhaps even a little impatient.

Express Peter's hurt in your voice.

times. Eagerly, Peter affirms his commitment to Jesus, but by the third question he is hurt and even more insistent. We are never told if Peter comes to recognize the hurt Jesus must have felt when Peter denied him or if Peter even connects the two experiences.

Each time Peter proclaims his love for Jesus, Jesus gives him a commission. Peter is to care for Jesus' "sheep," clearly members of the Christian community, those who themselves are committed to proclaiming the risen Lord. But Peter is also to "follow," for it is impossible for him to lead if he is not focused on Jesus.

The final section of the passage alludes to the death of Peter. The tradition of Peter's death by martyrdom in Rome is never told in the New Testament, but this passage affirms that indeed Peter met his fate at the hands of others and died for the sake of his faith.

Read the two sections of this passage as discrete units. The recognition scene in the first half has elements of the miraculous, and the disciples are in awe at the presence of the risen Jesus in their midst. But there is also humor, as Peter pulls on his clothes and jumps into the water to greet the Lord. The second half of the story turns serious. Let your voice be filled with compassion as you recount Jesus' questions and Peter's proclamation of the depth of his love. Conclude by addressing Jesus' command, "Follow me," to all the members of your assembly.

4TH SUNDAY OF EASTER

Lectionary #51

READING I   Acts 13:14, 43–52

Perga = PER-guh
Antioch = AN-tee-ahk
Pisidia = pih-SID-ee-uh

A reading from the Acts of the Apostles

Paul and *Barnabas* continued on from *Perga*
    and reached *Antioch* in *Pisidia*.
On the *sabbath* they entered the *synagogue* and took their *seats*.

Many *Jews* and worshipers who were *converts* to Judaism
    followed Paul and Barnabas, who *spoke* to them
    and *urged* them to remain *faithful* to the grace of *God*.

Emphasize the enormous size of the crowd that comes to hear Paul and Barnabas.

On the *following* sabbath almost the whole *city* gathered
    to hear the *word* of the *Lord*.
When the Jews saw the *crowds*, they were filled with *jealousy*
    and with violent *abuse* contradicted what Paul *said*.

Both *Paul* and *Barnabas* spoke out *boldly* and said,
    "It was *necessary* that the word of God be spoken to you *first*,
    but since you *reject* it
    and condemn *yourselves* as *unworthy* of eternal *life*,
    we now turn to the *Gentiles*.
For so the Lord has *commanded* us,
    I have made you a *light* to the *Gentiles*,
    that you may be an *instrument* of *salvation*
    to the ends of the *earth*."

The Gentiles were *delighted* when they heard this
    and *glorified* the word of the *Lord*.

READING I The Acts of the Apostles consistently presents the gospel being preached first to Jews, at least some of whom subsequently reject it, and only then to Gentiles. Paul describes himself as the apostle to the Gentiles and gives no hint that he first tried to preach to Jews. But the author of Acts strongly affirms Jesus' role as the fulfillment of the promises made to Israel, as well as his cosmic role as savior of the world.

The story of the earliest Christian communities is one in which initial success is followed by failure, often because of the objections of powerful members of the larger Jewish community. Here, we are told that many Jews were interested in the message of Paul and Barnabas, but the Jewish leaders and other prominent Jews impeded the progress of the gospel. The final note, however, is one of triumph; God overcomes all opposition.

Christianity's success among Gentiles is well known. This passage depicts Paul and Barnabas quoting from one of the suffering servant songs of the prophet Isaiah, in which the promises to Israel are extended to all the nations. Like the servant, the Christian community is to reach out to all peoples in order to bring salvation. You share the servant's mission: to proclaim the faith to all so that everyone may proclaim Christ's universal reign.

Read this passage with the same boldness that Paul and Barnabas must have felt as they proclaimed the word of God. Do not shrink from the reality of opposition that they experienced, but at the same time emphasize the success of their mission and the ultimate victory of God.

All who were destined for eternal *life* came to *believe,*
>   and the word of the *Lord* continued to *spread*
>   through the whole *region.*
The *Jews,* however, incited the *women* of prominence
>   who were *worshipers*
>   and the leading *men* of the city,
>   stirred up a *persecution* against Paul and Barnabas,
>   and *expelled* them from their *territory.*
So they shook the *dust* from their *feet* in protest *against* them,
>   and went to *Iconium.*
The disciples were filled with *joy* and the Holy *Spirit.*

READING II   Revelation 7:9, 14b–17

"Revelation," not "Revelations."

A reading from the book of Revelation

I, *John,* had a vision of a great *multitude,*
>   which no one could *count,*
>   from every *nation, race, people* and *tongue.*
They stood before the *throne* and before the *Lamb,*
>   wearing white *robes* and holding *palm* branches
>   in their hands.
Then one of the *elders* said to me,
>   "*These* are the *ones* who have survived the time
>   of great *distress;*
>   they have *washed* their *robes*
>   and made them *white* in the blood of the *Lamb.*

"For *this* reason they stand before God's *throne*
>   and *worship* him day and *night* in his *temple.*

READING II   John the seer continues to describe his visionary experience in today's reading, building upon the accounts we have been hearing throughout the Easter season. John witnesses the heavenly scene in which the righteous—purified and holy, including those martyrs who have been made victorious in death—stand before God (the throne) and Christ (the Lamb). Together with the heavenly host, they offer praise to God, who protects them.

Two key concepts deserve emphasis in this passage. The first is the universality of the righteous community. The righteous ones, as is made clear elsewhere in Revelation, include members from all the tribes of Israel but are not limited to the Jews. Instead, the redeemed are from every people and nation. Salvation is available to all who have "washed their robes" by trusting in the saving action of Jesus, the Lamb of God.

The second important aspect of the vision is the comfort and life-giving sustenance that Christ the shepherd provides for his sheep. They will have no want or discomfort but will be refreshed with the waters of life. The selection ends with the touching affirmation that there will no longer be pain or sorrow on that day.

In this Easter season, we celebrate the promise of John's vision and look forward to the day when all tears will be wiped away. Proclaim the beginning of this passage boldly, emphasizing the universality of salvation, and conclude with tenderness as you describe the joys of the eternal life.

Speak this promise with hope and a sense of comfort. All will be well.

The one who *sits* on the *throne* will *shelter* them.
They will not *hunger* or *thirst* any*more*,
      nor will the *sun* or any *heat* strike them.
For the *Lamb* who is in the *center* of the throne
      will *shepherd* them
      and *lead* them to springs of life-giving *water*,
      and God will wipe away every *tear* from their *eyes*."

GOSPEL   John 10:27–30

A reading from the holy gospel according to John

Since the gospel is so short, read it slowly and with extra care.

Jesus said:
"My *sheep* hear my *voice*;
      I *know* them, and they *follow* me.
I give them eternal *life*, and they shall never *perish*.
No one can take them out of my *hand*.
My Father, who has *given* them to me, is *greater* than *all*,
      and *no* one can take them out of the Father's *hand*.
The *Father* and I are *one*."

This statement suggests Jesus' lordship. Speak slowly and clearly.

GOSPEL   The gospel of John often uses the image of a sheep-fold to explain the relationship between Jesus and his followers. The shepherd guides and cares for the sheep, and the sheep follow willingly. Just as the shepherd risks his life to care for the sheep, so also Jesus gives his life for his flock.

The larger context of this passage is the conflict between the Jewish leadership and Jesus. When the leaders ask Jesus if he is the Messiah, Jesus responds with the pastoral imagery that fills this passage. But the thrust of his message is that those who

question him do not belong to him and do not listen to his message. Those who belong to him know him and he knows them. He gives them life, a life that is eternal and cannot be taken from them.

In addition to the loving care Jesus provides for his followers and their devotion to him, Jesus here affirms his oneness with God. In a remarkably strong statement of the unity of Jesus and the Father, Jesus claims to bear God's power and authority. It is this claim—"The Father and I are one"—that will stir up animosity among his Jewish

adversaries. It is too much for them to take, and they will threaten to stone him.

Offer this short passage to your assembly as a statement of Christ's profound love and care for the church. Speak tenderly but with authority, just as Jesus does. Give yourself plenty of time so that your listeners can ponder every word.

5TH SUNDAY OF EASTER

Lectionary #54

READING I   Acts 14:21–27

A reading from the Acts of the Apostles

After *Paul* and *Barnabas* had proclaimed the *good news*
    to that *city*
    and made a considerable number of *disciples*,
    they returned to *Lystra* and to *Iconium* and to *Antioch*.
They *strengthened* the spirits of the *disciples*
    and exhorted them to *persevere* in the *faith*, saying,
    "It is *necessary* for us to undergo many *hardships*
    to enter the *kingdom* of *God*."
They appointed *elders* for them in each *church* and,
    with *prayer* and *fasting*, *commended* them to the *Lord*
    in whom they had put their *faith*.

Then they traveled through *Pisidia* and reached *Pamphylia*.
After proclaiming the word at *Perga* they went down to *Attalia*.
From *there* they sailed to *Antioch*,
    where they had been *commended* to the grace of *God*
    for the *work* they had now *accomplished*.

And when they *arrived*, they called the church *together*
    and *reported* what God had *done* with them
    and how he had opened the *door* of *faith* to the *Gentiles*.

Lystra = LĪS-truh
Iconium = ī-KOH-nee-uhm
Antioch = AN-tee-ahk

Pisidia = pih-SID-ee-uh
Pamphylia = pam-FIL-ee-uh
Perga = PER-guh
Attalia = uh-TAHL-ee-uh

Stress the activity of God in their ministry.

READING I   Paul's first missionary journey ended with a return to Antioch in Syria, following stops in several of the cities he had visited earlier. Barnabas was Paul's faithful companion and coworker on that first journey, but they soon parted ways after an argument to pursue separate missionary careers.

The Acts of the Apostles presents Antioch as the community from which Paul began his missionary activity. Paul and Barnabas report back to the Christians in Antioch about their travels and their work among the Gentiles. The author also reports that Paul and Barnabas established church leadership in each of the communities they visited, a detail lacking in Paul's own letters. The author of Acts was writing several decades later than Paul did and may have depended on his own knowledge of contemporary church structure.

Given their own experience of rejection during their missionary work, it is not surprising that Paul and Barnabas find it necessary to encourage the newly-formed communities to withstand persecution. Their message that one enters the kingdom of God through persecution is strikingly similar to the message in Paul's letters that suffering is an essential component of the Christian life. Yet it is through suffering that Christians find deep joy.

This passage is a fairly straightforward account of the return of Paul and Barnabas to Antioch. Be sure to practice the place names until you are comfortable with them. Stress the message Paul and Barnabas convey to their churches and the fact that they are not working on their own. Rather, it is God who works through them.

"Revelation," not "Revelations."

READING II   Revelation 21:1–5a

A reading from the book of Revelation

Then I, *John*, saw a new *heaven* and a new *earth*.
The *former* heaven and the *former* earth had passed *away*,
    and the *sea* was no *more*.

I also saw the holy *city*, a new *Jerusalem*,
    coming *down* out of *heaven* from *God*,
    prepared as a *bride* adorned for her *husband*.

Speak with authority.

I heard a loud *voice* from the *throne* saying,
    "*Behold*, God's *dwelling* is with the human *race*.
He will *dwell* with them and they will be his *people*
    and God *himself* will always be *with* them as their *God*.

Lower your voice and speak tenderly.

He will wipe every *tear* from their *eyes*,
    and there shall be no more *death* or *mourning*, *wailing* or *pain*,
    for the *old* order has passed *away*."

Close strongly, with a bright voice, as you relay God's promise.

The One who sat on the *throne* said,
    "*Behold*, I make *all* things *new*."

READING II   As on previous Sundays during the Easter season, we again hear from the visionary John about his experience in the heavenly realm. Found near the end of the book of Revelation, the present passage describes the period of Christ's reign.

Christ's reign will usher in a new age, characterized by a new heaven and a new earth. In that coming age, a new Jerusalem, symbolic of the church, will be united with God, just as the earthly Jerusalem had once served as the center of God's activity on earth. God's union with the chosen people will be complete and final. In that new era, God will no longer be distant, reigning only in heaven. God's home will be among humankind. It will be a time of joy and peace, a time when the sting of death will no longer be felt.

The promises of Revelation have yet to be completely realized. They were written to give hope to a persecuted people, and they continue to provide hope for us today. Proclaim this passage as God's promise to your community and to all Christians. Let your voice be filled with hope as you share this message.

GOSPEL   The setting for this scene is Jesus' last meal with his disciples. Jesus speaks of his own glorification which, in this gospel, always refers to his death on the cross. Far from an ignominious, shameful death, it is the means by which Jesus is exalted and revealed as Lord of all. The author writes from the perspective of a believer in the risen Jesus, and Jesus speaks in this passage as the one

GOSPEL   John 13:31–33a, 34–35

A reading from the holy gospel according to John

Speak slowly and solemnly.

When Judas had *left* them, Jesus said,
   "*Now* is the Son of Man *glorified*, and *God* is glorified *in* him.
If God is glorified *in* him,
   God will also glorify *him* in *himself*,
   and God will *glorify* him at *once*.

Let your voice be filled with tenderness.

"My *children*, I will be with you only a *little* while *longer*.
I give you a *new* commandment: *love* one *another*.
As *I* have loved *you*, so you *also* should love one *another*.
This is how all will *know* that you are my *disciples*,
   if you have *love* for one *another*."

Offer this directly to your community, as both encouragement and challenge.

who is already exalted. Everything is spoken in the context of his death and resurrection. He is already glorified and gives glory to God by being raised up—exalted—on the cross.

The new commandment to love is a theme throughout this gospel and, indeed, throughout the New Testament. Here, however, it has a very specific meaning. It is the members of the church, the followers of the risen Jesus, who are to love one another.

There is no concern for the community beyond the church in this particular passage. This love stems from Jesus' own love for his followers and is a sign of their discipleship. Indeed, the early Christian community was characterized by its adherence to this command, and Christians were proud to know that others said of them, "See how they love one another."

Since this reading is being used during the Easter season, Jesus' words that he will remain only a little while longer might be understood to refer to his time on earth

before his ascension. It is not entirely necessary to concern your listeners with correct chronology. Emphasize instead the two themes of this short selection: Jesus' glorification and the command to love.

6TH SUNDAY OF EASTER

Lectionary #57

READING I   Acts 15:1–2, 22–29

A reading from the Acts of the Apostles

Some who had come down from *Judea* were instructing
    the brothers,
    "Unless you are *circumcised* according to the Mosaic *practice*,
    you cannot be *saved.*"
Because there arose no little *dissension* and *debate*
    by *Paul* and *Barnabas* with them,
    it was decided that *Paul, Barnabas* and some of the *others*
    should go up to *Jerusalem* to the *apostles* and *elders*
    about this question.

The *apostles* and *elders*, in agreement with the *whole* church,
    decided to choose *representatives*
    and to send them to *Antioch* with *Paul* and *Barnabas.*
The ones chosen were *Judas*, who was called *Barsabbas*,
    and *Silas, leaders* among the brothers.
This is the letter *delivered* by them:

"The *apostles* and the *elders*, your *brothers*,
    to the brothers in *Antioch, Syria* and *Cilicia*
    of Gentile *origin: Greetings.*
Since we have *heard* that *some* of our number
    who went *out* without any mandate from *us*
    have *upset* you with their teachings
    and *disturbed* your peace of *mind*,
    we have with one *accord* decided to choose *representatives*

This was a very emotional issue. Try to convey some of the anguish of the debate in your voice.

**Antioch = AN-tee-ahk
Barsabbas = bahr-SAH-buhs
Silas = SĪ-luhs**

Cilicia = sih-LISH-ee-uh

Dioceses in the United States are able to decide by region to move the celebration of the solemnity of the Ascension of the Lord from this Thursday, May 24, 2001, to next Sunday, May 27, 2001. In that case, the second reading and the gospel from the Seventh Sunday of Easter may be read today. Check with your liturgy coordinator or pastor to find out which readings will be used today.

READING I | **The most pressing issue facing the young church in the first century was the question of whether Gentiles were included in the salvation offered in Christ. Some people held that it was necessary to become Jewish in order to be Jesus' disciple, since Jesus himself said that he had come to save the lost sheep of Israel. Others, notably Paul, argued strongly for freedom in Christ and believed that the gospel was to be preached to everyone, Jews and non-Jews alike.**

Today's reading describes this conflict and the compromise solution envisioned by the author of Acts. As always in Acts, the Jerusalem community is central and has decision-making power. The Jerusalem Christians send delegates with a letter insisting that they had not been consulted about the Jewish-Christian claim that circumcision was necessary for all followers of Christ. Instead, they reject such a requirement but affirm the importance of certain dietary restrictions and ethical demands.

and to *send* them to you along with our beloved *Barnabas*
    and *Paul,*
who have dedicated their *lives* to the name of our
    Lord Jesus *Christ.*

"So we are sending *Judas* and *Silas*
    who will also convey this *same* message by word of *mouth*:
    'It is the decision of the Holy *Spirit* and of *us*
    not to place on you any *burden* beyond these *necessities*,
    namely, to abstain from *meat* sacrificed to *idols*,
    from *blood*, from meats of *strangled* animals,
    and from unlawful *marriage*.
If you keep *free* of these,
    you will be doing what is *right. Farewell.'*"

READING II   Revelation 21:10–14, 22–23

"Revelation," not "Revelations."

A reading from the book of Revelation

The angel took me in *spirit* to a great, high *mountain*
    and showed me the holy city *Jerusalem*
    coming *down* out of heaven from *God.*
It *gleamed* with the *splendor* of *God.*
Its *radiance* was like that of a precious *stone,*
    like *jasper,* clear as *crystal.*

Let your voice convey the beauty of the image.

It had a *massive,* high *wall,*
    with twelve *gates* where twelve *angels* were stationed
    and on which *names* were inscribed,
    the names of the twelve *tribes* of the *Israelites.*

We know from Paul's own letters that including all people in God's embrace was of paramount importance to him. Paul emphatically rejects the necessity of the Jewish law, although he continues to uphold ethical demands for Christians. In addition, Paul views himself as an apostle directly called by Christ, not one sent from the community in Jerusalem or any other place.

The solution to the question of circumcision offered by the Jerusalem community is one with biblical precedent. The specified regulations are those that were required of Gentiles who were dwelling among Jews. The author of Acts, therefore, upholds the importance of the Jewish law and the central claim that salvation is first for the Jews, while at the same time extending the possibility of salvation to all. By following the requirements to abstain from certain foods and from sexual immorality, the non-Jews are, in a strict sense, keeping the law of Moses as far as it was intended for them.

The central message of this passage is the universality of the Christian message.

Jesus came to save all nations, and all people are able to be his followers. Emphasize strongly this message of inclusion and acceptance of others.

READING II The seer John continues to describe his otherworldly vision, building on the images we have heard throughout the Easter season. In today's passage, he sees a vision of the heavenly Jerusalem. Jerusalem was regarded by the

There were *three* gates facing *east*,
    three *north*, three *south*, and three *west*.
The *wall* of the city had twelve courses of *stones*
        as its *foundation*,
    on which were inscribed the twelve *names*
    of the twelve *apostles* of the *Lamb*.

Begin this sentence with a tone of surprise, then conclude with conviction.

I saw *no temple* in the city
    for its *temple* is the Lord God *almighty* and the *Lamb*.
The city had no need of *sun* or *moon* to *shine* on it,
    for the *glory* of *God* gave it *light*,
    and its *lamp* was the *Lamb*.

GOSPEL   John 14:23–29

A reading from the holy gospel according to John

Jesus said to his disciples:
    "Whoever *loves* me will keep my *word*,
    and my *Father* will love *him*,
    and we will *come* to him and make our *dwelling* with him.
Whoever does *not* love me does *not* keep my words;
    yet the word you *hear* is not *mine*
    but that of the *Father* who *sent* me.

There is challenge in this message: Rejecting Jesus' word is to reject the Father who sent him.

"I have *told* you this while I am *with* you.
The *Advocate*, the Holy *Spirit*,
    whom the Father will *send* in my *name*,
    will teach you *everything*
    and *remind* you of all that I *told* you.

Jewish faithful and by Christians—Jewish and non-Jewish—as the spiritual center of the world. But it was destroyed by the Romans a few decades before John wrote Revelation. Jerusalem remains central to his thought, however, but the city he envision is a new Jerusalem, resplendent and holy.

The new Jerusalem has twelve gates, each bearing the name of one of the twelve tribes of Israel, and twelve foundation stones with the names of the apostles. These features confirm that the new Jerusalem is in fact the Christian church, built on the foundation of the apostles and the heritage of Israel. It is a priestly city, yet it has no need of a temple. In the temple's place is God and the Lamb who has been sacrificed. The city shines, bedecked in jewels and illuminated by the glory of God.

Meditate on this passage until you can proclaim with awe the splendor of God's people, imaged as the city of Jerusalem. Read the passage with wonder in your voice and also firm conviction of God's glory evident in the church.

GOSPEL   In the gospel of John, Jesus addresses his disciples in a farewell discourse prior to his arrest and crucifixion. It focuses on the centrality of love in the life of each of his followers and the unity in love of the Father and Jesus. Both of these aspects of the love command are found in today's gospel.

Loving Jesus has demands; it involves keeping his word, which is not simply his own but the word of the Father. But the primary feature of this word is precisely the

Speak with warmth and comfort.

"*Peace* I leave with you; my *peace* I *give* to you.
Not as the *world* gives do *I* give it to *you*.
Do not let your hearts be *troubled* or *afraid*.

"You heard me *tell* you,
  'I am going *away* and I will come *back* to you.'
If you *loved* me,
  you would *rejoice* that I am going to the *Father*;
  for the *Father* is *greater* than I.
And now I have *told* you this before it *happens*,
  so that when it *happens* you may *believe*."

importance of love. There are also rewards to keeping Jesus' command: God will come to dwell in those who adhere to his word. And when he is gone he will not leave his followers to struggle alone but will send the Spirit to teach and guide them.

In words that suggest he will soon depart, Jesus offers peace to his listeners. This peace is not simply the absence of conflict or lack of anxiety, but a deep, abiding peace. Although in the context of this passage Jesus' departure refers to his death (which, in this gospel, is identical with his

glorification), your listeners might understand it to refer to his ascension, to be celebrated later this week. Jesus goes away to take his rightful place with the Father, and those who love him should rejoice.

Read this passage slowly and carefully as a word of comfort and challenge to your assembly. Jesus offers peace to those who trust in him but also demands that Christian communities be places of profound love.

ASCENSION OF THE LORD

Lectionary #58

READING I   Acts 1:1–11

A reading from the Acts of the Apostles

Theophilus = thee-OF-uh-luhs
The name means "lover of God."

In the *first* book, *Theophilus,*
    I dealt with *all* that Jesus *did* and *taught*
    until the *day* he was taken *up,*
    after giving *instructions* through the Holy *Spirit*
    to the *apostles* whom he had *chosen.*
He presented himself *alive* to them
    by many *proofs* after he had *suffered,*
    appearing to them during *forty days*
    and *speaking* about the kingdom of *God.*

While meeting with them,
    he enjoined them *not* to *depart* from Jerusalem,
    but to *wait* for "the *promise* of the *Father*
    about which you have heard me *speak;*
    for *John* baptized with *water,*
    but in a *few* days *you* will be baptized with the Holy *Spirit."*

When they had gathered *together* they *asked* him,
    "*Lord,* are you at *this* time going to restore
    the *kingdom* to *Israel?"*
He answered them, "It is *not* for you to *know* the *times*
        or *seasons*
    that the *Father* has *established* by his own *authority.*

Dioceses in the United States are able to decide by region to move the celebration of the solemnity of the Ascension of the Lord from today to Sunday, May 27, 2001, in which case today's readings are used.

READING I   The opening section of the Acts of the Apostles tells of Jesus' presence with the disciples after the resurrection and of his ascension into heaven. Because he is said to have appeared among them for 40 days, this feast has been fixed on the calendar 40 days after Easter. In biblical terminology, 40 days indicates a considerable length of time; it is not to be taken at face value. In fact, this dating contradicts the gospel of Luke, to which the Acts of the Apostles is the sequel. In the gospel, Jesus ascends to heaven on the evening of Easter Sunday.

The events described in the opening chapters of the Acts of the Apostles (including the ascension and Pentecost) are not told as historical occurrences. Rather, the author is creatively making claims of faith about Jesus and his followers. The story of the ascension conveys that Jesus is glorified, that his rightful home is with God in heaven. Similarly, the story of Pentecost describes the disciples' experience of the Spirit of God in their lives.

What is important is that the 50 days from Easter to Pentecost are all included in the Easter season. This is the time when we ritually celebrate for an extended period the victory of Christ over death, his vindication after being executed, his exaltation and his continued presence, through the working of the Holy Spirit, with his followers on earth. The Easter season is one extended feast, although we concentrate on different aspects

But you will receive *power* when the Holy *Spirit* comes *upon* you,
   and you will be my *witnesses* in *Jerusalem*,
   throughout *Judea* and *Samaria*,
   and to the *ends* of the *earth.*"

When he had *said* this, as they were looking *on*,
   he was lifted *up*, and a *cloud* took him from their *sight.*
While they were looking *intently* at the sky as he was *going*,
   suddenly two men dressed in white *garments*
      stood *beside* them.

They said, "Men of *Galilee*,
   why are you standing there looking at the *sky*?
This *Jesus* who has been taken *up* from you into *heaven*
   will *return* in the *same* way as you have seen him
      going into *heaven.*"

READING II   Hebrews 9:24–28; 10:19–23

A reading from the letter to the Hebrews

Christ did not enter into a sanctuary made by *hands*,
   a *copy* of the true one, but heaven *itself*,
   that he might now appear before *God* on our *behalf.*
Not that he might *offer* himself *repeatedly*,
   as the high *priest* enters each *year* into the sanctuary
   with *blood* that is not his *own*;
   if *that* were so, he would have had to *suffer* repeatedly
   from the *foundation* of the *world.*
But *now* once for *all* he has *appeared* at the end of the *ages*
   to take away *sin* by his *sacrifice.*

of Christ's triumph at different times during the season.

Today's reading is an awe-inspiring account of Jesus' exaltation to his rightful place with God. As a good teacher, he instructs his followers right to the end and closes by giving them a commission to go forth in his name. In a manner similar to the women's discovery of the empty tomb, two men (presumably angels) appear to the apostles and tell them where Jesus is. Because they have yet to receive the gift of the Holy Spirit, the disciples remain confused, even after all that they have seen and heard.

There are several "voices" to adopt in the reading of this selection. It opens on a historical note, summarizing the gospel; this can be read in a straightforward manner. Raise your voice to proclaim the words of Jesus to his followers. Their question to him is asked innocently enough, ignorant though it may sound to us. Finally, the ascension itself is exciting, and the proclamation of the angels should be given due emphasis. Throughout, your goal is to make real to your listeners the great majesty of Jesus, now enthroned in heaven.

> There is a choice of second readings today. Speak with the liturgy coordinator or pastor to find out which reading will be used.

READING II   **HEBREWS.** The letter to the Hebrews contrasts the true and perfect heavenly sacrifice made by Christ, the heavenly high priest, with the sacrifice of the Jewish cult. Today's passage is an excellent summary of some of the main issues and claims.

Hebrews envisions a heavenly temple upon which the temple in Jerusalem was

Pause after "judgment," then raise your voice as if to start anew.

Just as it is appointed that *men* and *women* die *once*,
   and *after* this the *judgment*, so also *Christ*,
   offered *once* to take away the sins of *many*,
   will appear a *second* time, not to take away *sin*
   but to bring *salvation* to those who eagerly *await* him.

Speak warmly and confidently.

Therefore, brothers and sisters, since through the *blood* of *Jesus*
   we have *confidence* of entrance into the *sanctuary*
   by the *new* and living *way* he *opened* for us
     through the *veil*, that is, his *flesh*,
   and since we have "a *great priest* over the house of *God*,"
   let us *approach* with a sincere *heart* and in absolute *trust*,
   with our *hearts* sprinkled *clean* from an evil *conscience*
   and our bodies *washed* in pure *water*.
Let us hold *unwaveringly* to our confession that gives us *hope*,
   for he who made the *promise* is *trustworthy*.

Or:

READING II   Ephesians 1:17–23

A reading from the letter of Saint Paul to the Ephesians

This is a prayer; read it as such for your assembly.

Brothers and sisters:
May the *God* of our Lord Jesus *Christ*, the Father of *glory*,
   give you a Spirit of *wisdom* and *revelation*
   resulting in *knowledge* of him.

The author prays for the reader to know three things: the hope of God's call, the riches of glory, and the greatness of God's power. Plan your phrasing to make these three points stand out.

May the *eyes* of your *hearts* be *enlightened*,
   that you may *know* what is the *hope* that belongs to his *call*,
   what are the *riches* of *glory*

---

modeled. The Jerusalem temple was first and foremost a place of animal sacrifice, but it also contained within it an especially sacred area, the Holy of Holies. Once a year, on the feast of Yom Kippur, the high priest of the temple would enter into this holiest area of the building and emerge to pronounce the divine name. A scapegoat was then sent into the desert to carry away the people's sins. Animal sacrifices were also performed on a daily basis in the temple for other purposes: in thanksgiving, to ask for forgiveness, and so on.

The principal contrast here between Christ's sacrifice and that of the Hebrew cult is the uniqueness of Jesus' action. He entered heaven itself to offer himself once for all. The Jewish cult operated in a copy of the true sanctuary, and its sacrifices had to be repeated over and over again. The high priest could only offer inadequate animal sacrifices, but Jesus offered the perfect sacrifice of himself.

Jesus' entry into that heavenly sanctuary opens the way for all of his followers to enter as well. Because of what he has done, Christians can approach the gate of heaven

in sincerity and trust, knowing that we have been forgiven.

Although the imagery may be foreign to your listeners, the message of forgiveness and confidence in approaching God is one that we all need to hear. Address the second section of the passage directly to the members of your assembly, in order to encourage them to approach God boldly, knowing that forgiveness is theirs.

EPHESIANS. The author of Ephesians prays for the community he addresses; you can offer to God the same prayer for your community as you read this selection. The

in his *inheritance* among the *holy* ones,
and what is the surpassing *greatness* of his *power*
for us who *believe*,
in accord with the *exercise* of his great *might*,
which he *worked* in *Christ*,
raising him from the *dead*
and *seating* him at his *right hand* in the *heavens*,
far above every *principality*, *authority*, *power*, and *dominion*,
and every *name* that is *named*
not only in *this* age but also in the one to *come*.

And he put *all things* beneath his *feet*
and gave him as *head* over *all* things to the *church*,
which is his *body*,
the *fullness* of the one who *fills* all things in every *way*.

The mention of God's greatness inspires the author to praise God's work in Christ. Steadily raise your voice from here until the end.

GOSPEL   Luke 24:46–53

A reading from the holy gospel according to Luke

Jesus said to his disciples:
"*Thus* it is *written* that the *Christ* would *suffer*
and *rise* from the *dead* on the third *day*
and that *repentance*, for the forgiveness of *sins*,
would be *preached* in his *name*
to all the *nations*, beginning from *Jerusalem*.
You are *witnesses* of these things.
And *behold* I am sending the *promise* of my *Father* upon you;
but stay in the *city*
until you are clothed with *power* from on *high*."

Pause and take a breath after "day."

Speak forcefully the promise of heavenly power.

---

enlightenment for which you pray is that of knowing God better and receiving all that God has to give, including God's awesome power. Mention of that power leads the author to utter a prayer of praise to the glorified Christ.

The power of God was manifest most fully in Christ's resurrection and ascension into heaven. Christ is honored to such a degree that he rules over every power; he is worthy of every honorary title imaginable.

Raise your voice to unite your praises with those of the author. Slow down in the second half of the reading, and speak forcefully and with expression.

GOSPEL Both the gospel of Luke and its companion volume, the Acts of the Apostles, contain accounts of the ascension of Jesus into heaven; we read both passages today. The gospel account is simpler than the one in Acts, but both affirm that Jesus is exalted at the right hand of God, where he is given dominion and glory.

The disciples who witness the ascension have already participated in the great events of salvation. They were crushed by the reality of Jesus' death but have experienced his victory over death. They have been preaching about him and his offer of forgiveness. Now they see him exalted, and soon they will be given the gift of power.

Jesus' departure is relatively uneventful in the gospel account. He blesses his friends and takes leave of them. But their

Let your voice be filled with awe and peacefulness.

Then he led them *out* as far as *Bethany*,
    raised his *hands*, and *blessed* them.
As he *blessed* them he *parted* from them
    and was taken up to *heaven*.
They did him *homage*
    and then *returned* to Jerusalem with great *joy*,
    and they were continually in the *temple* praising *God*.

response is telling: They worship him and rejoice, knowing that he has prevailed and that what he has promised will occur.

We too have participated in the anguish of Jesus' death and the joy of knowing that he has triumphed over death. We too are witnesses to his name. Proclaim this passage as a call to the members of your assembly to open their hearts continually to the activity of the Spirit in their lives and to join their voices in praise to God.

7TH SUNDAY OF EASTER

Lectionary #61

READING I   Acts 7:55–60

A reading from the Acts of the Apostles

Stephen, filled with the Holy *Spirit*,
  looked up intently to *heaven* and saw the *glory* of *God*
  and *Jesus* standing at the right *hand* of God,
  and Stephen said, *"Behold*, I see the heavens *opened*
  and the Son of *Man* standing at the right *hand* of *God."*

But they cried *out* in a loud *voice*,
  covered their *ears*, and *rushed* upon him *together*.
They threw him out of the *city*, and began to *stone* him.
The *witnesses* laid down their *cloaks*
  at the *feet* of a young man named *Saul*.

As they were *stoning* Stephen, he called out,
  "Lord *Jesus*, receive my *spirit."*
Then he fell to his *knees* and cried out in a loud *voice*,
  "Lord, do not hold this sin *against* them";
  and when he *said* this, he fell *asleep*.

Speak Stephen's words with forcefulness and conviction. Then let your voice express the anger and hostility of the crowd.

Again, Stephen speaks with conviction and a sense of peacefulness.

Dioceses in the United States are able to decide by region to move the celebration of the solemnity of the Ascension of the Lord from Thursday, May 24, 2001, to today. In that case, the readings of the Ascension replace the readings of the Seventh Sunday of Easter.

READING I   Stephen is the first Christian martyr, the first person to suffer death for his faith. His fate resembles that of Jesus: He is innocent, but his detractors are filled with animosity; he prays for forgiveness for those who are taking his life; and he asks Jesus to receive his spirit.

Although Stephen is already on trial as the scene opens, it is his description of a vision that apparently stirs the ire of his accusers. Not only does he claim that Jesus was no longer dead, but he also declares that Jesus is exalted with God. Such talk must have sounded like blasphemy to the religious leadership.

Stephen's hearers attack him in anger, viciously dragging him out of the city and stoning him. Ironically, the only member of the mob who is named is Saul (later renamed Paul), the person who will figure prominently in the Acts of the Apostles as the missionary to the Gentiles and who will repeatedly risk his life for the sake of the gospel. Indeed, Paul himself admits that he zealously persecuted the Christians prior to his own encounter with the risen Lord.

The drama in this passage makes it especially interesting to read. Proclaim the opening vision with a sense of awe, then increase the tension in your voice as you

"Revelation," not "Revelations."

recompense = REK-uhm-pens

Alpha = AHL-fuh
Omega = oh-MAY-guh

Speak gently these words of comfort and promise.

Let each line stand on its own, and emphasize the word, "Come." Proclaim the final line of the reading as a fervent prayer of hope.

READING II   Revelation 22:12–14, 16–17, 20

A reading from the book of Revelation

I, *John*, heard a voice saying to me:
   "*Behold*, I am coming *soon*.
I bring *with* me the *recompense* I will give to *each*
      according to his *deeds*.
I am the *Alpha* and the *Omega*, the *first* and the *last*,
      the *beginning* and the *end*."

Blessed are they who *wash* their *robes*
      so as to have the *right* to the *tree* of *life*
      and enter the *city* through its *gates*.

"I, *Jesus*, sent my *angel* to give you this *testimony*
         for the *churches*.
I am the *root* and *offspring* of *David*,
      the *bright* morning *star*."

The *Spirit* and the *bride* say, "*Come*."
Let the *hearer* say, "*Come*."
Let the one who *thirsts* come *forward*,
      and the one who *wants* it receive the *gift* of life-giving *water*.

The one who gives this *testimony* says, "*Yes*, I am coming *soon*."
Amen! *Come*, Lord *Jesus*!

describe the fury of Stephen's attackers. Close with a declaration of Stephen's conviction and generous spirit.

READING II   John's vision concludes with Christ's promise to come again. The passages from Revelation that have been read during the Easter season have described persecution and terror, victory and triumph. Now John conveys the eschatological hope that Jesus will return to bring to completion the work he has begun. He is the first and last, the sum of everything,

beyond all human comprehension. He comes as judge to draw his own into the heavenly abode so that they may eat of the fruit of immortality.

In response to Jesus' promise to come soon, the Spirit and the bride (the Christian church) proclaim, "Come." All who hear are welcome to join in the appeal to the risen Lord. The cry of hope rises to heaven: "Come, Lord Jesus." But, in a paradoxical move, believers are also invited to come to the water of life available in baptism. All

Christian liturgy is an expression of the belief that there is yet more to come and that Jesus will return as a righteous judge.

We know that Jesus did not return immediately, as the early Christians hoped and expected. Yet we too can join our voices with theirs in a fervent prayer that God's work will be brought to completion in Jesus' return. Proclaim this text with joyful expectation and the profound belief that the risen Jesus is indeed first and last, the one who offers life in full and promises to draw all to himself.

GOSPEL John 17:20–26

A reading from the holy gospel according to John

Lifting up his eyes to *heaven,* Jesus *prayed* saying:
"Holy *Father,* I pray not only for *them,*
    but also for those who will *believe* in me through their *word,*
    so that they may *all* be *one,*
    as *you,* Father, are in *me* and *I* in *you,*
    that they *also* may be in *us,*
    that the *world* may *believe* that you *sent* me.
And I have given them the *glory* you gave *me,*
    so that they may be *one,* as *we* are one,
    I in *them* and *you* in *me,*
    that they may be brought to *perfection* as *one,*
    that the world may *know* that you *sent* me,
    and that you *loved* them even as you loved *me.*

"Father, they are your *gift* to me.
I wish that where *I* am they also may be *with* me,
    that they may see my *glory* that you *gave* me,
    because you *loved* me before the *foundation* of the *world.*

"Righteous *Father,* the world also does not *know* you,
    but *I* know you, and *they* know that you *sent* me.
I made *known* to them your *name* and I *will* make it *known,*
    that the *love* with which you *loved* me
    may be in *them* and *I* in them."

Offer this prayer for the members of your assembly, who have come to believe through the word of others.

Speak slowly and deliberately, so that the progression of thought will be clear.

Stress the unity of Jesus and the Father, and the love they share with one another and with us.

GOSPEL The prayer of Jesus at the Last Supper in the gospel of John speaks of his unity with the Father and his glorification. In this gospel, Jesus' glorification is always tied to his crucifixion. Jesus is exalted in glory precisely as he is raised up on the cross.

Jesus' prayer extends beyond his intimate followers to include all believers, especially those who come to believe without having experienced him directly. Jesus prays that they may be as intimately united with one another and with his heavenly Father as he is. This unity will serve to proclaim to the world the truth of Jesus' role as messenger of God's love.

Just as Jesus' true realm is heavenly, so also is the destiny of his followers. He prays that they might witness his exaltation. Most of all, Jesus insists that the love that the Father has for him inspires and enlivens his followers. Because Jesus and the Father are one, knowing Jesus means knowing God, and knowing God means abiding in God's love.

Proclaim this rich passage as the prayer that it is. Reflect on the members of your own community, and offer it for their sake, sincerely desiring their unity in love. Speak solemnly, yet with the hope that your prayer will be answered positively.

PENTECOST VIGIL

Lectionary #62

READING I   Genesis 11:1–9

A reading from the book of Genesis

The *whole* world spoke the same *language*, using the
    same *words.*
While the people were *migrating* in the *east*,
  they came upon a *valley* in the land of *Shinar* and *settled* there.
They said to one another,
  "*Come*, let us mold *bricks* and harden them with *fire.*"
They used *bricks* for *stone*, and *bitumen* for *mortar.*

Then they said, "*Come*, let us *build* ourselves a *city*
  and a *tower* with its top in the *sky*,
  and so make a *name* for ourselves;
  otherwise we shall be *scattered* all over the *earth.*"

The LORD came down to *see* the *city* and the *tower*
  that the people had *built.*
Then the LORD said: "If *now*, while they are *one* people,
  all speaking the *same* language,
  they have started to do *this*,
  nothing will later stop them from doing
    whatever they *presume* to *do.*
Let us then go *down* there and *confuse* their language,
  so that one will not *understand* what another *says.*"

Thus the LORD *scattered* them from there *all* over the *earth*,
  and they *stopped* building the *city.*

Shinar = SHĪ-nahr

bitumen = bih-TYOO-m*n

The sin is threefold: building a tower to the sky, seeking a great reputation, and remaining in one place.

There is a choice of first readings today. Speak with the liturgy coordinator or pastor to find out which reading will be used.

READING I **GENESIS.** The story of the Tower of Babel is about human sin and alienation from God. The writer recalls a time at the beginning of human history when human relations were not characterized by division and when there was no enmity between the divine and the human realms. But the writer's own experience is one of a world inhabited by many peoples who cannot communicate with one another and who are scattered widely over the earth. Today's reading explains what caused the change to occur.

The story of the Tower of Babel follows the tale of Noah, who was saved from the waters of the flood with his family because of his devotion to God. But they were not without sin, as Genesis makes clear. Noah's descendants build a city and a tower for the express purpose of "making a name" (that is, gaining fame) for themselves, and to remain together against the command of God. The result is disastrous and their hope for unity destroyed; God scatters them and they cease to speak the same language.

At the root of the crime committed by the people was a desire to exceed human limitations, to make themselves as great as God (the phrase "to make a name" is reserved for the actions of a ruler or of God).

Babel = BAB-*l
There is a play on words here between the name of the city and the Hebrew word for "confuse." It is somewhat like the English play on the words "Babel" and "babble."

That is why it was called *Babel*,
    because *there* the LORD *confused* the *speech* of all the *world*.
It was from *that* place that he *scattered* them all over the *earth*.

Or:

Speak these words solemnly.

Lighten your voice as you read this beautiful image of how God rescued the people.

READING I   Exodus 19:3–8a, 16–20b

A reading from the book of Exodus

Moses went up the *mountain* to God.
Then the LORD *called* to him and said,
"*Thus* shall you say to the house of *Jacob*;
    tell the *Israelites*:
    You have *seen* for *yourselves* how I treated the *Egyptians*
    and how I bore you *up* on *eagle* wings
    and *brought* you here to *myself*.

"Therefore, if you *hearken* to my voice and *keep* my covenant,
    you shall be my *special* possession,
    dearer to me than *all* other *people*,
    though *all* the earth is *mine*.
You shall be to *me* a kingdom of *priests*, a *holy* nation.
That is what you must tell the *Israelites*."

So *Moses* went and summoned the *elders* of the *people*.
When he set *before* them
    all that the LORD had *ordered* him to *tell* them,
    the people all answered *together*,
    "*Everything* the LORD has said, we will *do*."

Proclaim this slowly, so that your listeners can join in silently. Pause.

We know also that Near Eastern cultures built towers to the heavens in order to enter the realm of the gods. God acts to punish the pride of the humans and to keep them in their proper realm. As a result, they resume moving into the land as God had commanded, but without the ability to communicate with each other. Division and lack of understanding result.

    Pentecost provides a reversal of the Babel story. At Pentecost, the misunderstandings that occur because of language differences are nullified; the Spirit moves so that the hearers understand Jesus' disciples speaking in their own languages. Unity is restored, but it is a unity under God's rule, not one that threatens to usurp divine authority.

    Proclaim the reading with expression, communicating the arrogance of the people and the determination of God to correct their waywardness. Inspire your own community to seek unity and open communication, always acting under divine guidance.

    EXODUS. God's presence is sometimes revealed in spectacular ways, as the appearance of the Holy Spirit on Pentecost will demonstrate. In that story, there is a sound like rushing wind, and tongues as of fire appear over the believers' heads. In this reading God's direct presence is also signaled by fire and smoke, by a loud trumpet and by the mountain shaking. Although we know that God is always present, we can

God's presence is announced unmistakably. Speak with awe in your voice.

On the morning of the third *day*
    there were peals of *thunder* and *lightning*,
    and a heavy *cloud* over the *mountain*,
    and a very loud *trumpet* blast,
    so that all the *people* in the camp *trembled.*
But *Moses* led the people out of the camp to meet *God,*
    and they *stationed* themselves at the foot of the *mountain.*
Mount *Sinai* was all wrapped in *smoke,*
    for the LORD came down upon it in *fire.*
The smoke *rose* from it as though from a *furnace,*
    and the whole *mountain* trembled *violently.*
The *trumpet* blast grew *louder* and *louder,*
      while Moses was *speaking,*
    and *God* answering him with *thunder.*

Close quietly, with a sense of finality.

When the LORD came *down* to the top of Mount *Sinai,*
    he summoned *Moses* to the top of the *mountain.*

Or:

READING I   Ezekiel 37:1–14

A reading from the book of the prophet Ezekiel

The image is striking: God picks up Ezekiel and moves him into the valley.

The *hand* of the LORD came *upon* me,
    and he led me out in the *spirit* of the LORD
    and set me in the *center* of the *plain,*
    which was now *filled* with *bones.*

Imagine a scene of utter destruction in the middle of the desert. Try to convey this image to your listeners.

He made me *walk* among the bones in every *direction*
    so that I saw how *many* they were on the *surface* of the *plain.*

---

sometimes forget this reality. The dramatic signs described in these readings make God's presence unmistakable, both to those who experienced them and to us.

The present passage details part of Israel's encounter with God at Sinai. Immediately following this passage is the giving of the Ten Commandments by God. It is especially appropriate to hear this story today, since the Jewish feast of Pentecost (or Shavuot, the feast of Weeks) celebrates the giving of the law at Sinai. For both Christians and Jews, Pentecost is a time to recall the establishment of a covenant with God. But

covenant also involves accepting responsibility. The Israelites were to obey God and keep the law, while the first Christians were to go forth under the guidance of the Spirit and preach to all the good news of salvation in Christ.

Israel is reminded of all that God has already done for it before being asked to keep God's covenant. The people respond with a statement of profound commitment: "All that the Lord has said, we will do." This

is our inspiration today, as we renew our pledge of faith.

The passage you are reading contains plenty of drama. Summon up your skills to convey the great love of God for the people in choosing them, the positive response on the part of Israel, and the magnificence of God evident in the signs. Challenge your listeners as well to proclaim with Israel a willingness to obey and serve God in whatever is asked of them.

EZEKIEL. Ezekiel's vision of dry bones was also used on the Fifth Sunday of Lent, Year A (see that commentary). Ezekiel wrote

How *dry* they were!
He asked me:
     Son of *man*, can these *bones* come to *life?*
I answered, "Lord GOD, you *alone* know that."

Then he said to me:
     Prophesy over these bones, and say to them:
     Dry *bones*, *hear* the *word* of the LORD!
Thus says the Lord GOD to these *bones:*
     See! I will bring *spirit* into you, that you may come to *life.*
I will put *sinews* upon you, make *flesh* grow *over* you,
     cover you with *skin*, and put *spirit* in you
     so that you may come to *life* and *know* that *I* am the LORD.

I, Ezekiel, *prophesied* as I had been *told,*
     and even as I was *prophesying* I heard a *noise;*
     it was a *rattling* as the bones came *together, bone* joining *bone.*
I saw the *sinews* and the *flesh* come *upon* them,
     and the skin *cover* them, but there was no *spirit* in them.

Then the LORD said to me:
     Prophesy to the *spirit, prophesy,* son of man,
     and *say* to the spirit: *Thus* says the Lord *GOD:*
     From the four winds *come,* O spirit,
     and *breathe* into these *slain* that they may come to *life.*
I *prophesied* as he *told* me, and the spirit came *into* them;
     they came *alive* and stood *upright,* a vast *army.*

Then he said to me:
     Son of *man,* these *bones* are the whole house of *Israel.*
They have been *saying,*
     "Our *bones* are dried *up,*
     our *hope* is lost, and we are cut *off."*

prophesy = PROF-uh-sī

sinews = SIN-y<u>oo</u>z

The purpose of the bones coming to life is to acknowledge God. This is our purpose too, just as it was for Israel.

Although the bones appear human, they have life only with the coming of God's spirit.

during the Babylonian exile, when the leaders of the kingdom of Judah were separated from their beloved land and forced to live in exile. It was a time of near despair, when many lost hope that they would ever return or that they would again live freely as a people.

The vision of dry bones is fundamentally a vision of hope. Ezekiel sees a valley filled with dry, lifeless bones. When he speaks the word of the Lord, the bones come together and take on human form. But only when Ezekiel calls upon the breath or spirit to breathe into them do they truly come to life. It is God's spirit that gives life.

The renewed life accorded the bones is a symbol of the life that will come to Israel. God promises in this vision that Israel will be reconstituted, that it will once again exist as a nation. God has not abandoned Israel, but will always take care of the chosen people.

The life of the church also begins when the Holy Spirit breathes into the disciples on Pentecost. It is a powerful Spirit, one that can bring life where there is only death. Read this story as it was first offered to the people in exile, as a promise of new life under God's care. Inspire your readers to be renewed and filled with life and energy as they reflect on the power of the Holy Spirit in their lives.

JOEL. The prophet Joel believed that the people of Israel had become complacent and as a result deserved to experience the

This is a message of great hope to Israel, which considered itself dead in a foreign land.

Therefore, *prophesy* and *say* to them: *Thus* says the Lord *GOD:*
  O my *people*, I will *open* your *graves*
  and have you *rise* from them,
  and bring you *back* to the land of *Israel.*

Then you shall know that *I* am the LORD,
  when I *open* your *graves* and have you *rise* from them,
  O my *people!*
I will put my *spirit* in you that you may *live*,
  and I will *settle* you upon your *land;*
  thus you shall know that *I* am the LORD.
I have *promised*, and I will *do* it, says the LORD.

Speak this solemn vow with firmness.

Or:

READING I Joel 3:1–5

A reading from the book of the prophet Joel

Thus says the Lord:
I will *pour out* my *spirit* upon *all* flesh.
Your *sons* and *daughters* shall *prophesy*,
  your *old* men shall dream *dreams*,
  your *young* men shall see *visions;*
even upon the *servants* and the *handmaids*,
  in those days, I will *pour out* my *spirit.*
And I will work *wonders* in the *heavens* and on the *earth*,
  blood, *fire*, and columns of *smoke;*
the *sun* will be turned to *darkness*,
  and the *moon* to *blood*,

prophesy = PROF-uh-sī

judgment of God on the "great and terrible" Day of the Lord. But God chose not to act in wrath but to draw Israel close and give this promise: God's spirit will be given to all people, regardless of nationality, age, sex or social status. Then, when the Day of the Lord arrives, those who respond to God's spirit and are faithful will be saved. It is a promise of hope and a fitting introduction to the feast

of Pentecost, when the Holy Spirit is poured out on believers.

Offer this reading as a great promise of God's love and the inspiration of the Spirit. It is to be spoken forcefully, as a pledge made by God. Even the section about the sun turning to darkness and the moon to blood is a statement of God's sovereignty over all, including nature. Inspire your listeners to respond to the Spirit in their lives and to strive to be part of the faithful remnant.

READING II For Paul, all creation awaits fulfillment in God. Despite any sufferings he currently experiences, he is convinced that there is a glorious future to be revealed. In the present, the "first fruits" of the Spirit (like a first installment) have been given, but this is simply a promise of what lies ahead. "Adoption" is both a present reality and something not yet completed. Paul often claims that Christians have

at the *coming* of the *day* of the LORD,
   the *great* and terrible *day.*

Those who are faithful have nothing to fear.

Then *everyone* shall be *rescued*
   who *calls* on the *name* of the LORD;
for on Mount *Zion* there shall be a *remnant,*
   as the LORD has *said,*
and in *Jerusalem survivors*
   whom the LORD shall *call.*

READING II   Romans 8:22–27

A reading from the letter of Saint Paul to the Romans

Brothers and sisters:
We know that *all creation* is *groaning* in *labor* pains
      even until *now;*
   and not only *that,* but we *ourselves,*
   who have the *firstfruits* of the *Spirit,*
   we also groan *within* ourselves
      as we wait for *adoption,* the *redemption* of our *bodies.*

The "firstfruits" were the portions of a grain sacrifice that were harvested first and offered in the temple as a promise of what was to come.

For in *hope* we were *saved.*
Now hope that *sees* is not *hope.*
For who *hopes* for what one *sees?*
But if we hope for what we do *not* see, we wait with *endurance.*

The key word here is "hope."

In the *same* way, the *Spirit too* comes to the aid of our *weakness;*
   for we do not *know* how to *pray* as we *ought,*
      but the Spirit *himself* intercedes with inexpressible *groanings.*

While we are waiting in hope, the Spirit inspires us and prays through us.

been adopted into the family of God that is Israel, but in this passage, he says we still await adoption. This isn't all there is!

But the belief that there is more to come is part of the hope that saves us. We await it with patience; in the meantime, the Spirit moves through us, helping us to pray and interceding for us before God. In the end, everything will work for the good, and we will share in the glory of God.

The reading is straightforward but filled with reassurances. It is a reflection on what is and what is to be. Paul intends it as a way to instill hope in his readers. Offer it to the members of your community in the same manner, drawing them into a vision for the future in which all creation is united and at peace.

GOSPEL   The festival in question in today's gospel is the Feast of Tabernacles or Booths, an important pilgrimage feast in the first century. It was associated with the triumph of God on the Day of the Lord, but retained some of its agricultural origins as an occasion of prayer for rain. The importance of water was emphasized during the feast; each day, water was carried in procession from a spring to the

And the one who searches *hearts*
knows what is the intention of the *Spirit*,
because he *intercedes* for the *holy* ones
according to God's *will*.

GOSPEL   John 7:37–39

A reading from the holy gospel according to John

On the *last* and *greatest* day of the *feast*,
Jesus stood up and *exclaimed*,
"Let anyone who *thirsts* come to me and *drink*.
As Scripture says:
'*Rivers* of living *water* will flow from *within* him
who *believes* in me.'"

He said this in reference to the *Spirit*
that those who came to *believe* in him were to *receive*.
There was, of course, no *Spirit* yet,
because Jesus had *not* yet been *glorified*.

Lift your voice and speak invitingly.

The Spirit was given after Jesus' resurrection.

temple, where it was poured out and flowed onto the ground.

The emphasis on water apparently inspired Jesus to announce a truth about himself. He describes himself as a fountain from which the believer can drink to receive refreshment. The image of drinking from a fountain is used often in connection with Lady Wisdom, who satisfies the thirst for knowledge and right action. The Jewish scriptures hold Wisdom in high esteem. With God she cocreates the world. Jesus is the font of wisdom, or even Wisdom in the flesh.

It should be noted that there has long been discussion about the source of the flowing waters; the Greek is unclear. Either the believer is the source of the water, as in some translations, or Jesus is, implied here. Either way, the waters represent wisdom, a wisdom given by Jesus to those who seek it.

Although the water is a symbol of the teaching of Jesus, it is also identified by the redactor of the gospel as a representation of the Spirit, which will be given by Jesus after

his death and resurrection. We proclaim on the feast of Pentecost that the Spirit indeed fills our lives and inspires our actions.

Emphasize the words of Jesus in this short passage. Invite your listeners to approach him in confidence and to learn from him, filled with the fervent hope and faith inspired by God's gift of the Spirit.

PENTECOST

Lectionary #63

READING I   Acts 2:1–11

A reading from the Acts of the Apostles

When the *time* for *Pentecost* was *fulfilled*,
    they were *all* in one place *together*.
And *suddenly* there *came* from the *sky*
    a *noise* like a strong driving *wind*,
    and it *filled* the entire *house* in which they *were*.
Then there *appeared* to them *tongues* as of *fire*,
    which *parted* and came to rest on each *one* of them.
And they were all *filled* with the Holy *Spirit*
    and began to *speak* in different *tongues*,
    as the *Spirit* enabled them to *proclaim*.

Now there were devout *Jews* from every nation under *heaven*
    staying in *Jerusalem*.
At this *sound*, they gathered in a large *crowd*,
    but they were *confused*
    because each one heard them *speaking* in his own *language*.
They were *astounded*, and in *amazement* they asked,
    "Are not all these people who are speaking *Galileans*?
Then *how* does each of us *hear* them in his native *language*?
We are *Parthians*, *Medes*, and *Elamites*,
    inhabitants of *Mesopotamia*, *Judea* and *Cappadocia*,

Pentecost (which means "fifty") is Jewish in origin and developed into a celebration of the reception of the law at Sinai.

Proclaim this as though you are reading the most exciting part of a mystery novel.

Express their confusion in your voice.

Galileans = gal-ih-LEE-uhnz

Parthians = PAHR-thee-uhnz
Medes = meedz
Elamites = EE-luh-mīts
Mesopotamia = mes-uh-poh-TAY-mee-uh
Judea = joo-DEE-uh
Cappadocia = kap-uh-DOH-shuh

READING I   The presence of God at Pentecost is manifested in several ways. There is a roaring sound, tongues as of fire, and a distinct change in the disciples' ability to communicate. The description in Acts recalls the ancient predictions that God would pour out the Spirit upon all people and that God would renew the people and give them hope. The dramatic symbols of God's presence (the tongues as of fire and the sound like wind) remind one of similar events when the law was given at

Sinai. Most significant, the divisions created by differences in communication, said to have begun after the building of the Tower of Babel, are reversed. All people are able to hear about and understand the wondrous deeds God has done in Jesus.

In the Pentecost account, people from many nations can understand the disciples' preaching. The differences between Jews and Gentiles are wiped out. This is important for us to recall as well: We Christians do not have ownership of God's Spirit. We need to remember that God is much bigger than we

are and is able to include all peoples in a loving embrace.

Share the excitement of this story with your listeners so that they might also experience the Holy Spirit in their lives. Read the first part of the reading a bit breathlessly, in order to convey the sweeping movement of the Spirit and the astonishment of the disciples. Slow down a bit in the second part, but continue to allow your voice to be filled with amazement. Stress in the final line the power of God. You are a vehicle through

Pontus = PON-tuhs
Phrygia = FRIJ-ee-uh
Pamphylia = pam-FIL-ee-uh
Libya = LIB-ee-uh
Cyrene = sī-REE-nee
Cretans = KREE-tuhnz

Slow down and emphasize the final line.

Pontus and *Asia*, *Phrygia* and *Pamphylia*,
Egypt and the districts of *Libya* near *Cyrene*,
as well as travelers from *Rome*,
both *Jews* and *converts* to Judaism, *Cretans* and *Arabs*,
yet we hear them *speaking* in our own *tongues*
of the *mighty* acts of *God.*"

READING II   Romans 8:8–17

A reading from the letter of Saint Paul to the Romans

Brothers and sisters:
Those who are in the *flesh* cannot please *God.*
But *you* are *not* in the flesh;
    on the *contrary*, *you* are in the *spirit*,
    if only the Spirit of God *dwells* in you.
Whoever does not have the Spirit of *Christ* does not *belong*
        to him.

But if Christ is *in* you,
    although the body is *dead* because of *sin*,
    the *spirit* is *alive* because of *righteousness.*
If the Spirit of the *one* who *raised* Jesus from the dead *dwells*
        in you,
    the one who raised *Christ* from the *dead*
    will give *life* to *your* mortal bodies *also*,
    through his *Spirit* that *dwells* in you.

Consequently, brothers and sisters,
    we are not *debtors* to the *flesh*,
    to live *according* to the flesh.

Speak slowly and lift your voice in hopeful certitude.

whom God's Spirit moves in your community on this day. Inspire your listeners to open their hearts to God and to work to break down barriers to communication in their own lives.

There is a choice of second readings today. Speak with your liturgy coordinator or pastor to find out which reading will be used.

READING II **ROMANS.** In this passage Paul contrasts a mindset that is not fixed on God (which he calls being "in the flesh") with the proper Christian mindset (one that is "in the Spirit"). The "flesh" and the "body" are hallmarks of the corruptible world, the world not yet freed from sin and given the promise of life through Jesus. The Spirit is the one who dwells within and enlivens each believer.

It is this Spirit that makes each Christian an heir of God and a joint heir with Christ. The Christians of Rome already know this, says Paul, because of their experience of the Spirit in their prayer. It is the Spirit who inspires them to call out to God as Father, thus giving evidence of their status as adopted children of God. In a typical Pauline statement, the letter asserts that adoption as children of God is available to us through our willingness to suffer as Jesus did, but the future holds out hope of being exalted with Christ.

Offer this meditation to your community with sincerity and conviction. Speak slowly, so that the progression of thought will not be lost on your listeners.

This sentence interrupts the flow of the passage. Speak it more quickly and in a low voice.

For if you live according to the *flesh*, you will *die*,
　but if by the *Spirit* you put to *death* the deeds of the body,
　you will *live*.

Begin afresh with this thought.

For those who are led by the Spirit of *God* are *sons* of God.
For you did not receive a spirit of *slavery* to fall back into *fear*,
　but you received a spirit of *adoption*,
　through whom we cry, "*Abba, Father!*"
The Spirit *himself* bears *witness* with *our* spirit
　that we are *children* of *God*,
　and if *children*, then *heirs*,
　heirs of God and *joint* heirs with *Christ*,
　if only we *suffer* with him
　so that we may also be *glorified* with him.

Or:

READING II　1 Corinthians 12:3b–7, 12–13

A reading from the first letter of Saint Paul to the Corinthians

Brothers and sisters:
No one can say, "*Jesus* is *Lord*," except by the Holy *Spirit*.
There are different kinds of spiritual *gifts* but the same *Spirit*;
　there are different forms of *service* but the same *Lord*;
　there are different *workings* but the same *God*
　who produces *all* of them in *everyone*.
To each *individual* the *manifestation* of the *Spirit*
　is given for some *benefit*.

Pause before and after each element in this list. Emphasize the last line.

1 CORINTHIANS. The Corinthian community was an exuberant one, with lively worship services and energetic members. Paul needed to expend much effort to guide this energetic but sometimes confused community on the right path. The present passage was written in response to a Corinthian question regarding testing the actions of members of the community to see whether they were indeed inspired by God.

Because the Corinthians placed undue emphasis on the more spectacular gifts of the Spirit, such as speaking in tongues and prophesying, Paul insists that the Spirit works in many ways and all gifts of the Spirit should be appreciated. But despite such variety of gifts, the Spirit is not divisive. There is one Spirit who unites all people.

It is the Spirit who gives a person the ability to proclaim Jesus as Lord, a sure confession of faith and sign of the presence of the Spirit. Such a confession, which gives Jesus a title of honor applied to God, distinguishes the Christian from a nonbeliever. Beyond that common confession, the Spirit inspires each person according to what the good of the community requires.

The one Spirit of God unites people from various religious persuasions or from different social and economic circumstances into one body. The differences that had been so important before are no longer significant. This is an important message for us to take to heart, living in a society that sometimes makes it hard to cross the barriers that are established along racial, economic or educational lines.

Differences are essential, but the unity brought by the Spirit prevails.

As a body is *one* though it has many *parts*,
  and *all* the parts of the body, though *many*, are *one* body,
  so also *Christ*.
For in one *Spirit* we were all baptized into one *body*,
  whether *Jews* or *Greeks*, *slaves* or *free* persons,
  and we were *all* given to drink of one *Spirit*.

GOSPEL   John 14:15–16, 23b–26

A reading from the holy gospel according to John

Jesus said to his disciples:

Proclaim this directly to your community.

"If you *love* me, you will keep my *commandments*.
And I will ask the *Father*,
  and he will give you *another* Advocate to be with you *always*.

"Whoever *loves* me will keep my *word*,
  and my *Father* will love *him*,
  and we will *come* to him and make our *dwelling* with him.

There is challenge in this message. To reject Jesus' word is to reject the Father who sent him.

Those who do *not* love me do not keep my *words*;
  yet the word you *hear* is not *mine*
  but that of the *Father* who *sent* me.

Speak with warmth and comfort.

"I have told you this while I am *with* you.
The *Advocate*, the Holy *Spirit* whom the Father
    will send in my *name*,
  will teach you *everything*
  and *remind* you of all that I *told* you."

Or:

Address this reading to your assembly so that all might recognize the ways the Spirit is active in each member of your community. Inspire your listeners to look inside themselves to see the ministries they have to offer, whether visible and acknowledged or quiet but necessary. Challenge them to work always for unity with all other Christians, believing sincerely that there is one Spirit who inspires us all.

Note that there is a choice of gospel readings today.

GOSPEL   JOHN 14. Jesus' last discourse to his followers in the gospel of John lays out his primary teaching in this gospel: the command to love. If his followers truly love him, they will keep his commandments, and his commandment is precisely to love one another. Loving Jesus and keeping his command to love results in the indwelling of God in the

believer. Rejecting Jesus' words and failing to love is a rejection of the Father.

To strengthen and inspire his disciples, Jesus leaves the Holy Spirit to be with them after his return to the Father in glory. Although we celebrate this gift of the Spirit today, the gospel of John describes the experience differently than Luke does in Acts. In John, Jesus breathes his Spirit on his followers during an appearance to them, whereas Luke narrates a dramatic coming of the Spirit in wind and fire. Each author is

GOSPEL   John 20:19–23

A reading from the holy gospel according to John

On the *evening* of that *first* day of the week,
    when the *doors* were *locked*, where the disciples were,
    for *fear* of the *Jews*,
    Jesus came and *stood* in their *midst*
    and *said* to them, "*Peace* be with *you.*"
When he had *said* this, he showed them his *hands* and his *side*.
The disciples *rejoiced* when they saw the *Lord*.

Jesus said to them *again*, "*Peace* be with *you*.
As the *Father* has *sent* me, so I send *you.*"

And when he had *said* this, he *breathed* on them
        and said to them,
    "*Receive* the Holy *Spirit*.
Whose *sins* you *forgive* are *forgiven* them,
and whose sins you *retain* are *retained*."

Although Jesus is recognizable, he has been transformed. He is able to entered a locked room.

In the Hebrew scriptures, the Spirit of God is represented as the breath of God.

Forgiveness is a hallmark of the new people of God.

trying to provide an image to describe the tremendous outpouring of love and inspiration that the early Christians received after Jesus' departure from them. That same Spirit continues to work in each of us.

Proclaim this brief passage slowly and solemnly. Remind your listeners of God's great promise to send the Spirit, and affirm that God's promises last forever.

JOHN 20. The experience of the Spirit's presence in the lives of the evangelists was difficult to describe in concrete terms, leading to the two very different accounts we read in the Acts of the Apostles and in this passage from the gospel of John. Here, the Spirit is given on Easter Sunday, with Jesus still present. The spectacular occurrence of wind and fire has changed; now it is the astonishing ability of Jesus to enter a locked room that brings amazement and awe. What matters is not how the event is described but the reality that the Spirit has indeed been given to believers, drawing Christians of every way of life into one church.

And what Jesus brings, what the Spirit inspires, is peace. It is the deep, heartfelt peace of knowing that one is in right relationship with God, despite what might be happening in one's life or in the world. It is a peace that gives the strength to change the world. Jesus sends us, his followers, just as he was sent, and says that the hallmark of the life in the Spirit is forgiveness. Enmity and strife remain, but in the Spirit we can heal wounds and bring forgiveness and unity to a broken world.

Speak Jesus' words gently but firmly. Pray that the members of your community might also receive the Spirit, just as Jesus' first disciples did.

Lectionary #166

READING I Proverbs 8:22–31

A reading from the book of Proverbs

Thus says the *wisdom* of *God*:
"The LORD *possessed* me, the *beginning* of his *ways*,
   the *forerunner* of his prodigies of long *ago*;
from of *old* I was poured forth,
   at the *first*, before the *earth*.
When there were no *depths* I was brought *forth*,
   when there were no *fountains* or springs of *water*;
before the *mountains* were settled into *place*,
   before the *hills*, I was brought *forth*;
while as yet the *earth* and *fields* were not *made*,
   nor the first *clods* of the *world*.

"When the LORD established the *heavens* I was *there*,
   when he marked out the *vault* over the face of the *deep*;
when he made *firm* the skies *above*,
   when he fixed *fast* the foundations of the *earth*;
when he set for the *sea* its *limit*,
   so that the *waters* should not transgress his *command*;
then was I *beside* him as his *craftsman*,
   and I was his *delight* day by day,
playing before him all the *while*,
   playing on the surface of his *earth*;
   and I found *delight* in the human *race*."

Stress the words that describe the antiquity of Wisdom.

Speak in lofty tones of Wisdom's presence throughout creation.

Pause briefly before the word "then"; proceed with a strong voice filled with exuberance.

READING I In a beautiful declaration of her greatness, Wisdom claims that God created the world through her. Wisdom was present from the beginning and worked with God in establishing the world and all that is in it.

Christians have long associated the figure of Wisdom with the person of Christ, using the wisdom tradition to understand the relationship of the Father and the Son. Just as Wisdom asserts her participation in creation, so also Christians hold that all things came into being through Christ. Christians believe that Jesus, the Son of God, is the wisdom of God, which is why this passage is used for today's celebration of the Trinity.

Read this passage as though you are sharing exciting, breathtaking news. Close on a note of joy as you share the God's delight in the beauty of Wisdom.

READING II Romans 5:1–5

A reading from the letter of Saint Paul to the Romans

God's peace is the direct result of faith in Christ. Emphasize this concept.

Brothers and sisters:
Therefore, since we have been *justified* by *faith*,
> we have *peace* with God through our Lord Jesus *Christ*,
> through whom we have gained *access* by *faith*
> to this *grace* in which we *stand*,
> and we *boast* in *hope* of the *glory* of *God*.

Avoid a sing-song voice in these lines.

Not only *that*, but we even boast of our *afflictions*,
> knowing that *affliction* produces *endurance*,
> and *endurance*, proven *character*,
> and proven *character*, *hope*,
> and *hope* does not *disappoint*,
> because the love of *God* has been poured out into our *hearts*
> through the Holy *Spirit* that has been *given* to us.

READING II In a warm declaration of the peace that comes through Jesus and the working of the Holy Spirit, Paul discusses the centrality of faith in the Christian life. It is by faith in Jesus' saving actions that Christians are justified before God, which gives us hope that we shall one day share in God's glory.

But lest that message be misunderstood, Paul immediately highlights the importance of suffering for the faith. He knew from his own experience that some early churches often emphasized glorification over the necessity of suffering. Paul acknowledges a future glorification but asserts that our present reality often involves pain and struggle. But such pain can build character, making the Christian stronger and eager to serve God. Stronger character generates greater hope, a hope that is not in vain because it is confirmed by the love of God and the action of the Holy Spirit.

The church proclaims this passage today because of its reference to all three persons of the Trinity. It is not an exposition of trinitarian doctrine, however, which took several centuries to develop. As Paul intended it, it is a statement of encouragement to stand firm in the faith, trusting in God's goodness and love. Offer it as such to the members of your assembly.

GOSPEL   John 16:12–15

A reading from the holy gospel according to John

Jesus said to his disciples:
"I have much more to *tell* you, but you cannot *bear* it *now*.
But when he *comes*, the Spirit of *truth*,
   he will *guide* you to all *truth*.
He will *not* speak on his *own*,
   but he will speak what he *hears*,
   and will *declare* to you the things that are *coming*.
He will glorify *me*,
   because he will take from what is *mine* and *declare* it to you.
Everything that the *Father* has is *mine*;
   for *this* reason I told you that he will take from what is *mine*
   and *declare* it to you."

Pause after "comes" to set off the identifying phrase that follows it.

GOSPEL   In Jesus' farewell discourse in the gospel of John, Jesus tells the disciples what will happen to him and to them, and what they can expect when he is gone. Since the gospel was actually written many years after Jesus' death and resurrection, his words reflect the experience of the community that produced the gospel. In today's passage, it is the presence of the Spirit in the lives of Christians that gives rise to these promises of Jesus.

Jesus declares that there are many more things he wants to teach his followers, but it is the Spirit who will bring them greater understanding. The Spirit will guide Jesus' disciples—and Christians of all ages as well—and will instruct and comfort the faithful. But, as Jesus' words attest, the Spirit is always revealing and glorifying Jesus himself, and Jesus is so intimately united with the Father that he is able to claim in another passage, "The Father and I are one."

Emphasize the relationship of the Father, Son and Spirit, while remaining true to the thrust of the passage that the Spirit provides guidance for Christians as we await Jesus' return.

BODY AND BLOOD OF CHRIST

Lectionary #169

READING I   Genesis 14:18–20

Speak slowly and clearly throughout this short passage.
Melchizedek = mel-KEEZ-ih-dek
Salem = SAY-luhm

A reading from the book of Genesis

In those days, *Melchizedek*, king of *Salem*,
　　brought out *bread* and *wine*,
　　and being a *priest* of God Most *High*,
　　he *blessed* Abram with these *words*:
　　"Blessed be *Abram* by God Most *High*,
　　the creator of *heaven* and *earth*;
　　and blessed be *God* Most *High*,
　　who delivered your *foes* into your *hand*."
Then Abram gave him a *tenth* of *everything*.

Proclaim this line of praise with enthusiasm.

READING II   1 Corinthians 11:23–26

A reading from the first letter of Saint Paul to the Corinthians

Brothers and sisters:
I *received* from the *Lord* what I also handed on to *you*,
　　that the Lord *Jesus*, on the night he was handed *over*,
　　took *bread*, and, after he had given *thanks*,
　　broke it and said, "*This* is my *body* that is for *you*.
Do this in *remembrance* of *me*."

With Paul, you hand on this account of Jesus' words to your community.

Proclaim this solemnly.

READING I The figure of Melchizedek appears only in this passage, in Psalm 110, and in the letter to the Hebrews, where he prefigures Jesus as priest and king. Here he appears out of nowhere and yet is given honor and authority. As priest, he presides over a liturgy involving bread and wine, suggestive of the Christian eucharist and the reason we proclaim this passage today, the solemnity of the Body and Blood of Christ. Abraham (here still called Abram) offers Melchizedek a tithe—one-tenth—of his possessions, just as one-tenth of a person's resources were later offered to God at the temple in Jerusalem.

Melchizedek has the authority to bless Abram and offers a stirring praise of God. Abram was returning victorious from battle, winning despite all odds, and Melchizedek declares that it was God who had blessed Abram and given him victory.

Take your time in proclaiming this passage to your assembly, emphasizing the bread and wine offerings of Melchizedek and savoring every word of the blessings. Pause before you begin, so that you are assured of your listeners' rapt attention. Then speak with dignity.

READING II The first letter of Paul to the Corinthians contains the oldest known tradition about the eucharist. It is the one most familiar to us, since it is the model for the eucharistic prayers that we use each time we celebrate eucharist. It is not simply Paul's own understanding but something he received from the risen Lord, which he now passes on to the members of the Corinthian community. They, in turn, will

In the same way also the *cup*, after supper, saying,
"This *cup* is the *new covenant* in my *blood*.
Do this, as often as you *drink* it, in *remembrance* of *me*."
For as often as you *eat* this *bread* and *drink* the *cup*,
you proclaim the *death* of the Lord until he *comes*.

GOSPEL Luke 9:11b–17

A reading from the holy gospel according to Luke

Jesus spoke to the crowds about the kingdom of *God*,
and he *healed* those who needed to be *cured*.

As the day was drawing to a *close*,
the Twelve *approached* him and said,
"*Dismiss* the crowd
so that they can go to the surrounding *villages* and *farms*
and find *lodging* and *provisions*;
for we are in a deserted *place* here."

He said to them, "Give them some food *yourselves*."
They replied, "*Five loaves* and *two fish* are all we *have*,
unless we *ourselves* go and *buy* food for all these people."
Now the *men* there numbered about five *thousand*.

Then he said to his disciples,
"Have them sit *down* in groups of about *fifty*."
They *did* so and made them all sit *down*.

Are the disciples concerned about their own well-being or that of the crowd? Let your response to this question dictate your tone of voice.

Jesus speaks with confidence, but his disciples begin to panic.

Jesus takes control. Proclaim this with dignity.

share it with those who come after them. Faith is a communal event.

Although the words are familiar, it is important to reflect on them and pray about them before proclaiming them. Jesus gives thanks for the bread and shares it with his disciples. The act of sharing is central; we join together to partake of the eucharist and become one body of Christ because of what we share. It is Christ's body, a body that is broken and battered on the cross. His words look forward to his passion as he tells his friends to remember him. Indeed, we look back in each eucharist to that time when

heaven broke through into human life, when eternity invaded our temporal existence, when God became one of us.

Jesus also recalls the covenants established between God and the chosen faithful of old, especially the covenant with Abraham. Covenants were agreements between God and a person, in which God promised protection and the human partner pledged loyalty. The covenant was ratified with the sacrifice of an animal. Jesus looks forward to his death on the cross, declaring that his blood

is sufficient for ratifying this new covenant. No other need die to fulfill this covenant.

In addition to remembering Jesus when sharing the bread and cup, Christians also look to a future time when Christ's reign will be complete. Far from shrinking from the reality of Jesus' passion and death, Paul proclaims it, but he also looks forward in hope to future glory. As we wait in hope, we proclaim Jesus' death, for it is precisely in that moment of brokenness and pain that true peace has entered the world. We remember it at every eucharist.

Then taking the five *loaves* and the two *fish*,
    and looking up to *heaven*,
    he said the *blessing* over them, *broke* them,
    and gave them to the *disciples* to set before the *crowd*.

They all *ate* and were *satisfied*.
And when the leftover *fragments* were picked *up*,
    they filled *twelve* wicker *baskets*.

Proclaim this message to your listeners with great solemnity. Speak Jesus' words as though you are reading them for the first time, so that the members of your assembly may hear them with fresh ears, especially on this day when we reflect on the centrality of the eucharist in our lives.

GOSPEL The story of the loaves and fishes has long been a favorite of Christians. It speaks of sharing and of nourishment, of hospitality and of providing for others. Today's selection opens with Jesus providing for the crowds in several ways: by filling their spirits with teaching about God, and by healing their bodies of disease. But it concentrates on the way Jesus cares for the people by providing them with food.

The Twelve, the inner circle of Jesus' followers, see the mass of people and want to send them away. Perhaps they are concerned with the needs of the crowd, but they might also be overwhelmed by the mob. Jesus responds matter-of-factly: Feed them. When the Twelve are dismayed at the thought of having to share their meager supplies, Jesus takes action, blessing and sharing the food.

The text does not describe how the miracle occurs. (Did Jesus increase the food, or did he inspire generosity?) What it does teach is that we will find abundance when we include others in our embrace.

Give plenty of expression to the words of the Twelve, and speak Jesus' words with calm assurance. Close with conviction, drawing your hearers to see the eucharistic connotations of the closing paragraphs.

BIRTH OF JOHN THE BAPTIST VIGIL

Lectionary #586

READING I   Jeremiah 1:4–10

A reading from the book of the prophet Jeremiah

Speak God's words with tenderness.

In the days of King *Josiah*, the *word* of the LORD
    came to me, saying:
Before I formed you in the *womb* I *knew* you,
    before you were *born* I *dedicated* you,
    a *prophet* to the nations I *appointed* you.

There is a bit of fear in Jeremiah's words.

"Ah, Lord *GOD!*" I said,
    "I know *not* how to *speak*; I am too *young.*"
But the LORD answered me,
    Say *not*, "I am too *young.*"

Let your voice grow in intensity as you read God's response.

To whomever I *send* you, you shall *go*;
    whatever I *command* you, you shall *speak.*
Have no fear *before* them,
    because I am *with* you to *deliver* you, says the LORD.

Then the LORD extended his *hand* and touched
        my *mouth*, saying,
    See, I place my *words* in your *mouth!*
This *day* I set you
    over *nations* and over *kingdoms*,
    to *root* up and to tear *down*,
    to *destroy* and to *demolish*,
    to *build* and to *plant.*

Be careful not to become sing-song, but speak forcefully.

READING I   The prophet Jeremiah was active at the end of the seventh and beginning of the sixth centuries BCE, a time when Judah was threatened by a powerful nation from the north.

Jeremiah is often remembered as a prophet of doom, foretelling the defeat of the nation. But Jeremiah also spoke with tenderness and comfort in the face of Judah's impending defeat. He asserted that the exile would be temporary and that God intended it as a period of chastisement for the sake of teaching the people how to be truly faithful.

We read today from the account of Jeremiah's call to God's service as a prophet. The passage opens with the tender words of God, declaring God's knowledge and choice of this servant. Even before Jeremiah was born, indeed before he was even conceived, he was chosen to proclaim God's word.

Responding in humility and perhaps fear, Jeremiah argues with God. The prophets were often honest with God about their shortcomings, and they sometimes even tried to convince God to choose someone else. Jeremiah insists that he is too young and inexperienced, but God is not convinced.

God will provide both the words and the strength to speak; Jeremiah is compelled to go forth.

The lips of the prophet Isaiah were touched with a burning coal in order to purify his mouth for prophecy. In a similar gesture, God touches Jeremiah's mouth in order to infuse him with the word of God. He is given a mission, and much of the mission involves destruction. But in the end he will provide hope and encouragement.

We read this passage today because John the Baptist was similarly called (even from his mother's womb!) to be a prophet to

READING II   1 Peter 1:8–12

A reading from the first letter of Saint Peter

Beloved:
Although you have not *seen* Jesus Christ you *love* him;
  even though you do not see him *now* yet *believe* in him,
  you *rejoice* with an *indescribable* and *glorious joy*,
  as you attain the *goal* of your *faith*, the *salvation*
    of your *souls*.

Concerning this *salvation*,
  prophets who prophesied about the *grace* that was to be *yours*
  searched and *investigated* it,
  investigating the *time* and *circumstances*
  that the Spirit of Christ *within* them *indicated*
  when he testified in *advance*
  to the *sufferings* destined for *Christ*
  and the *glories* to *follow* them.

It was *revealed* to them that they were serving
    not *themselves* but *you*
  with regard to the things that have now been *announced*
    to you
  by those who preached the *good news* to you
  through the Holy *Spirit* sent from *heaven*,
  things into which *angels* longed to *look*.

Speak with certainty and encouragement.

This is a long sentence; practice your phrasing carefully.

The opening phrase is key; emphasize the word "you." Then speak in a more subdued voice, building in strength at the end.

Israel. He too was compelled to speak God's word, even if it was difficult for people to hear. But it is also a message that we all need to receive. God has called each of us, even before we were born, for a purpose. Only God knows completely what our mission is, but we know that God will give us the strength to speak the truth.

Proclaim this reading as a direct call to the members of your community. Share the opening scene with warmth and sensitivity. Jeremiah's own words are sincere, but God's reply is stronger. Speak with power and conviction.

READING II The first letter of Peter was written to Christians living in Asia Minor (modern Turkey), an area in which Paul was particularly active. It seeks to give them encouragement despite their sufferings. Government leaders were beginning to see that Christians were not simply a sect within Judaism, and the Christians' refusal to participate in the state cult made them vulnerable to charges of treason and insubordination. The author writes to build up the community's hope and faith in a time of persecution, speaking of the joy that knowledge of Christ brings, despite adversity.

Because of the victory of Jesus Christ over death, the Christian can look forward in joy despite present trials, moving ever closer to the goal of salvation. The Christian loves Jesus despite having never seen him; the Christian believes in him, although he is no longer present on earth. The author knows that the Christian life is a paradox and continues to point out the intricacies of the faith throughout this passage and the entire letter.

The author asserts that even though the Hebrew prophets lived long before Jesus, they were really instructing believers about him. They prophesied about the sufferings

Zechariah = zek-uh-RĪ-uh
Abijah = uh-BĪ-juh

Speak firmly, then with a tone of regret as you mention their childlessness.

The angel speaks comfortingly.

GOSPEL Luke 1:5–17

A reading from the holy gospel according to Luke

In the days of *Herod*, King of *Judea*,
     there was a priest named *Zechariah*
     of the priestly division of *Abijah*;
     his *wife* was from the daughters of *Aaron*,
     and her name was *Elizabeth*.
Both were *righteous* in the eyes of God,
     observing all the *commandments*
     and *ordinances* of the Lord *blamelessly*.
But they had no *child*, because Elizabeth was *barren*
     and both were *advanced* in *years*.

Once when he was serving
     as *priest* in his division's turn before *God*,
     according to the practice of the priestly *service*,
     he was chosen by *lot*
     to enter the *sanctuary* of the *Lord* to burn *incense*.
Then, when the whole assembly of the *people*
          was praying *outside*
     at the hour of the *incense* offering,
     the *angel* of the *Lord appeared* to him,
     standing at the *right* of the altar of *incense*.
Zechariah was *troubled* by what he saw, and *fear* came
          upon him.

But the angel said to him, "Do *not* be *afraid*, Zechariah,
     because your *prayer* has been *heard*.
Your wife *Elizabeth* will bear you a *son*,
     and you shall name him *John*.

that would befall Jesus, but they also predicted his glorification. They were able to do so precisely because the Holy Spirit spoke in them and inspired them. But now that same Spirit has been more fully revealed in the gospel of Jesus Christ.

This selection is an appropriate one to address to Christians of all eras. Speak boldly of the joy that comes from believing in Jesus, despite our distance from him in time and space. Although the author is probably speaking about the prophets of Israel, the passage is used today because John, the

direct precursor of Jesus, is the last and greatest of the Hebrew prophets.

GOSPEL | Only the gospel of Luke provides an account of John the Baptist's birth and of the visitation of Mary to Elizabeth. As he does throughout the gospel, the author begins by providing the historical setting for the events he describes, intimating that the events he recounts effect all of human history. The gospel writer places John's conception during the reign of King Herod in Judea.

John, the author tells us, was born into a priestly family; both his father and mother were of priestly lineage and were righteous in God's sight. They upheld the law of Moses and presumably raised their son to respect it. Throughout the gospel, Jesus is presented as a fulfillment of God's promises to Israel; his precursor likewise stands within the tradition of Israel.

As in the case of many Hebrew women before her (such as Sarah, Rebecca, Rachel and Hannah), John's mother, Elizabeth, had

Raise your voice in joy as you proclaim this promise.

"And you will have *joy* and *gladness*,
    and many will *rejoice* at his birth,
    for he will be *great* in the sight of the *Lord*.
John will drink neither *wine* nor strong *drink*.
He will be *filled* with the Holy *Spirit*
    even from his mother's *womb*,
    and he will turn many of the children of *Israel*
    to the *Lord* their *God*.

Emphasize the mention of the Spirit and the power that will fill John.

"He will go *before* him in the *spirit* and *power* of *Elijah*
    to turn their *hearts* toward their *children*
    and the *disobedient* to the understanding of the *righteous*,
    to prepare a *people* fit for the *Lord*."

no children in her old age. Into this sad situation an angel appears. While in the sanctuary of the temple, where only priests could enter, John's father, Zechariah, receives a message from God, delivered by the angel Gabriel, announcing the birth of a child. As in the annunciation to Mary, the angel's presence instills fear, but Zechariah is told not to be afraid. Zechariah is dumbfounded, unable to speak until after the child's birth.

The angel indicates the mission and temperament of the child. He is to be no ordinary child, but one whose birth will bring joy and whose life will be modeled after that of the prophets of old. He will be dedicated to God in the manner of the nazirites, who devoted themselves wholeheartedly—and visibly, by not cutting their hair—to serving God. Just as Elijah turned the hearts of Israel toward God, so also this child will be filled with a power that will lead many to righteousness and prepare them for God's presence. Although the author of this gospel never explicitly identifies John as Elijah, who was expected to return prior to the coming of the Messiah, John has much the same mission. He is a bold and courageous prophet to the people.

Even in this story of the announcement of John's birth, then, several key themes from the gospel are presented: These events have lasting impact and affect all of history; they fulfill the expectations of Israel; and the lives of Jesus and John are set squarely in the religious tradition of Jerusalem and the temple. Finally, the Holy Spirit enlivens John, even from the womb, preparing the people for the coming of the Messiah.

Summon your storytelling skills to offer this tale to your listeners with the joy and awe it is meant to evoke.

BIRTH OF JOHN THE BAPTIST

Lectionary #587

READING I   Isaiah 49:1–6

A reading from the book of the prophet Isaiah

Speak with tenderness and compassion.

Hear me, O *coastlands,*
  listen, O distant *peoples.*
The LORD *called* me from *birth,*
  from my mother's *womb* he gave me my *name.*

He made of me a sharp-edged *sword*
  and *concealed* me in the shadow of his *arm.*
He made me a polished *arrow,*
  in his *quiver* he *hid* me.

The identification of Israel as the servant comes as a bit of a surprise. Speak boldly.

There is regret and sadness in these lines.

You are my *servant,* he said to me,
  Israel, through whom I show my *glory.*
Though I thought I had toiled in *vain,*
  and for *nothing, uselessly,* spent my *strength,*
yet my *reward* is with the LORD,
  my *recompense* is with my *God.*

For now the LORD has *spoken*
  who formed me as his *servant* from the *womb,*
that Jacob may be brought *back* to him
  and Israel *gathered* to him;
and I am made *glorious* in the sight of the LORD,
  and my *God* is now my *strength!*

Raise your voice now and until the end, closing on a strong note.

READING I The book of Isaiah contains several "servant songs" in which God's servant speaks of facing adversity while steadfastly serving the divine will. In today's selection from Isaiah, the servant describes being chosen by God and the mission that awaits God's messenger. But this passage also adds an interesting twist to the picture of an individual servant found elsewhere; in this passage, the servant is Israel.

In a beautiful description of the intimacy that exists between God and the servant, the servant recognizes having been called by God, even before birth. This is not simply a general call; God knows the servant by name and calls the servant specifically. God has chosen this one from all the rest and gives the servant a message so sharp and true that it cuts like a sword. The servant is destined to draw the people into the relationship with God that is meant for them.

But the servant, Israel, has a bigger mission. Not only are God's chosen people to return to God, but Israel is to be a beacon for all the world to see. God's salvation is not for a chosen few but is available to all people. Israel must proclaim God's glory to the nations and thus draw all people to God.

We proclaim this passage in our celebration of John the Baptist's birth because John was also a servant who sought to restore the people to God. He too had an intimate relationship with God, spoke the truth without flinching, and, as we know from the gospel, was chosen even before he was born. But the message is for all of us as well. We too are called by name and given the task of preaching God's message to all the earth. Proclaim this passage with an eye to

It is too *little*, he says, for you to be my *servant*,
 to *raise* up the tribes of *Jacob*,
  and *restore* the survivors of *Israel*;
I will make you a *light* to the *nations*,
 that my *salvation* may reach to the ends of the *earth*.

READING II Acts 13:22–26

A reading from the Acts of the Apostles

In those days, *Paul* said:
"God raised up *David* as their *king*;
 of him he testified,
 'I have found *David*, son of *Jesse*, a man after my own *heart*;
 he will carry out my every *wish*.'

"From this man's *descendants* God, according to his *promise*,
 has brought to Israel a *savior*, *Jesus*.
John heralded his *coming* by proclaiming a baptism
  of *repentance*
 to all the people of *Israel*;
 and as John was *completing* his course, he would say,
 'What do you suppose that I *am*? I am not *he*.
Behold, one is coming *after* me;
 I am not *worthy* to unfasten the *sandals* of his *feet*.'

"My brothers, *children* of the family of *Abraham*,
 and those others *among* you who are *God*-fearing,
 to *us* this word of *salvation* has been *sent*."

**Sidebar notes (left margin):**

Paul begins with a brief reference to Israel's history, then asserts that all history is directed to the appearance of Jesus.

Pause before mentioning John, then proceed to tell this story as an independent unit, in order to draw attention to the role of the Baptist.

Pause again after John's words, then proclaim Paul's final statement with confidence.

the story of John but also as a challenge to your listeners to be a light to the nations.

READING II — John was remembered by the early church as one who pointed toward Jesus as God's chosen one. There are hints of tension in the gospels between the followers of Jesus and the followers of John, who were at first rival groups. So the gospel writers make clear that John is the lesser of the two figures; it is Jesus who is the savior of Israel.

Jesus does not simply come on the scene unannounced or unexpected. As Paul makes clear in his speech in the synagogue, God chose David to carry out God's plan and promised him that one of his descendants would always reign over Israel. Paul proclaims that this promise is fulfilled in Jesus, David's descendant. Jesus is the rightful heir to the promises of God.

To prepare for Jesus, John arrived preaching a baptism of repentance. John's message was to the chosen people of Israel, and his task was to draw the people back into a right relationship with God.

Proclaim this speech in a straightforward manner, emphasizing the greatness of Jesus over John. But give due emphasis to the Baptist, who prepared the way for the one who was greater than he, and whose feast we celebrate today.

GOSPEL — The story of the birth of John in the gospel of Luke parallels the infancy narrative of Jesus: An angel announces John's conception, name and mission; John's birth is greeted with great joy; and bystanders marvel at the events. But

GOSPEL   Luke 1:57–66, 80

A reading from the holy gospel according to Luke

When the time arrived for *Elizabeth* to have her *child*
   she gave birth to a *son*.
Her *neighbors* and *relatives* heard
   that the Lord had shown his great *mercy* toward her,
   and they *rejoiced* with her.

When they came on the *eighth* day to *circumcise* the child,
   they were going to call him *Zechariah* after his *father*,
   but his mother said in reply,
   "*No.* He will be called *John*."
But they answered her,
   "There is no one among your *relatives* who has this name."
So they made *signs*, asking his *father* what *he* wished him
    to be called.

He asked for a *tablet* and wrote, "*John* is his *name*,"
   and all were *amazed*.
Immediately his mouth was *opened*, his tongue *freed*,
   and he *spoke* blessing *God*.

Then *fear* came upon all their neighbors,
   and all these matters were *discussed*
   throughout the *hill* country of *Judea*.
All who *heard* these things took them to *heart*, saying,
   "*What*, then, will this child *be*?"
For surely the *hand* of the *Lord* was *with* him.

The child *grew* and became strong in *spirit*,
   and he was in the *desert* until the day
   of his *manifestation* to *Israel*.

This unexpected gift of a child is a sign of God's tremendous love.

Zechariah = zek-uh-RĪ-uh

Speak Elizabeth's words firmly.

Give this line great emphasis. Then pause before recounting the amazing events that follow.

Speak with awe and wonder.

Close with a firm tone.

the events surrounding Jesus' birth surpass those surrounding John's, for John is the precursor. Even the stories of their births make clear that John is of lesser significance than Jesus, although he still has an important role to play in the events of salvation.

Elizabeth and Zechariah were devout Jews and circumcised their child on the eighth day, as required by the Mosaic law. The child was named in the same ceremony. Both his parents agree that the name announced by the angel should be given him, despite the objections of relatives. Zechariah had been unable to speak since

his encounter with the angel in the temple. When the angel announced the impending birth of John, Zechariah had doubted, citing his and Elizabeth's advanced age. He was struck dumb because of his questioning and was allowed to speak only after obeying the angel's command to name the child John.

Zechariah's resolute stance and his renewed gift of speech inspire those present, who recognize that God's Spirit is upon this child. John grows strong in the Holy Spirit and lives a life set apart from others, a sign of his special status and mission. The wilderness is often a place of testing and

strengthening, and John uses the time well, emerging from his self-imposed exile as a powerful messenger of God.

Proclaim the sense of inspiration in this gospel passage. Express the joy of the birth, the doubt of Zechariah's relatives, and Zechariah's stalwart resolve. Then speak with awe as it becomes evident to everyone that God's Spirit is guiding John.

13TH SUNDAY IN ORDINARY TIME

Lectionary #99

READING I   1 Kings 19:16b, 19–21

A reading from the first book of Kings

The LORD said to *Elijah*:
  "You shall anoint *Elisha*, son of *Shaphat* of Abel*meholah*,
  as *prophet* to *succeed* you."

Elijah set *out* and came upon *Elisha*, son of *Shaphat*,
  as he was *plowing* with twelve yoke of *oxen*;
  he was following the *twelfth*.

Elijah went *over* to him and threw his *cloak* over him.
Elisha left the *oxen*, ran *after* Elijah, and said,
  "*Please*, let me kiss my father and mother *goodbye*,
  and I will *follow* you."

Elijah answered, "Go *back*!
Have *I* done anything to *you*?"
Elisha *left* him, and taking the yoke of *oxen*, *slaughtered* them;
  he used the *plowing* equipment for fuel to boil their *flesh*,
  and gave it to his people to *eat*.
Then Elisha *left* and followed *Elijah* as his *attendant*.

Elijah = ee-LĪ-juh
Elisha = ee-LĪ-shuh
Shaphat = SHAY-fat

Pause after "oxen."

READING I   The call of a prophet often involves a direct encounter between human and divine. Sometimes the encounter involves a heavenly vision; at other times the prophet may hear the voice of God. For Elisha, the call to prophetic activity involves a period of apprenticeship under the tutelage of Elijah. Elijah, guided by God, chooses Elisha to assume the prophetic mantle. Elisha's task is to respond in trust.

The description of Elisha plowing with twelve yoke of oxen, although probably an exaggeration, conveys how much he gave up in order to respond to God's call. But he does respond immediately, pausing only to notify his parents, thus fulfilling his family obligations. Inexplicably, Elijah seems to tell Elisha not to follow, but Elisha cannot be dissuaded.

Proclaim this story of Elisha's call with enthusiasm, emphasizing Elisha's willingness to follow Elijah without hesitation. It points forward to the lesson on discipleship in the gospel and is a fitting reminder to all of us that discipleship must be embraced wholeheartedly.

READING II   Paul's letter to the Galatians is his treatise on Christian freedom. In it, he chastises, cajoles and rebukes the Galatians in order to bring them to accept the freedom that Christ has won for them. The central issue is circumcision and whether non-Jews, including the members of the Galatian community, were required to keep the Jewish law. Paul preaches the centrality of faith and presents the law as a burden that interferes with freedom in Christ. Paul argues that circumcision binds one to obey every aspect of the Jewish law, an obedience that is impossible to maintain

READING II   Galatians 5:1, 13–18

A reading from the letter of Saint Paul to the Galatians

Brothers and sisters:
For *freedom* Christ set us *free*;
   so stand *firm* and do not submit again to the yoke of *slavery*.

For you were called for *freedom*, brothers and sisters.
But do not *use* this freedom
   as an opportunity for the *flesh*;
   rather, *serve* one another through *love*.
For the whole *law* is fulfilled in one *statement*,
   namely, "You shall love your *neighbor* as *yourself*."
But if you go on *biting* and *devouring* one another,
   beware that you are not *consumed* by one another.

I say, then: *live* by the *Spirit*
   and you will certainly not *gratify* the desire of the *flesh*.
For the flesh has desires *against* the Spirit,
   and the *Spirit* against the *flesh*;
   these are *opposed* to each other,
   so that you may not *do* what you *want*.
But if you are guided by the *Spirit*, you are *not* under the *law*.

and cannot bring salvation. Salvation is a gift offered in Christ; it is not something that can be earned with good behavior.

Today's passage does not deal directly with the question of circumcision but presents the issue of freedom in more general terms that are applicable today. Freedom is not simply the absence of law but the opportunity to act uprightly, to go beyond the letter of the law and truly love oneself and others. Real freedom is not freedom from responsibility but freedom for the responsibility of Christian life.

The Spirit provides the Christian with the moral guidance necessary to live in a way that is truly free. Paul contrasts the Spirit with the desires of the flesh, another way of speaking of slavery to sin. The sins Paul has in mind are not simply "fleshly" in a sexual sense but include desires such as greed, jealousy and selfishness. These are not from the Spirit and are not the fruits of freedom in Christ but are the condition of enslaved, sinful humanity. The Spirit, however, guides the Christian beyond the law, for the Spirit knows what is right and good.

Reflect on actions or desires of your own that sometimes feel overpowering and enslaving. Keep them in mind as you read this exhortation to freedom, and resolve to heed Paul's advice to be led by the Spirit.

GOSPEL Jesus' journey in the gospel of Luke, which we follow throughout the rest of the liturgical year, is always directed toward Jerusalem and his death. Today's passage is found at a transition point in the gospel, when Jesus finishes his ministry in his home area of Galilee and begins his journey toward Jerusalem.

GOSPEL   Luke 9:51–62

A reading from the holy gospel according to Luke

When the days for Jesus' being taken up were *fulfilled*,
  he resolutely determined to *journey* to *Jerusalem*,
  and he sent *messengers ahead* of him.

On the *way* they entered a Samaritan *village*
  to prepare for his *reception* there,
  but they would not *welcome* him
  because the destination of his journey was *Jerusalem*.

When the disciples James and John *saw* this they asked,
  "*Lord*, do you want us to call down *fire* from *heaven*
  to *consume* them?"
Jesus turned and *rebuked* them, and they journeyed
    to *another* village.

As they were proceeding on their *journey* someone said to him,
  "I will *follow* you wherever you *go*."
Jesus answered him,
  "*Foxes* have *dens* and *birds* of the sky have *nests*,
  but the Son of *Man* has nowhere to rest his *head*."

And to another he said, "*Follow* me."
But he replied, "Lord, let me go *first* and bury my *father*."
But he answered him, "Let the *dead* bury their *dead*.
But *you*, go and proclaim the *kingdom* of *God*."

And another said, "I will *follow* you, Lord,
  but *first* let me say *farewell* to my family at *home*."
To him Jesus said, "*No* one who sets a hand to the *plow*
  and looks to what was left *behind* is *fit* for the kingdom
    of *God*."

When Jesus meets with rejection, he simply continues on his way. There is no need for vengeance. Pause.

Read this as a direct response to the person's intent to follow wherever Jesus goes.

Is Jesus impatient here or resigned? Modify your voice according to your understanding.

Discipleship requires wholehearted focus on the goal ahead.

The journey from Galilee to Jerusalem often required passing through Samaritan territory. Although the Samaritans and Jews shared many of the same traditions and beliefs, Samaritans rejected the centrality of Jerusalem and the temple cult. As a result, Jews and Samaritans were hostile to one another. The Samaritans in today's gospel selection reject Jesus precisely because he is on his way to Jerusalem.

When James and John (the "sons of thunder") want to call down fire from heaven, Jesus rebukes them. Their request is reminiscent of a similar incident in the life of Elijah, when Elijah did call down fire to demonstrate the superiority of Israel's God to all others. But Jesus corrects his disciples; one cannot be a follower of Jesus and resort to violence.

The second half of the gospel selection presents Jesus' responses to those who wish to follow him. In the first, Jesus replies enigmatically to a would-be follower that the Son of Man has no place to lay his head. Following an itinerant preacher who advocates separation from the concerns of the world is not a life of leisure. To the second person, whose father has died, Jesus replies that discipleship involves ministry to the living. It is an active life of proclaiming God's reign. Finally, in response to the last would-be disciple, Jesus makes it clear that nothing is more important than following Jesus. The call to discipleship is a demanding one.

Read this passage with attention to the two distinct sections that form the whole. The second section has three parts. Offer it to your community as a call to greater fidelity to Jesus and a summons to follow him on his path to Jerusalem and death.

14TH SUNDAY IN ORDINARY TIME

Lectionary #102

READING I   Isaiah 66:10–14c

A reading from the book of the prophet Isaiah

Begin strongly, with a bright voice.

Thus says the LORD:
Rejoice with Jerusalem and be *glad* because of her,
    all you who *love* her;
exult, exult with her,
    all you who were *mourning* over her!

Lower your voice a bit and speak tenderly.

Oh, that you may suck *fully*
    of the milk of her *comfort*,
that you may *nurse* with *delight*
    at her abundant *breasts*!

This is a promise. Deliver it with boldness.

For *thus* says the LORD:
Lo, I will spread *prosperity* over Jerusalem like a *river*,
    and the wealth of the *nations* like an overflowing *torrent*.
As *nurslings*, you shall be carried in her *arms*,
    and *fondled* in her *lap*;
as a *mother* comforts her *child*,
    so will *I* comfort *you*;
    in *Jerusalem* you shall find your *comfort*.

Again, speak tenderly, then close with a confident declaration.

When you *see* this, your heart shall *rejoice*
    and your bodies *flourish* like the *grass*;
the LORD's *power* shall be known to his *servants*.

READING I   The book of the prophet Isaiah is divided into two main sections, the first of which comes from the time of the prophet himself and the second (itself divided into two sections) from two centuries later, after the Babylonian exile. Today's passage is from that latter half and celebrates the glory of Jerusalem. In the eyes of those who had longed for their beloved city and temple, both destroyed by the Babylonians, nothing could be more beautiful than Jerusalem's restoration.

Today's passage sings with joy at the prospect of the exiles being nurtured once again in their home. Previously they had mourned for Jerusalem and longed to see its splendor once again. The author depicts the city as a loving mother, providing for her beloved child's every need. Evoking the image of a nursing mother tenderly caressing her infant, the author speaks to the hearts of all who have known what it is to be away from home, to be lonely and heartbroken, and to return once again to a warm embrace.

The image changes as God promises a flood of prosperity to the holy city. Like a current that cannot be contained, all good things will come to Jerusalem. Once again she is a mother, playing with her children and holding them close. God is like a mother as well, comforting those who have been in mourning during the long exile and promising the renewal of the city. Every good will come to God's chosen ones.

Offer this beautiful declaration of God's love and care with gladness. Let your voice ring with joy and trust in God's goodness. If you are initially uncomfortable with the image of a woman nursing her child, practice the passage until you are confident that

READING II   Galatians 6:14–18

A reading from the letter of Saint Paul to the Galatians

Brothers and sisters:
May I never *boast* except in the *cross* of our Lord Jesus *Christ*,
   through which the *world* has been *crucified* to me,
   and *I* to the *world.*
For neither does *circumcision* mean *anything,*
      nor does *uncircumcision,*
   but only a new *creation.*

Peace and *mercy* be to all who follow this *rule*
   and to the *Israel* of *God.*
From now *on,* let no one make *troubles* for me;
   for I bear the marks of *Jesus* on my *body.*

The *grace* of our Lord Jesus Christ be with your *spirit,*
   brothers and sisters. *Amen.*

Speak firmly. Emphasize the word "cross" and speak the entire phrase with great conviction.

Let a freshness enter your voice as you speak about the new creation.

Paul is proud of his sufferings.

GOSPEL   Luke 10:1–12, 17–20

A reading from the holy gospel according to Luke

At that time the Lord appointed seventy-two *others*
   whom he sent *ahead* of him in *pairs*
   to every town and place he intended to *visit.*
He said to them,
   "The *harvest* is *abundant* but the *laborers* are *few;*
   so ask the *master* of the harvest
   to send out *laborers* for his *harvest.*

Speak this directly to your community. All Christians have a responsibility to help bring about the reign of God.

you can proclaim it as God's message of tender love. Speak God's words with confidence and hope.

READING II When the apostle Paul speaks of "boasting," he does not have in mind his own skills or triumphs. Instead he boasts about something that seems to make no sense: the cross of Jesus. Crucifixion was a means of torture and execution that was especially humiliating in the ancient world. The Romans used it for condemned traitors and insurrectionists.

For a Jew, it was a sign of being cursed by God. Yet Paul defiantly holds it up as the only reason for his boasting.

For Paul, the cross represents the only way salvation can come to the world. Because humans have chosen to reject the love God offers, because humans have chosen to act for their own glory rather than God's, because people have rejected the messenger of truth and Lord of justice, the cross is the sign of truth in a turbulent world. Jesus willingly gave himself for all humanity in order to right the wrongs of the

world. Embracing the cross means acknowledging the correct path to God and turning one's back on the falsehood of the world. Ordinary attitudes and expectations are turned upside down.

One of the principal concerns of Paul's ministry was the acceptance of non-Jews into the Christian community. Some people believed that everyone had to follow the Jewish law, which included circumcision of males, in order to follow Jesus. Paul emphatically rejects such an attitude and here considers it part of the folly of the world that has been crucified on the cross. All who

Go on your *way*;
  behold, I am sending you like *lambs* among *wolves*.
Carry no *money* bag, no *sack*, no *sandals*;
  and greet *no* one along the *way*.

Let a peacefulness enter your voice as you read this section. This is not, however, a sentimental peace but a serious, tough-minded realization of the truth.

"Into whatever house you *enter*, first say,
  '*Peace* to this *household*.'
If a *peaceful* person lives there,
  your peace will *rest* on him;
  but if *not*, it will *return* to you.
Stay in the same house and *eat* and *drink* what is *offered* to you,
  for the *laborer* deserves his *payment*.
Do not move *about* from one house to *another*.

"Whatever town you *enter* and they *welcome* you,
  eat what is set *before* you,
  cure the *sick* in it and say to them,
  'The kingdom of *God* is at *hand* for you.'

This is Jesus' own message. Preach it as though you are one of the missionaries.

"Whatever town you enter and they do *not* receive you,
  go out into the *streets* and say,
  'The *dust* of your town that clings to our *feet*,
  even *that* we shake off *against* you.'
Yet know *this*: the kingdom of *God* is at *hand*.
I tell you, it will be more tolerable for *Sodom* on that day
      than for *that* town."

God's judgment is harsh against those who refuse to listen.

The seventy-two returned *rejoicing*, and said,
  "Lord, even the *demons* are subject to us because
      of your *name*."
Jesus said, "I have observed *Satan* fall like *lightning*
      from the *sky*.

Express the disciples' joy and surprise.

recognize God's openness to all peoples will find peace.

Paul tells us elsewhere of some of the treatment he endured during his ministry, and the Acts of the Apostles confirms his sufferings. In today's reading, he defies anyone who would claim that his views make him a less-worthy follower of Christ and insists that the scars he bears as a result of his devotion to Jesus prove his faithfulness.

Paul had a strong personality and firm conviction. Try to express that as you read this passage. Speak boldly and confidently,

closing with a sincere offer of peace for all your listeners.

GOSPEL The mission of the seventy-two represents the spread of the good news to the entire world. Jewish tradition held that there were seventy-two nations in the world; that number came to represent all the peoples of the earth. The two-volume work of Luke-Acts is primarily concerned with the preaching of God's word to all the nations. Jesus' life and mission,

while rooted in the promises and opportunities of Judaism, has significance that extends beyond the twelve tribes of Israel. Israel had always seen itself as a "light to the nations," and the author of the gospel of Luke takes that mission seriously. There are many willing recipients of the gospel (a plentiful harvest) among the Gentiles and a great need for ministers who are willing to offer Jesus' message that the reign of God is near.

The missionaries are sent into the world with instructions: They are not to take any provisions with them, carrying only the knowledge of God and the peacefulness it

Build to this line. Speak slowly and with emphasis.

Behold, I have given you the *power* to 'tread upon *serpents'*
    and *scorpions*
  and upon the full force of the *enemy* and nothing will
    harm you.
Nevertheless, do not *rejoice* because the spirits are *subject* to you,
  but *rejoice* because your names are written in *heaven.*"

[Shorter: Luke 10:1–9]

brings. They are to offer peace to everyone in the homes they enter and are to be satisfied with whatever their hosts provide. If they are not welcomed, they are to leave, knowing that those who reject them face the judgment of God.

Although the ministry of the seventy-two is to consist of healing, thus continuing the work of Jesus, they return from their travels overjoyed with the power over demons that speaking Jesus' name provided them. To speak someone's name was to

claim that person's authority. Jesus' confirms that all evil powers are overcome in the present reign of God. Even Satan has fallen. Jesus goes on to claim that nothing can harm God's messengers, not even poisonous snakes or any other evil power.

Surely this victory over evil is cause for rejoicing. But Jesus clarifies that the real reason for rejoicing lies not in the signs and wonders performed at the hands of the missionaries but in the mission itself; participating in it ensures the inscription of the disciple's name in heaven.

The most significant attributes of the mission given to the disciples in this passage can be applied today as well. Simplicity, detachment and peacefulness must describe our lives as well. Think of your own ministry and the work of your community as you share this message with your assembly. Build in intensity until you reach the concluding statement that the goal of all ministry is beyond what we can see and know today.

15TH SUNDAY IN ORDINARY TIME

Lectionary #105

READING I Deuteronomy 30:10–14

A reading from the book of Deuteronomy

Moses said to the *people*:
"If *only* you would heed the *voice* of the LORD, your *God*,
    and keep his *commandments* and *statutes*
    that are *written* in this *book* of the *law*,
    when you *return* to the LORD, your God,
    with all your *heart* and all your *soul*.

"For this command that I *enjoin* on you today
    is not too *mysterious* and *remote* for you.
It is not up in the *sky*, that you should say,
    '*Who* will go up in the sky to *get* it for us
    and *tell* us of it, that we may carry it *out*?'

"Nor is it across the *sea*, that you should say,
    'Who will cross the sea to *get* it for us
    and *tell* us of it, that we may carry it *out*?'

"*No*, it is something very *near* to you,
    already in your *mouths* and in your *hearts*;
    you have *only* to carry it *out*."

Slow down as your proclaim this final phrase of the sentence. Speak clearly and forcefully.
This is meant to be reassuring; speak encouragingly.

Close with a tone that is at once comforting and challenging.

READING I Deuteronomy claims to contain the words of Moses addressed to the chosen people just before they entered the land of Canaan. The name of the book means "second law," and in it Moses proclaims the laws given by God at Mount Horeb (Sinai). He also reviews the history of Israel, offering the people motivation for keeping God's law.

In today's passage, Moses encourages Israel to take God's commandments to heart and observe them faithfully. But keeping the law involves more than simply adhering to a set of rules. It enables the people to turn to God "with all your heart and all your soul." Faithfulness is a matter of constant conversion, continually approaching God in sincerity of heart.

A key feature of Israel's belief regarding the law, beautifully summed up in this passage, is the idea that God's commands can be kept; they are not overly burdensome or difficult. They are not a distant reality that must be sought in the heavens or in the sea but are near and dear to Israel, part of Israel's everyday life. Keeping the law expresses a heartfelt desire to serve the Lord in everything.

This reading is addressed to us as well as to Israel. As Christians, we do not strictly observe the Mosaic law, yet we too strive to keep the spirit of God's commands in our hearts, observing God's will in our actions. We also strive to turn to God continually and to work toward the day when God's word will be so truly written in our hearts that everything we do will reflect God's will. Proclaim this selection boldly, then, addressing it directly to your listeners.

READING II Colossians 1:15–20

A reading from the letter of Saint Paul to the Colossians

Be sure you have the attention of the assembly before beginning. Then boldly proclaim this important first line.

Christ *Jesus* is the *image* of the invisible *God*,
the *firstborn* of all *creation*.
For in *him* were created *all* things in *heaven* and on *earth*,
the *visible* and the *invisible*,
whether *thrones* or *dominions* or *principalities* or *powers*;
all things were created *through* him and *for* him.

Pause briefly after "powers," then emphasize "all."

He is *before* all things,
and *in* him all things hold *together*.
He is the *head* of the *body*, the *church*.
He is the *beginning*, the *firstborn* from the *dead*,
that in *all* things he himself might be *preeminent*.

Soften your voice a bit, as if you are sharing a meaningful confidence. Close strongly.

For in *him* all the *fullness* was pleased to *dwell*,
and *through* him to reconcile *all* things *for* him,
making *peace* by the blood of his *cross*
through him, whether those on *earth* or those in *heaven*.

READING II The hymn from Colossians that you proclaim today presents Christ in the role occupied by Lady Wisdom in Hebrew wisdom literature. Just as Wisdom acts as cocreator with God in Proverbs, this letter presents Christ as the agent through whom everything has been made. He is above every other power and exists before everything else.

The author then turns to the question of Christ's redemptive work. Christ is the firstborn from the dead and thus brings life to all.

He is also worthy of all praise because of his exalted status. Lest the hymn be understood to refer only to the exalted Christ in heaven, however, the author clarifies that "the body" over which Christ reigns is precisely the earthly Christian church.

The entire hymn proclaims boldly the preexistence of Christ. Although he came into the world at a particular time and place, he has always been with the Father. Indeed, God dwells so fully in Jesus that Jesus is the very manifestation of God in the world, the one through whom God can draw all people into a loving embrace. Yet the author

stresses that it is through the painful reality of the cross that the reconciliation of the world with God is possible.

Offer this hymn of praise with a sense of awe as you sing the praises of Christ as the one exalted over every cosmic power. Let it be a reminder to your community that nothing is to be more important in the life of a Christian than God, who is manifest in Christ Jesus. Proclaim boldly the message that God is not distant but dwells fully in Christ, who has become one of us.

GOSPEL Luke 10:25–37

A reading from the holy gospel according to Luke

There was a scholar of the *law* who stood up to *test* him and said,
"*Teacher*, what must I *do* to inherit eternal *life*?"
Jesus said to him, "What is *written* in the *law*?
How do you *read* it?"
He said in reply,
"You shall *love* the LORD, your *God*,
with all your *heart*,
with all your *being*,
with all your *strength*,
and with all your *mind*,
and your *neighbor* as *yourself*."

He replied to him, "You have answered *correctly*;
do this and you will *live*."
But because he wished to *justify* himself, he said to Jesus,
"And *who* is my *neighbor*?"

Jesus replied,
"A *man* fell victim to *robbers*
as he went down from *Jerusalem* to *Jericho*.
They *stripped* and *beat* him and went *off* leaving him half-*dead*.
A *priest* happened to be going down that road,
but when he *saw* him, he passed *by* on the opposite *side*.
Likewise a *Levite* came to the place,
and when *he* saw him, he passed *by* on the opposite *side*.

Although the lawyer tests Jesus, he is not an entirely negative figure in this gospel; Jesus agrees with his understanding of the essential aspects of the law. Speak his question with sincerity.

Express the harshness of the beating.

GOSPEL Jesus' parable about the good Samaritan, found only in Luke's gospel, is one of the most beautiful and beloved parables of Jesus. In it, a lawyer—someone well versed in the Mosaic law—questions Jesus regarding eternal life. By linking Deuteronomy 6:4–5 and Leviticus 19:18, the lawyer asserts that the core of the Jewish legal tradition is summed up in the love of God and of neighbor. Jesus approves of his answer, but the lawyer presses him further. How far does this loving have to go? Jesus answers him by telling a story of how to act as a neighbor.

The story itself offers only tantalizing clues to questions we might bring to the text. We are not told the identity of the man who was beaten and robbed. Was he a trader, perhaps dishonest himself? Nor are we told what the priest and Levite were thinking as they passed him. Were they afraid that the man would die, making them unclean if they touched the corpse? Or were they afraid that they would be attacked, either by the man himself or by bandits waiting in ambush? Or were they simply unwilling to get involved?

Jesus does not address these questions or attempt to help his hearers understand the reasoning of the religious leaders, who pass on the other side of the road. Instead, he shocks his listeners by bringing in the figure of a Samaritan. Despite their common religious heritage, there was great animosity between Samaritans and Jews. The figure of the Samaritan introduces a religious and social enemy as the model of neighborliness.

Samaritan = suh-MAYR-uh-tuhn
Pause slightly before beginning to
speak of the Samaritan. Emphasize
the name in an attempt to shock
your listeners, perhaps even speaking
with a bit of disdain.

"But a *Samaritan* traveler who came upon him
was moved with *compassion* at the sight.
He *approached* the victim,
poured *oil* and *wine* over his *wounds* and *bandaged* them.
Then he lifted him up on his own *animal*,
took him to an *inn*, and *cared* for him.
"The *next* day he took out two silver *coins*
and gave them to the *innkeeper* with the instruction,
'Take *care* of him.
If you spend *more* than what I have *given* you,
I shall *repay* you on my way *back*.'

Emphasize the word "neighbor."

Address this to your assembly.

"*Which* of these three, in your opinion,
was *neighbor* to the robbers' *victim*?"
He answered, "The one who treated him with *mercy*."
Jesus said to him, "*Go* and do *likewise*."

In the end, the neighbor was not someone who had formal ties to the injured man
but the one who saw to his needs. The one
who showed mercy, the one who displayed
kindness, is the neighbor. Neighborliness
has nothing to do with kinship or being from
the same town. It involves doing what is best
for another, regardless of social responsibilities or position. The Samaritan, the outsider,
was neighborly enough to have compassion
and to recognize the need of the injured man.

Summon all your rhetorical skills to
proclaim this passage effectively. Try to
recapture some of the shock value that
would have been present for Jesus' listeners. Then let the story itself inspire your listeners to identify with the Samaritan and to
resolve to be people of action, getting
involved in the lives of others and working
for their welfare.

16TH SUNDAY ON ORDINARY TIME

Lectionary #108

READING I   Genesis 18:1–10a

A reading from the book of Genesis

terebinth = TAYR-uh-binth
Mamre = MAHM-ray

The LORD appeared to *Abraham* by the terebinth of *Mamre*,
    as he sat in the *entrance* of his *tent*,
    while the day was growing *hot*.
Looking *up*, Abraham saw three *men* standing *nearby*.
When he *saw* them, he *ran* from the entrance of the tent
        to *greet* them;
    and bowing to the *ground*, he said:
    "Sir, if I may *ask* you this *favor*,
    please do not go on *past* your servant.

Speak with excitement in order to convey Abraham's eagerness to honor the visitors.

Let some *water* be brought, that you may *bathe* your *feet*,
    and then *rest* yourselves under the *tree*.
Now that you have come *this* close to your servant,
    let me bring you a little *food*, that you may *refresh* yourselves;
    and *afterward* you may go on your *way*."
The men replied, "Very *well*, do as you have *said*."

Abraham *hastened* into the tent and told *Sarah*,
    "*Quick*, three measures of fine *flour*! *Knead* it and
        make *rolls*."

Again, convey Abraham's haste, and emphasize that he and Sarah are offering their finest foods to their guests.

He ran to the *herd*, picked out a tender, choice *steer*,
    and gave it to a *servant*, who quickly *prepared* it.
Then Abraham got some *curds* and *milk*,
    as well as the *steer* that had been prepared,

READING I In the ancient world, travel was risky, difficult and without many conveniences along the way, and hospitality was required of those who had the means to offer it. When the three men, presumably a manifestation of God, appear to Abraham, he instantly jumps up and greets them, offering refreshment and rest, and serving them the choicest foods. His is an example of true hospitality. The gratitude of the three visitors is shown when one of them promises that Abraham's wife Sarah will bear a son. Abraham and Sarah had both

given up hope for a child; in verses following those in today's passage, Sarah even laughs at the thought of bearing a child in her old age. But God's word is true and, through Isaac, Abraham and Sarah become the ancestors of a great people.

There are three points of emphasis in this passage: the hospitality Abraham and Sarah offer, the fact that they offer the very best that they have, and the promise that closes the story. Provide a rhythm to your proclamation that will allow these three

points to stand out. Slow down near the end so that the significance of God's promise can be fully appreciated.

READING II Paul was prone to boasting. He boasts not of his talents or accomplishments but "of the Lord" and of his own sufferings for Christ. In the letter to the Colossians, an admirer of Paul writes in his name and continues Paul's emphasis on suffering. Suffering is cause for rejoicing because it draws one into closer imitation of Jesus and demonstrates the true nature of one's faith.

and set these before the three *men;*
and he *waited* on them under the *tree* while they *ate.*

They asked Abraham, "Where is your wife *Sarah?*"
He replied, *"There* in the *tent.*"
One of them said, "I will surely *return* to you
    about this time *next* year,
and *Sarah* will then have a *son.*"

Pause before this final scene. The tone changes. Speak God's promise with great solemnity.

READING II   Colossians 1:24–28

A reading from the letter of Saint Paul to the Colossians

Brothers and sisters:
Now I *rejoice* in my *sufferings* for *your* sake,
    and in my *flesh* I am filling up
    what is *lacking* in the afflictions of *Christ*
    on behalf of his *body,* which is the *church,*
    of which I am a *minister*
    in accordance with God's *stewardship* given to *me*
    to bring to *completion* for you the *word* of *God,*
    the *mystery* hidden from *ages* and from generations *past.*

But now it has been *manifested* to his *holy* ones,
    to whom God chose to make *known* the *riches* of the *glory*
    of this *mystery* among the *Gentiles;*
    it is *Christ* in *you,* the hope for *glory.*
It is he whom we *proclaim,*
    admonishing everyone and *teaching* everyone
      with all *wisdom,*
    that we may present *everyone perfect* in Christ.

Speak with genuine joy, but also with a tone of seriousness as you reveal the cause of the joy, namely, suffering.

This sentence is long and complicated. Speak slowly and clearly. Emphasize the word "mystery."

Proclaim this with triumph, closing with firm conviction.

It is difficult to know precisely what is meant by the phrase "what is lacking in Christ's afflictions," but it might indicate that the sufferings of Christ are continued in those who suffer in his name. Although Jesus' passion and death were complete and need nothing added to them, Christians who continue to be persecuted for their faith make real his passion for the church in their own age. Paul's sufferings, then, incarnate in his body the passion of Jesus.

Central to today's reading is a discussion of ministry, which is a response to a call from God to reveal the mystery of God's plan of salvation. This mystery must be carried to the Gentiles, a mission important to Paul, so that they might know Christ. The importance of each minister proclaiming Christ is something we should keep in mind as well, so that we might not become too burdened with concerns about how "successful" we are in our ministries. If we keep our eyes on Christ, we are following our calling.

Meditate on this reading until you are comfortable that you can convey the importance of suffering and the meaning of ministry that the author expresses. Speak slowly in order to be clear, and proclaim the message with the same pride the author expresses.

GOSPEL The story of Martha and Mary, like that of Abraham and the three visitors, is a story about hospitality. But it is also a story that is somewhat disturbing, for Jesus seems to rebuke his friend Martha for offering precisely the type of generosity and care that is usually required of a host.

Martha knows how to open her home to a guest. She knows that Jesus is tired and

GOSPEL   Luke 10:38–42

A reading from the holy gospel according to Luke

Jesus entered a *village*
   where a woman whose name was *Martha welcomed* him.
She had a sister named *Mary*
   who sat beside the Lord at his *feet* listening to him *speak.*

Martha, burdened with much *serving, came* to him and said,
   "Lord, do you not *care*
   that my sister has *left* me by *myself* to do the *serving?*
Tell her to *help* me."

The Lord said to her in reply,
   "*Martha, Martha,* you are *anxious* and *worried*
      about many *things.*
There is need of only *one* thing.
Mary has chosen the *better* part
   and it will *not* be taken *from* her."

(margin notes)

Stress how welcoming Martha was. Mary is also introduced in a positive light.

Decide what emotions Martha is feeling and let that dictate your reading.

Jesus rebukes Martha, but it is a mild correction. Does he speak with resignation or with frustration? Speak the last line firmly.

needs refreshment. She knows that offering care to another involves effort. Anyone who has ever prepared a large meal alone knows what Martha is experiencing and can understand her exasperation at being left to do all the work by herself.

But it is Mary who receives praise from Jesus. She too is offering hospitality, but of a different sort. What appears to Martha to be laziness and irresponsibility is accepted by Jesus as attentiveness and peacefulness. Mary offers her ear and succeeds in making the guest feel comfortable.

Perhaps the central message of this story is not so much the contrast between the active life and the contemplative life—with Mary's contemplation seen as clearly superior to Martha's action. Perhaps instead the placement of this story immediately after the narrative of the good Samaritan can help us to understand the need for a balance between action and prayer. Hospitality does not consist solely in listening (at the expense of meeting a guest's physical needs), nor is it solely found in constant activity. Loving others is complicated business and involves

taking action when necessary, but it also includes active listening.

Proclaim this story so that the three characters come alive. Determine what emotion lies behind the words of the speakers and give expression to it. Don't be afraid to portray any of the characters in what might at first appear to be a negative light. There is no question that there is conflict in the story. But the author clearly gives greater weight to the type of hospitality that Mary offers.

17TH SUNDAY IN ORDINARY TIME

Lectionary #111

READING I   Genesis 18:20–32

A reading from the book of Genesis

In those *days*, the LORD said:
"The *outcry* against *Sodom* and *Gomorrah* is so *great*,
　　and their sin so *grave*,
　　that I must go down and *see* whether or not
　　their *actions* fully correspond to the cry *against* them
　　　　that *comes* to me.
I mean to find *out*."

While Abraham's visitors walked on farther toward *Sodom*,
　　the LORD remained standing before *Abraham*.
Then Abraham drew *nearer* and said:
　　"Will you sweep away the *innocent* with the *guilty*?
Suppose there were *fifty innocent* people in the city;
　　would you wipe *out* the *place*, rather than *spare* it
　　for the sake of the *fifty* innocent people *within* it?
Far be it from *you* to *do* such a thing,
　　to make the *innocent* die with the *guilty*
　　so that the *innocent* and the *guilty* would be treated *alike*!
Should not the judge of all the *world* act with *justice*?"
The LORD replied,
　　"If I find *fifty* innocent *people* in the city of *Sodom*,
　　I will *spare* the whole *place* for *their* sake."

Sodom = SOD-uhm
Gomorrah = guh-MOHR-ah

Use plenty of expression for Abraham's words. Decide if he is shocked and dismayed or simply being cunning.

Let your tone indicate how preposterous it is to think that God would be unjust.

READING I God reveals to Abraham the fate of the wicked, sinful cities of Sodom and Gomorrah. The Lord announces the plan, but Abraham speaks boldly, questioning the wisdom of destroying cities that might still have righteous inhabitants within them.

What ensues is an almost comical exchange, as God and Abraham bargain over the price of salvation for the cities of Sodom and Gomorrah. The scene comes straight out of a Middle Eastern marketplace, in which bargaining over the correct price is an accepted—and expected—practice. The limits are set at the beginning: God intends to destroy everything; Abraham begs mercy for the cities if there are fifty innocent people within them. Between these positions, anything is possible. Abraham gradually adjusts the figure until, by the end of the conversation, God has come around to a far more merciful position.

But the back-and-forth haggling is not simply a humorous means of dragging out the story. There is real risk involved for Abraham. Just as a buyer in the marketplace must take care not to push too much lest the seller take offense, so also Abraham needs to be cautious. He cannot risk offending God by reducing the number too quickly, lest God become angry and destroy the cities regardless of the number of righteous people.

The real message of the tale, however, is the mercy of God. Although God is portrayed here with human emotions, there is truth to the assertion that God has the right to punish the wicked. The author of goodness is also judge of the world. But God is a righteous judge and does not wish to take the lives of the innocent, even if it means

Abraham speaks humbly here.

Abraham spoke up again:
  "*See* how I am *presuming* to speak to my *Lord*,
    though I am but *dust* and *ashes*!
What if there are five *less* than *fifty* innocent *people*?
Will you destroy the *whole city* because of those *five*?"
He answered, "I will *not destroy* it, if I find forty-*five* there."

But Abraham *persisted*, saying "What if only *forty* are
    found there?"
He replied, "I will *forbear* doing it for the sake of the *forty*."
Then Abraham said, "Let not my Lord grow *impatient* if I go *on*.
What if only *thirty* are found there?"
He replied, "I will *forbear* doing it if I can find but *thirty* there."

Still Abraham went on,
  "Since I have *thus* dared to *speak* to my Lord,
    what if there are no more than *twenty*?"
The LORD answered, "I will not *destroy* it, for the sake
    of the *twenty*."
But he still persisted:
  "*Please*, let not my Lord grow *angry* if I speak up this last *time*.
What if there are at least *ten* there?"
He replied, "For the sake of those *ten*, I will not *destroy* it."

Although you may choose to express God's earlier words with different emphases, in this case be sure to speak with patience, devotion and love.

that the wicked majority receives mercy as well. God allows the many to go unpunished for the sake of the few.

Allow yourself to be playful with this story without losing the central message of forgiveness. If the seriousness of the conversation inhibits you from seeing the humor in the piece, imagine haggling at a local flea market or garage sale instead. It might help to add in your mind the word "say" before each number ("Suppose there were, say, *fifty* innocent people") in order to draw emphasis to each of the numbers Abraham proposes. Let Abraham's attitude change as

you see fit: Is he being sneaky, insistent, cajoling or subservient? Let God's responses also change: God might be resigned, angry, impatient or annoyed. Speak the final line with great seriousness and certainty, so that your listeners will be left with the sense that God's mercy is sure.

READING II The letter to the Colossians was written to believers who respected the authority of Paul but who had been led astray by the teachings of

unknown preachers. The author wrote in Paul's name to instruct the Colossians in the correct understanding of the gospel.

The letter begins with instruction to be Christ-centered, for in Christ God is revealed to the world. The author then highlights three of Paul's favorite themes: baptism, the rejection of circumcision, and the centrality of the cross.

For Paul, initiation involves a baptism into the death of Christ with a hope for future resurrection. Here, baptism is understood as burial with Christ but also resurrection with him. Paul always insists that the resurrected

READING II   Colossians 2:12–14

A reading from the letter of Saint Paul to the Colossians

Brothers and sisters:
You were *buried* with him in *baptism,*
    in which you were also *raised* with him
    through *faith* in the power of *God,*
    who *raised* him from the *dead.*

And even when you were *dead*
    in *transgressions* and the *uncircumcision* of your *flesh,*
    he brought you to *life* along *with* him,
    having *forgiven* us all our *transgressions;*
    obliterating the bond *against* us, with its legal *claims,*
    which was *opposed* to us,
    he also *removed* it from our *midst, nailing* it to the *cross.*

God is made known to the world through Jesus, the incarnate Son. Exult in this proclamation.
Lift your voice as you proclaim God's tremendous power.

Speak firmly and with gratitude for God's forgiveness.

GOSPEL   Luke 11:1–13

A reading from the holy gospel according to Luke

Jesus was *praying* in a certain *place,* and when he had *finished,*
    one of his disciples said to him,
    "*Lord,* teach *us* to *pray* just as *John* taught *his* disciples."
He said to them, "When you *pray,* say:
    Father, hallowed be your *name,*
    your kingdom *come.*
    Give us *each* day our daily *bread*
    and *forgive* us our *sins*

This version of the Lord's Prayer is somewhat different from the one most familiar to us. Pause after each line so that the force of the words can sink in.

---

life is in the future; believers must strive to be worthy of it. The author of Colossians agrees with Paul that the Christian life requires moral living but understands the new life to have already begun.

    Like Paul, the author does not think that circumcision is necessary for salvation, as some Jewish Christians insisted. The proof of this lies in the fact that the Colossians became believers and began their new life in Christ even when they were sinful and without benefit of circumcision. Because God forgives sin, its presence in someone's

life does not deter that person from trusting completely in Christ and the efficacy of his death and resurrection.

    Because the Colossians had lived in sin and had not known the truth of God's message, the author likens them to prisoners who have a bail note or bond written against them. But Jesus' death on the cross cancels that bond, freeing believers of the "debts" of sin, which have been symbolically nailed to the cross with Jesus.

    The central message of this selection is the importance of Christ's saving actions. Draw attention to the new life offered in him.

Speak slowly and carefully, so that the message will not be lost on your listeners.

| GOSPEL | The gospel of Luke portrays Jesus at prayer, especially at crucial points in his ministry. Prayer gives him strength and provides him with the guidance he needs on his journey. In response to a request from his disciples, Jesus teaches them to pray in a way that will identify them as his followers, just as John's disciples had adopted unique prayers. The prayer Jesus

for we *ourselves* forgive everyone in *debt* to us,
and do not *subject* us to the final *test*."

Pause before beginning. The tone becomes lighter as you tell this story.

And he said to them, "Suppose *one* of you has a *friend*
to whom he goes at *midnight* and says,
'*Friend*, lend me *three* loaves of *bread*,
for a *friend* of mine has arrived at my house from a *journey*
and I have nothing to *offer* him,'
and he says in reply from within,
'Do not *bother* me; the door has already been *locked*
and my *children* and I are already in *bed*.
I cannot get *up* to give you *anything*.'

"I *tell* you,
if he does not get *up* to give the visitor the loaves
because of their *friendship*,
he will get *up* to give him whatever he *needs*
because of his *persistence*.

Speak solemnly and with encouragement.

"And I *tell* you, *ask* and you will *receive*;
seek and you will *find*;
knock and the door will be *opened* to you.
For everyone who *asks*, *receives*;
and the one who *seeks*, *finds*;
and to the one who *knocks*, the door will be *opened*.

Pause again before this story.

"What *father* among you would hand his *son* a *snake*
when he asks for a *fish*?
Or hand him a *scorpion* when he asks for an *egg*?

Close with a tone of sincerity and trust.

"If *you* then, who are *wicked*,
know how to give *good* gifts to your *children*,
how much *more* will the Father in *heaven*
give the Holy *Spirit* to those who *ask* him?"

---

gives his disciples has become the unifying and identifying prayer of Christians.

The Lord's Prayer begins by acknowledging God's sovereignty and moves to petitions for the community. Far from being a private prayer, the Lord's Prayer expresses the petitions in the plural. *We* pray for *our* bread and ask forgiveness for *our* sins. As a community, we approach God in need and beg for mercy, while striving to offer mercy to others.

Jesus' instruction on prayer continues with a humorous story about the bothersome neighbor. Just as Abraham is persistent in

his dealings with God in today's first reading, so also each of us should be persistent with God in times of need. Such requests demonstrate our dependence on the divine. And, just as the homeowner in the gospel finally gets annoyed and grants his friend's request, so also God just might give in out of sheer fatigue!

The final story, of the father and child, tempers the lesson of the previous story. Our petitions are not simply to be self-centered demands. God desires what is good for us. And God grants us the most profound gift of

all, the Holy Spirit, who guides our prayer and brings us all that we need.

Treat each of these three sections separately, giving voice to the different lessons each offers. There is hyperbole in the stories; allow yourself to exaggerate along with the author. Give special emphasis to the final line concerning the Holy Spirit.

18TH SUNDAY IN ORDINARY TIME

Lectionary #114

READING I Ecclesiastes 1:2; 2:21–23

A reading from the book of Ecclesiastes

Vanity of *vanities*, says Qoheleth,
   vanity of *vanities*! All things are *vanity*!

Here is one who has labored with *wisdom* and *knowledge*
      and *skill*,
   and yet to *another* who has *not* labored over it,
   he must leave *property*.
This also is *vanity* and a great *misfortune*.

For what *profit* comes to man from all the *toil* and anxiety
      of *heart*
   with which he has *labored* under the *sun*?
All his days *sorrow* and *grief* are their *occupation*;
   even at *night* his mind is not at *rest*.
This *also* is *vanity*.

Cry out with desperation in these opening lines.

Let sadness fill your voice as you describe the situation.

There is deep pain in these words. Close with a sense of futility.

READING I Hebrew wisdom literature attempts to give direction on how to live daily life. The author of Ecclesiastes finds much of life to be futile, for the same fate awaits both the wicked and the righteous: death. Written before belief in an afterlife developed, the book does not look to a future vindication for the righteous but recognizes that life can be unfair. The author concludes that the answer is to live well and be happy.

Today's passage is a mournful lament about the "vanity" or futility of life. As the author has observed, those who work hard often do not get to enjoy the fruits of their labor. Someone else, one who did not engage in the work, will enjoy the benefits of the other's labor. In fact, the reward for hard work is really just pain and frustration.

This selection highlights a reality that we would probably prefer to avoid. Far from being encouraging or joyous, it leaves us with a deep sense of sadness. The author appears to be disillusioned and tired. Only faith in God's goodness can provide peace for such a troubled soul.

Do not shy away from the pain the author expresses here. Start with a cry of anguish, then speak in a subdued voice and with a sense of futility.

READING II The author of Colossians writes as an admirer of Paul to the early community in Colossae. The Colossian church was not founded by Paul, but the author clearly holds the community in high esteem. The author hopes that, by writing in Paul's name, Paul's influence will be felt in a community that had received some misguided teachings.

READING II Colossians 3:1–5, 9–11

A reading from the letter of Saint Paul to the Colossians

Brothers and sisters:
If you were *raised* with *Christ*, seek what is *above*,
    where *Christ* is seated at the right *hand* of God.

Think of what is *above*, not of what is on *earth*.
For you have *died*,
    and your life is *hidden* with Christ in *God*.
When *Christ* your *life appears*,
    then you *too* will appear with him in *glory*.

Put to *death*, then, the parts of you that are *earthly*:
    immorality, impurity, passion, evil *desire*,
    and the *greed* that is *idolatry*.

Stop *lying* to one another,
    since you have taken *off* the *old* self with its *practices*
    and have put on the *new* self,
    which is being *renewed*, for *knowledge*,
    in the image of its *creator*.

Here there is not *Greek* and *Jew*,
    circumcision and *uncircumcision*,
    barbarian, Scythian, slave, free;
    but *Christ* is *all* and *in* all.

Lift your voice and speak brightly and encouragingly.

Continue to speak with a strong voice but with disdain for the impure thoughts and actions these words describe.

Let your voice brighten again; end with a stirring announcement that Christ is everything.

Although Paul always speaks of dying with Christ and asserts that the resurrected life lies in the future, the author of Colossians indicates that Christians have been raised already, just as Christ has been. Because the new life has already begun, we are to live as inhabitants of a heavenly order rather than be ruled by the spirits of the temporal world. Always keeping our eyes on the exalted Christ, we are to live lives worthy of him. Our heavenly, glorified life will be revealed when Christ himself is revealed.

Since the glorified life is not fully revealed on earth, there are moral imperatives that Christians are to follow in the meantime. As true residents of heaven, we are to leave earthly things behind. All forms of sin and temptation are earthly, but the Christian is a new self, with new ways of living. In language reminiscent of the baptismal ritual, in which those to be initiated approach the water naked and are later clothed with pure, white garments, the author speaks of stripping off the old self and putting on the new.

The final paragraph recalls a baptismal formula found in a letter of Paul that was presumably used in the baptismal rituals of the Pauline churches. It affirms that Christian initiation erases all the divisions of the world. In baptism, all are united into one community regardless of the barriers that ordinarily separate people from one another. In the Christian church, Christ is everything; nothing else matters.

Proclaim this passage with an eye to the lofty ideas being expressed. Offer the instructions as sincere reminders of how best to live. Finally, close with a strong

GOSPEL   Luke 12:13–21

A reading from the holy gospel according to Luke

Someone in the crowd said to Jesus,
  "*Teacher*, tell my brother to share the *inheritance* with me."
He replied to him,
  "*Friend*, who appointed *me* as your *judge* and *arbitrator*?"

Then he said to the crowd,
  "Take care to *guard* against all *greed*,
  for though one may be *rich*,
  one's *life* does not consist of *possessions*."

Then he told them a *parable*.
"There was a *rich* man whose land produced a bountiful *harvest*.
He asked himself, 'What shall I *do*,
  for I do not have *space* to store my *harvest*?'
And he said, '*This* is what I shall do:
  I shall tear *down* my barns and build *larger* ones.
There I shall store all my *grain* and *other* goods
  and I shall say to myself, "Now as for *you*,
  you have so many good *things* stored up for many *years*,
  rest, *eat*, *drink*, be *merry*!"'

"But God said to him,
  'You *fool*, this night your life will be *demanded* of you;
  and the things you have *prepared*, to whom will *they* belong?'
Thus will it *be* for all who store up treasure for *themselves*
  but are not rich in what matters to *God*."

Jesus' rebuke is harsh. He has no desire to negotiate possessions in this world; his values are elsewhere.

Proclaim this with a strong voice, as if Jesus is speaking to the crowds.

Is the man wily or simply satisfied with his success? Let your answer determine your reading.

God's condemnation is strong.

---

voice, confident of the unity we have in Christ, who is all and in all.

GOSPEL The question about inheritance leads Jesus to tell a story about greed. The death of a family member and the subsequent division of property often led, both in Jesus' time and today, to examples of the unhealthy significance that money and possessions have in people's lives.

The man in the parable is already blessed with great abundance. He plans to do precisely what the author of Ecclesiastes suggests is the only way to be happy in life: eat, drink and be merry. By relaxing and enjoying what he has accumulated, he hopes to have a good, long life. But before he can enjoy his wealth, he is told he will die. Clearly his many possessions will offer him no comfort in death.

It is not so much the possessions themselves that are the problem here. The issue is the desire to accumulate and hoard, making wealth one's highest priority. Jesus reminds his listeners that true wealth comes from knowing and trusting God.

This passage is especially appropriate for our society, in which accumulation of assets is often an all-consuming goal. Even when we do not have many possessions, the desire to have more can eat away at our souls. Offer this challenging gospel reading to your community as a call to return to what is central and an encouragement to reflect on the many blessings we already have. Read it as a straightforward story, giving plenty of expression to the attitudes of the man and the strong response of God.

19TH SUNDAY IN ORDINARY TIME

Lectionary #117

READING I   Wisdom 18:6–9

A reading from the book of Wisdom

Pause after "passover" to make the setting clear to your listeners.

The night of the *passover* was known *beforehand* to our *fathers*,
    that, with sure *knowledge* of the oaths in which they
        put their *faith*,
    they might have *courage*.

Your people awaited the *salvation* of the *just*
    and the *destruction* of their *foes*.
For when you punished our *adversaries*,
    in *this* you glorified *us* whom you had *summoned*.

Emphasize this line. The glorification of God's chosen people is central.

For in *secret* the holy children of the *good* were offering *sacrifice*
    and putting into effect with one *accord* the divine *institution*.

READING II   Hebrews 11:1–2, 8–19

A reading from the letter to the Hebrews

Begin with a strong voice. Pause at the end of the first sentence.

Brothers and sisters:
Faith is the realization of what is *hoped* for
    and *evidence* of things not *seen*.
Because of *it* the ancients were well *attested*.

Stress the word "faith" wherever it is found in the reading.

By faith *Abraham* obeyed when he was *called* to go out to a place
    that he was to receive as an *inheritance*;
    he went *out*, not *knowing* where he was to *go*.

READING I The exodus from Egypt and all that surrounded it had a lasting impact on the Hebrew people and continues to inspire Jews today. Today's reading alludes to these events.

In the exodus, God repeatedly revealed that the Hebrew people were the chosen ones by offering protection and guidance through their trials. Before leaving Egypt, the Israelites celebrated the Passover, slaughtering a lamb and marking their doors with its blood to safeguard their children from death. Then they fled their homes and, with

God's help, crossed the Red Sea as their pursuers were engulfed by the water.

The author suggests that the Hebrew people knew about the divine victory of the Exodus before it happened; they were long aware of their special calling because of this knowledge. Knowing that God would prevail, they offered the Passover sacrifice, thereby assenting to the divine law even before it was formally given to Moses at Mount Sinai.

The context of this passage is not immediately apparent, making it a difficult reading to comprehend and proclaim. Emphasize "the night of the passover" in order to make the context more apparent. Speak clearly and strongly of God's wondrous works for Israel.

READING II The reflection on faith in this chapter of Hebrews begins with a beautiful statement of its perspective: The author looks forward to something unknown, confident that it will become a reality. The text then reflects on several

By *faith* he sojourned in the *promised* land as
in a *foreign* country,
dwelling in *tents* with *Isaac* and *Jacob*,
heirs of the same *promise*;
for he was looking forward to the *city* with *foundations*,
whose *architect* and *maker* is *God*.

By faith he received power to *generate*,
even though he was past the normal *age*
—and Sarah *herself* was *sterile*—
for he thought that the one who had *made* the promise
was *trustworthy*.
So it *was* that there came forth from *one* man,
himself as good as *dead*,
descendants as *numerous* as the *stars* in the *sky*
and as *countless* as the *sands* on the *seashore*.

All these *died* in *faith*.
They did not *receive* what had been *promised*
but *saw* it and *greeted* it from *afar*
and *acknowledged* themselves to be *strangers* and *aliens*
on earth,
for those who speak *thus* show that they are seeking
a *homeland*.
If they had been thinking of the *land* from which they had *come*,
they would have had opportunity to *return*.
But *now* they desire a *better* homeland, a *heavenly* one.
Therefore, God is not *ashamed* to be called their *God*,
for he has prepared a *city* for them.

By faith *Abraham*, when put to the *test*, offered up *Isaac*,
and he who had received the *promises* was ready
to offer his *only son*,
of whom it was *said*,

Speak brightly as you recount this promise to Abraham.

Pause before beginning this important example of faithfulness.

examples of faithfulness from Hebrew history, concentrating especially on the faith of Abraham. The examples are understood, however, entirely from a Christian perspective, as the reference to the binding of Isaac makes clear.

Abraham was an example of faithfulness throughout his lifetime. He left his homeland and set out for a land promised by God even though he did not know where he was going. Trusting in God's word, he lived as a foreigner in a foreign land and believed that more awaited him. Sarah, too, had faith

that they could have a child, even though she and Abraham were both advanced in years ("as good as dead" is clearly an exaggeration!). Although they never saw their numerous descendants, they believed God and knew that they would have as many descendants as there are grains of sand. In ancient Hebrew thought, the only concept of an afterlife was the hope of living on through one's descendants. The author of Hebrews accepts this, but alters it as well to conform to belief in a heavenly afterlife.

What characterizes the ancestors who are extolled in this passage is their willingness to believe in God's promises, even though they never saw their fulfillment. Only Abraham, in his offering of Isaac, was given immediate reward for his faithfulness when his son was returned to him alive.

The binding of Isaac is the example that is most useful to the author of Hebrews, for it points to the resurrection of Jesus. Abraham is anachronistically said to be able to see through the "raising" of his only son the fact that God can raise someone from the dead. Early Christians were fond

Speak of God raising someone from the dead as though you are sharing a great secret.

"Through *Isaac* descendants shall bear your *name*."
He reasoned that God was able to *raise* even from the *dead*,
   and he received Isaac *back* as a *symbol*.

[Shorter: Hebrews 11:1–2, 8–12]

GOSPEL   Luke 12:32–48

A reading from the holy gospel according to Luke

Speak these words of Jesus with gentleness and encouragement.

Jesus said to his disciples:
   "Do not be *afraid* any *longer*, little *flock*,
     for your Father is *pleased* to give you the *kingdom*.
Sell your belongings and give *alms*.
Provide *money* bags for yourselves that do not wear *out*,
     an inexhaustible *treasure* in *heaven*
     that no *thief* can *reach* nor moth *destroy*.
For where your *treasure* is, there also will your *heart* be.

Now your reading should become more urgent and forceful.

"Gird your *loins* and light your *lamps*
     and be like *servants* who await their master's *return*
        from a *wedding*,
     ready to open *immediately* when he comes and *knocks*.
Blessed are those servants
     whom the master finds *vigilant* on his *arrival*.
Amen, I *say* to you, he will *gird* himself,
     have them recline at *table*, and proceed to *wait* on them.
And should he come in the *second* or *third* watch
     and find them prepared in this way,
       blessed are those *servants*.

There is an ominous tone to these words.

"Be sure of *this*:
     if the *master* of the house had known the *hour*
     when the thief was *coming*,

---

of seeing in Isaac a precursor of Christ, the only Son who was brought back to life.

The image of the faithful ancestors is evoked here in order to provide inspiration to the community so that its members would hold fast to their faith, even if they did not immediately see its benefits. The hope in a heavenly future is projected back into the stories of the Hebrew forerunners to show that they too believed in promises that could not be fulfilled on earth. With such examples of confident trust, the author urges the community to pursue the goal that is ahead.

The reading itself is fairly straightforward. Begin on a strong note, then give honor to those faithful servants of God whose memory is evoked here, emphasizing always the centrality of faith in their decisions and actions. Close with a conscious allusion to the resurrection of Jesus, in whom all Christians have hope even though we have not seen him.

GOSPEL | The opening sentences of today's gospel continue the theme that was begun last Sunday. Possessions are of little use to one who is

focused on a far greater treasure, a treasure that cannot be stolen or destroyed. The treasure is a royal possession, the reign of God.

The rest of the passage discusses the issue of preparedness. Slaves are to be alert as they await their master's return from the wedding feast. The master, too, needs to be prepared. Only those who are ready will receive the good things that are to come.

In this section, the author seeks to answer questions regarding Jesus' return to earth. The gospel was written several decades after Jesus' ministry and also after Paul's letters, which display a fervent hope he would not have let his *house* be broken *into*.

"You *also* must be *prepared*, for at an hour you do not *expect*,
the Son of *Man* will *come*."

Then *Peter* said,
"*Lord*, is this parable meant for *us* or for *everyone?*"
And the Lord replied,
"*Who*, then, is the *faithful* and prudent *steward*
whom the master will put in charge of his *servants*
to distribute the *food* allowance at the proper *time?*
Blessed is that servant whom his master on *arrival* finds *doing* so.
Truly, I *say* to you, the master will put the *servant*
in charge of *all* his *property*.
But if that servant says to *himself*,
'My master is *delayed* in *coming*,'
and begins to *beat* the *men*servants and the *maid*servants,
to *eat* and *drink* and get *drunk*,
then that servant's *master* will come
on an *unexpected* day and at an unknown *hour*
and will *punish* the servant *severely*
and assign him a place with the *unfaithful*.

"That servant who *knew* his master's will
but did *not* make preparations nor act in *accord* with his will
shall be beaten *severely*;
and the servant who was *ignorant* of his master's will
but acted in a way *deserving* of a severe beating
shall be beaten only *lightly*.

"*Much* will be required of the person *entrusted* with *much*,
and still *more* will be demanded of the person *entrusted*
with *more*."

[Shorter: Luke 12:35–40]

Peter's question is a practical one, and, as usual, Jesus does not answer directly but tells another story.

Let your voice darken as you recount the viciousness of the irresponsible slave and the cruel fate that awaits such a person.

Pause before concluding on a strong, solemn note. Those of us who have been so richly blessed need to be ever mindful of this teaching.

in the imminent return of the exalted Jesus. Some Christians must have been wondering when Jesus would come again and what signs would indicate that his coming was near. The author of Luke-Acts suggests that there is no need to watch for the time; rather, it is imperative to be always ready.

We are far removed from the situation that gave rise to this urgent expectation of Christ's coming. But we too know that we will be called to stand before our maker and judge. We can never know precisely when we will die, but we must be ever watchful, always faithful and ready so that we might be worthy to share in the heavenly banquet.

Peter's question and Jesus' response direct the issue especially to leaders in the community. Slaves are again symbolic of the servants of God, but these slaves have greater responsibility than others. They are to be especially prepared, for they are responsible for the care of others as well as themselves. And those who know what is expected of them will be held to a higher standard than those who act in ignorance.

The issue of preparedness is one that needs to be addressed by every member of the community, for we live in a society of distractions. Speak boldly, challenging your listeners and especially those in leadership positions to reflect on how well their hearts are attuned to the concerns that really matter. Emphasize the last few lines and encourage your listeners to reflect on the many gifts they have received from God, with the knowledge that such blessings require lives of even greater action.

ASSUMPTION VIGIL

Lectionary #621

READING I 1 Chronicles 15:3–4, 15–16; 16:1–2

A reading from the first book of Chronicles

David assembled *all Israel* in *Jerusalem* to bring the *ark*
> of the LORD
to the place that he had *prepared* for it.
David *also* called together the sons of *Aaron* and the *Levites.*

The *Levites* bore the *ark* of *God* on their *shoulders* with poles,
> as Moses had *ordained* according to the *word* of the LORD.

David commanded the *chiefs* of the Levites
> to appoint their *kinsmen* as *chanters,*
> to play on musical *instruments, harps, lyres,* and *cymbals,*
> to make a *loud sound* of *rejoicing.*

They brought in the *ark* of *God* and set it within the *tent*
> which David had *pitched* for it.
Then they offered up *burnt offerings* and *peace offerings* to *God.*
When David had *finished* offering up the *burnt* offerings
> and *peace* offerings,
> he *blessed* the people in the *name* of the LORD.

A central concern of the author is to indicate that all of Israel serves God in Jerusalem. Emphasize the inclusion of "all Israel."
Levites = LEE-vīts
The descendants of Aaron were priests who offered sacrifice, while the Levites served as their assistants.

Allow the excitement of the celebration to be heard here.

Here the tone changes a bit; David makes a solemn offering to God. Allow your voice to become a bit more serious.

READING I | First and Second Chronicles retell the history of the monarchy in Israel, with emphasis on the importance of the temple in Jerusalem. Today's passage details how the ark of the covenant, the container for the tablets of the law given to Moses, was brought into Jerusalem with great fanfare.

The ark, containing the direct communication of God to the people of Israel, symbolized the presence of God in the midst of the people. Today's reading tells how it was brought into Jerusalem by David. Before the temple was built by David's son Solomon,

the ark of the covenant alone was the center of Israelite worship in Jerusalem.

This reading is chosen for today's feast because Mary, like the ark, is the bearer of the presence of God. The occasion described is one of great joy as well as reverence toward God. Convey in your voice the festive atmosphere and the importance that this event had for uniting Israel.

READING II | In his first letter to the Corinthians, Paul discusses the resurrection of the dead, which some

Corinthians were questioning. After insisting on its reality, he describes the need for a different body, one suited to the resurrected life. It would be a body that is not subject to decay but is imperishable, a body that will not die but is immortal. In this way, the words of the prophets quoted here are fulfilled. Death has been conquered; it can no longer claim victory.

Paul goes on to link death to the reality of sin. Death came about only because of sin; it is not part of the divine plan. According to Paul, adherence to the Jewish law suggests and even brings about sin, since the

READING II   1 Corinthians 15:54b–57

A reading from the first letter of Saint Paul to the Corinthians

immortality = im-ohr-TAL-ih-tee (not
immorality)

Read the quote triumphantly and slowly.

**Continue with a sedate pace, but conclude
with a joyous prayer of praise.**

Brothers and sisters:
When *that* which is *mortal* clothes itself with *immortality,*
    then the *word* that is *written* shall come *about:*
    "Death is swallowed up in *victory.*
    Where, O death, is your *victory*?
    Where, O death, is your *sting*?"

The *sting* of death is *sin,*
    and the *power* of sin is the *law.*
But *thanks* be to *God* who gives us the *victory*
    through our *Lord* Jesus *Christ.*

GOSPEL   Luke 11:27–28

A reading from the holy gospel according to Luke

**Pause before beginning to make sure your
listeners are attentive. This reading is so
short that you don't want anyone to miss
any of it!**

**Read the words of the woman and those of
Jesus with great solemnity and sincerity.**

While Jesus was *speaking,*
    a *woman* from the crowd called *out* and *said* to him,
    "Blessed is the *womb* that *carried* you
    and the *breasts* at which you *nursed."*

He replied,
    "Rather, blessed are those
    who *hear* the word of God and *observe* it."

---

law is so demanding it cannot be met in full. But none of this matters now since God has conquered death in Jesus Christ.

This passage is used for today's feast because of the belief that Mary's body was not subject to decay after her death. Mary is seen as an example of what Paul describes: Her perishable body has put on imperishability, her mortal body has become immortal. Read slowly and carefully, conveying the hope that Paul expresses for a future life and his conviction that death, powerful though it may be, is not the final victor.

GOSPEL   After Jesus was accused of bearing demonic power, the woman in today's reading speaks in support of him and his contention that he acts as God's agent. She offers a word of praise for Mary in terms that recall how central bearing and rearing children were to women in ancient Palestinian culture.

Jesus' response does not negate the woman's claim but indicates that biological connections are of secondary importance. Instead of celebrating earthly relationships, Jesus calls attention to those whose goal is to listen to God's word and put it into action.

Mary is remembered as the first disciple of Jesus, the first to "ponder in her heart" the significance of his life and teachings. This reading is an appropriate way to honor her today, both for her role as mother of Jesus and for her willingness to recognize his significance and be his disciple.

Because this reading is so short, be especially careful to read it slowly and savor it.

ASSUMPTION

Lectionary #622

"Revelation" not "Revelations."

A reading from the book of Revelation

God's *temple* in *heaven* was *opened*,
    and the *ark* of his *covenant* could be seen in the *temple*.

A great *sign* appeared in the *sky*, a *woman* clothed with the *sun*,
    with the *moon* beneath her *feet*,
    and on her *head* a crown of twelve *stars*.
She was with *child* and *wailed* aloud in *pain* as she labored
        to give *birth*.

The dragon is diabolical; speed up the tempo here in order to indicate the tensions inherent in the scene. diadems = DĪ-uh-demz

Then *another* sign appeared in the sky;
    it was a *huge* red *dragon*, with seven *heads* and ten *horns*,
    and on its *heads* were seven *diadems*.
Its *tail* swept away a *third* of the *stars* in the *sky*
    and *hurled* them down to the *earth*.
Then the *dragon* stood before the *woman* about to give *birth*,
    to *devour* her child when she gave *birth*.

This is the Messiah promised by the prophets.

Although there is still urgency in the "catching up" of the child and the flight of the woman, begin to calm your voice.

She gave birth to a *son*, a *male* child,
    destined to *rule* all the *nations* with an iron *rod*.
Her child was caught up to *God* and his *throne*.
The woman *herself* fled into the *desert*
    where she had a place *prepared* by *God*.

READING I The vision recounted in this passage is one of a great battle between forces of good and evil. The descriptions of the participants in the drama and the combat itself are drawn from both Greco-Roman and Jewish myths. The woman in labor appears to be Mary (or Israel) and the child is clearly the Messiah; elsewhere the woman seems to represent the church as her many offspring continue to be pursued by the dragon.

The apocalyptic imagery of this passage can be confusing. First, heaven is pictured as a great temple that contains the ark of the covenant, the ancient container that held the tablets of the Mosaic law. Then, as in a dream, the scene changes and the focus shifts to a woman about to give birth. She is beautifully clothed with the sun, moon and stars; she is the queen of heaven.

The dragon who earlier tried to grasp heavenly authority (by sweeping the stars out of heaven) now enters the scene, seeking to harm the woman's child. The appearance of the dragon (seven heads and ten horns) comes from the depiction of the enemies of the righteous in the book of Daniel; the seven heads recall imperial Rome, the city on seven hills, which is here seen as the enemy of Christianity.

The child is born and taken to be with God. The woman now represents the church, cared for by God for a limited time (1260 days) until the dragon is defeated. During this time the Messiah already reigns, however, as the voice from heaven proclaims.

Then I heard a loud *voice* in *heaven* say:
    "*Now* have *salvation* and *power* come,
    and the *kingdom* of our *God*
    and the *authority* of his *Anointed* One."

READING II   1 Corinthians 15:20–27

A reading from the first letter of Saint Paul to the Corinthians

Brothers and sisters:
Christ has been *raised* from the *dead*,
    the *firstfruits* of those who have fallen *asleep*.
For since *death* came through *man*,
    the *resurrection* of the dead came *also* through man.
For just as in *Adam* all *die*,
    so too in *Christ* shall all be brought to *life*,
    but *each* one in proper *order*:
    Christ the *firstfruits*;
    then, at his *coming*, those who belong to *Christ*;
    then comes the *end*,
    when he hands over the *kingdom* to his God and *Father*,
    when he has *destroyed* every *sovereignty*
    and every *authority* and *power*.

For *he* must *reign* until he has put all his *enemies* under his *feet*.
The *last* enemy to be destroyed is *death*,
    for "he subjected *everything* under his *feet*."

Proclaim this triumphant statement of divine rule with clarity and authority.

Pause briefly at the end of this line.

Pause.
Pause after "die."

Take a deep breath, and change your tone as you begin the next line. "Then" all things will be different and God will reign supreme. Celebrate this proclamation with joyful expectation in your voice.

Your voice should be a bit more subdued for this final sentence; pause after "destroyed."

This is a difficult but beautiful passage, chosen because of the imagery of the woman. Mary has often been depicted as ruling the cosmos, and her Son is the one enthroned with God in heaven. Read the selection with awe at the heavenly vision and the beauty of the woman, and with compassion for her pain. Convey also the danger of the dragon's threat. Finally, close with the triumphant realization that all will be kept safe by God, who reigns in majesty.

READING II After rejecting the claim of some Christians that there is no resurrection of the dead, Paul develops in this section the meaning of Christ's resurrection. In Jewish liturgical language, Christ is the "first fruits" of those who have died, the one who represents the whole. What he experienced in rising from the dead is available to all who die with faith in him.

Paul then alludes to his belief that death entered the world because of the sin of Adam. Christ—the second Adam—makes life possible both for Christians who have already died and for those who remain alive at Christ's second coming. Finally, after overcoming death and all other hostile powers, Christ will turn over all rule to God.

This reading has been chosen for the Assumption because of the belief that Mary has already followed her Son into heavenly glory. The tradition that she was taken into heaven after her death is a way of indicating that death was not the final word for her. Instead, she has already experienced a share in the resurrection promised to all who follow Jesus.

GOSPEL Luke 1:39–56

A reading from the holy gospel according to Luke

Mary set *out*
    and traveled to the *hill* country in *haste*
    to a town of *Judah*,
    where she entered the house of *Zechariah*
    and greeted *Elizabeth*.

When *Elizabeth* heard Mary's *greeting*,
    the infant *leaped* in her *womb*,
    and *Elizabeth*, *filled* with the Holy *Spirit*,
    cried out in a loud *voice* and said,
    "*Blessed* are you among *women*,
    and *blessed* is the *fruit* of your *womb*.
And *how* does this happen to *me*,
    that the mother of my *Lord* should *come* to me?
For at the moment the sound of your *greeting* reached my *ears*,
    the *infant* in my womb *leaped* for *joy*.
Blessed are *you* who *believed*
    that what was *spoken* to you by the Lord
    would be *fulfilled*."

And Mary said:
    "My *soul* proclaims the *greatness* of the *Lord*;
    my *spirit rejoices* in *God* my *Savior*
    for he has looked upon his lowly *servant*.
From *this* day all *generations* will call me *blessed*:
    the *Almighty* has done great *things* for me,
    and *holy* is his *Name*.
He has *mercy* on those who *fear* him
    in every *generation*.

Zechariah = zek-uh-RĪ-uh

Proclaim Elizabeth's words with sincerity and wonder. In order to avoid rattling through the familiar words, consciously try to slow down your diction, dwelling on every phrase.

Mary picks up the tone of praise.

Speak this and the following lines with a bit of disbelief in your voice; Mary must surely have been amazed at God's favor toward her.

The beginning of the passage is difficult. Proclaim it slowly, emphasizing the contrasts between death and resurrection, between Adam and Christ. The second half of the reading is a proclamation of God's reign and can be read as a word of praise.

| GOSPEL | The gospel of Luke is known for the hymns it contains, |

and the Magnificat, spoken by Mary in today's gospel, is one of the most beautiful. Although the hymn itself clearly draws on material from the Hebrew tradition, it is

the longest passage attributed to Mary in any gospel. It is not difficult to imagine a poor, unwed pregnant girl proclaiming these words, a celebration of God's compassion for the lowly and ability to humble the proud.

The context of the hymn is Mary's visit to Elizabeth. The mothers of two future itinerant preachers are brought together as friends and relatives. Since there was some tension between the followers of John and those of Jesus during their ministries and afterward, the author here makes it clear that Jesus is the greater, and the unborn

John and his mother rejoice at and are humbled by Mary's visit. Elizabeth utters a cry honoring Mary for her trust in God's promise to her.

Mary's response is a joyful, trusting song of reversal that celebrates God's activity in her life and in Israel's. While the hymn is a song of praise to God, it is fitting for a Marian feast since it illustrates Mary's humility and faith, including her belief in a righteous God who acts on behalf of the lowly.

With this line, let your voice become firmer and more insistent. The words Mary proclaims are those of upheaval; nothing is at it seems.

"He has shown the *strength* of his *arm*,
and has scattered the *proud* in their *conceit*.
He has cast down the *mighty* from their *thrones*,
and has *lifted* up the *lowly*.
He has filled the *hungry* with *good* things,
and the *rich* he has sent away *empty*.
He has come to the help of his servant *Israel*
for he has *remembered* his promise of *mercy*,
the *promise* he made to our *fathers*,
to *Abraham* and his children for *ever*."

Pause before continuing in a subdued but clear voice.

Mary remained with her about three *months*
and then returned to her *home*.

The first half of the hymn discusses the favor God has bestowed on Mary. Although she proclaims herself a handmaid or servant, one of the lowly ones, she will be called blessed because of the great things God has done for her and through her. In this way, the first half of the hymn foreshadows what follows: God deals with the individual servant Mary in much the same way as God has dealt with servant Israel. Both are blessed beyond measure, recipients of God's protection, compassion and lavish graciousness.

Not only is there divine favor for the lowly, but God acts decisively to eliminate systems of power and inequity. The haughty and proud, who have placed themselves on a level with God as they scorn the less fortunate, are shown their rightful place. The images are of political leaders; the message is that the land of Israel, occupied by a foreign power, will be vindicated. But Israel has within it also the individual poor, the hungry; they too shall be cared for.

Sing with Mary this song of praise and thanksgiving. Read the passage as a way of honoring her, especially easy to do when

quoting the words of Elizabeth. But read it also as a celebration of God's righteousness, the triumph of the poor and humble over the proud and strong. Then work to make the words a reality in your own community wherever there are discrepancies—whether ecclesiastical, political, social or economic in nature—between the proud and the lowly, the hungry and the rich.

20TH SUNDAY IN ORDINARY TIME

Lectionary #120

READING I Jeremiah 38:4–6, 8–10

A reading from the book of the prophet Jeremiah

In those *days*, the princes said to the *king*:
"*Jeremiah* ought to be put to *death*;
   he is *demoralizing* the soldiers who are *left* in this *city*,
   and *all* the *people*, by *speaking* such things to them;
   he is not interested in the *welfare* of our people,
   but in their *ruin*."

King Zedekiah answered: "He is in your *power*";
   for the *king* could do nothing *with* them.

And so they *took* Jeremiah
   and *threw* him into the *cistern* of Prince *Malchiah*,
   which was in the quarters of the *guard*,
   letting him down with *ropes*.
There was no *water* in the cistern, only *mud*,
   and Jeremiah *sank* into the *mud*.

Ebed-*melech*, a court *official*,
   went there from the *palace* and said to him:
"My lord *king*,
   these *men* have been at *fault*
   in *all* they have done to the prophet *Jeremiah*,
   casting him into the *cistern*.
He will die of *famine* on the *spot*,
   for there is no more *food* in the *city*."

Speak in a strong, angry voice.

Zedekiah = zed-uh-KĪ-uh

Malchiah = mal-KĪ-uh

Jeremiah's fate seems sure.

Ebed-melech = EH-bid–MEH-lik

Ebed-melech speaks with respect but boldness as he challenges the wrong that was done to Jeremiah.

READING I Jeremiah was a prophet in the southern kingdom of Judah in the late seventh and early sixth centuries BCE. Despite some beautiful messages about God's love and care for Israel, Jeremiah is often remembered as a prophet of doom who foretold the fall of Jerusalem and the monarchy. He often opposed other prophets (whom he considered "false") who tried to reassure the people and the king that God would save them.

During a time of political upheaval and threat from the powerful Babylonian empire, Jeremiah preached the necessity of submitting to Babylonian rule, arguing that Judah was not strong enough to withstand the threat. If Judah submitted, he reasoned, it might at least continue to exist, even if not as a completely independent nation. This was quite unpopular with those in power in

the royal court. Such pessimism caused discouragement and was considered dangerous to the city and state. Jeremiah's words, however, proved to be true, and Judah fell to the Babylonian empire.

In today's reading, Jeremiah is treated badly for speaking the truth but is saved from death by the intervention of one of the king's servants. Proclaim this story with an eye to the exciting drama that it is.

Cushite = KOOSH-ĭt

Then the king ordered Ebed-*melech* the *Cushite*
to take three *men* along *with* him,
and draw the prophet *Jeremiah out* of the cistern
before he should *die.*

READING II   Hebrews 12:1–4

A reading from the letter to the Hebrews

Brothers and sisters:
Since we are *surrounded* by so great a cloud of *witnesses,*
let us *rid* ourselves of every *burden* and *sin* that *clings* to us
and *persevere* in running the *race* that lies *before* us
while keeping our eyes fixed on *Jesus,*
the *leader* and *perfecter* of *faith.*
For the sake of the *joy* that lay *before* him
he endured the *cross, despising* its shame,
and has taken his *seat* at the right of the *throne* of *God.*

Consider how he endured such *opposition* from *sinners,*
in order that you may not grow *weary* and lose *heart.*
In your *struggle* against *sin*
you have not yet *resisted* to the point of shedding *blood.*

Allow a tone of wonder to enter your voice.

Draw attention to Jesus' actions and central role in inspiring faith. This sentence is long; prepare it well.

READING II A great cloud of witnesses who trusted in God's promises surrounds us; some of them were mentioned in last week's reading from Hebrews. Their examples of faith have inspired Christians throughout the ages and continue to inspire us today.

The author employs the image of a race to describe the Christian life. Full of eager longing, we are urged to set our sights on our goal and pursue it with all our energy.

And our goal is precisely Jesus, who is both the inspiration for our faith and the one who gives us the strength to continue to believe.

Jesus himself is an example of such faithfulness, for he endured the pain and humiliation of death on a cross, trusting that God's righteousness would prevail. Because of his faithfulness, Jesus is now glorified with God. We who have not had to suffer as Jesus did should look to him for strength.

This short passage contains several long sentences that will have to be prepared well in advance. Begin by urging your listeners to persevere, but close with a tone of comforting encouragement.

GOSPEL Far from the frail, syrupy Jesus of so many movies and much preaching, the Jesus of today's gospel is harsh and demanding, speaking of a great conflagration and an immersion into his death. The fire he brings is a purifying

Jesus' words are fiery and strong. Speak them as such.

Do not shy away from these harsh words.

A reading from the holy gospel according to Luke

Jesus said to his disciples:
 "I have come to set the earth on *fire*,
  and how I *wish* it were already *blazing!*
There is a *baptism* with which I must be *baptized*,
  and how great is my *anguish* until it is *accomplished*!

"Do you think that I have come to establish *peace* on the earth?
No, I tell you, but rather *division*.
From now *on* a household of *five* will be *divided*,
  three against *two* and *two* against *three*;
  a *father* will be divided against his *son*
  and a *son* against his *father*,
  a *mother* against her *daughter*
  and a *daughter* against her *mother*,
  a *mother*-in-law against her *daughter*-in-law
  and a *daughter*-in-law against her *mother*-in-law."

one; it will burn away all imperfection. For this reason Jesus longs for it. Fire is often associated with the day of judgment, when the righteous will be gathered into God's reign and the wicked cast into the fires of damnation. This image of impending judgment recalls last week's gospel theme of preparedness.

Jesus also anticipates the terror and anguish of the "baptism" of his death. He does not shy away from it but in fact longs for its completion. Surely he wants it to be over, but he also knows it is necessary. And his disciples must share the baptism Jesus

will undergo, suffering rejection as well as physical pain. In this gospel there are no shortcuts to discipleship.

Jesus goes on to describe the division his followers will experience. In recent weeks, we have seen that discipleship involves letting go of possessions and even the desire to possess. It requires sharing with those in need. It means being watchful and ready, always alert for the return of the master. And today we learn that discipleship will bring dissension, pitting family members against one another.

Proclaim this difficult reading with all the fire that burns in your soul. Do not quench the flames, but let the harshness of Jesus' words ring out. Although the radical message might make some uncomfortable, it is important for us to reflect on the demands of the Christian life. Are we ready to commit ourselves so totally to following Jesus that we will go wherever he goes, forsaking all we have and creating division?

21ST SUNDAY IN ORDINARY TIME

Lectionary #123

READING I   Isaiah 66:18–21

A reading from the book of the prophet Isaiah

Thus says the LORD:
I know their *works* and their *thoughts*,
and I come to gather *nations* of every *language*;
   they shall *come* and see my *glory*.

I will set a *sign* among them;
   from *them* I will send *fugitives* to the *nations*:
   to *Tarshish, Put* and *Lud, Mosoch,. Tubal* and *Javan*,
   to the distant *coastlands*
   that have never *heard* of my fame, or seen my *glory*;
   and they shall *proclaim* my *glory* among the *nations*.

They shall bring *all* your brothers and *sisters* from all the *nations*
   as an *offering* to the LORD,
   on *horses* and in *chariots*, in *carts*, upon *mules*
      and *dromedaries*,
   to *Jerusalem*, my holy *mountain*, says the LORD,
   just as the *Israelites* bring their *offering*
   to the *house* of the LORD in clean *vessels*.

Some of these I will take as *priests* and *Levites*, says the LORD.

Open with a tone of majesty.

Tarshish = TAHR-shish
Put = <u>poot</u>
Lud = luhd
Mosoch = MOH-sok
Tubal = T<u>OO</u>-bahl
Javan = JAY-vuhn

Imagine a colorful procession coming from the four corners of the earth and converging at the center of the world, the city of Jerusalem. Proclaim this vision with wonder.

READING I   The book of Isaiah closes with a vision of a glorious Jerusalem, which will be a haven not only for the Jewish people but even for people of all nations. With the long exile in Babylon over, Jerusalem will be restored, and the people will once again rest in her arms. Jerusalem will be vindicated and will lead the world in singing praises to God.

Today's verses, close to the end of the book of Isaiah, form part of this vision. The passage itself is a bit unclear; there are references to the scattered members of the house of Israel and to those outside Israel, the Gentiles. All peoples will be gathered together and will know God's greatness.

Jews throughout the Diaspora will declare God's glory to those who do not know it. The cities and regions mentioned represent much of the known world, from North Africa to Asia Minor, perhaps extending westward to Spain or eastward to India. God's message will reach even the farthest ends of the world.

In a procession that recalls the return of the exiles to Jerusalem, the passage asserts that the Gentiles will bring back the descendants of Israel to the holy city. It is not entirely clear if the last line refers to these Diaspora Jews, who are worthy to serve in the temple despite having been dispersed, or if even the Gentiles will be allowed to serve as priests and Levites. What is clear is that all the nations will come to honor God.

Read this selection as a message of hope and encouragement, recognizing God's tremendous glory.

READING II   Hebrews 12:5–7, 11–13

A reading from the letter to the Hebrews

These words are meant to be reassuring. Read them forcefully, but with a tone of comfort.

Brothers and sisters,
You have *forgotten* the exhortation addressed to you as *children*:
"My *son*, do not disdain the *discipline* of the *Lord*
    or lose *heart* when *reproved* by him;
  for whom the Lord *loves*, he *disciplines*;
  he *scourges* every son he *acknowledges*."

Endure your trials as "*discipline*";
  God treats you as *sons*.
For what "*son*" is there whom his father does not *discipline*?

At the *time*,
  all discipline seems a cause not for *joy* but for *pain*,
  yet *later* it brings the peaceful fruit of *righteousness*
  to those who are *trained* by it.

Pause before these final lines. Speak with sincere encouragement.

So *strengthen* your drooping *hands* and your weak *knees*.
Make straight *paths* for your *feet*,
  that what is *lame* may not be disjointed but *healed*.

GOSPEL   Luke 13:22–30

A reading from the holy gospel according to Luke

Jesus passed through *towns* and *villages*,
  teaching as he went and making his way to *Jerusalem*.
Someone asked him,
"*Lord*, will only a *few* people be *saved*?"

READING II In a beautiful passage that recalls the anguish of every parent who wants to teach a child what is right, the author extols the need for discipline and compares God with a parent. The author exhorts the readers to accept the necessary discipline that comes from God, who offers it out of love. God uses adversity to teach Christians; it is to be understood, then, as a loving corrective, despite how unpleasant it may feel. In the end, a person is stronger for having endured it.

The passage provides encouragement to people who have been Christians for some time and have experienced persecution. They are encouraged to hold fast to their faith and to rely on one another when faced with outside threats or internal fatigue. Although they may be weary, they should recognize that they can be healed and strengthened.

Many times our own communities are like the one Hebrews addressed. We grow tired and need encouragement. We also need to hear that the trials we face are for our benefit, if we but endure. Address this to your community, then, keeping in mind especially those who are struggling. Offer it as a message of hope to a weary people.

GOSPEL The gospel of Luke does not mince words in demanding the wholehearted devotion of every Christian, a devotion first and foremost to following the path that Jesus walks, accompanying him on his journey to suffering and death. Discipleship requires a focus on what lies

Passing through the narrow door requires effort. Speak Jesus' words forcefully.

He answered them,
"*Strive* to enter through the *narrow* gate,
    for *many*, I tell you, will *attempt* to enter
    but will not be *strong* enough.

"After the *master* of the house has *arisen* and locked the *door*,
    then will you stand *outside* knocking and saying,
    '*Lord*, open the *door* for us.'
He will say to you in reply,
    'I do not *know* where you are *from*.'

There is desperation in their voices. Jesus' response is harsh.

"And you will say,
    'We *ate* and *drank* in your *company* and you taught
      in our *streets*.'
Then he will say to you,
    'I do not *know* where you are *from*.
Depart from me, all you *evildoers*!'

"And there will be *wailing* and grinding of *teeth*
    when you see *Abraham*, *Isaac* and *Jacob*
    and all the *prophets* in the kingdom of *God*
    and you *yourselves* cast *out*.

Allow your voice to be a bit gentler as you envision this procession of peoples. Close slowly, on a solemn note.

And people will come from the *east* and the *west*
    and from the *north* and the *south*
    and will recline at *table* in the kingdom of *God*.

"For *behold*, some are *last* who will be *first*,
    and some are *first* who will be *last*."

ahead and a willingness to endure trials for the sake of the good news. Today's gospel reading indicates that few will have the strength necessary to be so single-minded.

Jesus uses the image of a house, with himself as the owner, to make his point. The door is not wide for the masses to enter but narrow, and only the most faithful and noble may pass. Once the door is closed, there is no way to force it open. It will not be enough to have known Jesus or heard his message; the follower of Jesus must demonstrate total commitment to him.

Although the door is closed, those waiting outside are able to catch a glimpse of the wonders within, including the presence of Israel's righteous ones. Although the patriarchs and prophets have entered God's reign, the chosen people of old do not have exclusive claim to it. People from every nation will be able to enter if they devote themselves to Jesus' message.

This harsh and challenging passage contains good news as well as rebuke. It was intended to remind Israel that Gentiles will also find God's favor. But it is important

for us to hear as well, lest we become complacent in our lives of faith. Offer this message to your listeners (and yourself!) as a challenge to be ever more faithful, unwilling to be complacent or self-satisfied.

22ND SUNDAY IN ORDINARY TIME

Lectionary #126

READING I   Sirach 3:17–18, 20, 28–29

Sirach = SEER-ak

Although the theme is humility, the words are offered as loving instruction. Speak with encouragement.

A reading from the book of Sirach

My *child*, conduct your affairs with *humility*,
   and you will be loved *more* than a giver of *gifts*.
Humble yourself the *more*, the *greater* you are,
   and you will find *favor* with *God*.
What is too *sublime* for you, seek *not*,
   into things beyond your *strength search* not.

The mind of a *sage* appreciates *proverbs*,
   and an attentive *ear* is the joy of the *wise*.
Water quenches a flaming *fire*,
   and *alms* atone for *sins*.

Read with a quiet, reflective tone.

Close with finality.

READING II   Hebrews 12:18–19, 22–24a

A reading from the letter to the Hebrews

Brothers and sisters:
You have not *approached* that which could be *touched*
   and a blazing *fire* and gloomy *darkness*
   and *storm* and a *trumpet* blast
   and a *voice* speaking *words* such that those who heard
     begged that no message be further *addressed* to them.

Begin strongly. The first line is extremely important; everything that follows it is parenthetical.

READING I Jewish wisdom literature often seems disjointed, and today's selection is no exception. There are three proverbs here, and each deals with a separate issue.

The first and most important message concerns humility. Wisdom literature in general is directed toward the wealthy and educated, often members of the royal court or other leading citizens. But a lesson on the importance of humility could be addressed to anyone.

Humility is extolled over wealth, even a wealth that is generously shared. Even those who extend compassion should do so with humility rather than use charity as a way to exalt themselves over others. Although they may doing good for another person, those who lord it over others will not be loved as much as those who place themselves on par with the ones they are trying to help. The author recognizes that this message will be especially hard for those who are in positions of prominence to hear, but it is they who most need to hear it.

There are still things that even the most educated and respected will not be able to understand. Humility remains necessary, but it is also helpful to learn from the wisdom of others. The proverbs found in wisdom literature are a good place to start, since they offer practical, everyday lessons about life.

Finally, the author implies that everyone fails, but there is an antidote for sin. Sin is like a fire that needs to be put out, and giving alms is an effective means of doing so. Surely the first lesson of today's reading needs to be recalled—charity must be accompanied by humility—but an attitude of generosity must also be cultivated.

Proclaim this short passage slowly and carefully. Provide lengthy pauses between

There is both promise and fulfillment in these words. Proclaim them with confidence.

No, you have approached Mount *Zion*
  and the *city* of the living *God*, the heavenly *Jerusalem*,
  and countless *angels* in festal *gathering*,
  and the assembly of the *firstborn* enrolled in *heaven*,
  and *God* the judge of *all*,
  and the *spirits* of the *just* made *perfect*,
  and *Jesus*, the mediator of a *new* covenant,
  and the sprinkled *blood* that speaks more *eloquently*
    than that of *Abel*.

Pause briefly before the mention of Jesus, then close firmly.

GOSPEL   Luke 14:1, 7–14

A reading from the holy gospel according to Luke

On a *sabbath* Jesus went to *dine*
  at the home of one of the leading *Pharisees*,
  and the *people* there were observing him *carefully*.

He told a *parable* to those who had been *invited*,
  noticing how they were choosing the places of *honor*
    at the table.
"When you are *invited* by someone to a *wedding* banquet,
  do *not* recline at table in the place of *honor*.
A more *distinguished* guest than *you* may have been
    invited by him,
  and the host who invited *both* of you may approach *you*
    and say,
  'Give your place to *this* man,'
  and then you would proceed with *embarrassment*
    to take the *lowest* place.

The first few lines are introductory. Read them as such, then begin afresh with Jesus' words.

Is the host speaking harshly, or warmly and apologetically? Let your answer inform your reading.

the three sections so that each can be understandable to your listeners.

READING II   The letter to the Hebrews celebrates and builds on the experiences of the Jewish people and God's revelation to them. Hebrews recalls the holy people of old and their righteousness, looks back at God's saving works on behalf of the Israelites, and reflects on the superiority of Christ's sacrifice to the temple cult. In today's passage, the author contrasts two mountains, first recalling the

encounter between God and Israel at Sinai. That experience pales in comparison with the Christian's approach to another holy mountain: the heavenly Jerusalem.

At Sinai, only Moses was able to approach and commune with God. The experience was too powerful for the rest of the community. The Israelites recognized the awesome majesty of God in the fire, darkness, storms and trumpet blasts that announced the divine presence.

Christians, too, recognize the glory of God—symbolized by angels and the appearance of God as judge—and yet need not be

afraid to approach God's throne because Jesus mediates a new covenant between God and humankind. We need no longer cower in fear but can be confident that God will judge us favorably because of the saving action of Jesus, who with his blood has ratified a new covenant with God.

The sentences in this passage are long and difficult. Emphasize the first line of each and then speak parenthetically as you finish the description. The final line of the selection should also be emphasized; it is because of Jesus' role in establishing the new covenant

Let this sentence resound; it is the key to Jesus' teaching today.

"*Rather*, when you are *invited*,
   go and take the *lowest* place
   so that when the *host* comes to you he may say,
   'My *friend*, move up to a *higher* position.'
Then you will enjoy the *esteem* of your companions at the *table*.
For every one who *exalts* himself will be *humbled*,
   but the one who *humbles* himself will be *exalted*."

Then he said to the host who *invited* him,
   "When you hold a *lunch* or a *dinner*,
   do not invite your *friends* or your *brothers*
   or your *relatives* or your wealthy *neighbors*,
   in case they may invite you *back* and you have *repayment*.
Rather, when you hold a *banquet*,
   invite the *poor*, the *crippled*, the *lame*, the *blind*;
   blessed *indeed* will you *be* because of their *inability*
      to repay you.
For you will be *repaid* at the *resurrection* of the *righteous*."

Slow down here to make the meaning clear. True generosity does not expect repayment.

that the author can contrast these two mountaintop experiences.

GOSPEL The gospel of Luke repeatedly reverses the expected social order. From the Magnificat, in which Mary proclaims that God will exalt the lowly while humbling the mighty, to the crucifixion, in which the king of the cosmos is reviled and nailed to a cross, the author turns all expectations upside down. In today's passage, Jesus equates the desire of guests to find comfortable seating near the host with arrogance. Even the host should not invite friends but should instead welcome those who were excluded from ritual meals and forbidden to worship at the temple.

As is so often true in this gospel, the story operates on two levels. It is a story about both human relationships and the need for humility. On the level of relationships, it challenges all who have been blessed with plenty to reach out in concern to those who are struggling. Gift-giving takes on a new dimension if we are generous to those who really need assistance, rather than to those who return our favors. On the level of humility, those who strive for honor in this life are missing something of far greater significance. Only by acting in humility and a spirit of true generosity can we hope to be honored at the "resurrection of the righteous."

The message of this passage needs to be heard again and again. Meditate on it and strive to live your life in accordance with it. Then offer it as both a challenge to the members of your community and as a promise that there is more to life than what we now know.

23RD SUNDAY IN ORDINARY TIME

Lectionary #129

READING I   Wisdom 9:13–18a

A reading from the book of Wisdom

Who can know God's *counsel*,
    or who can *conceive* what the LORD *intends*?
For the deliberations of *mortals* are *timid*,
    and *unsure* are our *plans*.
For the corruptible body *burdens* the soul
    and the earthen *shelter* weighs down the *mind*
        that has many *concerns*.

And *scarce* do we *guess* the things on *earth*,
    and what is within our *grasp* we find with *difficulty*;
        but when things are in *heaven*, who can search them *out*?
Or who ever knew your *counsel*, except you had given *wisdom*
    and sent your holy *spirit* from on *high*?
And thus were the paths of those on *earth* made *straight*.

Let a tone of incredulity enter your voice. Of course no one can really do these things!

Change your voice to reflect the inadequacies of human beings.

The final sentence provides an answer to all the questions. It is through wisdom that "the paths of those on earth" are made straight.

READING I Today's selection is part of a larger prayer to God that asks for wisdom. The author praises Lady Wisdom and reflects on Wisdom's presence with God in creation. The present passage appears in this context.

The reading opens with what the author considers to be rhetorical questions. After describing Wisdom's greatness and asking for her guidance, the author expresses the obvious: No human can discern the mind of God without the counsel of Wisdom. Human beings are simply unable to comprehend God's majesty without the assistance of one who can teach and direct their thoughts.

The Greek philosopher Plato taught that the soul is imprisoned in the body and must be released; human beings must flee the body and everything material. Similarly, the author of the book of Wisdom declares that the body weighs down the soul and impedes the mind. It is impossible for humans to understand God because of the body; we have trouble understanding even what we can see and know. Only those endowed with wisdom and given the spirit of God can begin to comprehend God's ways.

The concluding line of the passage actually begins a section of the book that reflects on Lady Wisdom's role in salvation history. As it stands in today's reading, it is a fitting conclusion to the assertion that humanity needs Wisdom. The assistance she has given in the past is still available for those who seek her today.

Proclaim the lofty ideas of this reading with a sincere and passionate tone. Read the questions in such a way as to make clear that the answer to each is "no one." Close with a tone of finality.

READING II   Philemon 9b–10, 12–17

A reading from the letter of Saint Paul to Philemon

Paul writes as a respected leader. Speak with solemnity and authority.

Onesimus = oh-NES-ih-muhs

I, *Paul*, an old *man*,
>   and now also a *prisoner* for Christ *Jesus*,
>   *urge* you on behalf of my child *Onesimus*,
>   whose *father* I have become in my *imprisonment*;
>   I am *sending* him, that is, my own *heart*, *back* to you.

Express Paul's fervent plea with a tone of longing.

I should have liked to *retain* him for *myself*,
>   so that he might *serve* me on your *behalf*
>   in my *imprisonment* for the *gospel*,
>   but I did not want to do *anything* without your *consent*,
>   so that the *good* you do might not be *forced* but *voluntary*.

Speak with dignity. Paul wants cooperation, not capitulation.

Perhaps *this* is why he was *away* from you for a *while*,
>   that you might have him back *forever*,
>   no longer as a *slave*
>   but *more* than a slave, a *brother*,
>   beloved *especially* to *me*, but even *more* so to *you*,
>   as a *man* and in the *Lord*.

Let your voice be filled with warmth.

So if you regard me as a *partner*, *welcome* him as you would *me*.

Onesimus is to be treated with the same honor and respect as Paul himself.

READING II ▪ The letter to Philemon is unique among Paul's correspondence. It is not a general letter, as are Paul's other writings to the communities he had founded or visited, but is addressed to three people and the church that meets in their house. Paul writes in a very personal tone, appealing to have the slave Onesimus freed and sent back to him.

Onesimus had fled from his master and turned to Paul, accepting Christianity. Paul sends him back to his owner but also writes this letter subtly asking for the return of Onesimus. He had found the slave particularly helpful in his ministry and knows that Philemon, who owned Onesimus, owes a debt to Paul for having led him to Christ. By referring to this debt of gratitude and comparing Onesimus to himself, Paul hopes to win freedom for Onesimus and gain an assistant for himself.

It is clear that Paul is asking for the slave's freedom, but he does not challenge the legality of slavery itself in doing so. In fact, he actually returns Onesimus to his owner as the law requires. Speak with sensitivity to the tensions that may exist in your community with regard to this issue but also with the same boldness and compassion that Paul displays.

GOSPEL ▪ The gospel of Luke is subversive. The author does not mince words when it comes to what discipleship entails. The same author speaks of bringing down the powerful and exalting the homeless, the poor and the most sinful. This gospel often makes us squirm.

Following Jesus means leaving everything behind. Human relationships and responsibilities, even one's own life, cannot

GOSPEL Luke 14:25–33

A reading from the holy gospel according to Luke

Great *crowds* were *traveling* with Jesus,
    and he turned and *addressed* them,
      "If anyone *comes* to me without *hating* his *father* and *mother*,
    wife and *children*, *brothers* and *sisters*,
    and even his own *life*,
    he *cannot* be my *disciple*.
Whoever does not carry his own *cross* and come *after* me
    cannot be my *disciple*.

"*Which* of you wishing to construct a *tower*
    does not *first* sit down and calculate the *cost*
    to see if there is *enough* for its *completion*?
Otherwise, after laying the *foundation*
    and finding himself *unable* to *finish* the work
    the onlookers should *laugh* at him and say,
    '*This* one began to *build* but did not have the resources
      to *finish*.'

"Or what *king* marching into *battle* would not first sit *down*
    and decide whether with *ten* thousand troops
    he can successfully *oppose another* king
    advancing upon him with *twenty* thousand troops?
But if *not*, while he is still far *away*,
    he will send a *delegation* to ask for *peace* terms.

"In the *same* way,
    anyone of *you* who does not *renounce* all his *possessions*
    cannot be my *disciple*."

The demands of discipleship are great. Do not attempt to lessen them.

The questions are rhetorical. Give them full expression, then offer the alternative with a tone of regret.

Pause before this line, then close strongly.

---

get in the way of devotion to Jesus and his message. The Greek word for "hate" in the opening lines is a strong one. How strange that the one who commands us to love our enemies and act compassionately toward our neighbors asks us to despise our families!

What Jesus demands is not that his followers act without justice or compassion but that commitment to him must take precedence over everything else. Discipleship involves turning one's back on anything that might get in the way of focusing on the goal ahead. This idea of striving toward a goal

clarifies the two examples that Jesus offers. In both instances, the protagonist must carefully consider what is necessary to reach the goal and prepare accordingly.

In the same way, the followers of Jesus must prepare for a life of discipleship by freeing themselves from any obstacles that might impede their progress. Chief among these are possessions. Throughout this gospel, the author argues that wealth and possessions can take hold of a person, rendering one bound to them. Only by being freed of the entrapments of worldly goods can we truly follow Jesus.

Speak boldly, and do not try to soften the message of this text. It is not easy to hear these words, and we often fail. But offer Jesus' demands to the members of your assembly as a challenge to turn their lives ever more fully over to God. Stress especially the opening and closing sections, reading the two middle sections as examples of preparedness.

Lectionary #132

READING I   Exodus 32:7–11, 13–14

A reading from the book of Exodus

The LORD said to *Moses*,
"Go down at *once* to your *people*,
   whom you brought out of the land of *Egypt*,
   for they have become *depraved*.
They have *soon* turned *aside* from the way I pointed *out* to them,
   making for themselves a molten *calf* and *worshiping* it,
   sacrificing to it and crying out,
   '*This* is your *God*, O Israel,
   who brought you *out* of the land of *Egypt!*'

"I see how stiff-*necked* this *people* is," continued the LORD
     to *Moses*.
"Let me *alone*, then,
   that my *wrath* may blaze up *against* them to *consume* them.
Then I will make of *you* a great *nation*."

But Moses *implored* the LORD, his God, saying,
"*Why*, O LORD, should your wrath blaze *up* against your
     own *people*,
   whom you brought out of the land of *Egypt*
   with such great *power* and with so strong a *hand*?
Remember your servants *Abraham*, *Isaac*, and *Israel*,
   and how you *swore* to them by your own *self*, saying,
   'I will make your *descendants* as *numerous* as the *stars*
     in the *sky*;

God is angry. Speak forcefully.

Speak with scorn as you recount God's quotation of Israel's words. How ironic that God, the one who brought Israel out of Egypt, must give voice to this idolatry.

Speak with anger and impatience.

Moses is bold but respectful.

Speak with sincerity.

READING I   The famous incident of the golden calf, recounted in this reading, comes after Moses has been on Mount Sinai for a very long time. The people were told not to attempt to look upon God; instead all communication between God and Israel was to be mediated by Moses. During Moses' time on the mountain, God gave instructions for proper living (both general and specific) and told Moses how to build the ark of the covenant that was to serve as a visible reminder of God's presence and guidance.

Moses remained on the mountain for such a long time that the people must have thought he was deserting them. They rebel, building an image of a calf, a sign of youthfulness and strength. While their true God and deliverer is giving the law to Moses, the people proclaim that the calf—which they have fashioned—is the god who brought them out of Egypt.

God observes the people's idolatry and sends Moses down to intervene. God, portrayed here with human emotions, is furious.

Although Moses and God had just been discussing the covenant God wants to establish with Israel and how Israel should live as God's chosen people, God is now willing to abandon them and establish a covenant with Moses and his descendants. Moses must defend the people against God's wrath.

Moses reminds God of the promises made to Abraham, Isaac and Israel (Jacob). God had promised lasting fidelity and had even sworn allegiance to this people. God is convinced by Moses' plea and abandons the punishment planned for the people.

and *all* this land that I *promised,*
I will give your *descendants* as their perpetual *heritage.'"*

Pause before the final sentence, then proclaim it with certainty.

So the LORD *relented* in the *punishment*
he had threatened to *inflict* on his *people.*

READING II   1 Timothy 1:12–17

A reading from the first letter of Saint Paul to Timothy

Beloved:
I am *grateful* to him who has *strengthened* me, Christ *Jesus*
    our *Lord,*

Speak with a deep sense of gratitude.

    because he considered me *trustworthy*
    in appointing me to the *ministry.*

The tone changes here to one of apology.

I was once a *blasphemer* and a *persecutor* and *arrogant,*
    but I have been *mercifully* treated
    because I acted out of *ignorance* in my *unbelief.*

Stress the overwhelming nature of God's grace.

Indeed, the *grace* of our Lord has been *abundant,*
    along with the *faith* and *love* that are in Christ *Jesus.*

This saying is *trustworthy* and deserves full *acceptance:*
    Christ *Jesus* came into the world to save *sinners.*
Of *these* I am the *foremost.*

Speak with humility.

But for that *reason* I was mercifully *treated,*
    so that in *me,* as the *foremost,*
    Christ *Jesus* might display all his *patience* as an *example*
    for those who would come to *believe* in him for everlasting *life.*

Raise your voice in praise to God!

To the *king* of *ages, incorruptible, invisible,* the only *God,*
    honor and *glory* forever and *ever. Amen.*

In many ways, Moses is the true hero in this story, and it is no wonder that he has long been held in high esteem by the Jewish people. He rejects having his own posterity be the sole recipients of the promises made to Abraham, Isaac and Jacob, in order to hold God to the earlier covenant.

Proclaim this selection with vigor. Speak God's words forcefully and angrily. Moses responds sincerely but also insistently. The last line should be spoken calmly but firmly; the theme of God's forgiveness will continue through all the readings today.

READING II The present passage offers an account of Paul's life before his call to serve Christ. But the personal nature of the account does not detract from our ability to identify with its content.

As we know from the Acts of the Apostles and from Paul's own letters, Paul had once zealously persecuted the early followers of Christ. But he had an experience of the risen Christ's presence and was called not only to be a disciple but to serve the Lord by proclaiming the gospel to the Gentiles. He applied the same energy and zeal to spreading the good news as he had to persecuting Christians.

The present passage is a reflection on Paul's life, but one to which any Christian can relate. Only by receiving mercy and being strengthened by God can we serve Christ. Although not all of us formerly persecuted others, we know that we have done what is wrong, thus harming ourselves and others, and turning away from God's love. But there is hope, for Jesus came to save sinners. With the author, we can each hope that God will

GOSPEL   Luke 15:1–32

A reading from the holy gospel according to Luke

Tax collectors and *sinners* were all drawing near to *listen* to Jesus,
  but the *Pharisees* and *scribes* began to *complain*, saying,
  "This man welcomes *sinners* and *eats* with them."

So to *them* he addressed this *parable*.
"*What* man *among* you having a hundred *sheep*
    and losing *one* of them
  would not leave the ninety-*nine* in the *desert*
  and go after the *lost* one until he *finds* it?
And when he *does* find it,
  he sets it on his *shoulders* with great *joy*
  and, upon his arrival *home*,
  he calls together his *friends* and *neighbors* and *says* to them,
  '*Rejoice* with me because I have *found* my lost *sheep*.'
I *tell* you, in just the *same* way
  there will be more *joy* in *heaven* over one sinner who *repents*
  than over ninety-nine *righteous* people
  who have no *need* of repentance.

"Or what *woman* having ten *coins* and losing *one*
  would not light a *lamp* and *sweep* the *house*,
  searching *carefully* until she *finds* it?
And when she *does* find it,
  she calls together her *friends* and *neighbors*
  and *says* to them,
  '*Rejoice* with me because I have found the *coin* that I *lost*.'

"In just the *same* way, I *tell* you,
  there will be *rejoicing* among the *angels* of *God*
  over one *sinner* who *repents*."

Imagine a famous person—especially a well-known teacher or religious leader—who socializes with criminals. How would you respond? Express your response accordingly.

Express the shepherd's joy and excitement.

Again, speak with exuberance.

---

continue to work in our lives, forgiving us even when we sin repeatedly.

Reflect on this selection before attempting to read it in the assembly. Think of your own life and the mistakes you have made, then consider God's abundant grace, in which you have been offered mercy and called to a life of faithful service. Attempt to make the words your own as you share this message with your community. Speak with humility but certainty, and close with a fervent prayer of praise.

GOSPEL   Today's gospel divides up neatly into two sections. The first has to do with questions of value: What are things really worth to us? The second section is the much-loved tale of the prodigal son, a story found only in the gospel of Luke. Both sections take our assumptions about life and our dealings with others and turn them on their heads. Nothing is ever as simple as it seems.

The passage opens with a complaint from the religious leadership. Jesus was fraternizing with despicable people: tax collectors, who were widely reviled as cheats, and "sinners," probably those who could or would not keep the law of Moses. Adhering to the proverb "You are known by the company you keep," the Pharisees speak disparagingly of Jesus. In typical fashion, Jesus responds with parables.

The parables of the lost sheep and the lost coin challenge the Pharisees' value system—and ours. The shepherd, in an

Start fresh here, reading slowly and with expression, as though reading this story for the first time.

Then he said,
 "A *man* had two *sons*, and the *younger* son said to his father,
 '*Father* give me the share of your *estate* that should *come*
 to me.'
So the father *divided* the property *between* them.

"After a few *days*, the *younger* son collected all his *belongings*
 and set off to a distant *country*
 where he *squandered* his inheritance on a life of *dissipation*.
When he had freely spent *everything*,
 a severe *famine* struck that *country*,
 and he found himself in dire *need*.
So he hired himself *out* to one of the local *citizens*
 who sent him to his *farm* to tend the *swine*.
And he *longed* to eat his fill of the *pods* on which the swine *fed*,
 but *nobody* gave him *any*.

"Coming to his *senses* he thought,
 'How *many* of my father's hired *workers*
 have *more* than enough *food* to eat,
 but here am *I, dying* from *hunger*.
I shall get *up* and go to my *father* and I shall *say* to him,
 "*Father*, I have sinned against *heaven* and against *you*.
I no longer *deserve* to be called your *son*;
 treat me as you would treat one of your hired *workers*."'

Speak with sincere humility.

"So he got *up* and went back to his *father*.
While he was still a long way *off*,
 his father caught *sight* of him,
 and was filled with *compassion*.
He *ran* to his son, *embraced* him and *kissed* him.
His son said to him,
 '*Father*, I have sinned against *heaven* and against *you*;
 I no longer *deserve* to be called your *son*.'

The father is ecstatic.

Again, speak sincerely.

attempt to save one lost sheep, risks the safety of the rest of the fold. The woman turns her house upside down in hopes of finding her lost coin. Is it really worth it to risk so much in order to gain so little?

Jesus makes clear that he is really speaking of the value of a single human life. It is easy to affirm in theory that each life matters, that each person is worthy of being saved. But isn't it easier to focus on serving the needs of an entire group—whether a parish community, a class of students, a

group of colleagues—than to focus on one demanding individual? Jesus' words challenge us to see the needy person, the nuisance or the incorrigible delinquent as worthy of our time and effort.

The story of the prodigal son illustrates in concrete terms the importance of forgiveness. The relationships described—family members, siblings competing with one another—are so common that it is easy to identify with the story. The author uses it to respond further to the Pharisees' question about Jesus' association with sinners.

The story opens with arrogance. The younger son, who clearly was living a comfortable life in his father's home, demands his inheritance. In Jesus' day, as now, it was unusual for a parent to divide an estate before death, although it did occasionally occur. The son's question, then, displays not only his greed for the wealth he hoped to obtain but also his complete disregard for his father. It is as though he wishes his father were dead.

Express the father's excitement and love.

"But his father ordered his *servants,*
　'*Quickly* bring the *finest* robe and put it *on* him;
　put a *ring* on his *finger* and *sandals* on his *feet.*
Take the fattened *calf* and *slaughter* it.
Then let us *celebrate* with a *feast,*
　because this *son* of mine was *dead,* and has come to *life* again;
　he was *lost,* and has been *found.*'
Then the celebration *began.*

The tone changes as the older son enters the scene.

"Now the *older* son had been out in the *field*
　and, on his way *back,* as he neared the *house,*
　he heard the sound of *music* and *dancing.*
He called one of the *servants* and asked what this might *mean.*
The servant said to him,
　'Your *brother* has returned
　and your *father* has slaughtered the fattened *calf*
　because he has him back *safe* and *sound.*'
He became *angry,*
　and when he *refused* to enter the *house,*
　his father came *out* and *pleaded* with him.
He said to his father in reply,

Speak with a righteous indignation. Everything the older son says is true.

　'*Look,* all these *years* I *served* you
　and not *once* did I disobey your *orders;*
　yet you never gave *me* even a young *goat* to *feast* on
　　with my *friends.*
But when your *son* returns,
　who *swallowed* up your property with *prostitutes,*
　for *him* you slaughter the fattened *calf.*'

As if the younger son's arrogance were not enough, he has the audacity to take his inheritance and waste it. The older son later tells us that his brother not only "squandered" his wealth, but spent it on "loose women," adding insult to injury. As so often happens, however, his behavior catches up with him, and he soon hits rock bottom. Jesus' listeners would have recognized this when they learned he was living with pigs, which made one ritually unclean according to Jewish law.

In desperation, the son reflects on his former life and regrets what he has done. But he still has some pride. The younger son realizes that he has wronged his father and resolves to demand nothing of him. Yet he also knows his father's kind, loving nature, expressed even to servants, and turns to him in humility. The son's sincerity is evident when he sticks to his resolve and asks to be treated as a servant, even after his father warmly embraces him.

The older son, who had faithfully stayed by his father's side while his brother acted irresponsibly, now emerges as resentful and

obstinate. Although his attitude is understandable, the contrast with his father's response to the younger son is striking. The older son was not wronged, yet he refuses to forgive his brother. The father was treated despicably, yet he opens his heart and his home, and lavishly celebrates the return of his beloved son. The older son's refusal to forgive makes one wonder if there is still, indeed, a lost son.

On one level, the story deals with human relationships and the importance of forgiveness. On another level, of course, the father

Is the father impatient, sad or tender? Let your answer determine your tone. Close with a sense of peaceful joy.

"He said to him,
  'My *son*, you are here with me *always*;
  everything I *have* is *yours*.
But now we must *celebrate* and *rejoice*,
  because your *brother* was *dead* and has come to *life* again;
  he was *lost* and has been *found*.'"

[Shorter: Luke 15:1–10]

represents God's loving embrace of sinners and gentle rebuke of the self-righteous. The religious leaders who had questioned Jesus' behavior must have been squirming at the implications of this parable. Could God really grant the same forgiveness and favor to cheats and sinners as to them?

This final parable, then, affirms the truth found in the first two stories. God forgives the sinner, and all of heaven rejoices when one person repents. But the story of the prodigal son also challenges all of us to act with the wronged father's compassion, forgiveness and generosity. It is a demanding lesson.

Although the reading is long, it is well worth the time you will need to devote to it. Do not rush through it, but savor the stories, letting each one sink in before turning to the next. Give plenty of expression to the characters in the final parable, and close with a tone of joy and compassion.

Lectionary #135

READING I   Amos 8:4–7

A reading from the book of the prophet Amos

Begin strongly. Amos is angry.

Hear *this*, you who *trample* upon the *needy*
    and *destroy* the *poor* of the *land*!

Allow a tone of whining and greed to enter your voice. Pause briefly after "sabbath."

"*When* will the new moon be *over*," you ask,
    "that we may sell our *grain*,
    and the *sabbath*, that we may display the *wheat*?

ephah = EE-fah
shekel = SHEK-*l

We will *diminish* the *ephah*,
    add to the *shekel*,
    and fix our *scales* for *cheating*!

Speak with arrogance toward the poor.

We will buy the *lowly* for *silver*,
    and the *poor* for a pair of *sandals*;
    even the refuse of the *wheat* we will *sell*!"

Let your voice thunder with divine wrath.

The *LORD* has *sworn* by the pride of *Jacob*:
    Never will I forget a *thing* they have *done*!

READING I   The prophet Amos preached to the people of the northern kingdom of Israel in the eighth century BCE, spreading a message of justice and compassion. Today's passage is a stinging rebuke of those who are cheating and oppressing the poor for their own gain.

Amos was active during a time of great prosperity for Israel. There was relatively little threat from foreign powers (although a short time later the northern kingdom of Israel did fall to the Assyrians) and this, combined with agricultural success, resulted in a flourishing economy. Many of the leading citizens were growing gluttonous and lazy, often at the expense of the poor.

Each new moon and each Sabbath was a religious holiday during which no business could be conducted. Amos chastises the storeowners not only for their greed but also for their religious insincerity. They pretended to observe feasts but were really contemplating their future sales. Even on the Sabbath, they plotted to cheat others in order to fatten themselves. They had no concern for the poor and needy but intended to take advantage of them in order to make more money. God swears that these deeds will not be forgotten.

This is an especially appropriate message for us in our affluent society. Especially during times of widespread prosperity, when we hear how strong our economy is, we tend to forget the truly needy in our communities. Not everyone is enjoying abundance or is able to take long, leisurely vacations (or any vacation at all). Despite apparently widespread wealth, the gap between rich and poor grows greater all the time. Proclaim this passage, then, as an urgent reminder to the members of your community to practice

READING II   1 Timothy 2:1–8

A reading from the first letter of Saint Paul to Timothy

Beloved:
First of all, I ask that *supplications*, *prayers*,
    petitions and *thanksgivings* be offered for *everyone*,
    for *kings* and for all in *authority*,
    that we may lead a *quiet* and *tranquil* life
    in all *devotion* and *dignity*.
This is *good* and *pleasing* to God our *savior*,
    who wills *everyone* to be *saved*
    and to come to *knowledge* of the *truth*.

For there is *one* God.
There is also one *mediator* between *God* and *men*,
        the man Christ *Jesus*,
    who gave *himself* as ransom for *all*.
This was the *testimony* at the proper *time*.

For *this* I was appointed *preacher* and *apostle*
    —I am speaking the *truth*, I am not *lying*—
    teacher of the *Gentiles* in *faith* and *truth*.

It is my *wish*, then, that in every *place* the men should *pray*,
    lifting up holy *hands*, without *anger* or *argument*.

Read slowly through the list of prayers.

Pause before this line, then speak decisively.

Speak with pride in this ministry.

Read this final sentence with strength.

---

fairness in all transactions, to be sincere in their religious practices, and to have compassion for those in need. Do not try to soften the message but proclaim it forcefully.

READING II The "pastoral letters" (First and Second Timothy, and Titus) were written by an admirer of Paul to deal with concerns that Paul himself had never faced. The present passage from First Timothy gives instructions on prayer, discusses God's relationship with the human race through the person of Jesus, and reflects on Paul's own ministry.

The author begins by urging constant prayer, a theme that resonates throughout much of the Pauline correspondence. A unique aspect of the prayer enjoined here is that it is to be offered for kings and government officials. The relationship between Christians and the government in the early centuries after Jesus' death was varied. Some civil authorities violently persecuted Christians and denied them the right to worship freely. Sometimes Christians resisted; at other times, however, Christians sought to endear themselves to the authorities in the

hope that they would be able to practice their new religion in peace.

Paul, like Jesus, seems to have had a somewhat ambivalent attitude toward civil authorities. He did not advocate active resistance but was concerned about order within the Christian community, regardless of its wider environment. It is surprising, then, that this author speaks confidently about praying for civil leaders.

The author's point is that all people have the capacity to know God. There is one God, and God wants everyone to be saved. That is accomplished through Jesus, who is

GOSPEL   Luke 16:1–13

A reading from the holy gospel according to Luke

Jesus said to his *disciples*,
"A *rich* man had a *steward*
    who was *reported* to him for *squandering* his *property*.

"He *summoned* him and said,
    'What is this I *hear* about you?
Prepare a full *account* of your *stewardship*,
    because you can no *longer* be my *steward*.'

"The steward said to himself, 'What shall I *do*,
    now that my *master* is taking the position of *steward*
        away from me?
I am not *strong* enough to *dig* and I am *ashamed* to *beg*.
I know what I shall *do* so that,
    when I am *removed* from the stewardship,
    they may *welcome* me into their *homes*.'

"He called in his master's *debtors* one by *one*.
To the *first* he said,
    'How *much* do you owe my *master*?'
He replied, 'One *hundred* measures of *olive* oil.'
He said to him, '*Here* is your *promissory* note.
Sit *down* and quickly write one for *fifty*.'
Then to *another* the steward said, 'And *you*,
        how much do *you* owe?'
He replied, 'One *hundred* kors of *wheat*.'
The steward said to him, '*Here* is your *promissory* note;
    write one for *eighty*.'

The man speaks firmly, in a demanding tone.

He is a bit frantic, but also shrewd.

Surely the recipients of his dishonest acts of generosity would have been grateful, as he had hoped.

---

the mediator between God and humanity precisely because he is both human and divine. His life was given for all people, including those in positions of authority.

The mention of Jesus' role and his saving death prompt the author to reflect on the ministry of Paul, whose role was to preach the cross of Christ to the Gentiles.

The passage closes with a desire that people pray in purity, free from ill feelings. The author uses the image of one who praises God by lifting hands toward heaven. The teaching that negative thoughts and feelings must be released before entering into prayer rings true for many of us.

Proclaim this passage as an urgent reminder to your listeners of the importance of prayer. Because Jesus has already bridged the gap between God and humankind, we can approach God freely, turning over everything in our hearts to the one who loves us beyond our imagining.

GOSPEL | The parable of the unjust steward is sometimes difficult to read, much less proclaim in the assembly. Jesus actually seems to praise the steward for his dishonesty or "shrewdness." This is especially surprising to find in the gospel of Luke, which preaches the necessity of giving up possessions and even family relationships in order to follow Jesus. But perhaps the message of the story is even more radical than we first expect.

Because he was either incompetent or dishonest with his master's property, the steward loses his job. He first responds with panic but then realizes he can turn the situation to his advantage. As the one responsible for holding the receipts indicating the amounts owed by each of his master's

Let surprise be heard in your voice.

"And the master *commended* that dishonest steward
   for acting *prudently*.
For the *children* of this *world*
  are more *prudent* in dealing with their *own* generation
  than are the children of *light*.

"I *tell* you, make *friends* for yourselves with dishonest *wealth*,
  so that when it *fails*, you will be *welcomed*
    into eternal *dwellings*.
The person who is *trustworthy* in very *small* matters
  is also trustworthy in *great* ones;
   and the person who is *dishonest* in very *small* matters
  is also dishonest in *great* ones.
If, therefore, you are not trustworthy with *dishonest* wealth,
  who will trust you with *true* wealth?
If you are not *trustworthy* with what belongs to *another*,
who will give you what is *yours*?

Proclaim the final paragraph in a strong voice.

"No *servant* can serve two *masters*.
He will either *hate* one and love the *other*,
  or be *devoted* to one and *despise* the other.
You cannot serve both *God* and *mammon*."

[Shorter: Luke 16:10–13]

debtors, he still wields power. He instructs the debtors, each of whom is no more honorable than he, to rewrite the terms of their agreement with his master. The steward hopes they will be indebted to him when he is unemployed.

Perhaps the most surprising line in the entire passage is Jesus' recommendation of friendship with such dishonest wealth. Is this the same Jesus who demands that people leave everything behind in order to follow him? But Jesus says that even the proper use of dishonest wealth can ensure heavenly blessings. The disciple must be so completely detached from money that its presence or absence is insignificant. What matters is that what is accomplished—with or without wealth—is of such quality that it will reap an eternal reward.

All the riches of the world seem to fall under the title "dishonest wealth" in this story. Dealing with wealth—unimportant though it is in itself—can prepare one for truly significant responsibilities. In the end, though, as the final section makes clear, it is important to be detached from the wealth one uses in this world. The purpose of using it is to serve God. Any other goal is idolatrous, placing something material above God.

Proclaim this passage boldly, trusting that the message of detachment from wealth will be heard. Do not shy away from the difficulties, but draw special attention to the final section in order to clarify the main point of the passage.

26TH SUNDAY IN ORDINARY TIME

Lectionary #138

READING I   Amos 6:1a, 4–7

A reading from the book of the prophet Amos

The message is dire. Begin in a booming voice.

Thus says the LORD the God of *hosts*:
Woe to the *complacent* in *Zion*!

Let contempt fill your voice.

Lying upon beds of *ivory*,
    stretched *comfortably* on their *couches*,
they eat *lambs* taken from the *flock*,
    and *calves* from the *stall*!
Improvising to the music of the *harp*,
    like *David*, they devise their *own* accompaniment.
They drink *wine* from *bowls*
    and *anoint* themselves with the best *oils*;

Fairly shout the final line.

    yet they are not made *ill* by the collapse of *Joseph*!

Speak this word of judgment with finality but also with sadness.

Therefore, now they shall be the *first* to go into *exile*,
    and their wanton *revelry* shall be done *away* with.

READING II   1 Timothy 6:11–16

A reading from the first letter of Saint Paul to Timothy

Pause after each item in the list, in order to give each its due weight.

But *you*, man of *God*, pursue *righteousness*,
    devotion, *faith*, *love*, *patience* and *gentleness*.
Compete *well* for the *faith*.

READING I The prophet Amos lived in the eighth century BCE and preached to the people of the northern kingdom of Israel. His was a message of righteousness, calling the people to do justice to one another. Amos often speaks with anger and sarcasm, chastising the wealthy for their treatment of the poor.

The complacency of the wealthy is particularly irksome to Amos. Oblivious to the needs of the poor, they lounge in luxury and eat the choicest foods. In utter self-indulgence, they idly make music, drink from bowls rather than cups, and anoint themselves with costly perfumes.

In an ominous warning, Amos seems to predict the fall of Israel and the exile of its people. He speaks ironically of the prominent and wealthy members of the community, unconcerned as they are about the impending demise of the nation, who will retain their foremost positions when the country is defeated: They who were first in luxury will be first in exile!

Proclaim this reading as a wake-up call to your community. Do not be afraid to speak forcefully and with a note of disdain in your voice. Close with a sense of doom.

READING II The first letter to Timothy was written as a letter of support from a wise older teacher to a younger minister. It provides encouragement, instruction and hope as the author urges Timothy to remain faithful in his own life and true to his calling as a minister of Christ.

The reference to Timothy's "noble confession" of faith is probably intended as an allusion to his initiation. His baptismal confession in front of many witnesses opens for

Speak fervently.

Lay *hold* of eternal *life*, to which you were *called*
    when you made the noble *confession* in the presence
        of many *witnesses*.

Lift your voice boldly and direct this challenge to your community.

I *charge* you before *God*, who gives *life* to all *things*,
    and before Christ *Jesus*,
        who gave *testimony* under Pontius *Pilate*
            for the noble *confession*,
    to keep the *commandment* without *stain* or *reproach*
    until the *appearance* of our Lord Jesus *Christ*

This long section should be spoken as a sincere word of praise. Let your voice build in intensity through the entire section.

    that the *blessed* and only *ruler*
    will make *manifest* at the proper *time*,
    the King of *kings* and Lord of *lords*,
    who *alone* has *immortality*, who *dwells*
        in unapproachable *light*,
    and whom no human *being* has *seen* or can *see*.
To *him* be *honor* and eternal *power*. Amen.

GOSPEL   Luke 16:19–31

A reading from the holy gospel according to Luke

Jesus said to the *Pharisees*:

Let your voice be filled with mock admiration for the extravagance.

"There was a *rich* man who dressed in purple *garments*
        and fine *linen*
    and dined *sumptuously* each day.

The tone changes. Speak woefully about the plight of Lazarus.

And lying at his *door* was a *poor* man named *Lazarus*,
        covered with *sores*,
    who would *gladly* have eaten his fill of the *scraps*
        that fell from the rich man's *table*.
Dogs even used to come and *lick* his *sores*.

---

him the possibility of eternal life. Christ's testimony before Pilate is called by the same name—a "noble confession"—suggesting that what Timothy has confessed is of the highest quality.

The reference to the "commandment" is unclear but may refer to a teaching of Paul, to the call to serve the community in active ministry, or to the baptismal pledge. Whatever it is, Timothy is to preserve it until the coming of Jesus.

The mention of Jesus inspires the author to burst into a beautiful hymn of praise. Jesus is extolled as the King of Kings and Lord of Lords.

Lift your voice in the final section and sing out your praises to Jesus the Lord.

GOSPEL   The gospel of Luke is filled with teachings about wealth and the proper attitude toward money. Today's parable contrasts extreme wealth with absolute poverty. As so often happens

in this gospel, while Jesus' teaching pertains primarily to the life anticipated after death, it also applies to attitudes and actions that are necessary in this life.

The beginning of the story is not that hard to imagine. The rich man of the parable lives in comfort, dressed in finery and enjoying his wealth, completely oblivious to the destitute beggar outside his door. The story has a ring of truth to it, even if the situations of the protagonists are exaggerated for greater effect.

Raise your voice to express a petition from afar.

"When the poor man *died*,
   he was carried away by *angels* to the bosom of *Abraham*.
The *rich* man *also* died and was *buried*,
   and from the *netherworld*, where he was in *torment*,
   he raised his *eyes* and saw *Abraham* far *off*
   and *Lazarus* at his *side*.
And he cried out, 'Father *Abraham*, have *pity* on me.
Send *Lazarus* to dip the tip of his *finger* in *water* and cool
        my *tongue*,
   for I am suffering *torment* in these *flames*.'

Abraham speaks warmly but firmly.

"Abraham replied,
   'My *child*, remember that *you* received
   what was *good* during your lifetime
   while *Lazarus* likewise received what was *bad*;
   but now he is comforted *here*, whereas *you* are *tormented*.
Moreover, between *us* and *you* a great *chasm* is established
   to *prevent* anyone from *crossing* who might wish to go
   from *our* side to *yours* or from *your* side to *ours*.'

"He said, 'Then I *beg* you, father,
   send him to my *father's* house, for I have five *brothers*,
   so that he may *warn* them,
   lest they *too* come to this place of *torment*.'

The law of Moses and the prophetic teachings stress justice for the downtrodden and care for the poor.

"But Abraham replied, 'They have *Moses* and the *prophets*.
Let them listen to *them*.'
He said, 'Oh *no*, father Abraham,
   but if someone from the *dead* goes to them, they will *repent*.'
Then Abraham said, 'If they will not listen to *Moses*
        and the *prophets*,
   neither will they be persuaded if someone should *rise*
        from the *dead*.'"

Speak sadly but with conviction. Surely the author wants us to think of what happened to Jesus himself.

But the situation becomes more complicated after each man dies. Each receives his just reward, but the rich man, now in torment, wants to change his situation. After all, he had always had the means to do so in life. But he is not overly demanding; he does not ask to join Lazarus in the comforting bosom of Abraham. He desires only a drop of water to soothe his suffering and begs Abraham to send Lazarus to deliver it to him.

In the standard mode of this gospel, everything one usually expects is turned upside down. The rich man was accustomed to making demands of others. Now he is told that he has already received more than his share of good things; it is Lazarus's turn. The gulf that separates the heavenly abode from the realm of fire contrasts with the proximity of the rich man and Lazarus on earth. When he had the chance, the rich man did not help Lazarus; now Lazarus is unable to help him.

The final exchange serves to alert the reader to the main point of the gospel message. The rich man says that his brothers would listen to someone who came to them from the dead. The author has Abraham disagree with the man's assertion, well aware that people continued to reject the Christian message that Jesus has conquered death. Nothing, not even someone rising from the dead, will be able to convince the obstinate. Faith is essential in order for people to open their hearts and allow themselves to be guided by God in service to their neighbor.

Offer this message to your listeners as a challenge to resolve to follow Jesus, keeping wealth in its proper place and serving the poor and needy. Give plenty of expression to the various characters in the reading, while remembering that the author is using hyperbole to make a point.

27TH SUNDAY IN ORDINARY TIME

Lectionary #141

READING I   Habakkuk 1:2–3; 2:2–4

Habakkuk = HAB-uh-kuhk

Speak with heartfelt longing.

This is a genuine question. Habakkuk cannot understand how God can allow this.

Speak God's words firmly but calmly.

The final line is key. Emphasize it strongly, especially the word "faith."

A reading from the book of the prophet Habakkuk

How *long*, O LORD? I *cry* for *help*
    but you do not *listen!*
I cry out to you, *"Violence!"*
    but you do not *intervene.*
Why do you let me see *ruin;*
    why must I look at *misery?*
Destruction and *violence* are *before* me;
    there is *strife*, and clamorous *discord.*

Then the LORD *answered* me and said:
    Write *down* the vision *clearly* upon the *tablets,*
    so that one can read it *readily.*
For the *vision* still has its *time,*
    presses on to *fulfillment*, and will not *disappoint;*
if it *delays*, *wait* for it,
    it will surely *come*, it will not be *late.*
The *rash* one has no *integrity;*
    but the *just* one, because of his *faith*, shall *live.*

READING I Habakkuk expresses a concern common to many people of faith, both in the Bible and elsewhere: the apparent absence of God and the injustice of life. How can a good God allow violence and injustice to occur? Where is God when the suffering cry out?

Habakkuk preached at a time when a foreign army was threatening the southern kingdom of Judah; the Babylonians eventually conquered the tiny state. But Habakkuk's complaints do not always refer to threats from outside. It is possible that the prophet refers to the unjust actions of the king of Judah himself.

God responds to Habakkuk's complaints with an answer that is commonly given to prophets: Write down what you know. The content of Habakkuk's vision concerns the time when God will intervene: It is coming soon. The promise of God's intervention is a message of judgment for the proud but one of hope for those who walk in justice. These righteous ones live by faith, absolutely confident in God's reliability. Habakkuk has complained about God's absence, and God responds by saying that those who are righteous should trust in God's presence and love.

There is a timeless quality to the words of Habakkuk. Express his exasperation and longing with sincerity and heartfelt pleading. God answers firmly and reassuringly. Close on a strong note as you describe the faith of the righteous.

READING II The pastoral letters (First and Second Timothy, and Titus) were written in Paul's name and encourage fidelity to his teachings. They are

Speak confidently and boldly.

READING II   2 Timothy 1:6–8, 13–14

A reading from the second letter of Saint Paul to Timothy

Beloved:

I *remind* you, to stir into *flame*
    the gift of *God* that you *have* through the imposition
        of my *hands*.
For *God* did not give us a spirit of *cowardice*
    but rather of *power* and *love* and self-*control*.
So do not be *ashamed* of your *testimony* to our *Lord*,
    nor of *me*, a *prisoner* for his *sake*;
        but bear your *share* of *hardship* for the *gospel*
        with the *strength* that comes from *God*.

Take as your *norm* the sound *words* that you *heard* from me,
    in the *faith* and *love* that are in Christ *Jesus*.
Guard this rich *trust* with the help of the Holy *Spirit*
    that dwells *within* us.

---

addressed to individuals but express concern for the entire community.

Based on the two letters that bear his name, it seems that Timothy was a leader in his community. He apparently looked to Paul for advice, and Paul had encouraged him as he began his ministry. The mention of Paul laying hands on Timothy in today's reading suggests an ordination rite. It also points to a period after Paul's life and ministry, since such practices developed only later. The pastoral letters were actually written by an admirer of Paul seeking to preserve Paul's teachings and style of ministry.

Today's selection could be addressed to anyone involved in serving the Christian community, but especially those in leadership. The author seeks to inspire greater devotion to service and greater zeal for the gospel. God provides the courage to face adversity; to give in to fear is to be ashamed of the gospel, an attitude the author deplores. Despite hardship, the Christian is to press on, relying on divine assistance.

The author reminds the young minister of the truths that have been passed on to him. Pastoral leadership—indeed the Christian faith itself—is not an individual matter. The teachings of the faith are part of a treasure that is entrusted to each community and generation of Christians. This precious tradition is to be safeguarded. But the Christian faith is not static. The Holy Spirit lives within each believer, actively guiding the church.

Reflect on those in leadership positions in your community as you share this message with your listeners. But address it as well to the entire assembly, encouraging each person to be courageous in proclaiming the love of God for all to hear. Speak warmly and reassuringly.

GOSPEL   Luke 17:5–10

A reading from the holy gospel according to Luke

The apostles said to the Lord, *"Increase* our *faith."*
The Lord replied,
"If you have *faith* the size of a *mustard* seed,
   you would say to this *mulberry* tree,
   'Be *uprooted* and planted in the *sea,'* and it would *obey* you.

"Who *among* you would say to your *servant*
   who has just come in from *plowing* or tending *sheep*
      in the *field,*
   'Come here *immediately* and take your place at *table'*?
Would he not *rather* say to him,
   'Prepare something for me to *eat.*
Put on your *apron* and *wait* on me while I *eat* and *drink.*
You may eat and drink when I am *finished'*?
Is he *grateful* to that servant because he did what
      was *commanded*?
So should it be with *you.*
When you have done *all* you have been *commanded,*
   say, 'We are unprofitable *servants;*
   we have done what we were *obliged* to do.'"

Speak slowly but with confidence.

Imagine yourself in charge of a work crew, and speak as one insisting that your employees put in a good day's work. Speak kindly but firmly.

GOSPEL   Jesus' disciples, recognizing the importance of the gift of faith, ask for more. Jesus responds with a teaching about the strength of even a little faith. The tiniest amount can work wonders. More importantly, Jesus' message teaches that the gift of faith, like any other gift, cannot be demanded; it can only be appreciated.

The parable that follows teaches a similar lesson. One who is working in service to another cannot expect a reward. Service is a requirement of discipleship.

It is difficult for many of us to hear this story. We react with horror at the thought of owning another human being; we deplore the lack of gratitude and appreciation shown by the master. The author does not question the institution of slavery, however, but simply lays out its rules. And they apply particularly to service for the gospel.

When applied to church ministry or the Christian life in general, the meaning of the parable is clear. Those serving God cannot simply stop working and expect gratitude. Rather, out of gratitude to God for the gift of faith and for God's tremendous love, we must share our faith with others and strive to bring God's justice to reality on earth. We do not minister for the sake of ourselves; instead, we act out of gratitude for the undeserved gifts we have already received.

Proclaim this passage with boldness in order to convey the importance of faith and service to the gospel. But be sensitive to the emotions that Jesus' example might stir.

28TH SUNDAY IN ORDINARY TIME

Lectionary #144

READING I 2 Kings 5:14–17

A reading from the second book of Kings

Naaman = NAY-uh-muhn
Elisha = ee-LĪ-shuh

Speak with wonder.

Naaman went down and *plunged* into the Jordan seven *times*
    at the word of *Elisha*, the man of *God*.
His *flesh* became again like the flesh of a little *child*,
    and he was *clean* of his *leprosy*.

Naaman speaks humbly and gratefully.

Naaman *returned* with his whole *retinue* to the man of *God*.
On his *arrival* he stood before *Elisha* and said,
    "Now I *know* that there is no God in all the *earth*,
    except in *Israel*.
Please accept a *gift* from your *servant*."

Read Elisha's words with stubborn pride.

Elisha replied, "As the LORD *lives* whom I *serve*, I will not
        take it,"
    and despite Naaman's *urging*, he still *refused*.

With Naaman, resolve to serve God faithfully, then speak his closing words with conviction.

Naaman said: "If you will not *accept*,
    please let *me*, your *servant*, have two *mule*-loads of *earth*,
    for I will no longer offer *holocaust* or *sacrifice*
    to any other *god* except to the LORD."

READING I · Today's passage begins midway through the story of Naaman and Elisha. Naaman the Syrian was an important and powerful man, but he was stricken with leprosy. He heard that there was a prophet in Israel named Elisha who could cure him, and so he approached Elisha for help. But he arrogantly turned away when Elisha sent a servant to talk with him rather than coming himself and curing Naaman immediately. Although Naaman began to leave, he reconsidered and agreed to Elisha's cure—immersing himself in the waters of the Jordan—which is where today's story begins.

Naaman is proud, but he is not ignorant. When his flesh is cleansed he recognizes the greatness of the prophet Elisha and the superiority of Israel's God. In gratitude, he offers a gift to Elisha from the wealth he had brought with him, but Elisha refuses.

Naaman's response seems odd at first. He asks Elisha for some dirt to take back with him, declaring that he will sacrifice only to the Lord. The idea behind this is that a god could be worshipped only in the land of the people who worshiped that god. To worship the God of Israel, Naaman must take some of Israel's earth back with him.

When you understand the context of this reading, you will be able to proclaim it as the interesting story of healing and conversion that it is. Express amazement at the miracle that occurs, and stress the conviction of both Naaman and Elisha. Naaman is sincere in his gratitude, and Elisha is equally serious. Speak the final line expressing Naaman's devotion to God with forcefulness.

READING II 2 Timothy 2:8–13

A reading from the second letter of Saint Paul to Timothy

Beloved:
Remember Jesus *Christ*, raised from the *dead*,
    a descendant of *David*:
      such is my *gospel*, for which I am *suffering*,
    even to the point of *chains*, like a *criminal*.
But the word of *God* is *not* chained.

Therefore, I bear with *everything* for the sake of those
    who are *chosen*,
      so that they *too* may obtain the *salvation* that is
      in Christ *Jesus*,
      together with eternal *glory*.

This saying is *trustworthy*:
If we have *died* with him
    we shall also *live* with him;
if we *persevere*
    we shall also *reign* with him.
But if we *deny* him
    he will deny *us*.
If we are *un*faithful
    he remains *faithful*,
      for he *cannot* deny *himself*.

Be sure you have the attention of the assembly before you begin, then proclaim this message in a strong voice.

Speak harshly of the hardships of ministry. Then pause, lower your voice, and quietly but firmly proclaim the line about God's word.

Slow down and proclaim each line separately, in order to avoid becoming sing-song. Build in intensity to the end.

READING II The second letter to Timothy was written by an admirer of Paul many years after Paul's death. The author writes as if Paul is still alive and refers to events in Paul's life. The author also upholds Pauline teaching and encourages faithfulness to Paul's preaching.

Paul was often imprisoned for the sake of the gospel during his missionary travels, and the author alludes to his suffering. While in prison, Paul wrote letters to the churches he had founded and others he had visited. Even while imprisoned, he worked to spread the gospel to the Gentiles—who were his special responsibility—and to build up the communities of Christians he had known. Today's reading opens with a reference to Paul's imprisonment and to his evangelism while in chains. In a powerful statement of the force of the gospel despite all human efforts to squelch it, the author claims that the word of God cannot be chained. It has a life of its own.

The author emphasizes key Pauline themes: the hope in Christ's resurrection; the significance of suffering for the gospel; and the eagerness to endure whatever is necessary in order to bring others to salvation.

The final section of the passage is taken from an ancient Christian hymn. The Christian has died with Christ (in the waters of baptism) but has hope of living with him. The Christian life involves endurance, but we can also look forward to the fulfillment of God's promises. God's love is eternal.

Reflect on your own ministry as you read these words. Although you might not be asked to witness to your faith from prison, think of the suffering you have endured for your principles. Then speak confidently as you share this message with your assembly.

GOSPEL Luke 17:11–19

A reading from the holy gospel according to Luke

As Jesus continued his journey to *Jerusalem*,
   he traveled through *Samaria* and *Galilee*.

As he was entering a *village*, ten *lepers met* him.
They stood at a *distance* from him and raised their *voices*, saying,
   "Jesus, Master! Have *pity* on us!"

And when he *saw* them, he said,
   "Go *show* yourselves to the *priests.*"
As they were *going* they were *cleansed.*
And *one* of them, *realizing* he had been healed,
   returned, glorifying *God* in a loud *voice;*
      and he fell at the feet of *Jesus* and *thanked* him.
He was a *Samaritan.*

Jesus said in reply,
   "Ten were cleansed, were they *not?*
Where are the *other* nine?
Has none but this *foreigner* returned to give thanks to *God?"*

Then he said to him, "Stand *up* and *go;*
   your *faith* has *saved* you."

Because of the contagious nature of skin diseases, lepers were required to keep their distance and call out to others to stay away. These lepers instead call out for mercy.

Jews were suspicious of Samaritans. This one displays knowledge of and gratitude for God's work in him.

Speak gently and kindly.

GOSPEL The gospel story today has many similarities with the first reading. Both include a cure of leprosy, thankfulness for God's goodness, and a foreigner who expresses faith and gratitude.

The law of Moses indicates that a cure of leprosy is to be confirmed by a priest. Jesus sends the lepers he encounters to the priests; on the way they are cured. Nine continue their journey, but one, a Samaritan, returns to thank Jesus and praise God.

Samaritans and Jews were at odds with one another, despite a common heritage. They differed over the contents of scripture and over the proper place and manner of worship. Jews were suspicious of Samaritans and tried to avoid contact with them whenever possible.

The author of this gospel repeatedly surprises the reader by suggesting that unexpected people prove to be truly righteous. Surely no Jew would have expected the single righteous leper to be a Samaritan. Jesus emphasizes the importance of the man's faith. True healing and well-being go beyond the merely physical.

In our own day, the Samaritan in this story would be someone from a religious background or ethnic group different from our own, or perhaps a drug addict or convict. Keep that image in mind as you tell this story with enthusiasm. Speak Jesus' words clearly, so that your listeners can join with the Samaritan leper in praising God.

29TH SUNDAY IN ORDINARY TIME

Lectionary #147

READING I — Exodus 17:8–13

A reading from the book of Exodus

Amalek = AM-uh-lek

In *those* days, *Amalek* came and waged war against *Israel*.
Moses, therefore, said to *Joshua*,
   "Pick out certain *men*,
      and *tomorrow* go out and engage *Amalek* in *battle*.
I will be *standing* on top of the *hill*
      with the staff of *God* in my *hand*."

So Joshua did as Moses *told* him:
   he engaged Amalek in *battle*
      after Moses had climbed to the top of the *hill*
         with *Aaron* and *Hur*.

Hur = her

As long as Moses kept his hands raised *up*,
   Israel had the *better* of the *fight*,
   but when he let his hands *rest*,
   Amalek had the better of the *fight*.
Moses' *hands*, however, grew *tired*;
   so they put a *rock* in place for him to *sit* on.
Meanwhile *Aaron* and *Hur* supported his *hands*,
   one on *one* side and one on the *other*,
   so that his hands remained *steady* till *sunset*.

Speak this final sentence quietly. The real point of the story has already been made.

And Joshua *mowed* down Amalek and his *people*
   with the edge of the *sword*.

READING I — The battle between Israel and the Amalekites takes place while the Israelites are wandering in the desert after their flight from Egypt. Shortly before Israel arrived at Mount Sinai—where Moses conversed with God and received instructions for the people—Amalek and his warriors attacked the Israelites. In the account that forms today's first reading, Israel is victorious because of the intervention of God through Moses.

Moses is clearly the authority not only when it comes to prophecy but even in military matters. Although Joshua is here and elsewhere the general in charge of the troops, Moses gives instructions and presides over the events.

The image of Moses holding the staff of God and standing with outstretched arms suggests that he was acting as a military standard. Ancient peoples would often go into battle with a statue of their god as a standard in order to inspire courage in the troops. Since Israel's God cannot be depicted, Moses acts in God's place, representing God's presence and power. With the assistance of other leaders of the community, Moses is able to withstand weariness, staunchly remaining in his designated position for the entire day. As a result, Israel overcomes its adversaries.

It can be difficult to read about a military victory with enthusiasm. But the point of this story is Moses' steadfastness and God's faithful protection of Israel. Proclaim the narrative in a straightforward manner.

READING II   2 Timothy 3:14—4:2

A reading from the second letter of Saint Paul to Timothy

Beloved:

Remain *faithful* to what you have *learned* and *believed*,
   because you know from whom you *learned* it,
   and that from *infancy* you have known the sacred *Scriptures*,
   which are capable of giving you *wisdom* for *salvation*
   through *faith* in Christ *Jesus*.

All *Scripture* is inspired by *God*
   and is useful for *teaching*, for *refutation*, for *correction*,
   and for training in *righteousness*,
   so that one who *belongs* to God may be *competent*,
   equipped for every good *work*.

I *charge* you in the presence of *God* and of Christ *Jesus*,
   who will *judge* the living and the *dead*,
   and by his *appearing* and his kingly *power*:
proclaim the *word*;
   be *persistent* whether it is *convenient* or *inconvenient*;
convince, reprimand, encourage through all *patience*
    and *teaching*.

This sentence is long. Practice it well so that you know when to pause, then speak slowly.

Pause briefly, then announce firmly, "proclaim the word." This line needs to be stressed more than any other in this passage.

READING II   We do not come before God alone but as part of a community. If it were not for our parents, family, teachers and others, we might not know anything about God. The author of today's selection recognizes the importance of instruction and encourages the members of the community to cling to the faith that has been passed on to them.

Especially important among the religious traditions that are handed from generation to generation is scripture. For the author, "scripture" means the Hebrew scriptures. The stories of Israel's journey toward

greater understanding of God, the prophetic messages, and the instruction in right living that characterizes Hebrew wisdom literature can all form the Christian in righteousness.

Finally, the author begins to look forward to the future, to the time when Jesus will return as judge and ruler of the world. In a bold statement, the author encourages the readers to proclaim their faith in all situations, even when it is not easy, and to instruct others with patience.

This passage can be directed to all the members of your assembly since its message is timeless. In proclaiming it, you do

precisely what the author says to do: You encourage a respect for God's word in scripture, and you instruct your own community to hold fast to the faith and to proclaim it with enthusiasm. Read with encouragement and patience in your voice.

GOSPEL   The first line of today's gospel states the message Jesus wants to convey in the parable that follows: Pray always. The story of the unjust judge illustrates the importance of persistence in prayer.

GOSPEL Luke 18:1–8

A reading from the holy gospel according to Luke

Jesus told his disciples a *parable*
    about the necessity for them to pray *always*
        without becoming *weary.*

He said, "There was a *judge* in a certain *town*
    who neither feared *God* nor respected any human *being.*
And a *widow* in that town used to *come* to him and say,
    'Render a *just* decision for me against my *adversary.'*

"For a *long* time the judge was *unwilling*, but *eventually*
      he thought,
    'While it is *true* that I neither fear *God* nor respect
      any human *being*,
    because this *widow* keeps *bothering* me
    I shall deliver a just *decision* for her
    lest she finally come and *strike* me.'"

The Lord said, "Pay *attention* to what the dishonest *judge* says.
Will not *God* then secure the rights of his *chosen* ones
    who call *out* to him *day* and *night*?
Will he be *slow* to *answer* them?
I *tell* you, he will see to it that *justice* is done for them *speedily*.
But when the Son of *Man* comes, will he find *faith* on *earth*?"

Margin notes (left):

It appears that he was corrupt, caring only for himself and his own benefit.

Resolve in your heart that the answer to this question is a resounding "Yes!"

Jesus is not afraid to use a dishonorable figure to illustrate his point. In another parable, he even praises the shrewdness and dishonesty of a steward who falsifies the notes of debt owed to his master. Rather than excoriate the judge in today's story, Jesus compares him with God! Although he is a poor excuse for a judge, he illustrates the faithfulness and devotion of the judge of the world.

The judge is clearly not fulfilling his duties on a regular basis. He does not care about God nor is he concerned about other members of his community. He does not seek justice or uphold what is right. Yet a poor, powerless widow is able to turn him around with her irritating persistence.

Widows in antiquity—women without a husband or family to care for and protect them—often faced danger and had few resources. They were among the downtrodden, depending on the kindness of strangers to meet their needs. You may decide for yourself if the widow in this story is meek and quiet (although persistent!) or if she is assertive and demanding. Either way, it is her unwillingness to give up that finally makes a difference.

Just as the widow refused to give up in asking for what she needed, so also the Christian can turn to God in everything, unwilling to stop asking and trusting in God's mercy and love.

Give plenty of expression to the characters in this story as you encourage the members of your assembly to pray always. The final line is spoken directly to each of us. If we take the message of the parable to heart, we will be able to affirm that we can indeed trust completely in God.

30TH SUNDAY IN ORDINARY TIME

Lectionary #150

READING I   Sirach 35:12–14, 16–18

A reading from the book of Sirach

The LORD is a God of *justice*,
    who knows no *favorites*.
Though not *unduly* partial toward the *weak*,
    yet he *hears* the cry of the *oppressed*.
The LORD is not *deaf* to the wail of the *orphan*,
    nor to the *widow* when she pours out her *complaint*.

The one who serves God *willingly* is *heard*;
    his *petition* reaches the *heavens*.
The prayer of the *lowly pierces* the clouds;
    it does not *rest* till it reaches its *goal*,
nor will it *withdraw* till the Most High *responds*,
    judges *justly* and affirms the *right*,
and the LORD will not *delay*.

READING I   The book of Sirach is a relatively late book of Jewish wisdom literature, a body of texts offering advice about right living. The present passage reflects on the proper attitude of the human person before God and how that posture affects God's response to prayer. First, however, the author discusses God's response to human social and economic positions, and to those who are less fortunate than others.

God is fair to all, whether rich or poor, powerful or powerless, strong or weak. But God also recognizes that some people suffer disadvantage in society and need special protection. Orphans and widows, two categories of people who had little legal protection or wealth in Hebrew society, are singled out. But they represent all the disadvantaged and oppressed. God listens and responds willingly to the poor and powerless when they cry out in need.

The passage then moves to the type of person whose prayer is most favorable to God. The one who serves God with enthusiasm and prays with humility will be heard. If we look ahead to the gospel reading, we see the same message expressed in a different way: The Pharisee's prayer, filled with self-righteousness for his many accomplishments, is not as pleasing to God as the sincere supplication of the humble tax collector, who recognizes his unworthiness before God.

The message of this passage is timeless. Reflect on your own attitudes, and then offer this reading to your community with sincerity and humility. Speak with conviction but also with compassion.

READING II   The author of the second letter to Timothy recalls the suffering Paul endured before his death. Yet

READING II   2 Timothy 4:6–8, 16–18

A reading from the second letter of Saint Paul to Timothy

Beloved:
I am *already* being poured out like a *libation*,
    and the time of my *departure* is at *hand*.
I have competed *well*; I have finished the *race*;
    I have *kept* the *faith*.

From now *on* the crown of *righteousness* awaits me,
    which the *Lord*, the just *judge*,
    will *award* to me on that *day*, and not only to *me*,
    but to *all* who have longed for his *appearance*.

At my *first* defense *no* one appeared on my *behalf*,
    but everyone *deserted* me.
May it *not* be held *against* them!

But the *Lord* stood by me and gave me *strength*,
    so that through *me* the proclamation might be *completed*
    and all the *Gentiles* might *hear* it.
And I was *rescued* from the lion's *mouth*.

The Lord will *rescue* me from every evil *threat*
    and will bring me *safe* to his heavenly *kingdom*.
To *him* be *glory* forever and *ever*. Amen.

Speak solemnly and slowly.

Let your voice be filled with regret rather than anger.

Proclaim this with strength and conviction. Close with joyful confidence.

the author speaks with hope and confidence, looking forward to life with God in glory. Throughout, Paul's experiences reflect those of Jesus.

Just as Jesus spoke of the wine as his blood at the Last Supper, so also the author characterizes his life as a libation, a drink offering poured out during worship. Early Christians suffering persecution often connected their bodies and their lives with the eucharist, an offering to God that could also give life to others.

Using image of an athlete, the author speaks with satisfaction of having endured to the end. Just as winning athletes received a victor's crown, so also God reserves a crown of righteousness for the victorious Christian. It will be given on the day when Christ is revealed as judge of the world.

In very personal terms, the author alludes to having been abandoned at his trial, just as Jesus was. But, like Jesus, he prays for others even as he approaches death himself. He relies on God's strength to support him through his tribulations, knowing that he can proclaim the gospel even from prison.

Proclaim this text solemnly and with a bit of sadness. But do not lose sight of the firm faith that undergirds the author's words. Even when speaking of the abandonment the author expresses, proclaim his belief in God's mercy. The closing verses express the hope of one who is certain to die soon but still trusts in God and looks forward to joining God in eternity; such hope causes the author to break into praise. Join with him in lifting your voice to God.

GOSPEL The story of the Pharisee and the tax collector in the gospel of Luke is a tale that hits home, if we let it. It is a story of righteousness and sin,

GOSPEL   Luke 18:9–14

A reading from the holy gospel according to Luke

Jesus addressed this *parable*
　　to those who were *convinced* of their own *righteousness*
　　and *despised* everyone *else.*

Do not give away the conclusion of the parable with your voice. Speak the Pharisee's words sincerely and genuinely.

"Two *people* went up to the *temple* area to *pray;*
　　one was a *Pharisee* and the other was a *tax* collector.
The *Pharisee* took up his *position* and spoke this *prayer*
　　　to *himself,*
　　　'O God, I *thank* you that I am not like the *rest* of humanity—
　　　greedy, dishonest, adulterous—or even like this *tax* collector.
I *fast* twice a *week,* and I pay *tithes* on my whole *income.'*

The tax collector speaks simply and sorrowfully. Pause.
Speak Jesus' words forcefully.

"But the *tax* collector stood off at a *distance*
　　and would not even raise his *eyes* to *heaven*
　　but beat his *breast* and *prayed,*
　　　'O *God,* be *merciful* to me a *sinner.'*

"I *tell* you, the *latter* went home *justified,* not the *former;*
　　for whoever *exalts* himself will be *humbled,*
　　and the one who *humbles* himself will be *exalted.*"

but not in the places we usually expect to see them.

Since the gospels often portray Jesus in conflict with Pharisees, we can sometimes forget that the Pharisees were concerned with proper living, extending the legal precepts of the temple to all of life. They taught that people should live holy lives in their homes and daily affairs. Pharisees also believed in the resurrection of the dead, in contrast to the Sadducees, the priestly caste of the Jerusalem temple.

Jesus had much in common with the Pharisees but also found them prone to self-righteousness. The Pharisee in the story has devoted himself to God and has even gone beyond what the law requires. But he is also proud of his good behavior and consequently looks down on others.

Tax collectors were known as cheaters, often charging more than was required in order to line their own pockets. The tax collector in the story seems to acknowledge that his actions have been less than admirable. He knows he is a sinner. Yet Jesus claims that the tax collector demonstrates the proper attitude of one approaching God in prayer! As is typical in the gospel of Luke, all expectations are turned upside down. The religious leader is criticized, while the sinner is praised.

Anyone who seeks to live the moral life can fall into the same trap that snared the Pharisee. We sometimes find it easy look down others whom we presume to be sinners. Yet Jesus' challenge falls directly on us. While not advocating sinful behavior, he insists on honesty and humility before God.

Do not be afraid of the shock that should accompany this story. Share its challenge with your listeners so that all in the assembly can together grapple with its meaning.

ALL SAINTS

Lectionary #667

READING I   Revelation 7:2–4, 9–14

"Revelation," not "Revelations."

A reading from the book of Revelation

I, *John*, saw another *angel* come up from the *East*,
    holding the *seal* of the living *God*.
He cried out in a loud *voice* to the *four angels*
    who were given *power* to damage the *land* and the *sea*,
    "Do *not* damage the *land* or the *sea* or the *trees*
    until we put the *seal* on the foreheads of the *servants*
        of our *God*."
I heard the number of those who had been *marked* with the *seal*,
    one *hundred* and forty-four *thousand* marked
    from *every tribe* of the *Israelites*.

After this I had a vision of a great *multitude*,
    which no one could *count*,
    from every *nation*, *race*, *people*, and *tongue*.
They stood before the *throne* and before the *Lamb*,
    wearing white *robes* and holding *palm* branches in their *hands*.
They *cried out* in a loud *voice*:
    "*Salvation* comes from our *God*,
    who is *seated* on the *throne*,
    and from the *Lamb*."

All the *angels* stood around the *throne*
    and around the *elders* and the four living *creatures*.
They *prostrated* themselves before the *throne*,
    worshiped God, and *exclaimed*:

Pause before reading the words of the crowd, then proclaim them loudly and clearly.

READING I   The seer John tells of being taken before the throne of God, where he sees angels and a lamb (Christ) who has been slain. After the lamb opens a sealed scroll, an angel bears the instrument for the final seal, the seal of God. In antiquity, seals were used to close documents and to mark possessions. Here the divine seal, a sign of ultimate authority, is used to mark those faithful to God.

Those eligible for marking with the seal are a vast number. The number 144,000 is intended to signify the complete nation of Israel. Not only the Israelites, but Gentiles of every race and nation are included among the chosen ones of God. The number of Gentiles is so great that it cannot be determined. Although these numbers are sometimes used to justify exclusion and the superiority of a few, the idea is really one of inclusion: Anyone faithful to God is worthy to be counted as one of God's servants.

The faithfulness of this crowd becomes evident as the vision continues. The white robes and palm branches indicate those martyred for their faith. This is confirmed by the elder, who tells John that these faithful have "washed their robes . . . in the blood of the Lamb." They cry out with the angels before the throne of God.

The purpose of apocalyptic writing is to encourage those who are struggling and who might even face persecution for the faith. Just as those dressed in white have been vindicated and now bask in God's presence, so also anyone who faithfully endures trial now will be justified by God and made to share in the heavenly glory.

Today's feast is a feast of memories, family stories and inspiring saints. As we remember today all the saints—those widely recognized for their holiness and those

Read this quotation slowly and with great emphasis on each term of honor. Pause slightly after "God," and be sure not to swallow the final "Amen."

"Amen. Blessing and *glory, wisdom* and *thanksgiving, honor, power,* and *might*
be to our *God forever* and *ever. Amen."*

Then one of the elders spoke up and *said* to me,
  "Who are *these* wearing white *robes,* and where did they
    come from?"
I said to him, "My *lord, you* are the one who *knows."*
He said to me,
  "These are the ones who have *survived* the time
    of great *distress;*
  they have *washed* their *robes*
  and made them *white* in the blood of the *Lamb."*

Speak this as the message of comfort it was intended to be.

READING II 1 John 3:1–3

A reading from the first letter of Saint John

Beloved:
See what *love* the Father has *bestowed* on us
  that we may be called the *children* of *God.*
Yet so we *are.*
The reason the world does not *know* us
  is that it did not know *him.*

Beloved, we are *God's* children now;
  what we *shall* be has not yet been *revealed.*
We *do* know that when it *is* revealed we shall be *like* him,
  for we shall *see* him as he *is.*

Everyone who has this *hope* based on *him* makes himself *pure,*
  as *he* is *pure.*

Speak tenderly and lovingly throughout this selection. Read slowly.

Pause briefly before and after this line. Read it with conviction.

This is both a statement of reality and an exhortation to your listeners to be pure.

---

known only to a few—we realize that we belong to a community of faith. We recall those who have instilled faith in us, and who have gone ahead to experience the full revelation of God. We would not be here, would not be joining our voices in praise of God, were it not for them. And so we take comfort in knowing that they are part of that multitude standing before the throne of God, free of all pain and anxiety.

READING II Building on the promise of today's first reading, this passage from the Johannine correspondence is addressed both to the recipients of the letter and to us. It affirms the tremendous love bestowed on us by God. We are not simply God's creatures, nor are we recipients from afar of God's goodness. Rather, we are part of the family of God, heirs to all God's blessings. The great chasm that divides imperfect mortals from the magnificent, immortal God is bridged, and we are called children of God.

The author offers this message, just as the mystic John did in the first reading, to encourage those who are facing adversity.

"The world" does not recognize the identity of these children of God, but that does not change the reality. But there is still more: The final outcome for our lives is still shrouded in mystery. The author makes two claims about that future reality: On that day we shall be like God; and we shall share in the beatific vision of a God fully revealed.

This is a message of hope for the future and encouragement for the present. The final line makes it clear that those who hope to become like God and to see God must now live lives of purity worthy of their calling.

Do not try to rush through the beatitudes. Speak each one as a distinct unit before moving on to the next. If it seems right to you to emphasize "blessed" more than is indicated here, feel free to do so. But be careful not to make each line sound exactly the same.

GOSPEL Matthew 5:1–12a

A reading from the holy gospel according to Matthew

When Jesus saw the *crowds*, he went up the *mountain*,
    and after he had sat *down*, his disciples *came* to him.
He began to *teach* them, saying:
"*Blessed* are the *poor* in *spirit*,
    for *theirs* is the kingdom of *heaven*.
Blessed are they who *mourn*,
    for they will be *comforted*.

"Blessed are the *meek*,
    for they will *inherit* the *land*.
Blessed are they who *hunger* and *thirst* for *righteousness*,
    for they will be *satisfied*.

"Blessed are the *merciful*,
    for they will be shown *mercy*.
Blessed are the *clean* of *heart*,
    for they will see *God*.

"Blessed are the *peacemakers*,
    for they will be called *children* of *God*.
Blessed are they who are *persecuted* for the sake
      of *righteousness*,
    for *theirs* is the kingdom of *heaven*.

Direct this line to your listeners.

The final sentence indicates the attitude that is to greet adversity; there is a promise of good things yet to come.

"Blessed are *you* when they *insult* you and *persecute* you
    and utter every kind of *evil* against you *falsely* because of *me*.
Rejoice and be *glad*,
    for your *reward* will be great in *heaven*."

This selection requires a slow, sincere and thoughtful rendering. Although the term "child of God" might be familiar, meditate on its significance. Share some of your joy with the members of your assembly as your address these words to them.

GOSPEL The beatitudes in Matthew "spiritualize" the concerns expressed also in the beatitudes in Luke. In Luke the needs are concrete: the poor are really poor, the hungry are really starving. Here, however, the ones who are blessed are not only those struggling to survive or those mistreated by the powerful but anyone who loves righteousness and is willing to suffer for it. Each beatitude tells of a present reality and offers a promise for the future that turns the present experience upside down or bestows a reward of heavenly magnitude. What we know now is not all that there is to know.

The beatitudes offer an assurance that the faith-filled pilgrims who have preceded us on this journey, having steadfastly endured the trials of their age, now enjoy peace and happiness in the presence of God. They are also a promise to us, living in a world filled with sorrow and slander, that there is more to come. The beatitudes in the gospel of Matthew in particular are a challenge to us who live in comfort to share in the struggle to create a just, compassionate world.

The natural rhythm of this passage makes it easy to proclaim but also offers pitfalls to the inattentive. Each blessing must be spoken sincerely and simply, with a pause before reading the "reward." Listen to your own words as though you are hearing the passage for the first time, so that it can truly provide comfort and challenge to your listeners.

31ST SUNDAY IN ORDINARY TIME

Lectionary #153

READING I   Wisdom 11:22—12:2

A reading from the book of Wisdom

Before the LORD the whole *universe* is as a *grain* from a *balance*
    or a drop of morning *dew* come down upon the *earth*.
But you have *mercy* on *all*, because *you* can do all *things*;
    and you *overlook* people's *sins* that they may *repent*.

For you *love* all things that *are*
    and loathe *nothing* that you have *made*;
    for what you *hated*, you would not have *fashioned*.
And how could a thing *remain*, unless you *willed* it;
    or be *preserved*, had it not been called *forth* by you?

But you *spare* all things, because they are *yours*,
    O LORD and *lover* of *souls*,
    for your imperishable *spirit* is in all *things*!
Therefore you *rebuke* offenders little by *little*,
    warn them and *remind* them of the *sins* they are *committing*,
    that they may *abandon* their *wickedness* and *believe* in you,
        O LORD!

Speak in awe and wonder, then change your tone to proclaim God's mercy.

Declare God's tremendous love with certainty and gratitude.

Although you are speaking of divine correction, it is given gently. Speak encouragingly.

READING I   The Wisdom of Solomon is a late work of Jewish wisdom literature (it does not actually claim to have been written by King Solomon). Wisdom literature teaches how one should live in order to merit the afterlife prepared for the righteous. But it also speaks eloquently of the nature of God. Today's selection reflects on God's relationship with the created world and especially with sinful humanity.

The passage begins by reflecting on God's majestic grandeur, with which nothing can compare. Insignificant as the universe is in God's eyes, God has created it and loves it. Everything that God has made is worthy of preservation, for God has willed its very existence.

Above all, God is able to forgive our sinfulness. God can do anything, of course, but human beings are especially singled out for mercy. Despite our many failings, we still have God's spirit. Yet God does not simply forgive sinful humanity without trying to make it better. God chastises and instructs so that we might learn to do what is right and be free from all sin, faithful to God.

This reading deserves to be proclaimed with special care. Reflect on the divine glory present in creation and especially on the tremendous love and forgiveness of God. Think about a time when you might have experienced God's gentle correction and its outcome. Then allow all the hope and gratitude in your heart to rise to your lips as you share with your community the splendor of God's creation and love. Read the closing sentence as an encouragement and a reminder that divine chastisement serves a greater purpose.

READING II 2 Thessalonians 1:11—2:2

A reading from the second letter of Saint Paul to the Thessalonians

Brothers and sisters:
We always *pray* for you,
   that our *God* may make you *worthy* of his *calling*
   and *powerfully* bring to *fulfillment* every good *purpose*
   and every effort of *faith*,
   that the *name* of our Lord *Jesus* may be *glorified* in you,
   and *you* in *him*,
   in accord with the *grace* of our *God* and Lord Jesus *Christ*.

We *ask* you, brothers and sisters,
   with regard to the *coming* of our Lord Jesus *Christ*
   and our *assembling* with *him*,
   not to be *shaken* out of your minds *suddenly*, or to be *alarmed*
   either by a "*spirit*," or by an oral *statement*,
   or by a *letter* allegedly from *us*
   to the effect that the *day* of the *Lord* is at *hand*.

Let your voice be filled with love and encouragement.

Change your tone here to one that is firm and instructive.

Speak the last line slowly.

READING II Paul opens every letter to his communities with a prayer. He was particularly fond of the Thessalonians and speaks with joy and gratitude for them and for their faith. Although this letter may have been written by someone other than Paul himself, it admirably recounts Paul's values and teachings.

The author begins by praying that the Thessalonians may be worthy of what God asks of them. But the author is confident that God can work through them, acting with power to bring about what is good. Through their actions, Jesus will be glorified. The author also speaks of the Thessalonians being glorified in the Lord, apparently in a new age. All of this is in accordance with God's grace.

The letter then turns to a problematic issue rooted in Paul's own teachings. In his earliest surviving correspondence, First Thessalonians, Paul expresses a fervent belief that Jesus will return soon. In today's passage from Second Thessalonians, the author has to temper the expectations of members of the community, who believed that Jesus' return was imminent.

Apparently, there were some members of the community who had prophesied about the immanent second coming of Jesus, and others pointed to Paul's earlier letter to support the view. While upholding Pauline authority, the author modifies Paul's teaching, downplaying the possibility of Christ's imminent return to make the gospel relevant to the contemporary Thessalonian community.

Speak fondly but powerfully as you offer the prayer in this passage, sincerely intending it for your own community. Continue to be sincere in the second half of the selection, knowing that Christians today

---

GOSPEL   Luke 19:1–10

A reading from the holy gospel according to Luke

At that *time*, Jesus came to *Jericho* and intended
  to pass *through* the town.
Now a man there named *Zacchaeus*,
  who was a chief *tax* collector and also a *wealthy* man,
  was seeking to see *who* Jesus *was*;
  but he could not *see* him because of the *crowd*,
  for he was *short* in *stature*.

So he ran *ahead* and climbed a *sycamore* tree in order to see *Jesus*,
  who was *about* to pass that *way*.
When he *reached* the place, Jesus looked *up* and said,
  "*Zacchaeus*, come down *quickly*,
  for *today* I must stay at *your* house."

And he came down *quickly* and received him with *joy*.
When they all *saw* this, they began to *grumble*, saying,
  "He has gone to stay at the *house* of a *sinner*."

But Zacchaeus *stood* there and said to the Lord,
  "*Behold, half* of my *possessions*, Lord, I shall give to the *poor*,
  and if I have *extorted* anything from *anyone*
  I shall *repay* it *four* times *over*."

And Jesus *said* to him,
  "*Today salvation* has come to this *house*
  because this man *too* is a descendant of *Abraham*.
For the Son of *Man* has come to *seek*
  and to *save* what was *lost*."

Zacchaeus = zuh-KEE-uhs

Express the eagerness of Zacchaeus.

Jesus speaks urgently but kindly.

Zacchaeus is sincere in his generosity.

Close with conviction.

---

should also guard against being too easily swayed by easy expectations of what is in store for us.

GOSPEL | The gospel of Luke is fond of tax collectors. Although such people were reviled in antiquity (and often today as well!), the author enjoys giving them important, positive roles in Jesus' ministry and stories. Tax collectors had the habit of charging taxpayers more than was actually required and then pocketing the difference. They had a well-deserved reputation for dishonesty.

Zacchaeus is a comical figure, so short that he needed to climb a tree to see the preacher everyone was talking about. Often in the gospels, sinful people approach Jesus with trembling, only to be praised for their faith. In this case, however, Jesus reaches out to Zacchaeus. Jesus did not simply tolerate the "scum" of society; he eagerly embraced them. No wonder his action was met with such disapproval.

Just by his presence, Jesus inspires Zacchaeus to do what is right. Zacchaeus eagerly announces that he will not only right any wrongs he has committed, but will go far beyond what is required, giving four times the necessary amount. He also intends to provide for the poor. Jesus declares that Zacchaeus is saved.

Reflect on your own ministry and that of your community. Do you reach out to those who have bad reputations, or do you try to avoid them? How can you seek them out lovingly, as Jesus did, without compromising your own ideals?

Proclaim this interesting story with plenty of expression. Speak the words of Zacchaeus with eagerness, and close with a solemn but caring pronouncement by Jesus.

32ND SUNDAY IN ORDINARY TIME

Lectionary #156

READING I   2 Maccabees 7:1–2, 9–14

A reading from the second book of Maccabees

Speak with great conviction and a tone of defiance.

It *happened* that seven *brothers* with their *mother* were *arrested*
　　and *tortured* with whips and *scourges* by the *king*,
　　to force them to eat *pork* in violation of God's *law*.
One of the brothers, speaking for the *others*, said:
　　"What do you expect to *achieve* by *questioning* us?
We are ready to *die* rather than transgress the laws
　　of our *ancestors*."

The brother speaks with disdain for the king but hope in God's promise of life.

At the point of *death* he said:
　　"You accursed *fiend*, you are depriving us of this *present* life,
　　but the King of the *world* will raise us *up* to *live* again *forever*.
It is for *his* laws that we are *dying*."

After *him* the *third* suffered their cruel sport.
He put out his tongue at *once* when told to *do* so,
　　and *bravely* held out his *hands*, as he spoke these noble *words*:
　　"It was from *Heaven* that I *received* these;
　　for the sake of his *laws* I *disdain* them;
　　from *him* I hope to receive them *again*."

Express their surprise and admiration.

Even the *king* and his *attendants marveled*
　　at the young man's *courage*,
　　because he regarded his *sufferings* as *nothing*.

After he had *died*,
　　they *tortured* and maltreated the *fourth* brother
　　in the same *way*.

READING I   The story of the torture and death of the seven brothers and their mother has served for centuries to inspire people in times of persecution. Today's passage is part of the story of Jewish resistance to persecution at the hands of Antiochus IV Epiphanes, the Seleucid king controlling Palestine at the time. Antiochus and his armies overran Palestine about 150 years before the time of Jesus, desecrating the temple in Jerusalem and forbidding fulfillment of the Jewish law. The Jews, led by the Maccabean brothers, revolted and eventually drove the Seleucids out of the land,

cleansing and rededicating the temple. The present story shows the tremendous courage of the brothers and expresses a belief in an afterlife, echoed in today's gospel.

The belief in resurrection developed relatively late in Jewish thought, during the persecution of Antiochus. While expressed in several writings from this period and later, it was still a matter of discussion and disagreement in Jesus' day. Initially, an afterlife was anticipated only for those who were righteous. The wicked were not expected to suffer eternal punishment but would suffer a

far worse fate. They would simply die and cease to exist.

Today's reading details only a small portion of the whole story told in Second Maccabees. Each brother courageously submits to torture but resists attempts to make him violate God's law. The first brother asserts that he and his brothers are willing to die rather than break the Jewish law. The third brother willingly offers his tongue and hands to be cut off, declaring that they have been given to him by God but keeping them is less important than keeping God's law. He declares his hope that God will restore what

Proclaim the end of the reading with finality and hope.

When he was near *death*, he said,
"It is my *choice* to die at the hands of *men*
with the hope *God* gives of being raised *up* by him;
but for *you*, there will be *no* resurrection to *life*."

READING II   2 Thessalonians 2:16—3:5

**A reading from the second letter of Saint Paul
to the Thessalonians**

Brothers and sisters:
May our *Lord* Jesus Christ *himself* and God our *Father*,
who has *loved* us and given us everlasting *encouragement*
and good *hope* through his *grace*,
encourage your *hearts* and *strengthen* them
in every good *deed* and *word*.

Plan your phrasing well. Speak with joy and peace.

Finally, brothers and sisters, *pray* for us,
so that the *word* of the *Lord* may speed *forward* and be *glorified*,
as it did among *you*,
and that we may be delivered from *perverse* and wicked *people*,
for not *all* have *faith*.

This is a sincere plea. Offer it to your listeners as such.

But the *Lord* is *faithful*;
he will *strengthen* you and *guard* you from the *evil* one.
We are *confident* of you in the Lord that what we *instruct* you,
you are *doing* and will *continue* to do.
May the Lord direct your *hearts* to the love of *God*
and to the *endurance* of *Christ*.

Read these final lines with a firm and reassuring voice.

---

has been destroyed. Finally, the fourth brother makes clear the source of the hope and courage that inspires them. Although he chooses to die rather than to break the law, he has hope that he will be raised again. Yet he declares that his persecutors will know no afterlife but will simply perish.

The story of the torture and great courage of the brothers and their mother teaches a lesson about the importance of following God's commands. It also instructs us about the source of their hope, as well as ours: There is more than this life; we trust that something greater awaits us. But the

tale also serves to inspire all who might be forced to sacrifice their ideals. The courage of the brothers can be emulated by anyone who sincerely strives to do what is right.

Proclaim this fascinating story with plenty of expression. Speak the brothers' words clearly and firmly. Then let the story speak for itself.

READING II   Second Thessalonians was written to encourage the community to hold fast to the teachings its

members had received from Paul and to continue to live responsibly. The present passage is a prayer of hope and encouragement.

The Christian faith is grounded in the love of God, who is revealed in Jesus. Only by relying on God will people truly receive strength and encouragement.

The author asks for prayer also for those who are involved in the ministry of evangelization. Paul traveled throughout the Mediterranean region spreading the gospel, and this text claims that it was especially well received by the Thessalonians. In an ambiguous statement, the author refers to

GOSPEL Luke 20:27–38

A reading from the holy gospel according to Luke

Sadducees = SAD-yoo-seez
The Sadducees are trying to trap Jesus.
Speak their words with mock sincerity.

Some *Sadducees*, those who *deny* that there is a *resurrection*,
  came *forward* and put this question to *Jesus*, saying,
  "*Teacher, Moses* wrote for us,
  'If someone's *brother* dies leaving a *wife* but no *child*,
  his brother must *take* the wife
  and raise up *descendants* for his *brother.*'
Now there were seven *brothers*;
  the *first* married a woman but died *childless.*

"Then the *second* and the *third* married her,
  and likewise *all* the seven died *childless.*
Finally the woman *also* died.
Now at the *resurrection whose* wife will that woman *be*?
For all *seven* had been *married* to her."

Jesus responds firmly and clearly. They
entirely misunderstand the teaching about
the afterlife. And they certainly
underestimate him!

Jesus said to them,
  "The children of *this* age *marry* and *remarry*;
  but those who are deemed *worthy* to attain to the *coming* age
  and to the *resurrection* of the *dead*
  neither *marry* nor are *given* in marriage.
They can no longer *die*,
  for they are like *angels*;
  and they are the *children* of *God*
  because *they* are the ones who will *rise.*

---

evil, faithless people who are apparently opposed to the gospel. It is not clear precisely who these evil ones were or what they taught.

But the author asserts that the Lord is faithful and will protect the community, and speaks confidently of the Thessalonians' faith, praying fervently that they remain rooted in God's love, always trusting in Christ.

This selection is especially easy to proclaim to your community. Address the members of the assembly directly as you encourage them, alluding to their faith and good works. Conclude with a sincere prayer

that your listeners will turn their hearts to God, always confident of Christ's faithfulness.

GOSPEL In order to understand the present passage, one must remember that there was an active debate about the resurrection of the dead at the time of Jesus. The belief in resurrection was a relatively new one, and the conservative faction in charge of the temple (the Sadducees) was slow to accept it. The Pharisees, on the other hand, believed in the resurrection, and Jesus agrees with them.

The other piece of information that is helpful in comprehending the question posed to Jesus is that the practice described in the question was indeed prescribed by the Mosaic law. In an era when there was no belief in an afterlife, it was essential to have children in order to carry on one's name and heritage. Children were the closest thing to life after death. In that context, the practice of levirate marriage—in which the brother of a deceased, childless man married his brother's widow to produce heirs for the dead man—developed.

Proclaim this final line with firm conviction.

"That the dead will *rise*
     even *Moses* made known in the passage about the *bush*,
     when he called out '*Lord*,'
     the God of *Abraham*, the God of *Isaac*, and the God of *Jacob*;
     and he is not God of the *dead*, but of the *living*,
     for to *him all* are *alive*."

[*Shorter: Luke 20:27, 34–38*]

The question is clearly intended to trap Jesus, but Jesus refuses to be caught. Marriage itself does not apply in heaven. Human existence and human relationships will be different than they are in this world. Jesus then reinforces his point by asserting that the God of Israel is the God of the living. Unfortunately, the story about the burning bush has nothing to do with the question of the resurrection of the dead. But the argument reflects a belief that the holy people of old live in heaven.

Although the practice of levirate marriage is foreign to us, the story provides an intriguing means of teaching about resurrection. Just as Jesus had hope in a future resurrection, so also we trust that there is more to life than what we know now. Proclaim this story with enthusiasm, as you express the Christian hope that death is not the final word.

33RD SUNDAY IN ORDINARY TIME

Lectionary #159

READING I   Malachi 3:19–20a

Malachi = MAL-uh-kī

Let your voice be filled with urgency.

A reading from the book of the prophet Malachi

Lo, the *day* is *coming, blazing* like an *oven,*
    when all the *proud* and all *evildoers* will be *stubble,*
and the *day* that is *coming* will set them on *fire,*
    leaving them neither *root* nor *branch,*
    says the LORD of *hosts.*

Lift your voice in hope and joy.

But for *you* who fear my *name,* there will arise
    the *sun* of *justice* with its healing *rays.*

READING II   2 Thessalonians 3:7–12

**A reading from the second letter of Saint Paul
    to the Thessalonians**

Offer this message with a tone of pride rather than arrogance. Sincerely strive to be a model for others in your life.

Brothers and sisters:
You *know* how one must *imitate* us.
For we did not act in a *disorderly* way among you,
    nor did we eat *food* received *free* from anyone.
On the *contrary,* in *toil* and *drudgery,* night and *day*
    we worked, so as not to burden *any* of you.

READING I As we draw to the end of the liturgical year, we reflect on the end times and the day of God's judgment. The end of the world is to be feared by wicked, but for those who delight in the Lord it will be a joyous day.

The Day of the Lord is often invoked by the Hebrew prophets as a day of judgment, when God will be fully revealed and will give each of us what we deserve. Malachi's vision of the day of judgment makes use of the image of fire. Fire is powerful and destructive, but it is also necessary, providing light and warmth.

The prophet first alludes to fire's ability to cause widespread devastation. Evoking the image of a wildfire sweeping over the land, the prophet speaks of the proud being swallowed up in an all-consuming conflagration. They are like the stubble from crops that is left in the field after the grain has been harvested, which farmers sometimes burn in order to clear the field of the residue from past years and to prepare the ground for a new planting. God's judgment of fire will consume the evildoers completely.

Those who do what is right, however, have nothing to fear. For them, the fire will bring not destruction but the warm glow of the sun, shining as righteousness. The sunrise of the Day of the Lord will bring healing, creating wholeness.

Do not shy away from Malachi's harsh message of judgment. At the same time, however, be sure to give emphasis to the hopefulness of the final sentence. Direct the prophet's message of hope to your listeners.

READING II Paul believed that Jesus would return soon to bring God's judgment to the world. He also taught the Christian communities he founded to

Proclaim this with a sense of outrage and righteous concern. Close in a firm voice.

Not that we do not have the *right*.
Rather, we wanted to present ourselves as a *model* for you,
  so that you might *imitate* us.
In fact, when we were *with* you,
  we *instructed* you that if anyone was *unwilling* to *work*,
  neither should that one *eat*.

We hear that *some* are conducting themselves among you
    in a *disorderly* way,
  by not keeping *busy* but minding the business of *others*.
Such people we *instruct* and *urge* in the Lord Jesus *Christ*
    to work *quietly*
  and to eat their *own* food.

GOSPEL Luke 21:5–19

A reading from the holy gospel according to Luke

While some *people* were speaking about
  how the temple was *adorned* with costly *stones*
    and *votive* offerings,
  Jesus said, "All that you *see* here—
  the *days* will *come* when there will not be *left*
  a *stone* upon *another* stone that will not be thrown *down*."

Does Jesus speak sadly or in an ominous tone? Reflect your opinion in your voice.

Then they asked him,
"*Teacher*, when will this *happen*?
And what *sign* will there be when all these *things*
    are about to *happen*?"

---

look forward to Christ's second coming. Unfortunately, some Christians thought it was therefore unnecessary to work and were idly awaiting Jesus' return. They became a burden on the larger community and caused dissension with idle gossip.

This situation resulted in the message we read today. The author reprimands those who are unwilling to work. It is important to keep in mind, however, that the author is addressing a very specific situation. The instruction that those who are unwilling to work should not eat is not meant as an argument against food programs or government

services. It is directed to those who are fully capable of supporting themselves but who choose not to do so.

Paul often presents his own life and ministry as an example to the members of his fledgling communities. The present passage picks up that theme and suggests that the recipients of the letter look to their own ministers in order to see how to live genuine, faith-filled lives. A believer can fervently hope for Jesus' return while at the same time continuing to accept the daily responsibilities that life entails.

Emphasize for the members of your community the importance of honest work. But the most important theme is the disruption caused by the unwillingness of some to do their part, expressed in the final paragraph.

GOSPEL The apocalyptic discourse in Luke's gospel describes what will happen in the end times. Even while predicting woes, the author also makes clear that catastrophe does not necessarily point to the end of the world. The most important message is the perseverance

Now Jesus speaks a stern warning. Address his concerns to your assembly, then continue in a tone of warning.

He answered,
"*See* that you not be *deceived,*
    for *many* will come in my *name,* saying,
    'I am *he,*' and 'The *time* has *come.*'
Do not *follow* them!

"When you hear of *wars* and *insurrections,*
    do not be *terrified;* for such things must happen *first,*
    but it will not *immediately* be the *end.*"

Then he said to them,
"*Nation* will rise against *nation,* and *kingdom* against *kingdom.*
There will be powerful *earthquakes, famines* and *plagues*
    from place to *place;*
    and awesome *sights* and mighty *signs* will come from the *sky.*

Pick up the tempo slightly, and let a note of terror enter your voice at this dire prediction.

"*Before* all this happens, however,
    they will *seize* and *persecute* you,
    they will hand you *over* to the *synagogues* and to *prisons,*
    and they will have you led before *kings* and *governors*
    because of my *name.*

There is comfort in these words. Suffering is not in vain, nor must the Christian endure it without assistance.

"It will *lead* to your giving *testimony.*
Remember, you are *not* to prepare your *defense beforehand,*
    for I *myself* shall give you a *wisdom* in *speaking*
    that all your adversaries will be *powerless* to resist or *refute.*

"You will *even* be handed over by *parents, brothers,*
    relatives and *friends,*
    and they will put *some* of you to *death.*
You will be hated by *all* because of my *name,*
    but not a *hair* on your *head* will be *destroyed.*

Close with a tone of reassurance.

By your *perseverance* you will secure your *lives.*"

required of Jesus' followers, regardless of the situation that surrounds them.

The story opens with Jesus' proclamation that the temple in Jerusalem will be destroyed and a question about when the destruction will occur. Jesus' own relationship with the temple was mixed: Although he worshiped in the temple and revered it, he also questioned whether worship of God was properly understood by those who engaged in it. When the author of Luke was writing, the temple had already been destroyed by the Romans after a period of resistance by the Jews to Roman rule.

Jesus then discusses the horrifying events that will precede the end of the world. His followers should not be misled by those who claim to know when the end will come, but they can be sure that it will be preceded by tribulation. Jesus' disciples will also suffer in some way for their faith. Jesus predicts persecution and imprisonment, events that will allow the gospel to be proclaimed even more broadly.

Because of our experience of history, the predictions in this passage do not seem to apply to us. We know that the temple has been destroyed and has never been rebuilt.

We know that there are wars and famines throughout the world, and often feel powerless to stop them. And few of us have had the experience of being thrown into prison or tortured. But we can respond to the challenge to preach the gospel in whatever circumstances we find ourselves.

Proclaim this reading forcefully, giving special emphasis to the teachings that will probably benefit your community the most: the need to resist deceivers, and the encouragement to persevere against all odds.

CHRIST THE KING

Lectionary #162

A reading from the second book of Samuel

In those *days, all* the tribes of *Israel* came to David
> in *Hebron* and said:
"Here we *are,* your *bone* and your *flesh.*
In days *past,* when *Saul* was our king,
> it was *you* who led the Israelites *out* and brought them *back.*
And the LORD said to you,
> 'You shall *shepherd* my people *Israel*
> and shall be *commander* of Israel.'"

When all the elders of *Israel* came to David in *Hebron,*
> King *David* made an *agreement* with them there
> > before the LORD,
> and they *anointed* him *king* of *Israel.*

Hebron = HEB-ruhn

The elders speak with gratitude and loyalty.

Speak triumphantly.

READING I   David's encounter with the Israelite tribes at Hebron is a classic story of the establishment of a covenant, this time not between God and humankind but between a leader and his people. David was able to unite all of the tribes under a single monarchy, despite the strife that had characterized the reign of his predecessor, Saul, and the divisions that remained after Saul's death.

The union of the monarch with his people is expressed in the assurance the elders give that they are David's "bone and flesh." They pledge such great loyalty and devotion

to him that they consider themselves his body. They acknowledge as well that he will protect them. David had already distinguished himself while Saul was king, and the elders recognize him as God's chosen ruler.

David will later establish Jerusalem, on the border dividing the northern and southern tribes, as his capital. But for now it is to the southern city of Hebron (a city closely associated with Abraham) that the leaders of Israel come to forge a pact with David and anoint him as their king.

Proclaim this reading in a straightforward manner. Speak fondly of David and with a tone of triumph. This was the beginning of Israel's glory days.

READING II   The beautiful hymn about Christ featured in our reading today is found near the beginning of the letter to the Colossians. The passage opens with the injunction to give thanks to God. The reason for the gratitude is the opportunity to live in the heavenly abode, a promise made possible by Christ's redemptive action.

READING II   Colossians 1:12–20

A reading from the letter of Saint Paul to the Colossians

Brothers and sisters:
Let us give *thanks* to the *Father*,
    who has made you *fit* to share
    in the *inheritance* of the *holy* ones in *light*.

He *delivered* us from the power of *darkness*
    and *transferred* us to the *kingdom* of his beloved *Son*,
    in whom we have *redemption*, the forgiveness of *sins*.

He is the *image* of the invisible *God*,
    the *firstborn* of all *creation*.
For in *him* were *created* all *things* in *heaven* and on *earth*,
    the *visible* and the *invisible*,
    whether *thrones* or *dominions* or *principalities* or *powers*;
    all things were created *through* him and *for* him.
He is *before* all things,
    and *in* him all things hold *together*.

He is the head of the *body*, the *church*.
He is the *beginning*, the *firstborn* from the *dead*,
    that in *all* things he himself might be *preeminent*.
For in *him* all the *fullness* was pleased to *dwell*,
    and *through* him to reconcile *all* things *for* him,
    making *peace* by the blood of his *cross*
    through *him*, whether those on *earth* or those in *heaven*.

Sincerely offer your own thanks to God, and invite your community to pray with you.

Pause before beginning the hymn. Then speak in a tone of wonder and conviction.

The phrasing is odd here, making the final sentence very difficult to proclaim. "Whether those on earth or those in heaven" describes what is meant by "all things" two lines earlier. Let your tone convey that the phrase "making peace by the blood of his cross through him" is parenthetical, in order to link the final phrase with "all things."

The mention of God's beloved Son inspires the author to launch into the hymn itself. Through Christ, human beings can see and know God. The invisible, ineffable God is made visible through him. He has been with God always, and through him the world was created. The author adopts language that was used in Hebrew wisdom literature to describe Lady Wisdom, who is depicted there as cocreator with God.

The author then builds on the Pauline image of the body and its many parts. In other passages, Paul compares members of the Christian community to body parts in order to argue that each person has an indispensable gift to offer to the rest of the community. This author presents Christ as the head of that body, its ruler and guiding force. Because of his role as the conqueror of death, who makes it possible for believers to experience life eternal (he is "firstborn" from the dead), Christ is to be given the foremost place in everything. He is first in death and in life, and is worthy to be honored in eternity.

The fundamental Christian belief that in Jesus God is revealed to the world is linked to the idea of salvation through the cross. The fullness of God dwells in Jesus, who is both divine and human. Because Jesus is both human and divine, he can bridge the gap between God and humanity, despite our propensity to turn away. Through his death, Jesus restored us to right relationship with God.

This selection is a joy to share with your community. Invite your listeners to give thanks with you as you proclaim the wondrous deeds of God in Jesus. Speak with a sense of awe.

GOSPEL   Luke 23:35–43

A reading from the holy gospel according to Luke

Speak in a mocking tone.

The rulers *sneered* at Jesus and said,
    "He saved *others*, let him save *himself*
    if he is the *chosen* one, the *Christ* of *God*."
Even the *soldiers* jeered at him.
As they *approached* to offer him *wine* they called out,
    "If *you* are King of the *Jews*, *save* yourself."
Above him there was an *inscription* that read,
    "*This* is the King of the *Jews*."

Proclaim this line with pride, although it was not intended to be understood this way by Jesus' persecutors.

Now one of the *criminals* hanging there *reviled* Jesus, saying,
    "Are *you* not the *Christ*?
Save yourself and *us*."

There is righteous indignation in this criminal's voice.

The *other*, however, *rebuking* him, said in reply,
    "Have you no fear of *God*,
    for you are subject to the *same condemnation*?
And indeed, *we* have been condemned *justly*,
    for the sentence *we* received corresponds to our *crimes*,
    but *this* man has done nothing *criminal*."
Then he said,
    "*Jesus, remember* me when you come into your *kingdom*."

Speak with sincere humility.

Jesus responds firmly but lovingly.

He replied to him,
    "Amen, I *say* to you,
    today you will be with me in *Paradise*."

GOSPEL   The irony of reading about the crucifixion on the feast of Christ the King is overwhelming. Just as we are proclaiming that Jesus is the exalted Lord, the "firstborn of all creation," the fulfillment of the promises to David, we see him bruised and beaten, dying on the cross. It is indeed the supreme irony of the Christian faith that the one who is Lord of all was willing to give his life for us, suffering a lonely, painful and humiliating death.

The gospel of Luke is fond of presenting such paradoxes. All our expectations about society, personal responsibility and our relationship with the things of this world are turned on their head in this gospel. The lowly are exalted, sinners are called righteous, the one who dies gives life. We close this liturgical year with the ultimate paradox: The one to whom we offer glory and honor and praise is lifted high for all to see—powerless, hanging on the cross.

The inscription on Jesus' cross proclaims that he is king of the Jews. What his tormentors thought was a joke or a condemnation, however, was indeed the truth. But, in another example of irony, a convicted criminal recognizes Jesus for who he is. He acknowledges his own guilt and Jesus' innocence, and confesses that Jesus will soon be entering his true realm.

Remember as you proclaim this passage that you are sharing it with your assembly on the feast that proclaims Christ as king. Read with an underlying note of triumph in your voice, despite the horrors you describe. Share the encounter of the just criminal and Jesus with compassion.